streets of paris

teNeues | MENDO

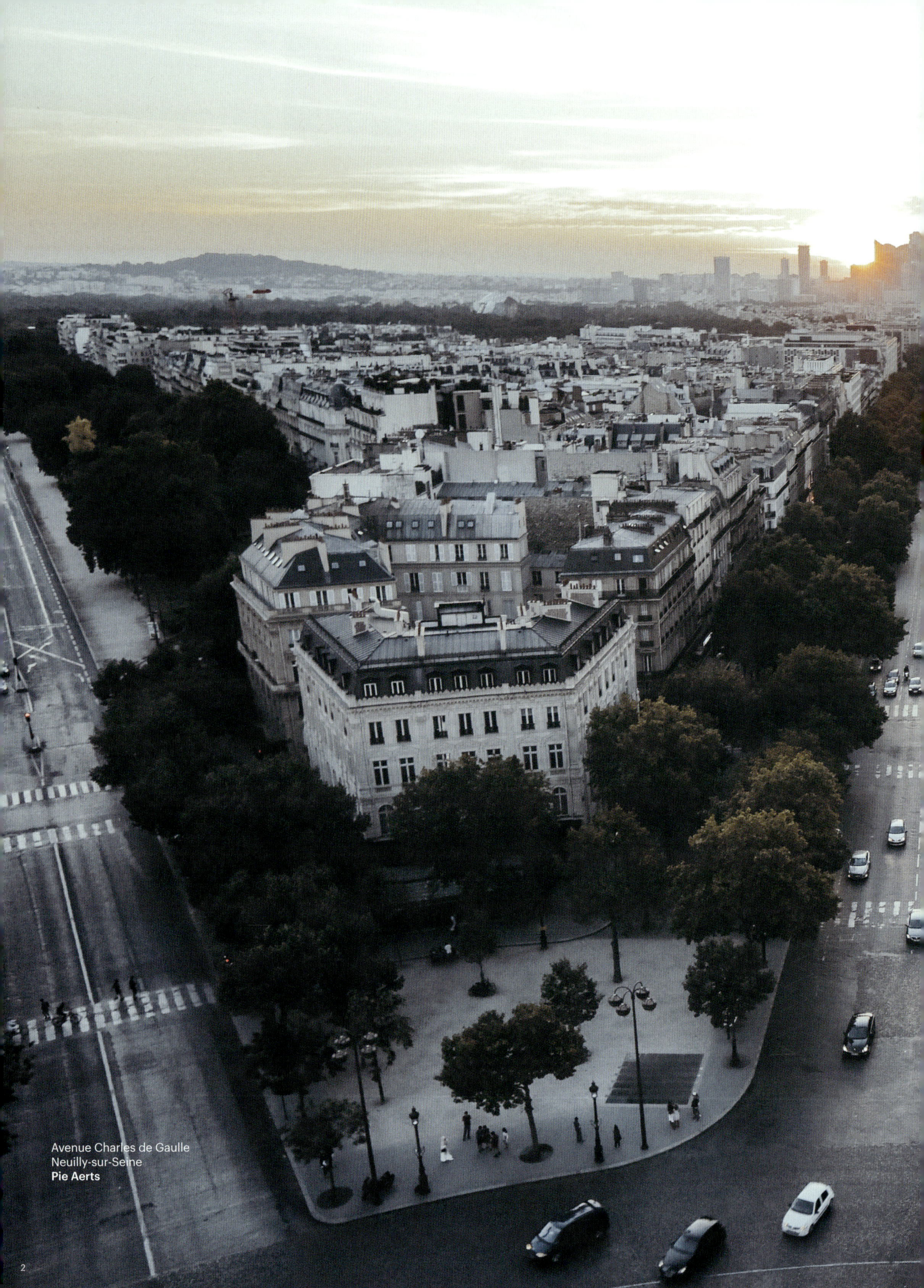

Avenue Charles de Gaulle
Neuilly-sur-Seine
Pie Aerts

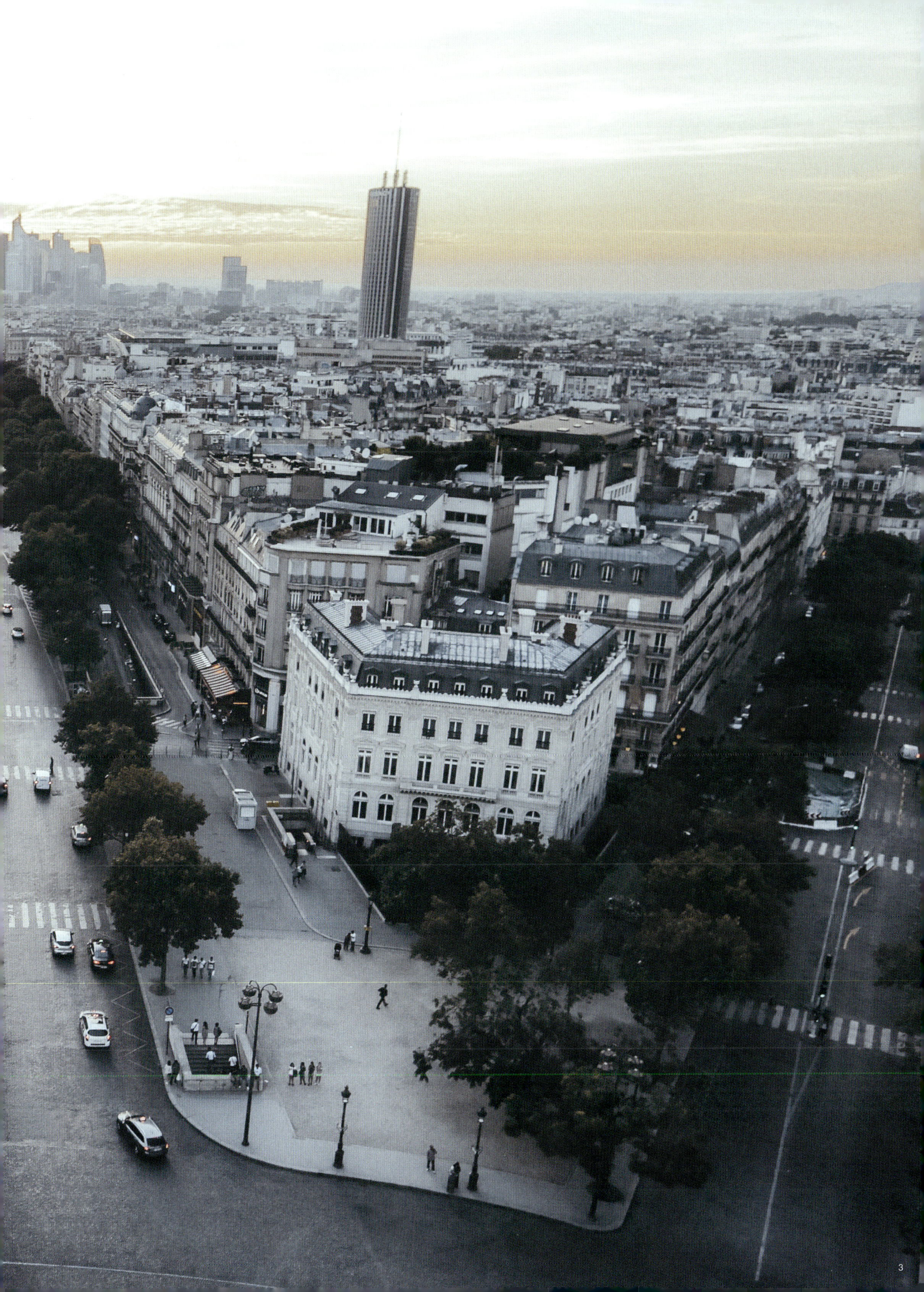

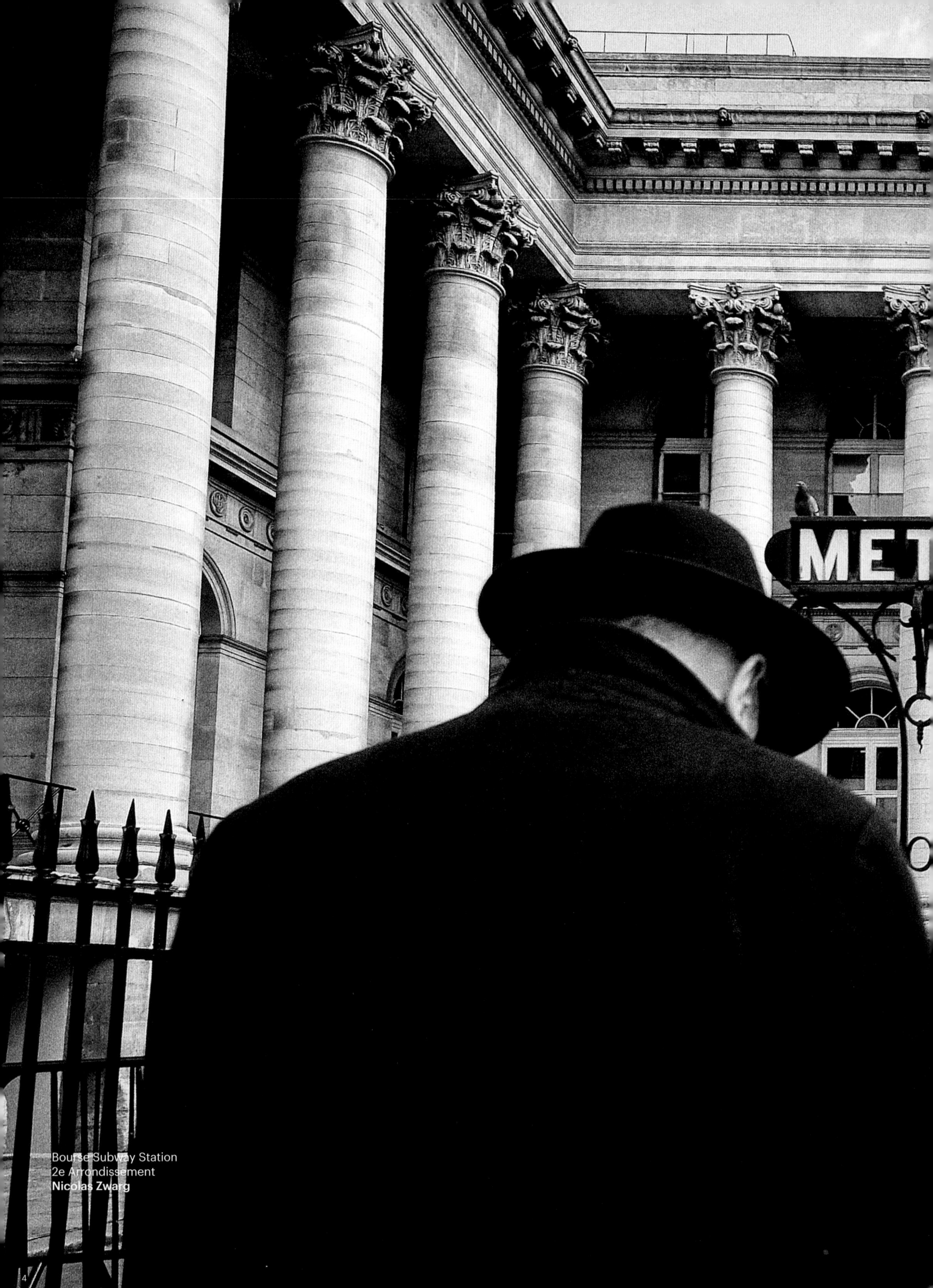

Bourse Subway Station
2e Arrondissement
Nicolas Zwarg

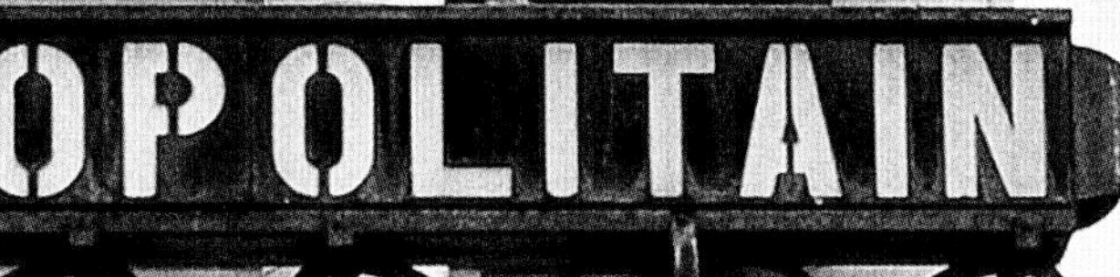
OPOLITAIN
M 3
Fermeture entre Villiers
et République du 31 mars
au 2 avril inclus

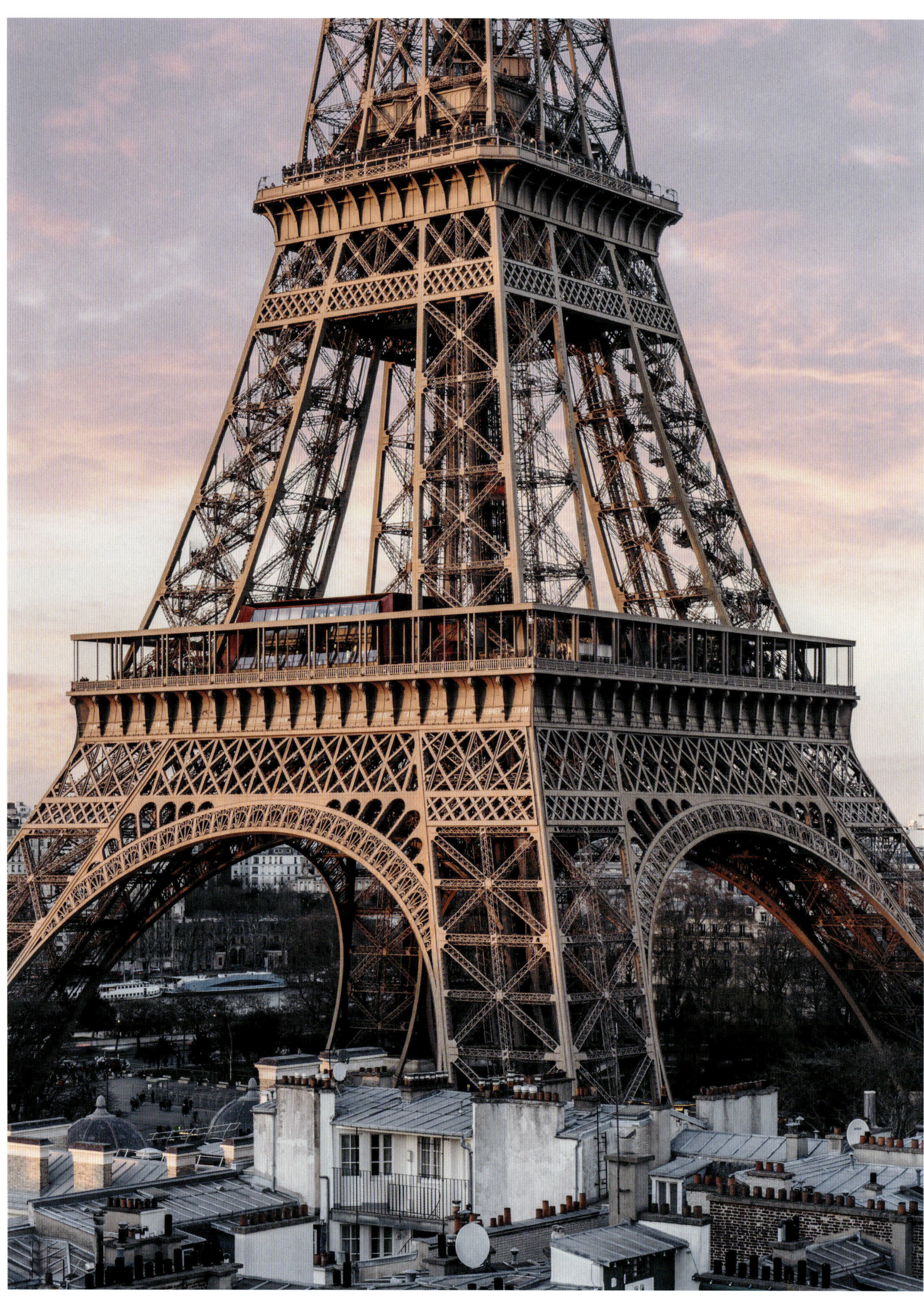

Photography is like writing with light.

—Amedeo Abello

Eiffel Tower
7e Arrondissement
Guillaume Dutreix

In love with Paris

Words Joost Bastmeijer
IG handle @joostbastmeijer

It's the City of Light, because of the early access to electricity and its leading role in the Age of Enlightenment. It's the City of Love, mainly because of the numerous romantic movies that are set in Paris. It's called Paname, Pantruche, Babylone. The city of Paris has many names and just as many faces. And that shouldn't be too surprising: this is the capital of the most visited country in the world.

Whoever walks the streets of Paris could easily fall in love. I sure did, when my parents almost yearly used the city as a stopover on our trips from The Netherlands to more southern, warmer destinations. I can vividly remember the city's famous joie de vivre, which is unmissable when you see the packed terraces where Parisians sit with a glass of wine to go with their déjeuner. No Paris terrorist attack or harsh winter comes between the French and their terraces.

The long history of the city is meticulously marked in the city center's buildings, engraved in the architecture, visible through all the famous landmarks, and vividly tangible when you look over the crooked rooftops with numerous chimneys. To this day, Paris is the capital of both exquisite French cuisine and, of course, extraordinary fashion.

Every self-respecting fashion brand has one or more stores in the French capital. Nowhere in the world is it more tempting to get a new outfit, whether it's in one of the famous shopping malls or in the endless number of boutique shops that line the Rue de Charonne, whether you go to the stores around Canal Saint-Martin or take a stroll through the Le Marais neighborhood—it's hard not to leave Paris with an empty wallet.

In these shopping neighborhoods, you will encounter a variety of people of many nationalities, because of the large quantities of tourists that roam the streets of Paris. Outside the city center, you will find just as diverse a crowd, even though the dynamic is completely different: people from all over the world live here and use the subway to commute to their jobs in the city.

All these landmarks—the charming neighborhoods with bars and restaurants, the famous architecture, the rougher parts of town and the multicultural allure of Paris—are captured in the photo book you are holding at this very moment: all the different faces of this metropolis can be seen through the lenses of contemporary photographers. It shows you that there will always be new angles, perspectives, and takes to discover on this magnificent city.

Gros-Caillou
Pie Aerts

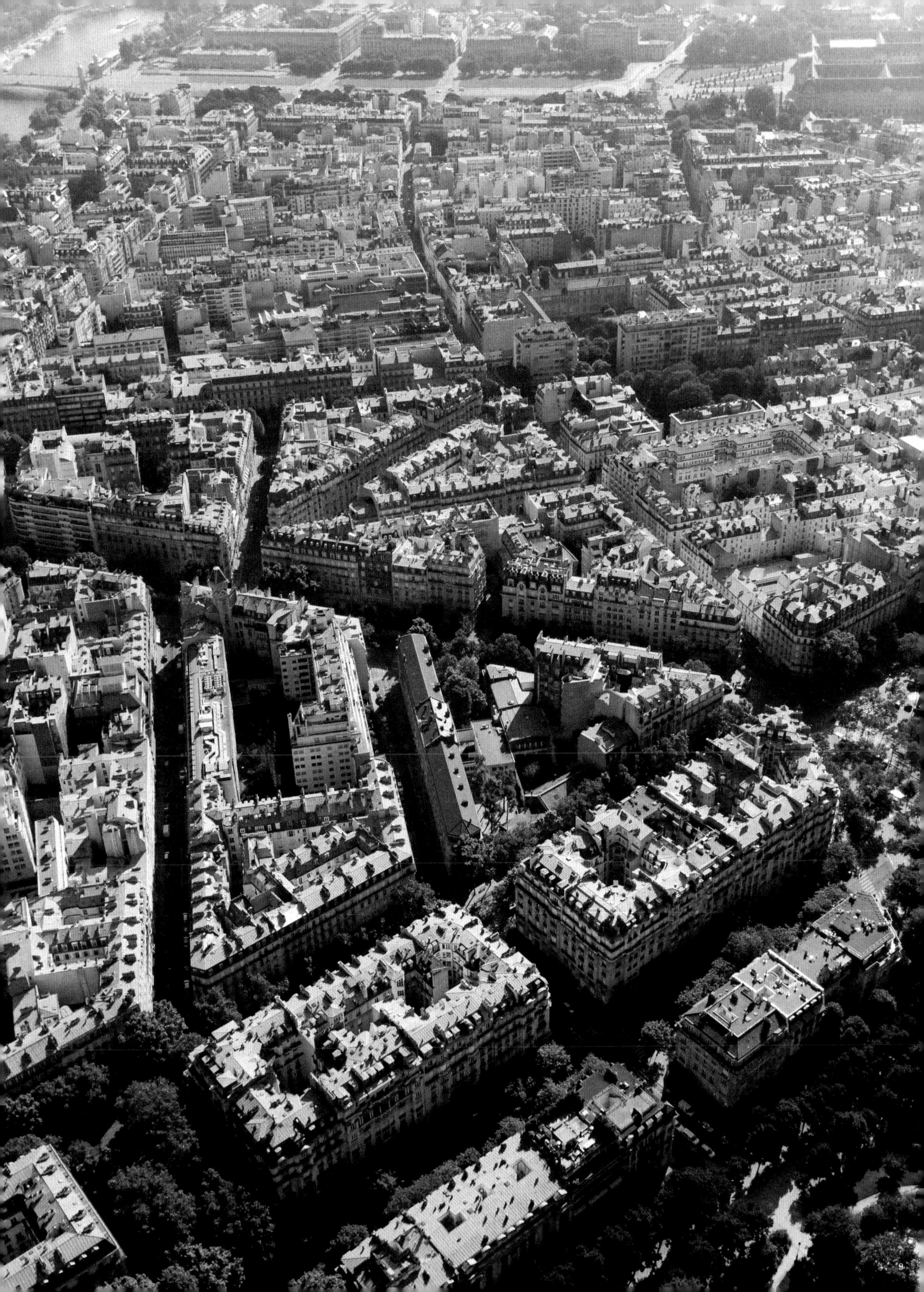

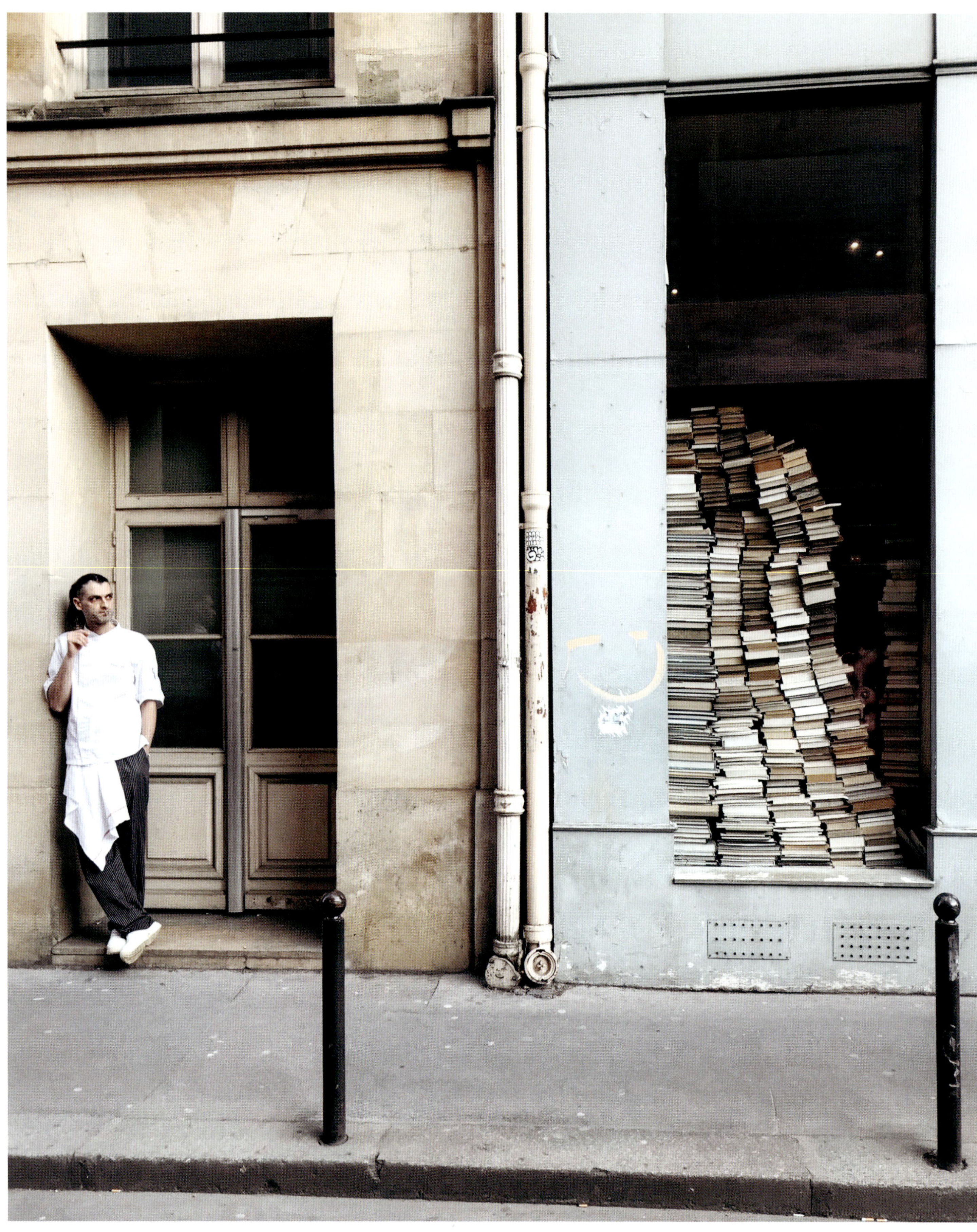

Outside Galerie Vivienne
Vivienne
Laurent Dassencourt

Verliebt in Paris

Words Joost Bastmeijer
IG handle @joostbastmeijer

Man nennt sie die Stadt des Lichts, denn sie war Pionierin in Sachen Elektrizität und spielte eine führende Rolle im Zeitalter der Aufklärung. Sie ist die Stadt der Liebe, denn dort spielen unzählige romantische Filme. Man nennt sie Paname, Pantruche, Babylon. Paris hat viele Namen und ebenso viele Gesichter. Doch das ist wenig überraschend, denn sie ist die Hauptstadt des meistbesuchten Landes der Welt.

Wer durch Paris schlendert, kann sich leicht verlieben. Mir ist es auf jeden Fall so ergangen, denn meine Eltern legten dort fast jedes Jahr auf der Durchreise von den Niederlanden in südlichere, wärmere Gefilde einen Zwischenstopp ein. Ich erinnere mich noch gut an die berühmte joie de vivre, unverkennbar, wenn man die Pariser auf den überfüllten Terrassen beim Mittagessen mit einem Glas Wein sitzen sieht. Und ihre geliebten Terrassen lassen sich die Franzosen weder durch einen Angriff auf Paris noch einen strengen Winter madig machen.

Die lange Historie der City spiegelt sich en détail wider in den Gebäuden im Zentrum, eingemeißelt in die Architektur, erkennbar an all den berühmten Wahrzeichen und deutlich spürbar beim Blick über die schiefen Dächer mit den zahllosen Kaminen. Bis heute verkörpert Paris das Zentrum der französischen Küche – und natürlich auch der Mode.

Jedes Modelabel, das etwas auf sich hält, hat einen oder mehrere Läden in der französischen Hauptstadt. Nirgends auf der Welt ist es verlockender, ein neues Outfit zu erstehen, sei es in einer der berühmten Einkaufspassagen oder der unzähligen Boutiquen entlang der Rue de Charonne, sei es beim Bummel durch die Szene-Läden am Canal Saint-Martin oder beim Gang durch das Viertel Le Marais – Paris nicht mit leerer Geldbörse zu verlassen, das ist schon eine Kunst.

Als Ziel Tausender von Touristen, die sich durch die Pariser Straßen schieben, trifft man in den Einkaufsvierteln Menschen aus aller Herren Länder. Ein ebenso bunt gemischtes Publikum findet sich in den Außenbezirken der Stadt, doch herrscht dort eine völlig andere Dynamik: Von dort aus pendeln Menschen aus der ganzen Welt mit der Metro zu ihrem Arbeitsplatz in der City.

Die Vielzahl der Wahrzeichen, die pulsierenden Viertel mit ihren Bars und Restaurants, die berühmte Architektur, die raueren Stadtteile und der multikulturelle Anstrich von Paris sind in diesem Bildband, den Sie in Händen halten, vereint: die vielen Gesichter der Metropole, gesehen durch das Objektiv zeitgenössischer Fotografen. Ein Bildband, der Sie einlädt, immer neue Blickwinkel, Perspektiven und Ansichten in dieser zauberhaften Stadt zu entdecken.

Par amour de Paris

Words Joost Bastmeijer
IG handle @joostbastmeijer

C'est la Ville Lumière – pour l'électricité dont elle a bénéficié très tôt et pour son rôle durant le Siècle des Lumières. C'est la Ville de l'Amour – principalement pour les nombreux films romantiques dont elle est le cadre. On l'appelle Paname, Pantruche ou encore, Babylone. Paris possède de nombreux noms, et autant de visages. Ce qui n'a rien de surprenant : elle est la capitale du pays le plus visité au monde.

Quiconque déambule dans les rues de Paris, peut aisément en tomber amoureux. Ce que j'ai assurément vécu année après année, lorsque mes parents choisissaient la capitale française comme escale de nos pérégrinations depuis les Pays-Bas vers des contrées plus chaudes et méridionales. J'ai un vif souvenir de cette célèbre joie de vivre qu'on ne peut manquer de rencontrer sur les terrasses bondées où les Parisiens s'installent devant un déjeuner, avec un verre de vin. Nul attentat, nul hiver rude ne peut s'interposer entre les Français et leurs terrasses.

La longue histoire de la ville est inscrite avec précision dans chacun des édifices qui se dressent en son centre, incarnée par l'architecture, visible dans chaque monument célèbre, et perceptible de façon saisissante lorsqu'on regarde les toits biscornus aux multiples cheminées. Jusqu'à ce jour, Paris est restée la capitale d'une gastronomie exquise et d'une mode extraordinaire.

Toute marque en vogue se doit de posséder une ou plusieurs boutiques dans cette capitale. Nulle part ailleurs dans le monde, il n'est aussi tentant d'acheter une tenue nouvelle, que ce soit dans l'un des célèbres grands magasins, dans l'un des innombrables magasins qui bordent la rue de Charonne ou le canal Saint-Martin, ou encore, au terme d'une virée dans le quartier du Marais – difficile de ne pas quitter Paris avec un porte-monnaie vide.

Dans les quartiers commerçants se côtoient toutes sortes de nationalité, en raison du grand nombre de touristes qui écument la capitale. Hors du centre, la foule y est tout aussi variée, même si l'énergie en est complètement différente : on y rencontre des habitants venus du monde entier qui font la navette en métro, entre leur lieu de travail et leur domicile.

Chaque monument, chaque lieu de charme, avec ses bars et ses restaurants, chaque édifice célèbre, mais aussi, les quartiers plus rudes ou le multiculturalisme de Paris, sont présents dans l'ouvrage que vous tenez entre vos mains en cet instant : les différents visages de la métropole se révèlent au travers de l'objectif de photographes contemporains - prouvant qu'il est toujours de nouveaux angles, de nouvelles perspectives ou images à découvrir dans cette ville superbe.

Forum des Halles
Les Halles
Maxime Roig

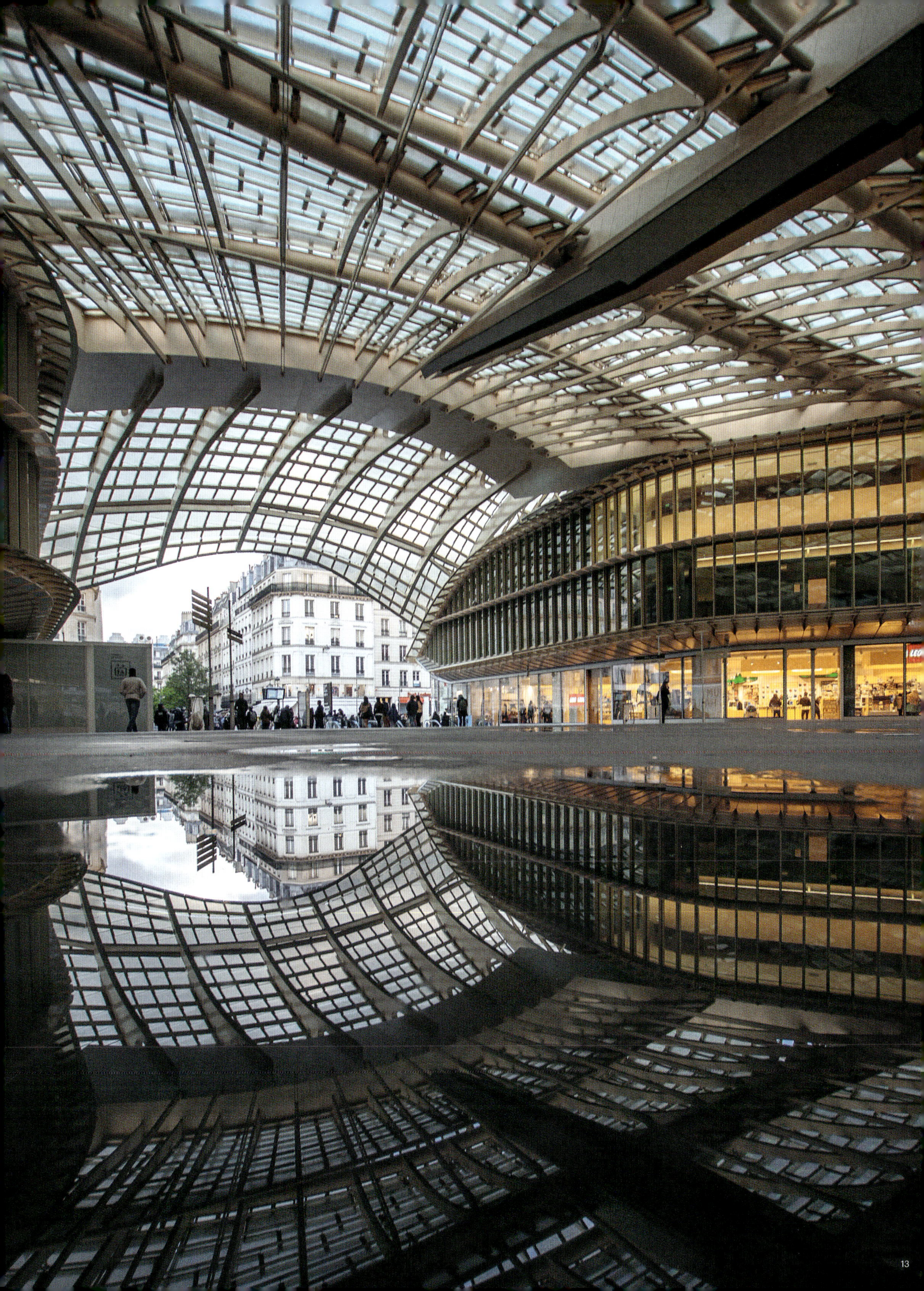

Palais Garnier, Opéra National de Paris
9e Arrondissement
Roel Ruijs

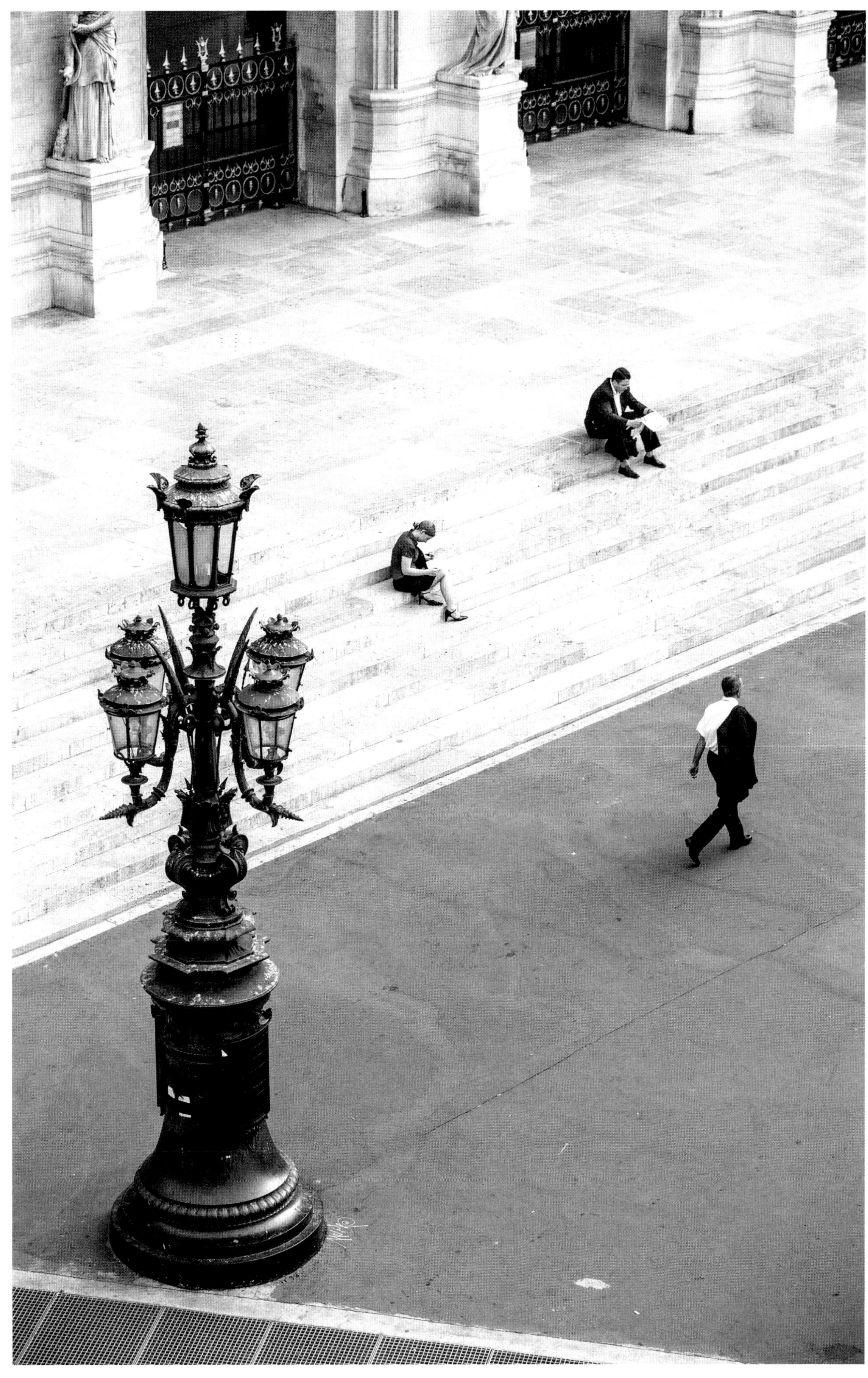

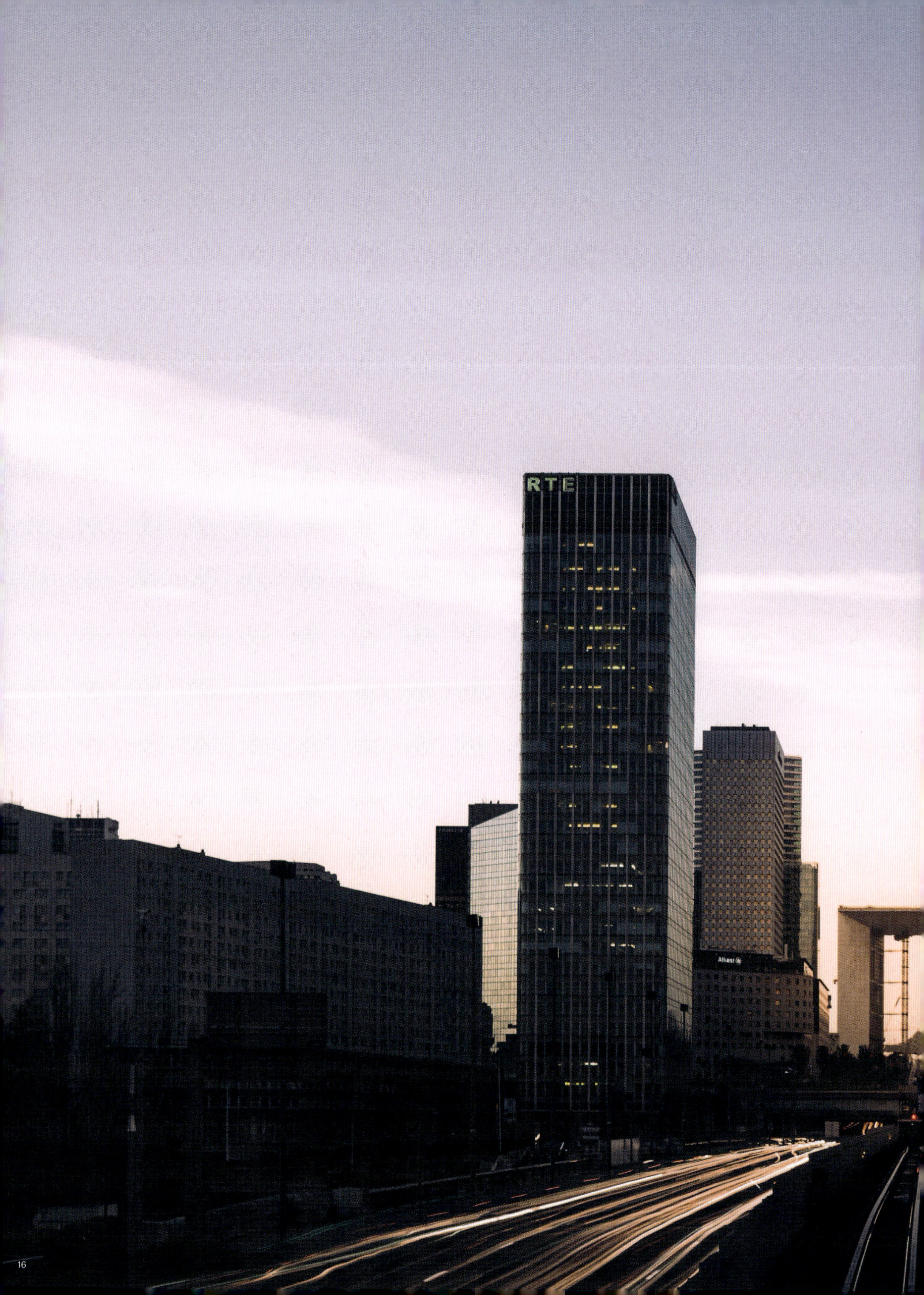
RTE
Allianz

La Défense
Nicolas Zwarg

Auber Subway Station
9e Arrondissement
Sulay Kelly

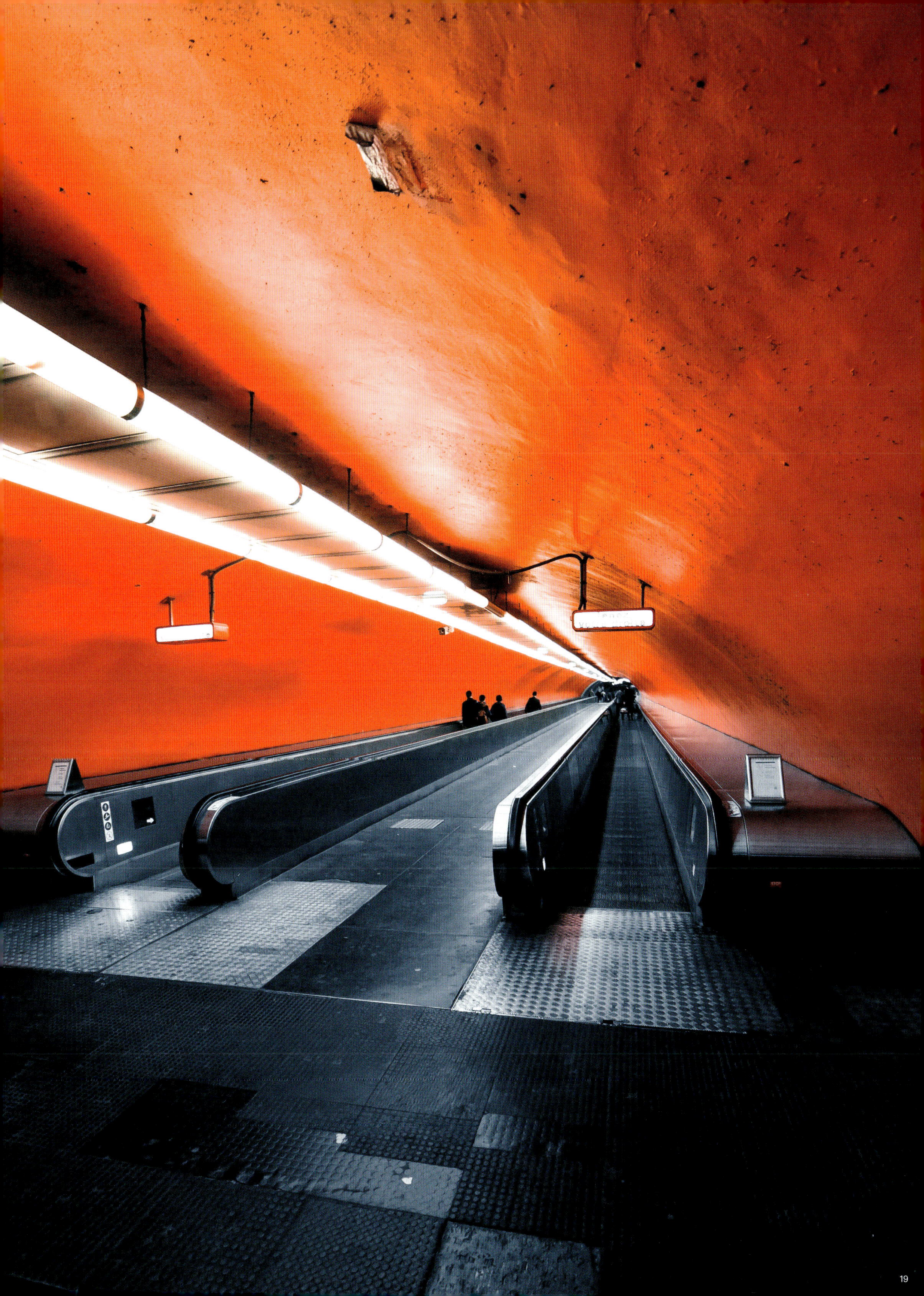

Amedeo Abello

hometown Paris, France
IG handle @amedeoabello

"The secret is to get lost," says photographer Amedeo Abello. "I always try to find new parts of the city to photograph. I'm more stimulated by new places and tend to avoid clichés." So, when Amedeo joined his filmmaker friend Giuletta Vacis in the Paris suburbs, he took a lot of pictures. "When I first saw Lac de la Sourderie, I was blown away. It is a place out of this the world: a dilapidated popular building that stands in the middle of a vast artificial lake. Wow." Abello got into photography because of his mentor, Antonio Azzano, who gave him an old Leica M3. "I started out taking pictures for pure pleasure and it became a sort of drug. My approach is all about material, substance, and being close to analogue, since I am nostalgic about analogue photography. Photography is like writing with light. The process of getting to know the world and its people, is either through light or text." Amedeo tries to create something that has social importance as much as an aesthetic appeal. "In the suburbs, I like photographing colorful and joyful scenes. I think they express a condition of positive marginality, like: 'I live in the suburbs and I enjoy it.' For me, it is essential to say something about the times we live in. We live in an era where everything occurs in a short span of time; you just need a click: from precooked food to any kind of online shopping." Amedeo likes to focus on the good and the bad side of Paris. "My aim is to collect, through a visual photographic experiment, the essence and contradictions that lie behind our society and era."

„Das Geheimnis ist, sich zu verlaufen", sagt der Fotograf Amedeo Abello. „Ich versuche immer, neue Teile der Stadt zu entdecken, die ich fotografieren kann. Neue Orte regen mich an, und ich versuche Klischees zu vermeiden." Immer, wenn Amedeo mit seiner Freundin aus der Filmbranche, Giuletta Vacis, in den Pariser Vororten unterwegs war, machte er unzählige Fotos. „Als ich zum ersten Mal den Lac de la Sourderie sah, war ich überwältigt. Der Ort ist nicht von dieser Welt: ein bekanntes verfallenes Gebäude inmitten eines riesigen künstlichen Sees. Wow!"Abello fing mit der Fotografie an, als er von seinem Mentor Antonio Azzano eine alte Leica M3 bekam. „Ich machte Fotos aus reinem Vergnügen, und ich wurde süchtig danach. Ich fotografiere das Materielle, Substanzielle, ganz nah am Analogen, denn was die analoge Fotografie anbelangt, da bin ich altmodisch. Die Fotografie ist für mich wie Schreiben mit Licht. Du lernst die Welt und die Menschen entweder durch das Licht oder durch den Text kennen." Amedeo möchte etwas von gesellschaftlicher Bedeutung mit ästhetischem Anstrich kreieren. „In den Vororten fotografiere ich immer bunte und fröhliche Szenen. Ich glaube, dass sie einen Zustand positiver Marginalität ausdrücken, so etwas wie: ‚Ich lebe in der Vorstadt und das gefällt mir'. Es ist sehr wichtig für mich, etwas über die Zeit, in der wir leben, auszudrücken. Wir leben in einem Zeitalter, wo alles innerhalb kurzer Zeit passiert, und man braucht immer nur einen Klick: vom fertig gekochten Essen bis zum grenzenlosen Online-Shopping." Amedeo beschäftigt sich gerne mit den guten und den schlechten Seiten von Paris. „Ich möchte durch ein visuelles fotografisches Experiment das Wesentliche in und die Widersprüche hinter unserer Gesellschaft und unserer Zeit entdecken."

« Le secret, c'est de se perdre, affirme le photographe Amedeo Abello. J'essaie chaque fois de découvrir de nouveaux quartiers à photographier. Les lieux inconnus me stimulent particulièrement, et je m'efforce d'éviter les clichés ». Aussi, lorsqu'il rejoint en banlieue parisienne son amie cinéaste, Giuletta Vacis, prend-il de nombreuses photographies. « Lorsque, pour la première fois, j'ai vu le Bassin de la Sourderie, j'ai été soufflé. C'est un lieu en-dehors du monde : un bâtiment populaire et délabré, au milieu d'un vaste lac artificiel. Waouh ». Abello se lance dans la photographie grâce à son mentor, Antonio Azzano, qui lui fait don d'un vieux Leica M3. « J'ai commencé à prendre des images par pur plaisir, et c'est devenu une sorte de drogue. Mon travail se concentre sur la matière, la substance, et tente de rester proche de la photographie argentique, dont je suis nostalgique. Photographier, c'est en quelque sorte écrire avec la lumière. Le processus qui consiste à connaître le monde et ceux qui l'habitent, s'opère par le truchement de la lumière ou du texte ». Amedeo s'efforce d'aboutir à des créations qui possèdent une valeur sociale autant qu'un attrait esthétique. « Ce que j'aime photographier dans les banlieues, ce sont des scènes colorées et joyeuses. Il me semble qu'elles expriment une forme de marginalité positive, du type : 'je vis en banlieue et j'aime ça'. Pour moi, il est essentiel de dire quelque chose sur l'époque qui est la nôtre. Nous vivons dans un temps où tout advient dans de brefs délais, il n'est besoin que d'un clic : de la nourriture pré-cuite aux diverses courses en ligne ». Amedeo aime à se concentrer sur les bons et les mauvais côtés de Paris. « Mon but est de recueillir, au travers d'une expérience visuelle et photographique, l'essence et les contradictions à l'œuvre derrière notre société et notre époque ».

Lac de la Sourderie
Montigny-le-Bretonneux
Amedeo Abello

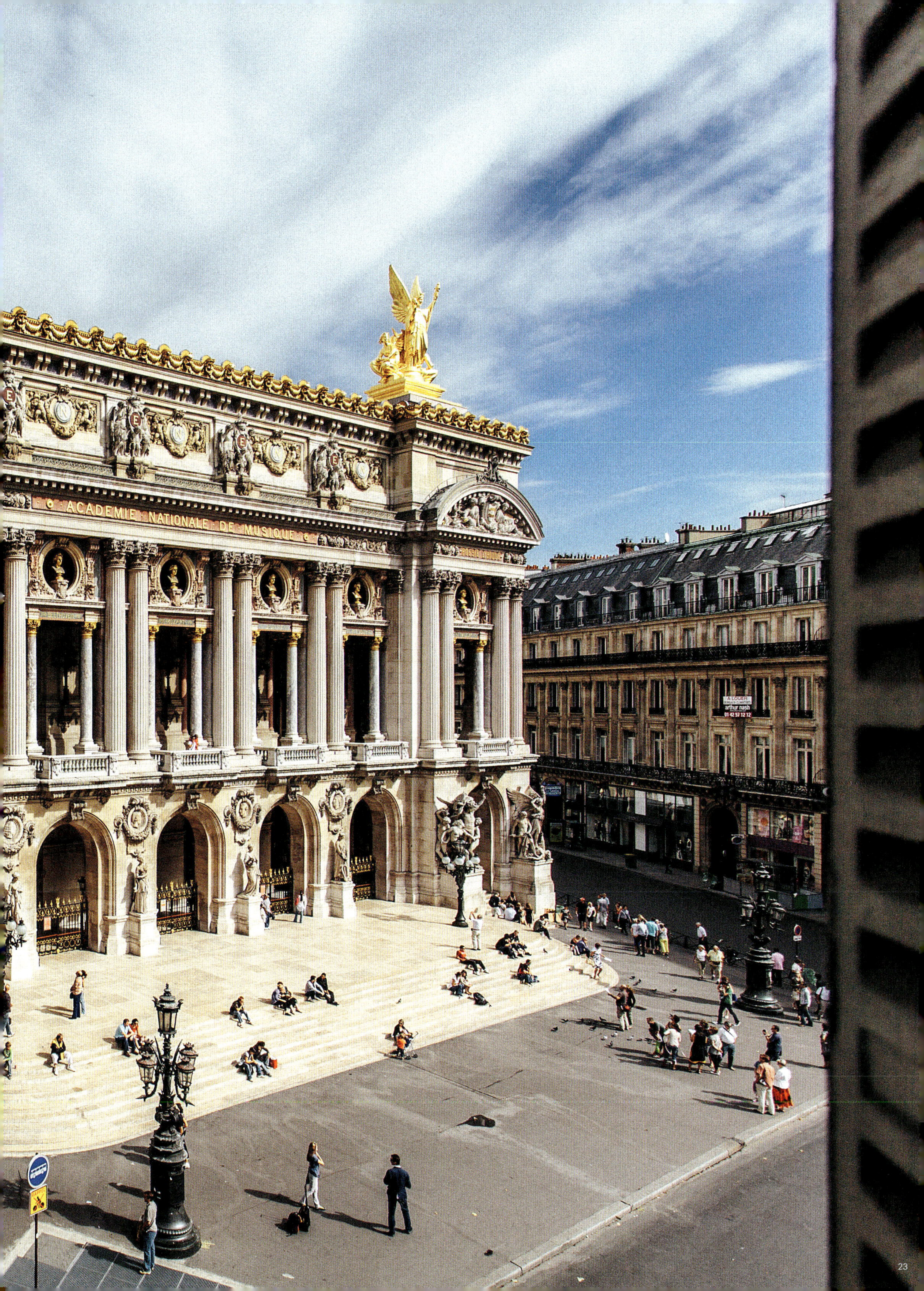
ACADEMIE NATIONALE DE MUSIQUE

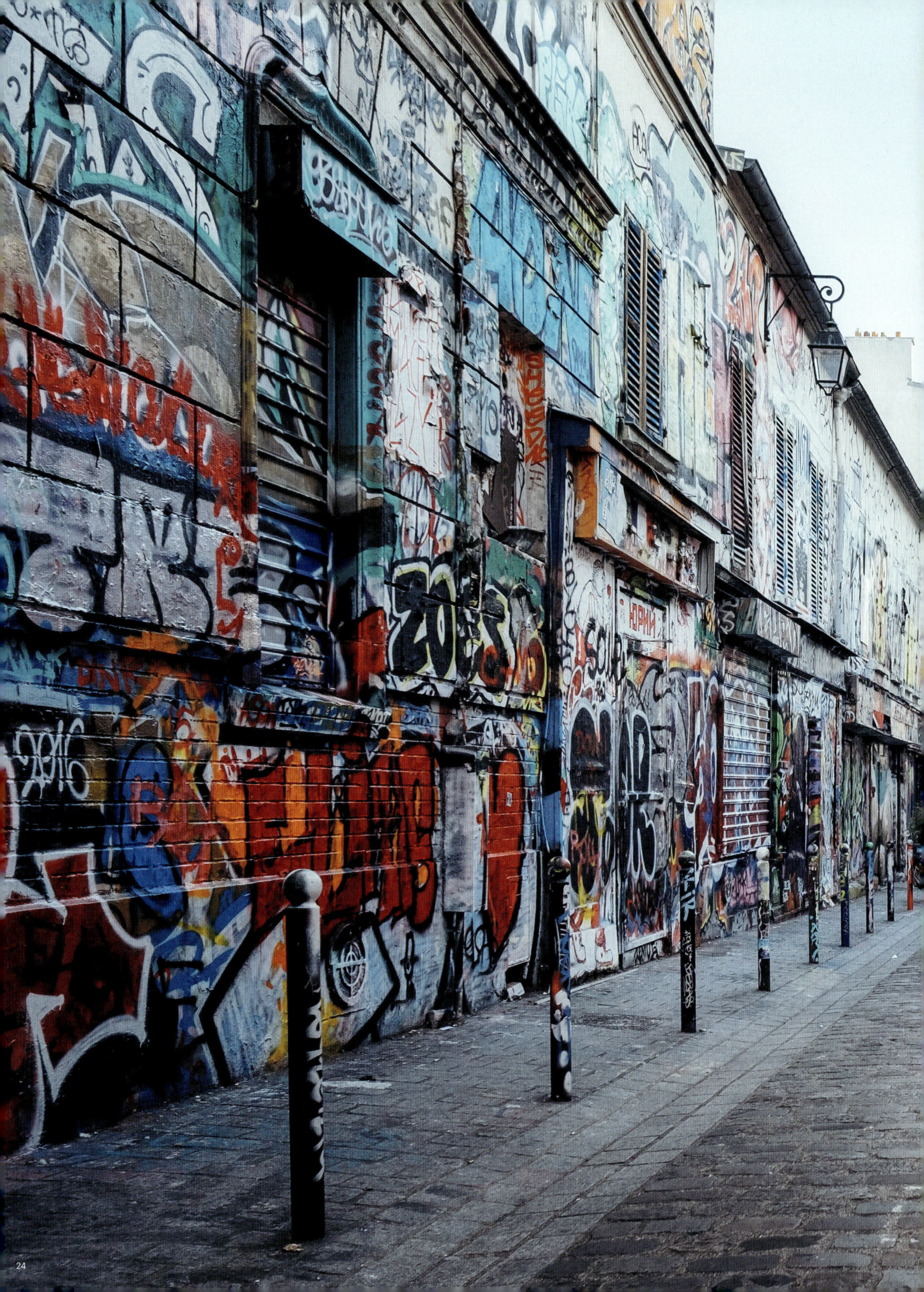

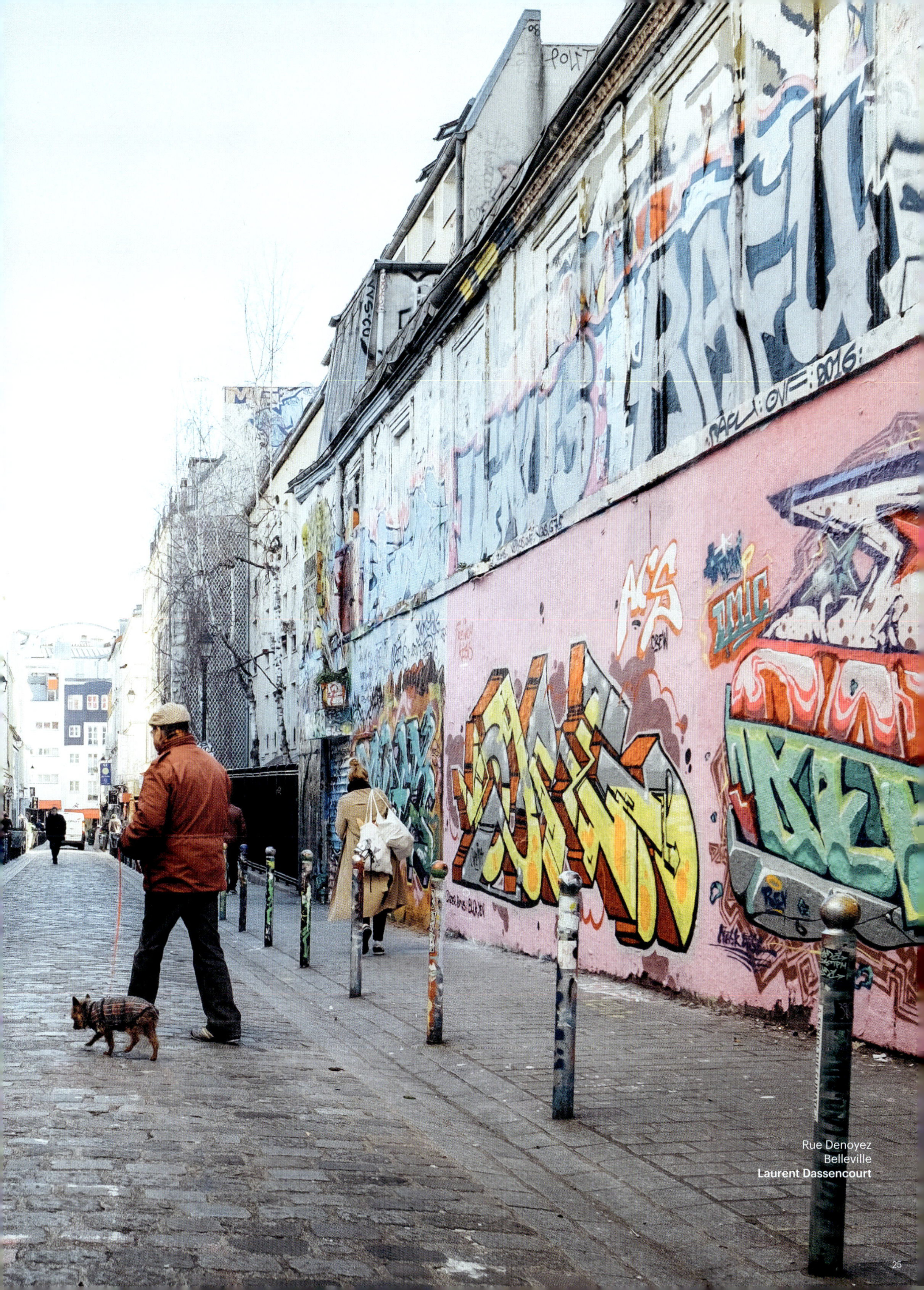

Rue Denoyez
Belleville
Laurent Dassencourt

Rue des Petites-Écuries
10e Arrondissement
Sarah van Rij

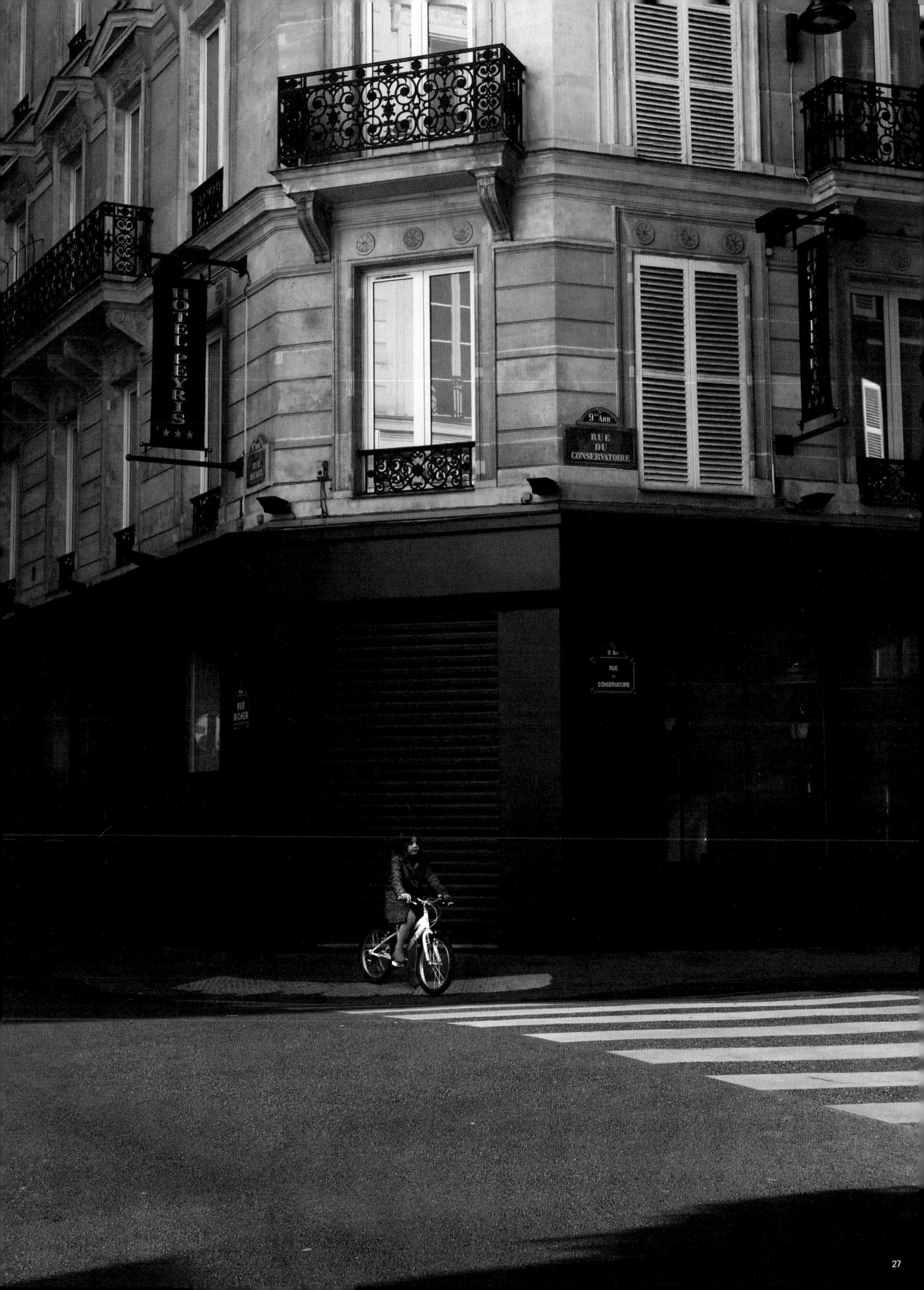
HOTEL PEYRIS
RUE DU CONSERVATOIRE

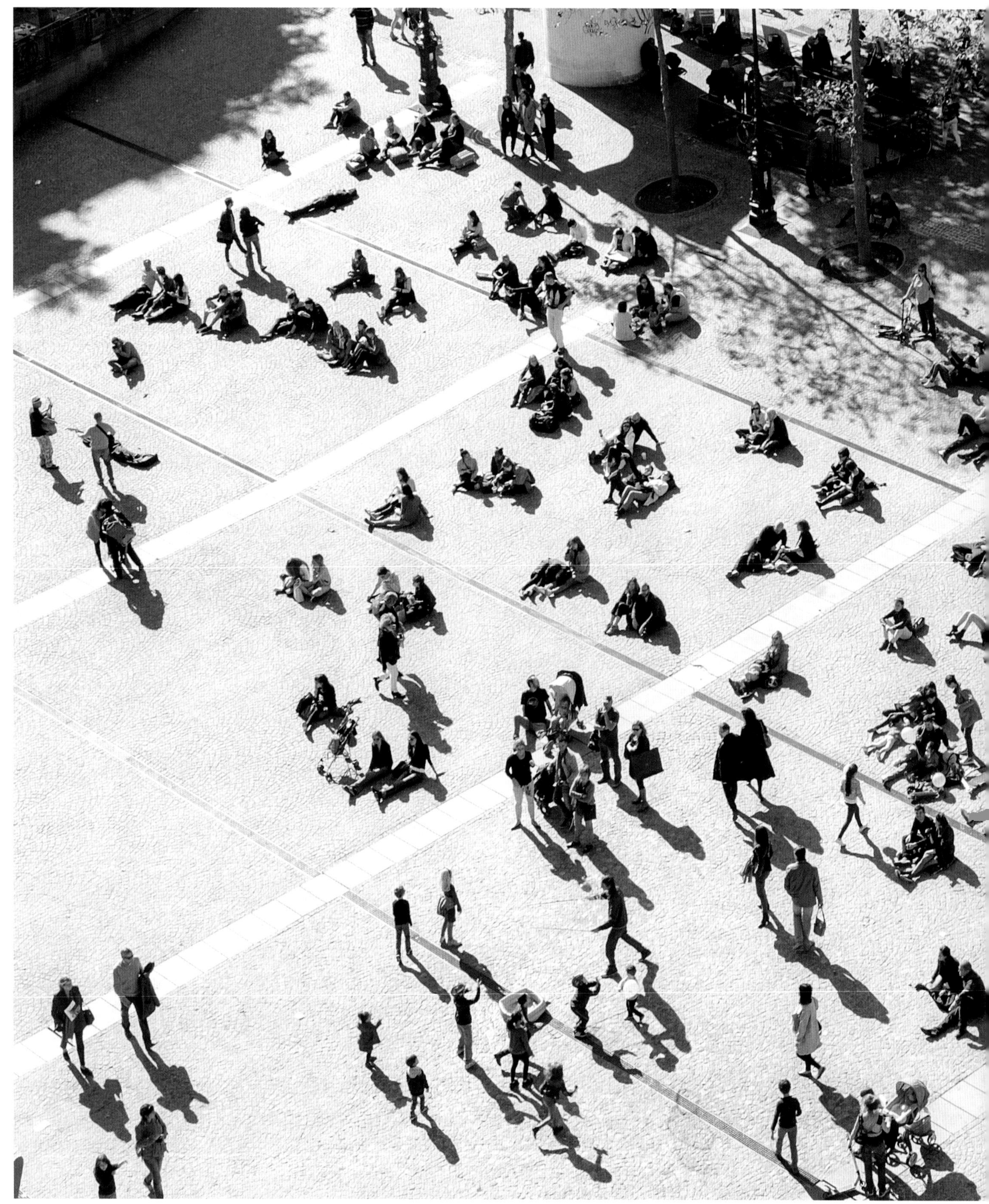

Place Georges Pompidou
4e Arrondissement
Laurent Dassencourt

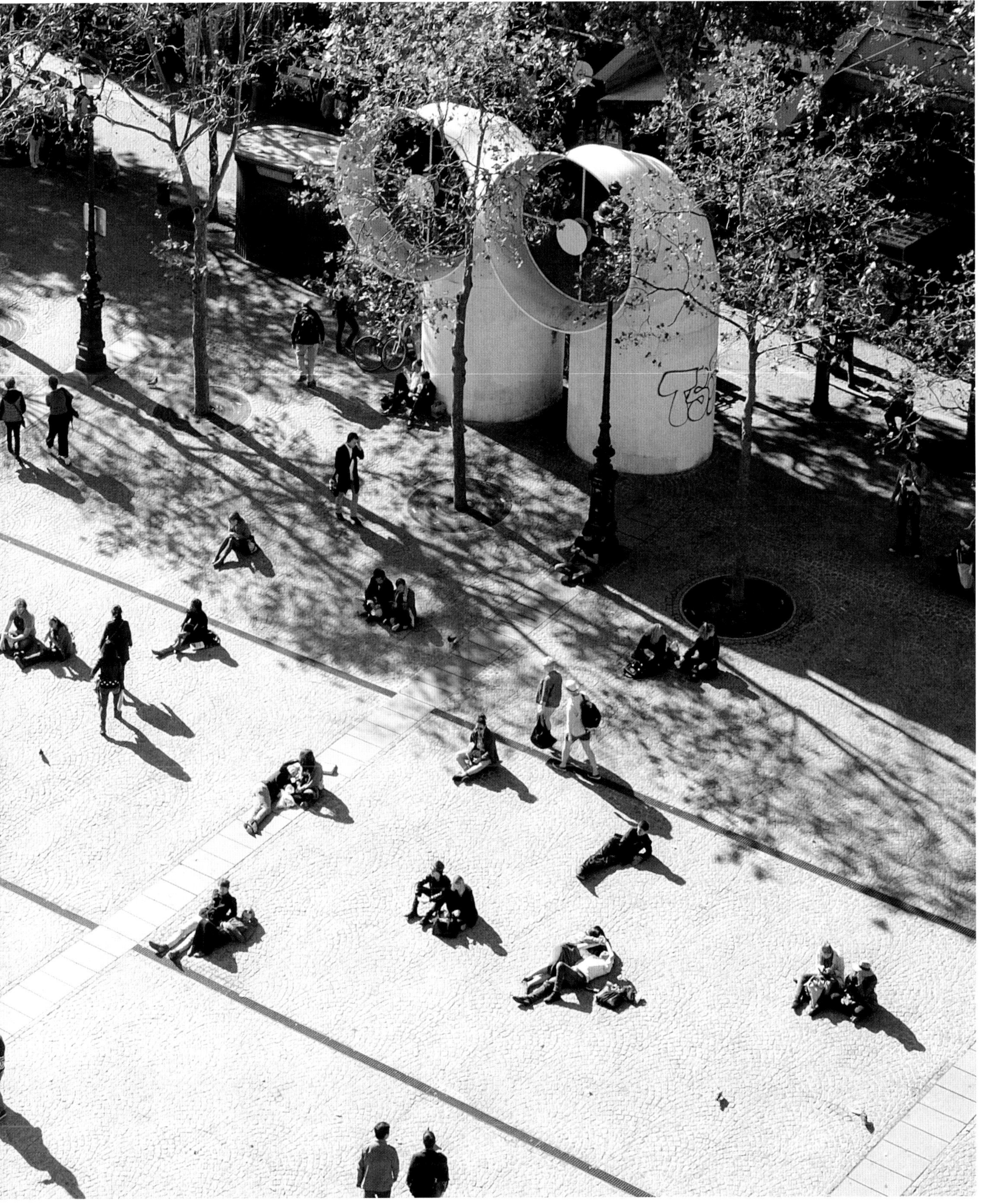

There is just a certain feel about Paris and France in general that screams out love and romance.

—Erica Gonzalez

Sainte-Chapelle Church
4e Arrondissement
Sulay Kelly

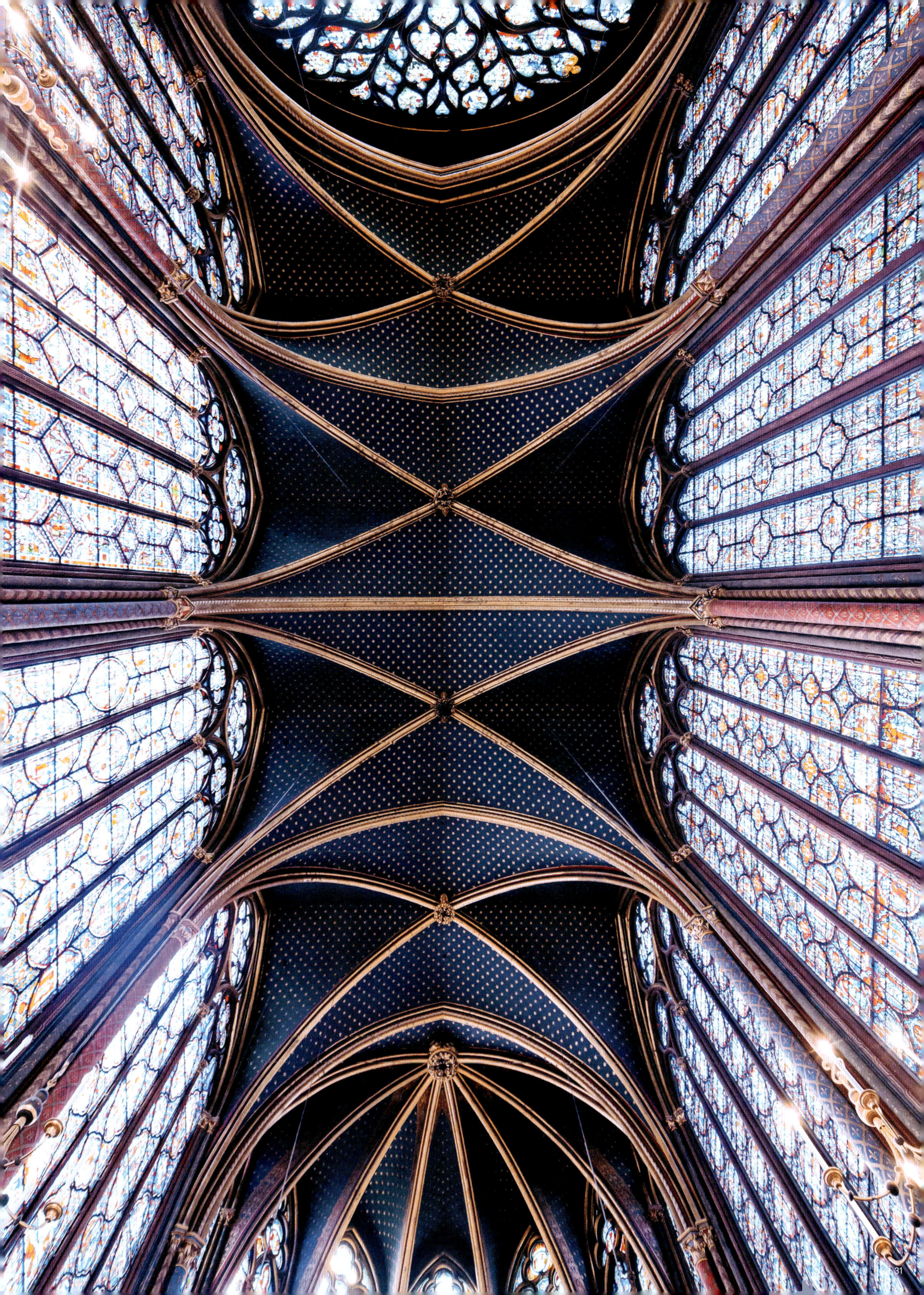

Jardin du Luxembourg
6e Arrondissement
Joseph Jabbour

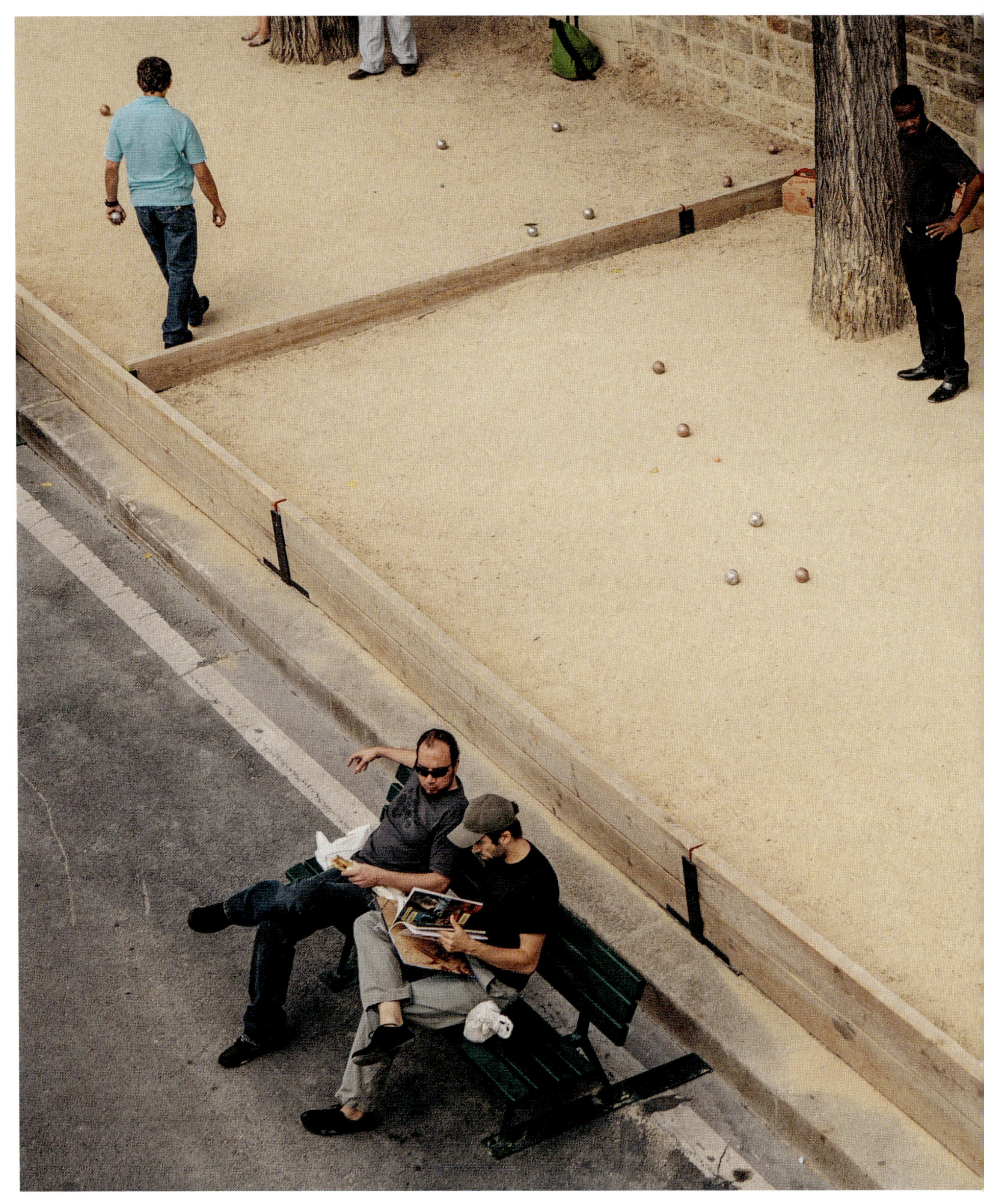

Petanque
Parc Rives de Seine
Roel Ruijs

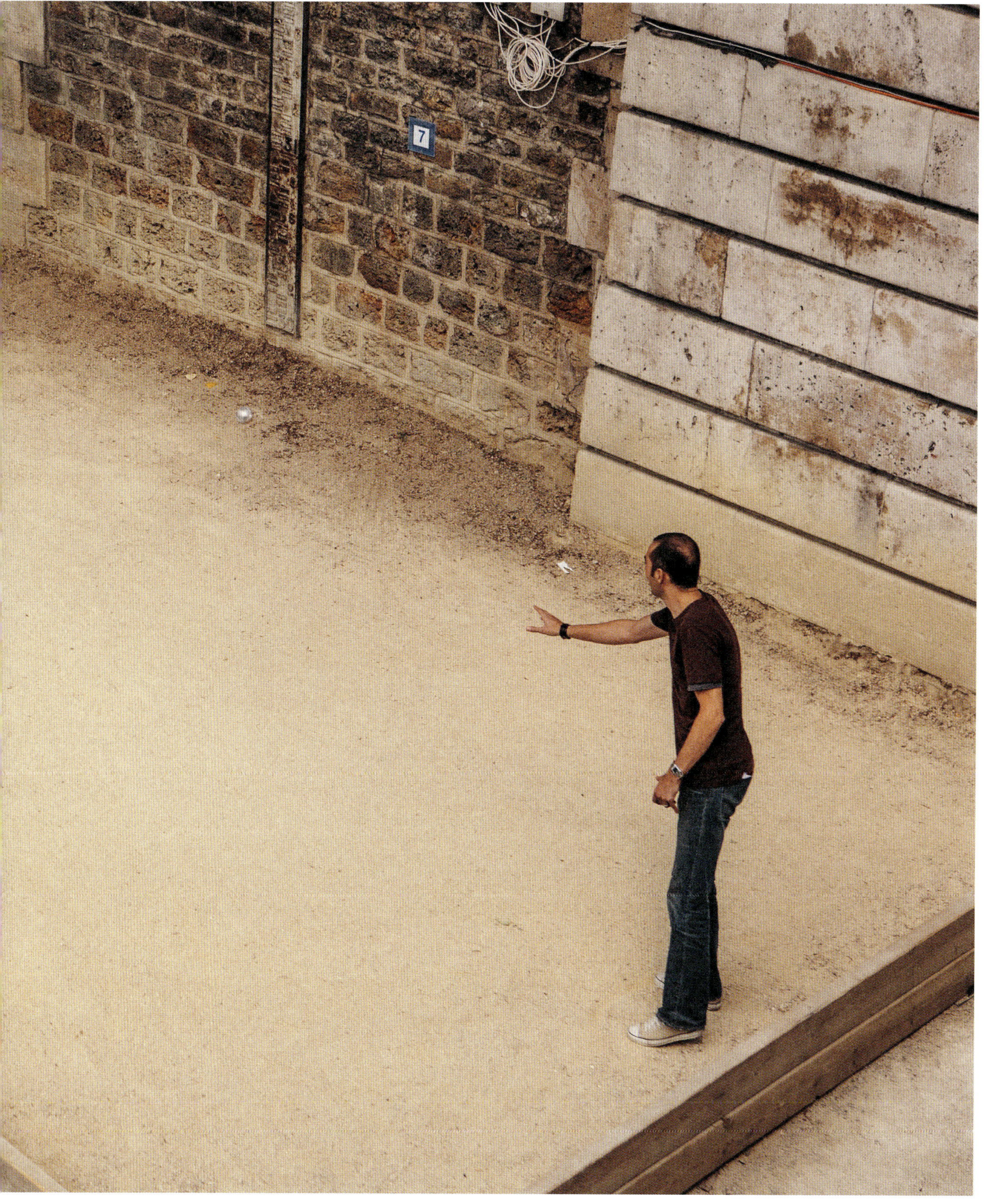
7

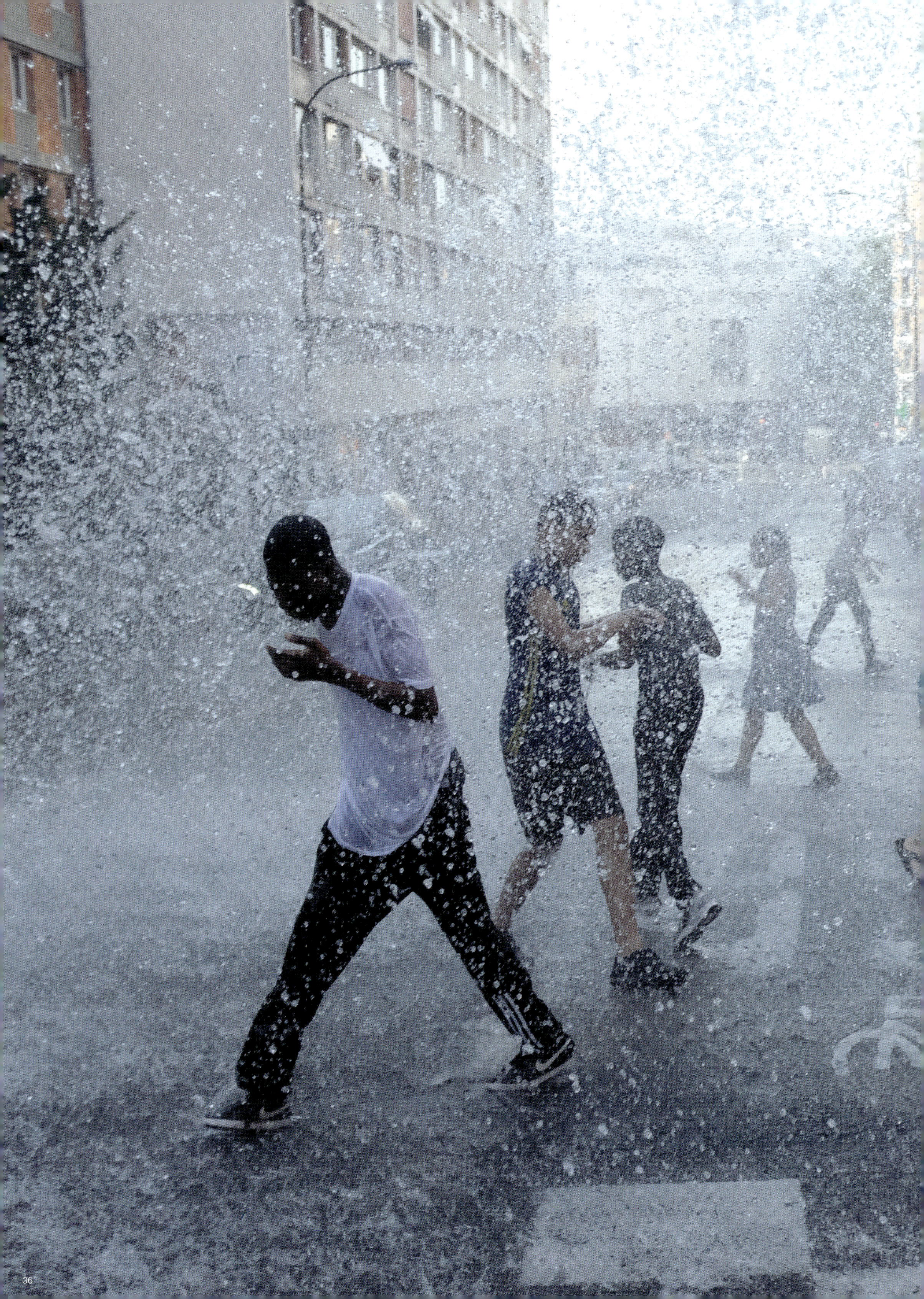

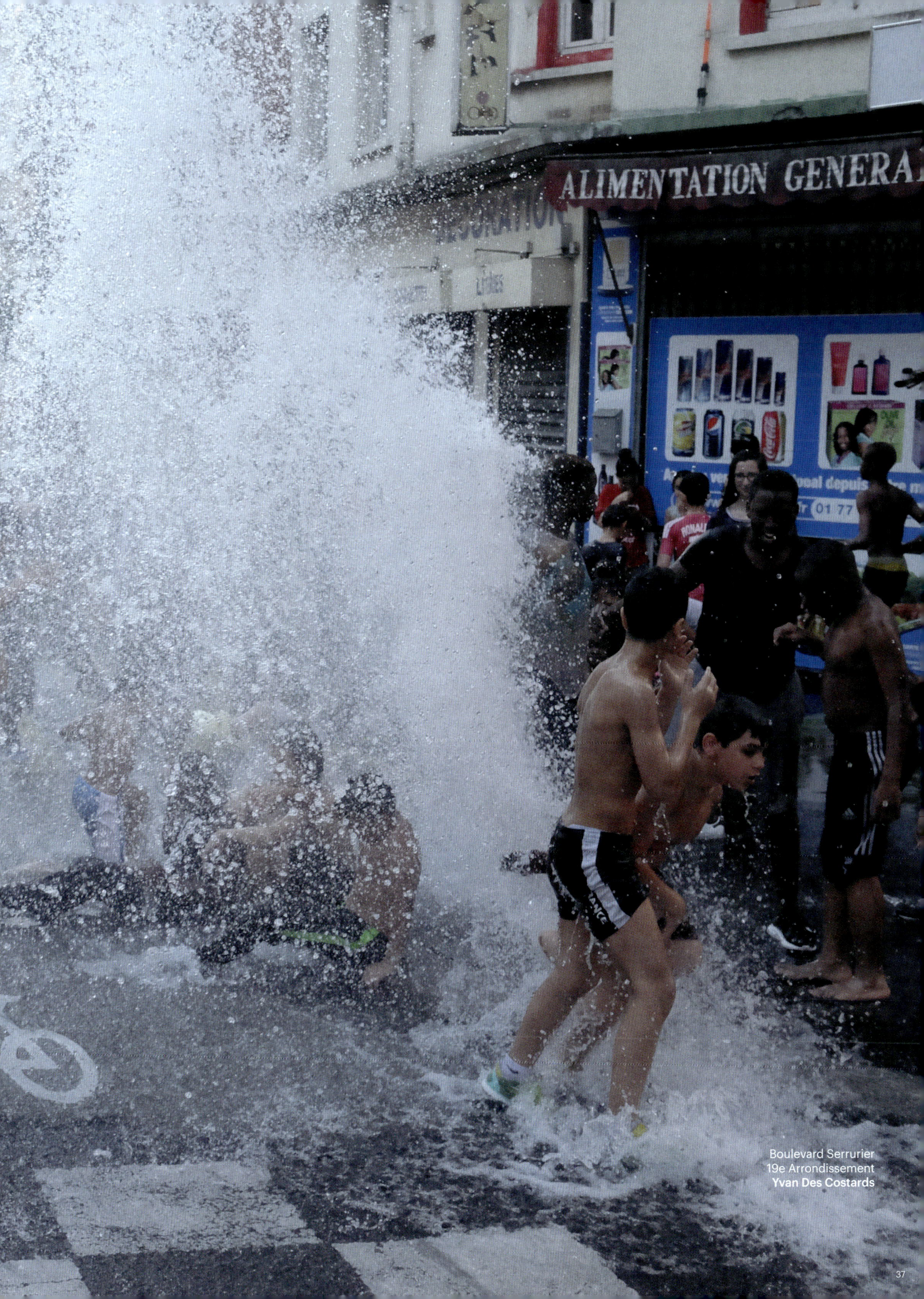

Boulevard Serrurier
19e Arrondissement
Yvan Des Costards

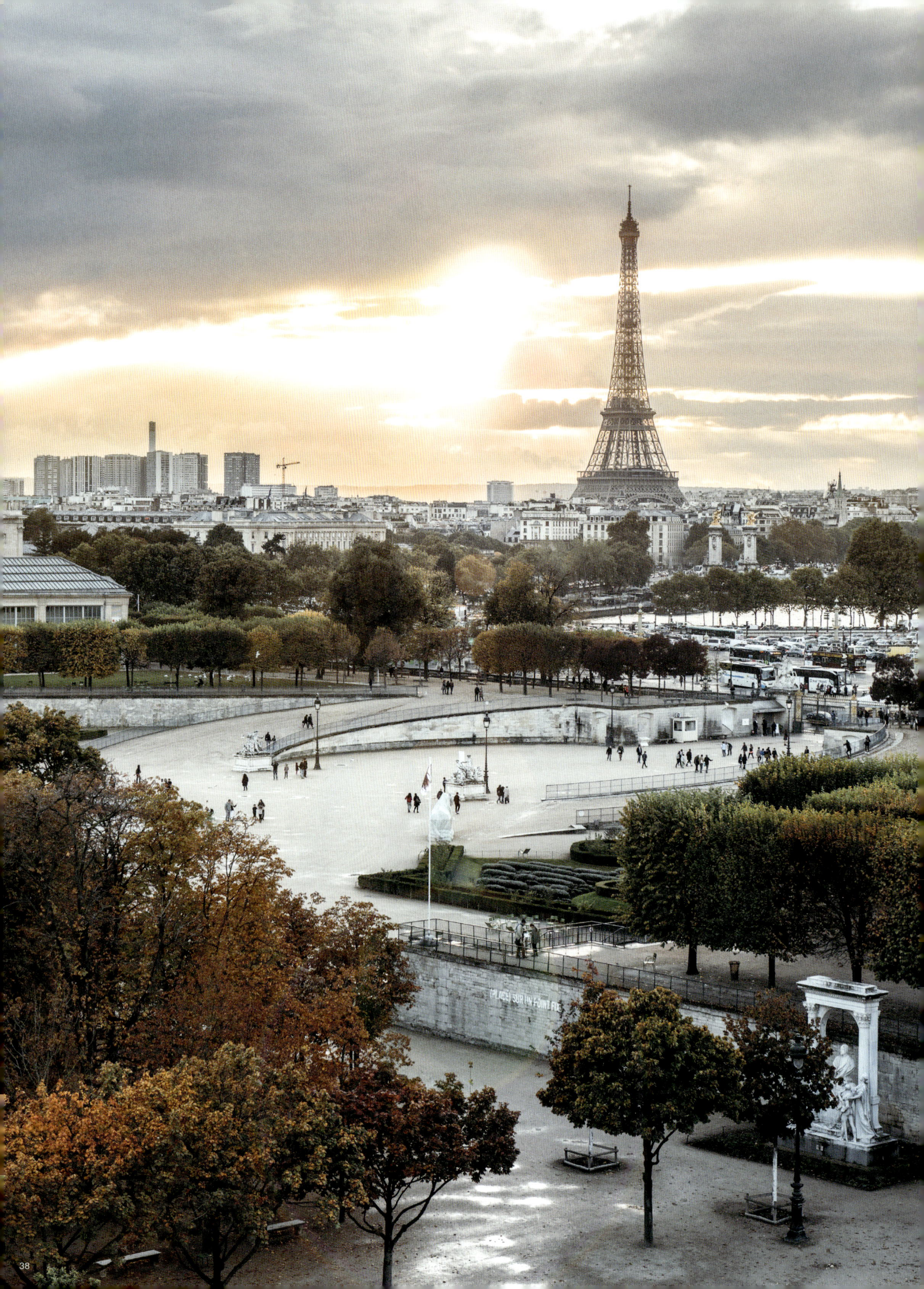

Guillaume Dutreix

hometown Paris, France
IG handle @guillaume_dx

Born and raised in Paris, Guillaume Dutreix dreamt of being a great illustrator, until he found out he wasn't the most talented at drawing and turned to photography instead. "I like to play with reality," he explains. "With a camera, you can turn something ordinary into something beautiful. It's a great feeling to know that a simple click can change a perspective." After living in Paris for 36 years, Guillaume says it's not always easy to see the city's beauty. "My relationship with Paris is like a relationship between two old, long-time lovers. Sometimes, everyday life catches up with you and it can be hard to take pictures because of tourists or ugly cars. But then, whenever I take a simple walk in the historical center, the architecture always reminds me how unique this city actually is." It's these typical Haussman-era buildings that regularly feature in Guillaume's work, which is also defined by its symmetrical compositions. "I like my images to be soothing to the eye. It's satisfying to look at something harmonious. The buildings I photograph are so subtle and elegant, full of small details. All the good architecture in Paris boasts symmetry, and photography is a great way to pay homage to the city's architects."

Guillaume Dutreix, gebürtig in Paris und dort aufgewachsen, träumte davon, ein berühmter Illustrator zu werden. Doch dann fand er heraus, dass sein Talent nicht unbedingt zeichnerischer Art war und wandte sich der Fotografie zu. „Ich spiele gerne mit der Realität", erklärt er. „Mit einer Kamera kann man etwas ganz Normales in etwas Schönes verwandeln. Es ist ein tolles Gefühl, mit einem einfachen Klick die Perspektive zu wechseln." Nach 36 Jahren in Paris ist es für Guillaume nicht immer leicht, die Schönheit der Stadt zu erkennen. „Meine Beziehung zu Paris ist für mich wie die zwischen einem alten Liebespaar. Manchmal holt dich der Alltag ein und du kannst vor lauter Touristen oder hässlicher Autos keine Fotos machen. Doch dann gehe ich einfach mal durch die Altstadt und merke an der Architektur, wie einzigartig diese Stadt doch ist." Die typischen Gebäude aus der Haussmann-Ära finden sich immer in Guillaumes Arbeit wieder, die ebenfalls von einer gewissen Symmetrie gekennzeichnet ist. „Ich möchte, dass meine Fotos dem Auge wohltun. Es tut gut, auf etwas Harmonisches zu schauen. Die Gebäude auf meinen Fotos sind so subtil und elegant, voller kleiner Details. Die schönen Bauten in Paris strotzen vor Symmetrie, und mit der Fotografie kann man den Architekten dieser Stadt auf wundervolle Weise Ehre erweisen."

Né à Paris où il grandit, Guillaume Dutreix rêve de devenir un célèbre illustrateur, avant de réaliser que le dessin n'est pas le plus grand de ses talents et de se tourner vers la photographie. « J'aime jouer avec la réalité, explique-t-il. L'appareil photo permet de transformer l'ordinaire en quelque chose de beau. Savoir qu'un simple clic peut bouleverser une perspective procure un sentiment incroyable ». Après avoir vécu dans la capitale 36 ans durant, Guillaume constate qu'il n'est pas toujours aisé de percevoir la beauté de la ville. « La relation que j'entretiens avec Paris ressemble à celle de vieux amants qui se connaissent depuis longtemps. La vie quotidienne, parfois, vous emporte, et il peut être difficile de prendre des photographies avec tous ces touristes ou ces affreuses voitures. Et puis voilà, il suffit que je me promène dans le centre historique, pour que l'architecture me rappelle combien cette cité est en réalité unique ». Les édifices typiquement haussmanniens apparaissent régulièrement dans son travail, qui se caractérise également par des compositions symétriques. « J'aime que mes images soient apaisantes pour le regard. Contempler une harmonie procure un sentiment de satisfaction. Les bâtiments que je photographie sont d'une telle subtilité, d'une telle élégance, fourmillants de détails. Les meilleurs d'entre eux se caractérisent par la symétrie, et la photographie est un merveilleux moyen de rendre hommage aux architectes de la ville ».

Jardin des Tuileries
1e Arrondissement
Guillaume Dutreix

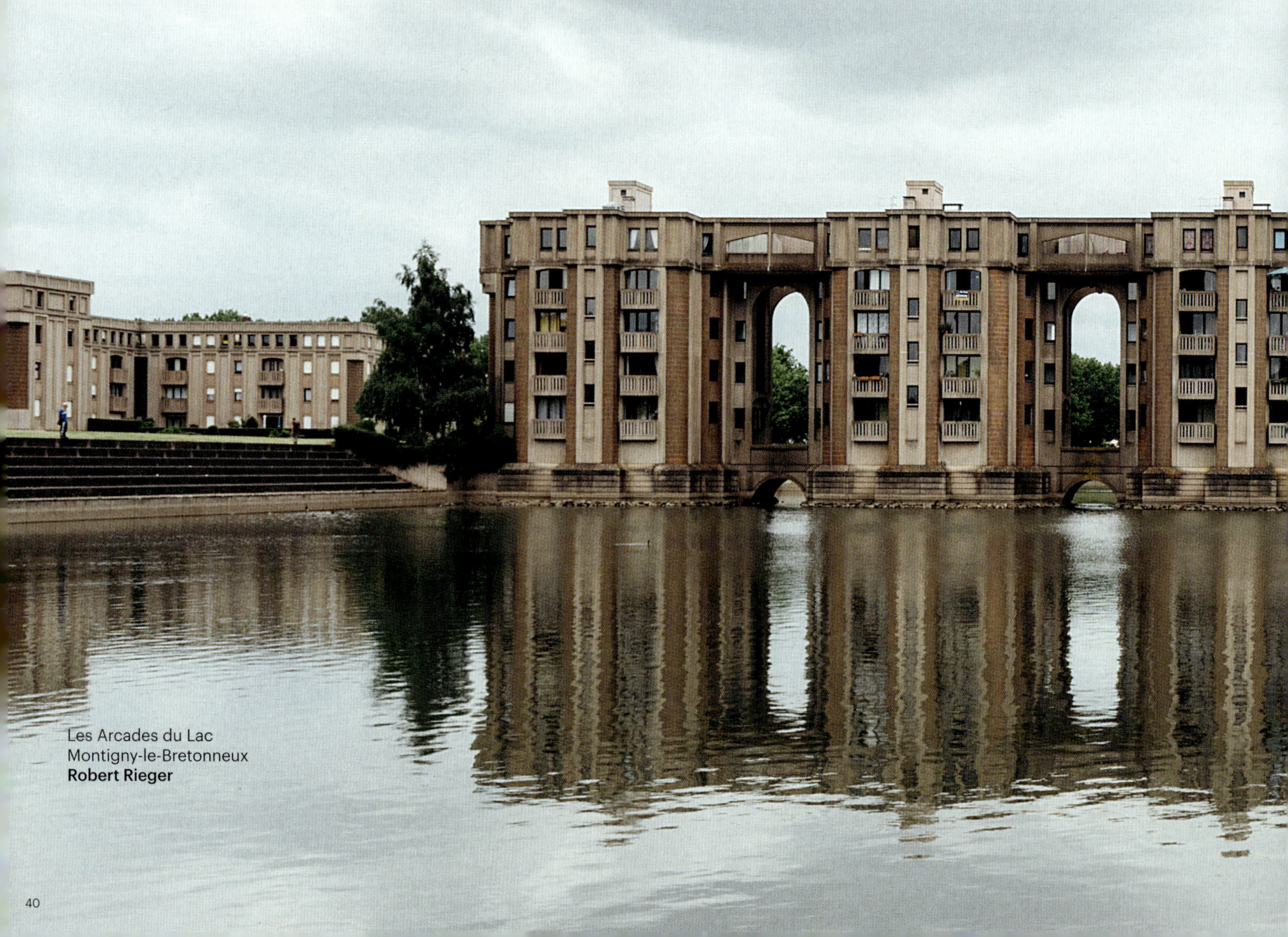

Les Arcades du Lac
Montigny-le-Bretonneux
Robert Rieger

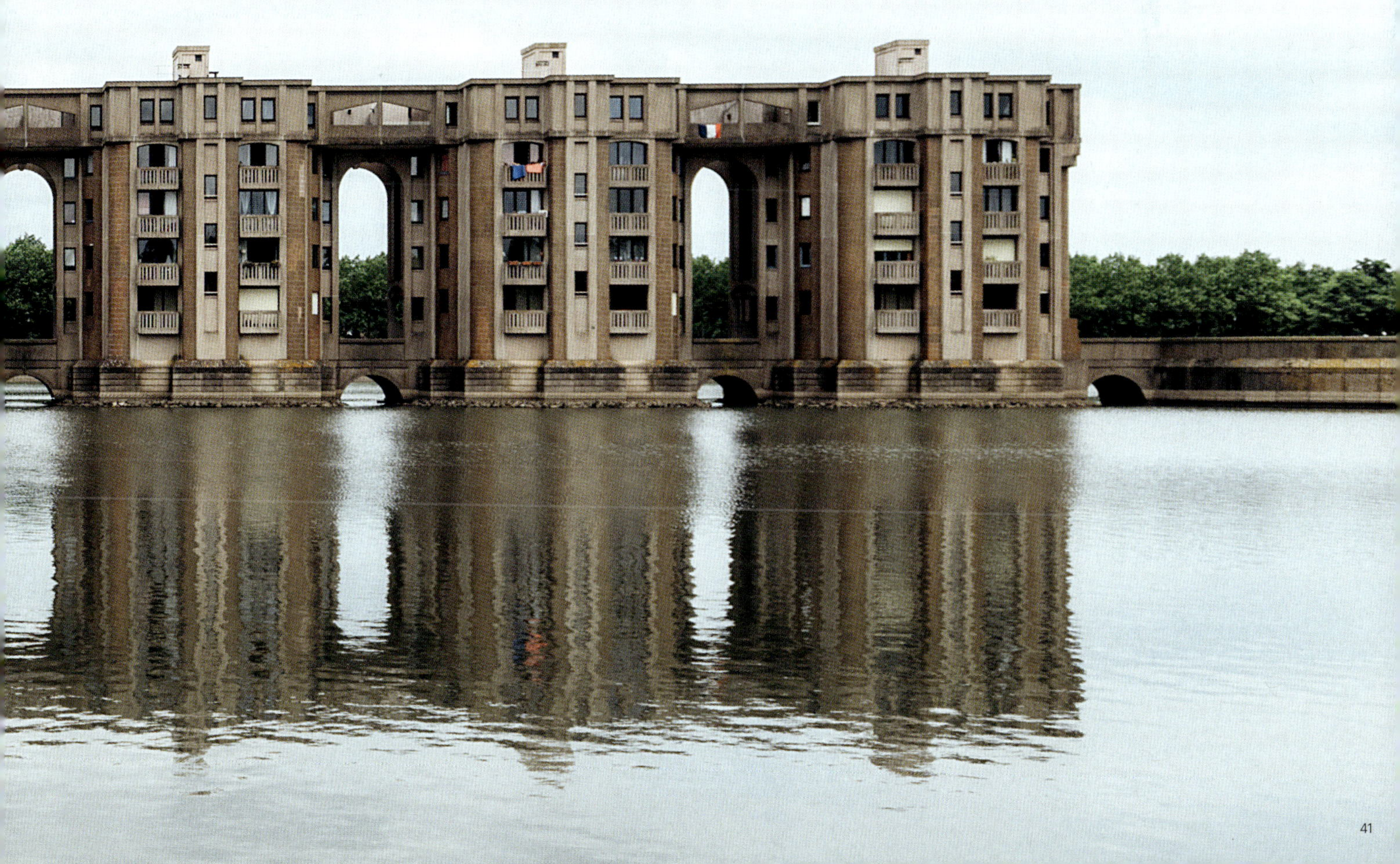

Rue de Rivoli
1e Arrondissement
Juan Jerez del Valle

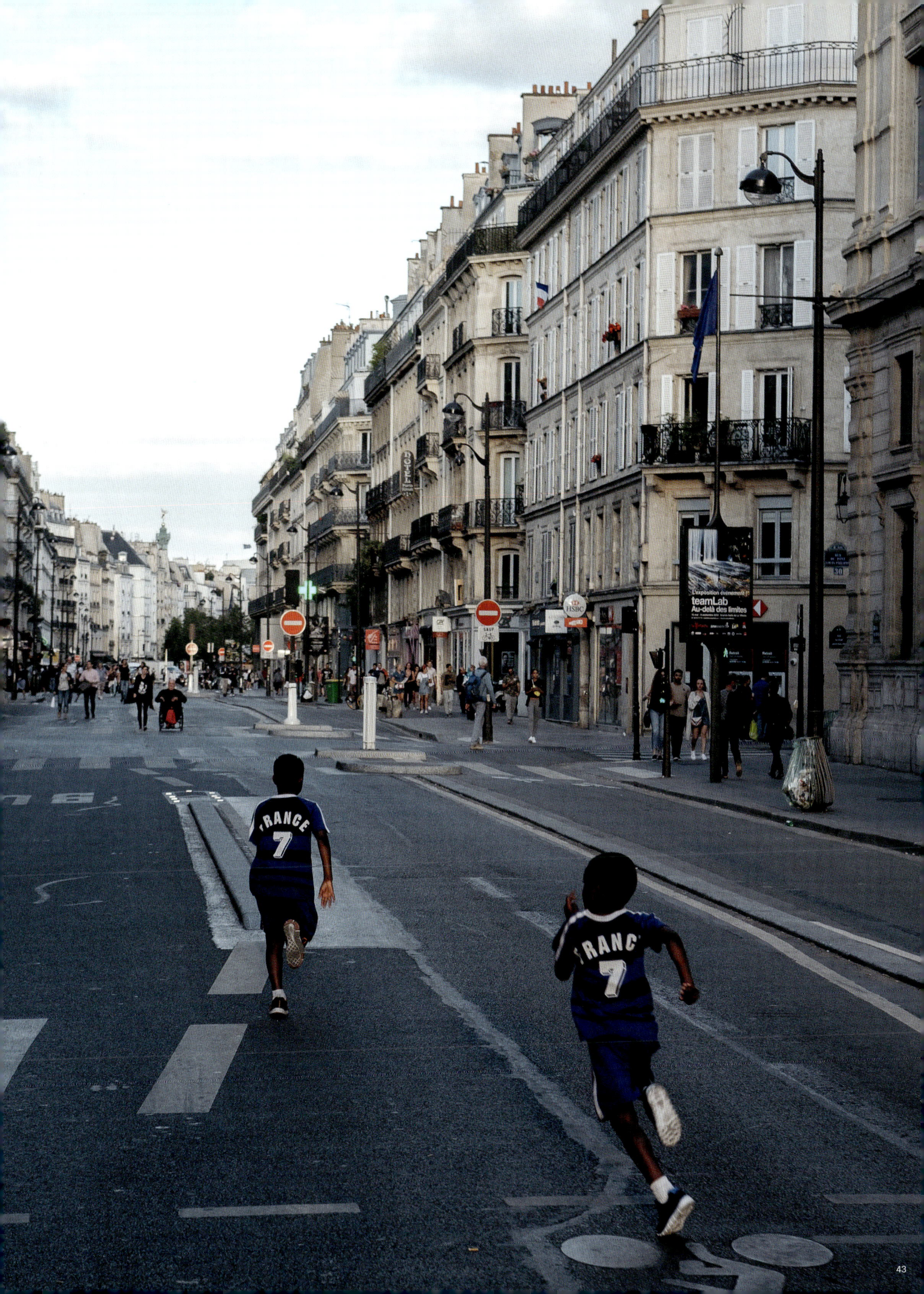
FRANCE
7
teamLab
Au-delà des limites
HSBC

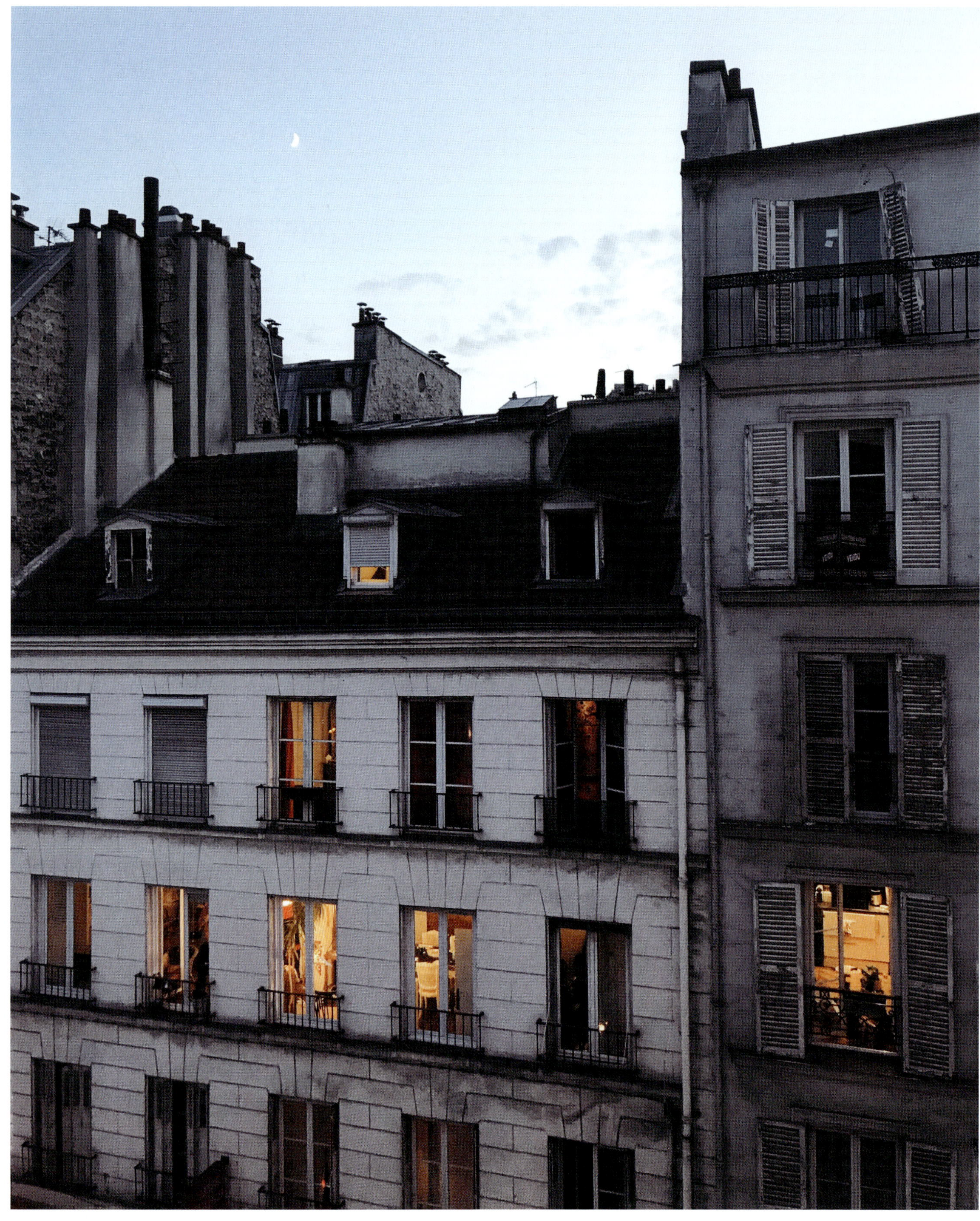

Rue Clignancourt
Montmartre
Laurent Dassencourt

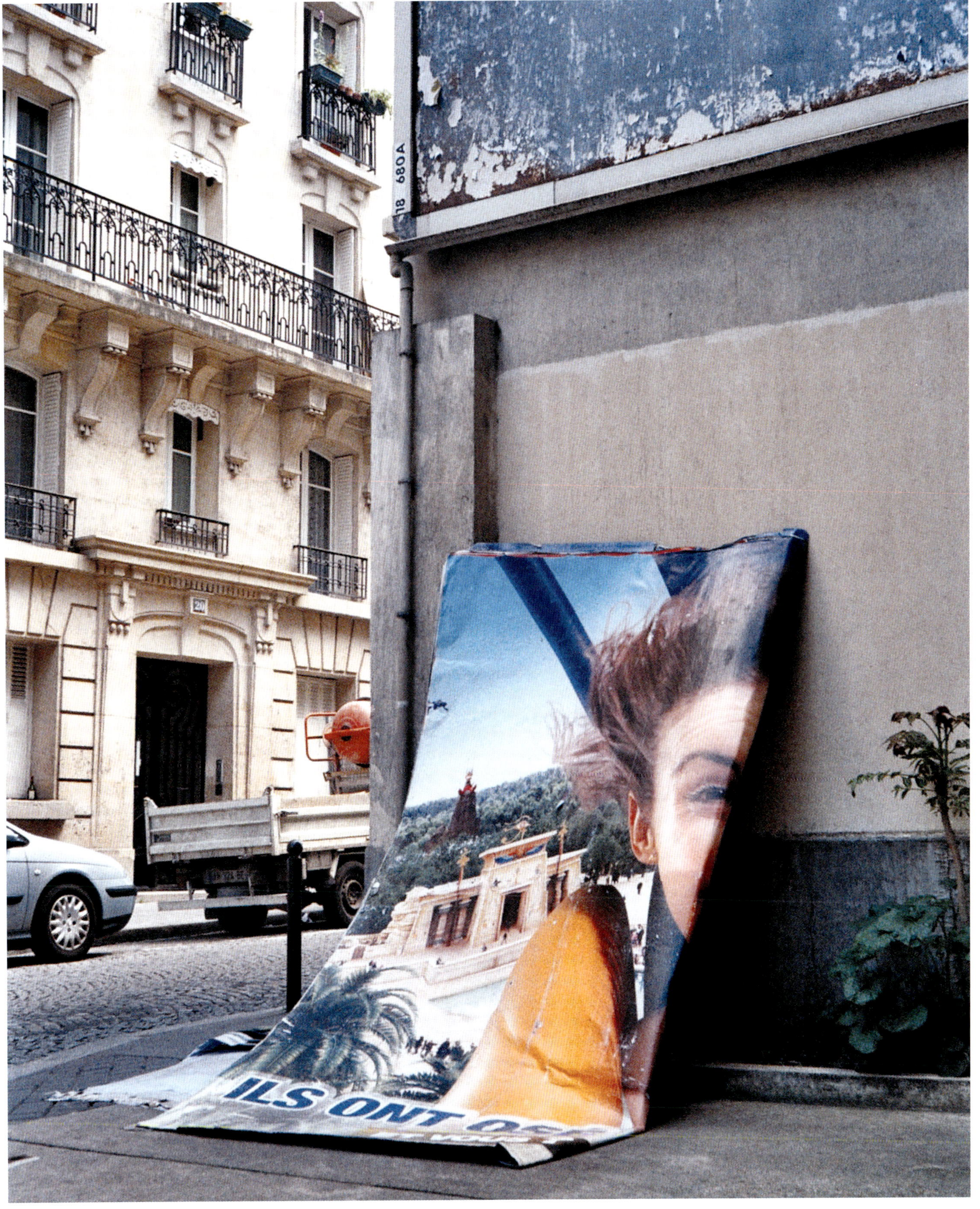

Place de Clichy
19e Arrondissement
IZBERG

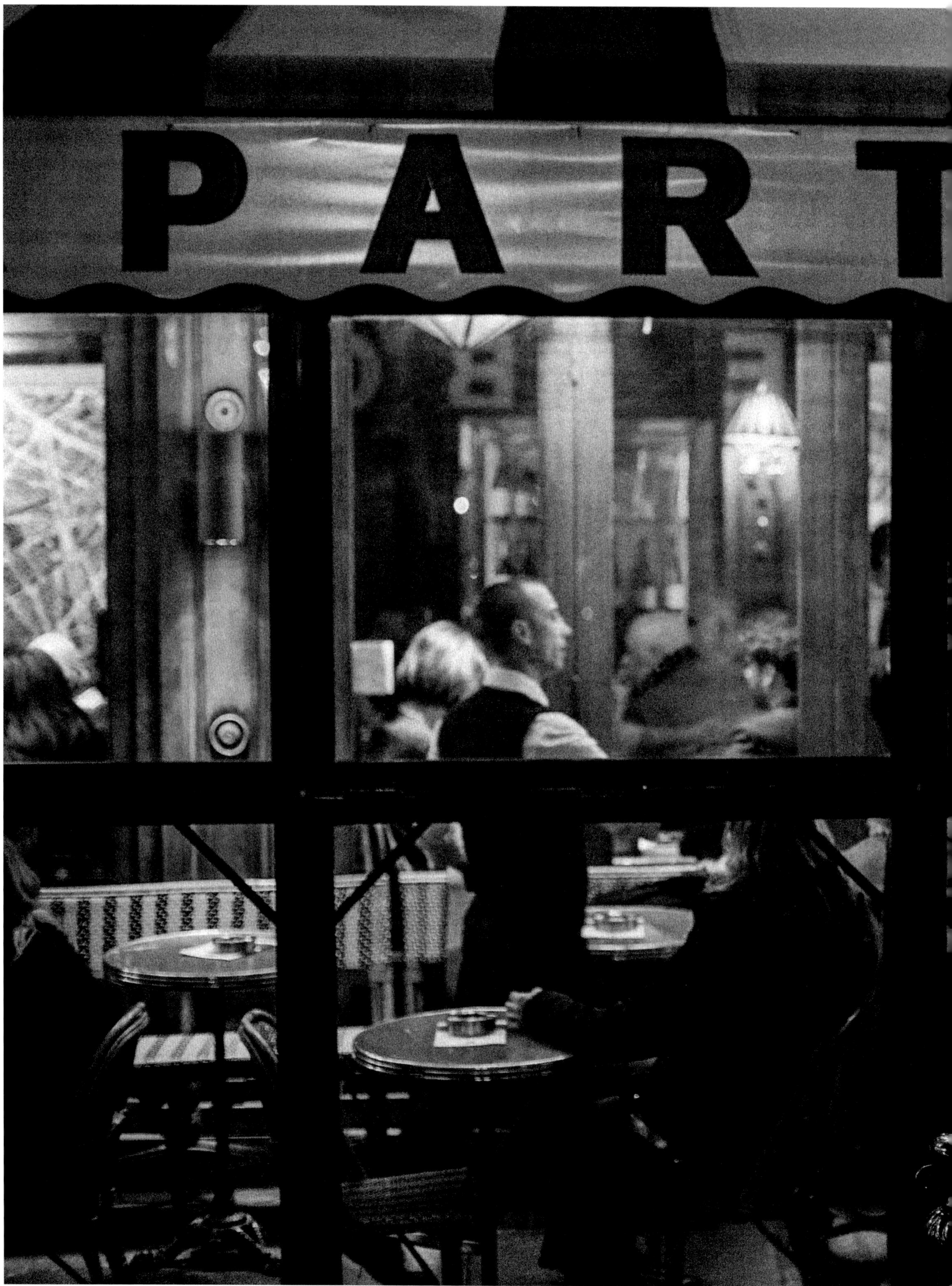
PART

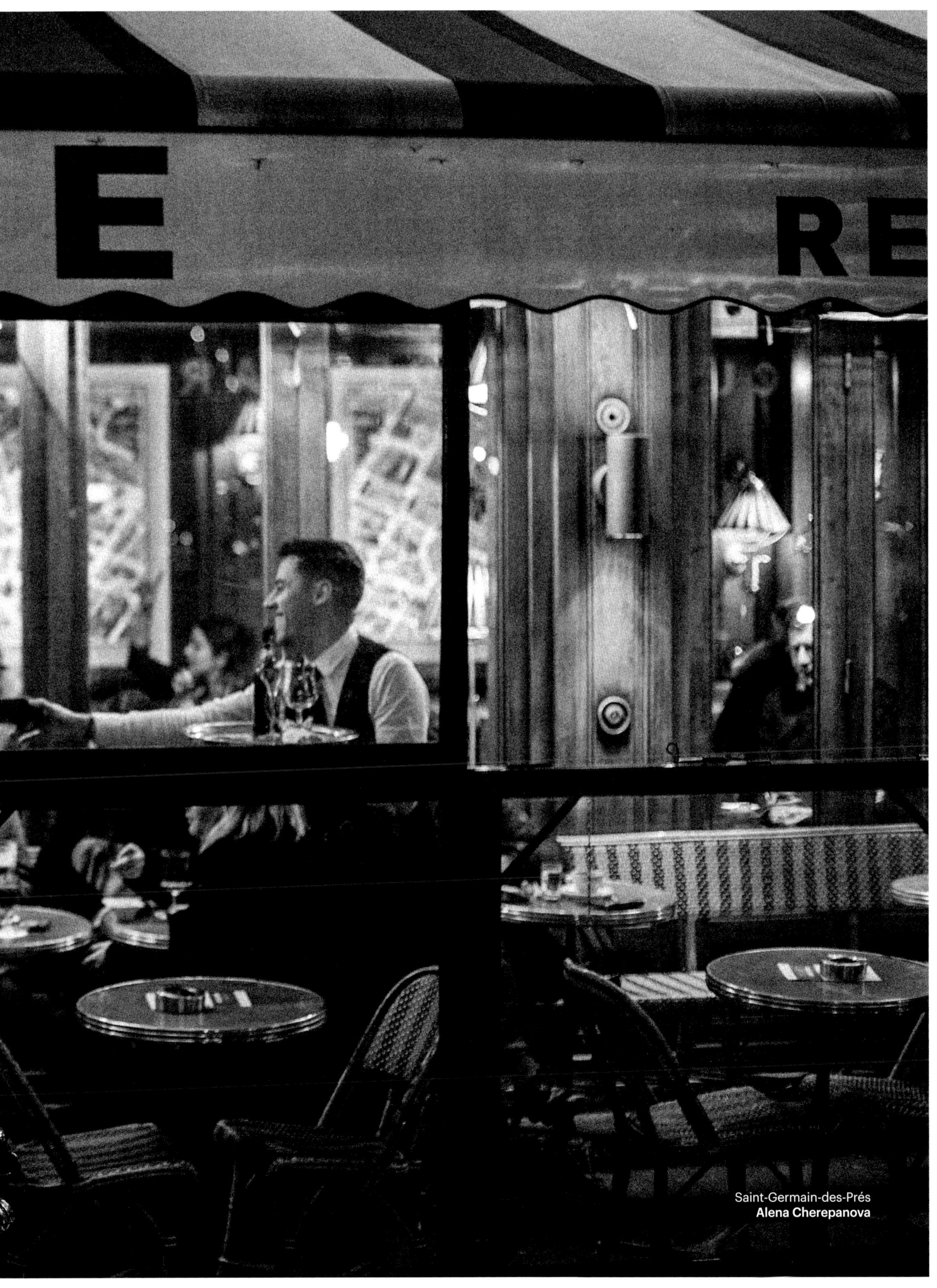

Saint-Germain-des-Prés
Alena Cherepanova

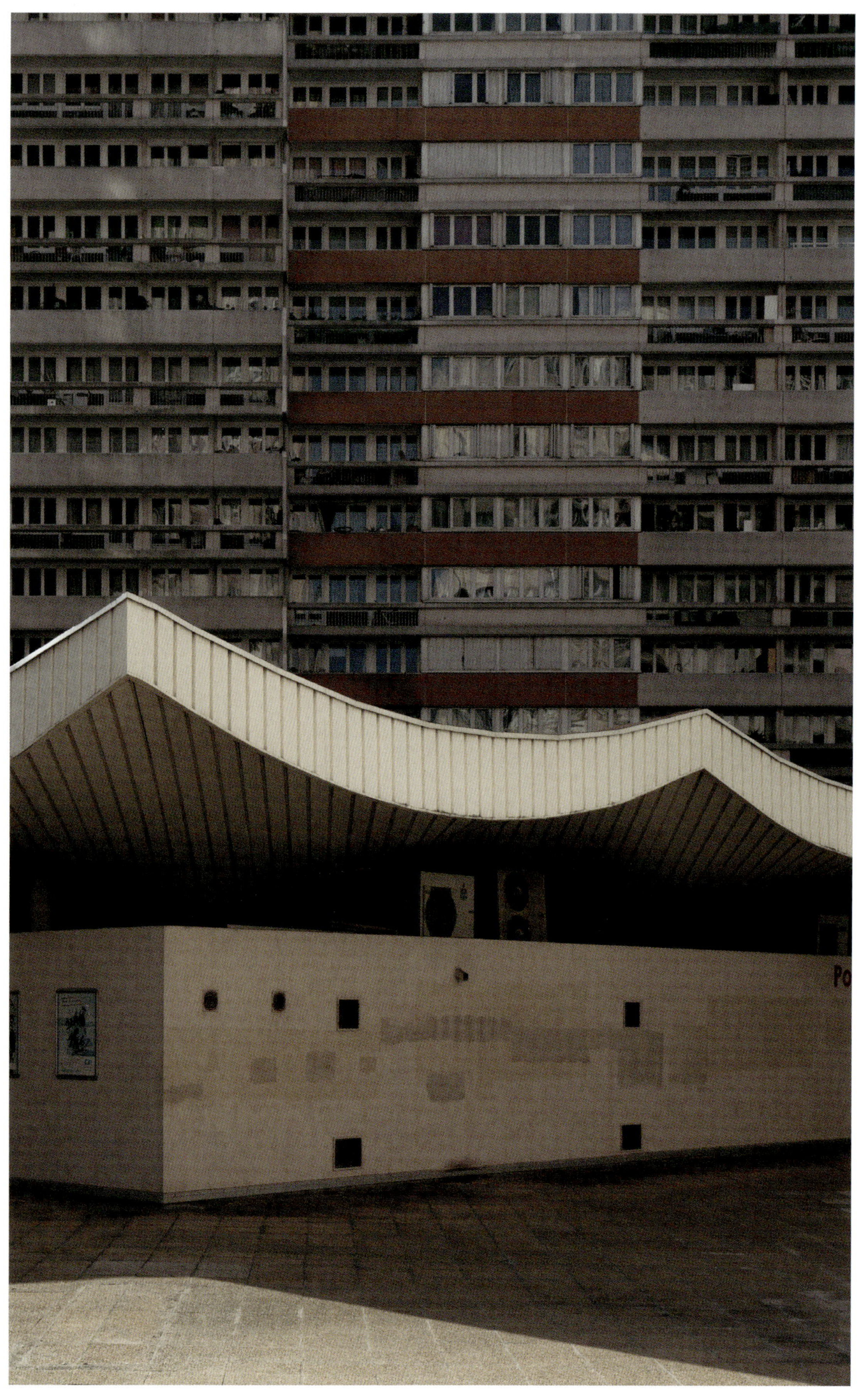

Quartier de la Gare
Dariusz Jasak

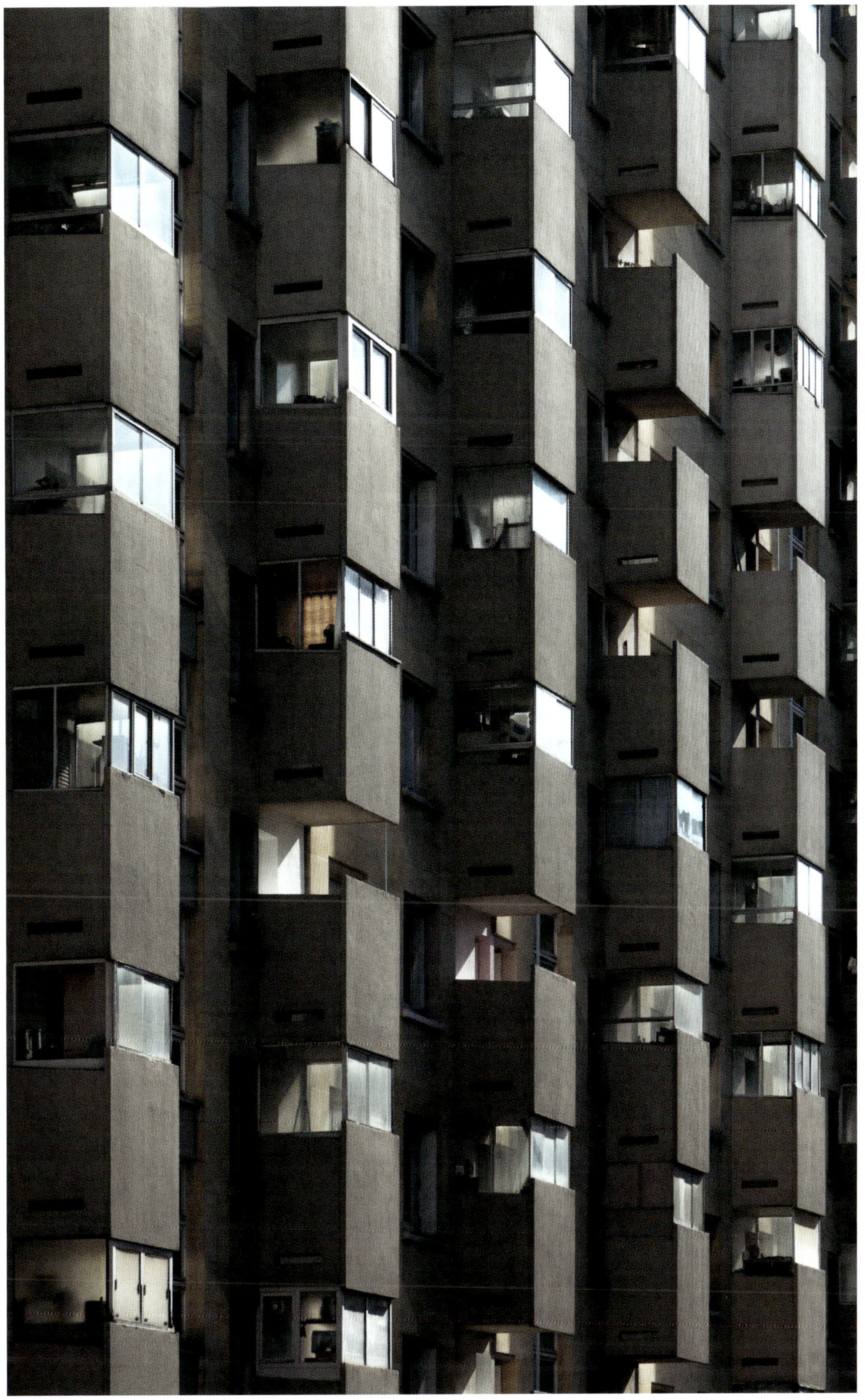

13e Arrondissement
Dariusz Jasak

Basilique du Sacré-Cœur
Montmartre
Willem Sizoo —

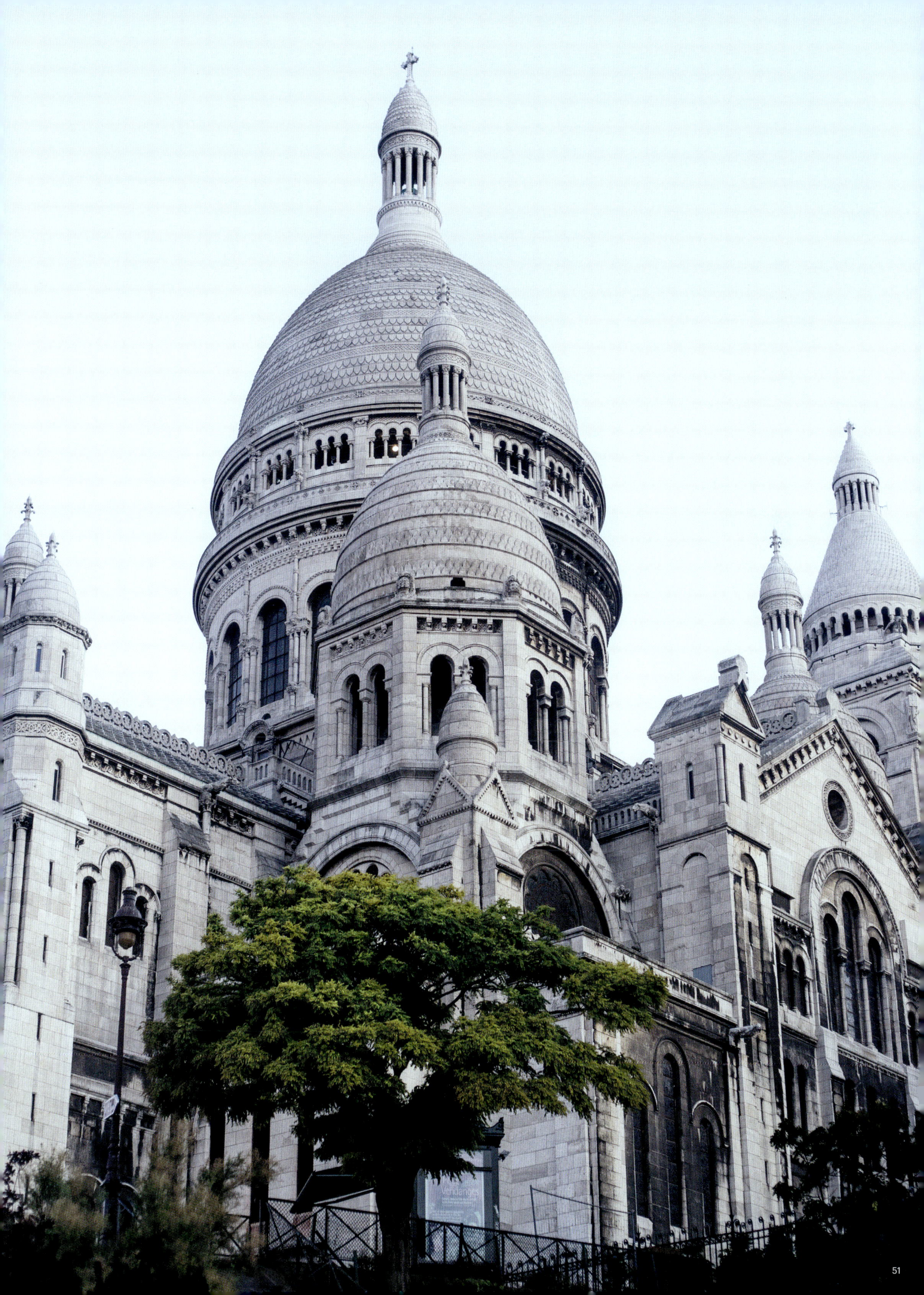

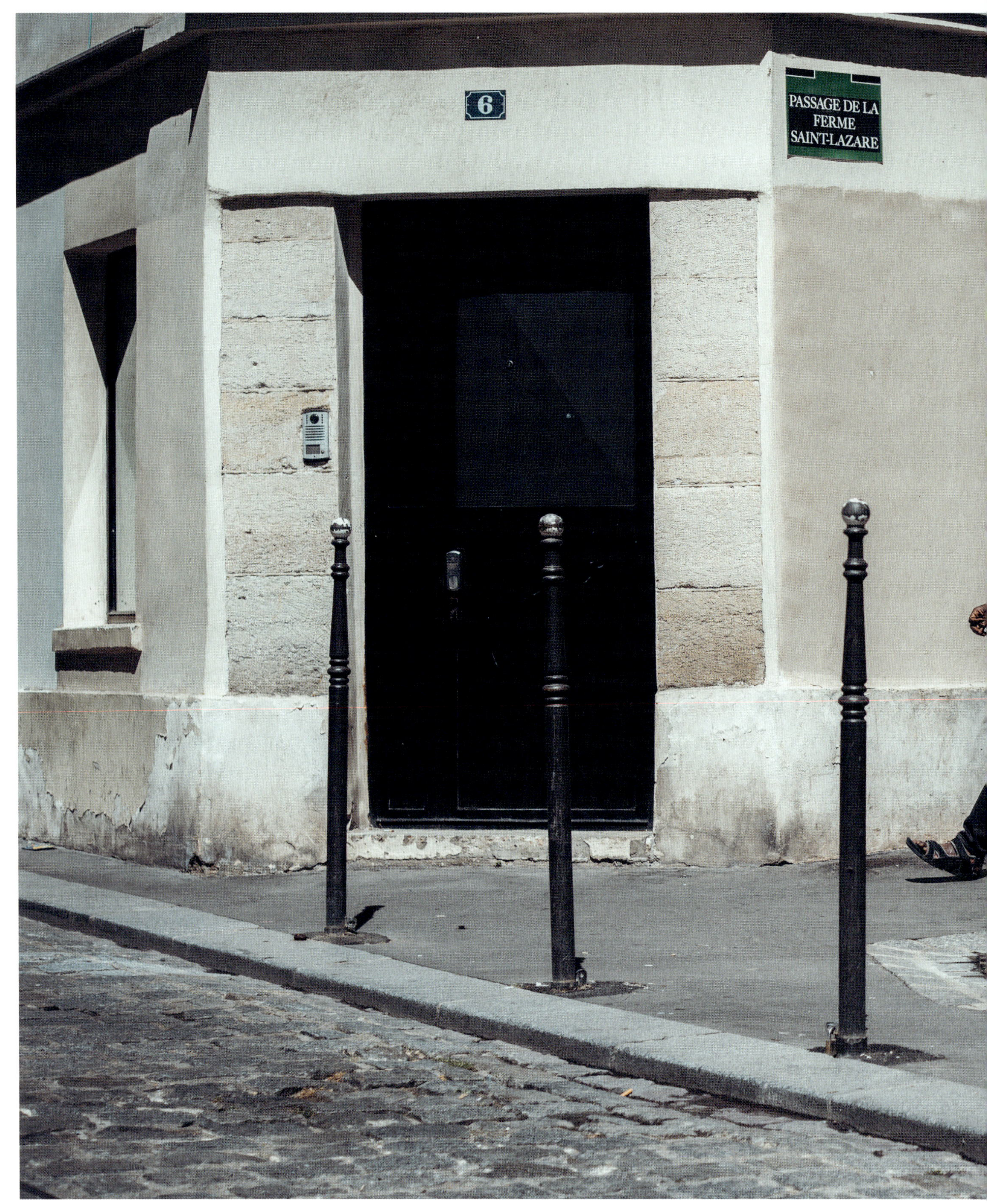

Le passage de la Ferme Saint-Lazare
10e Arrondissement
Stijn Hoekstra

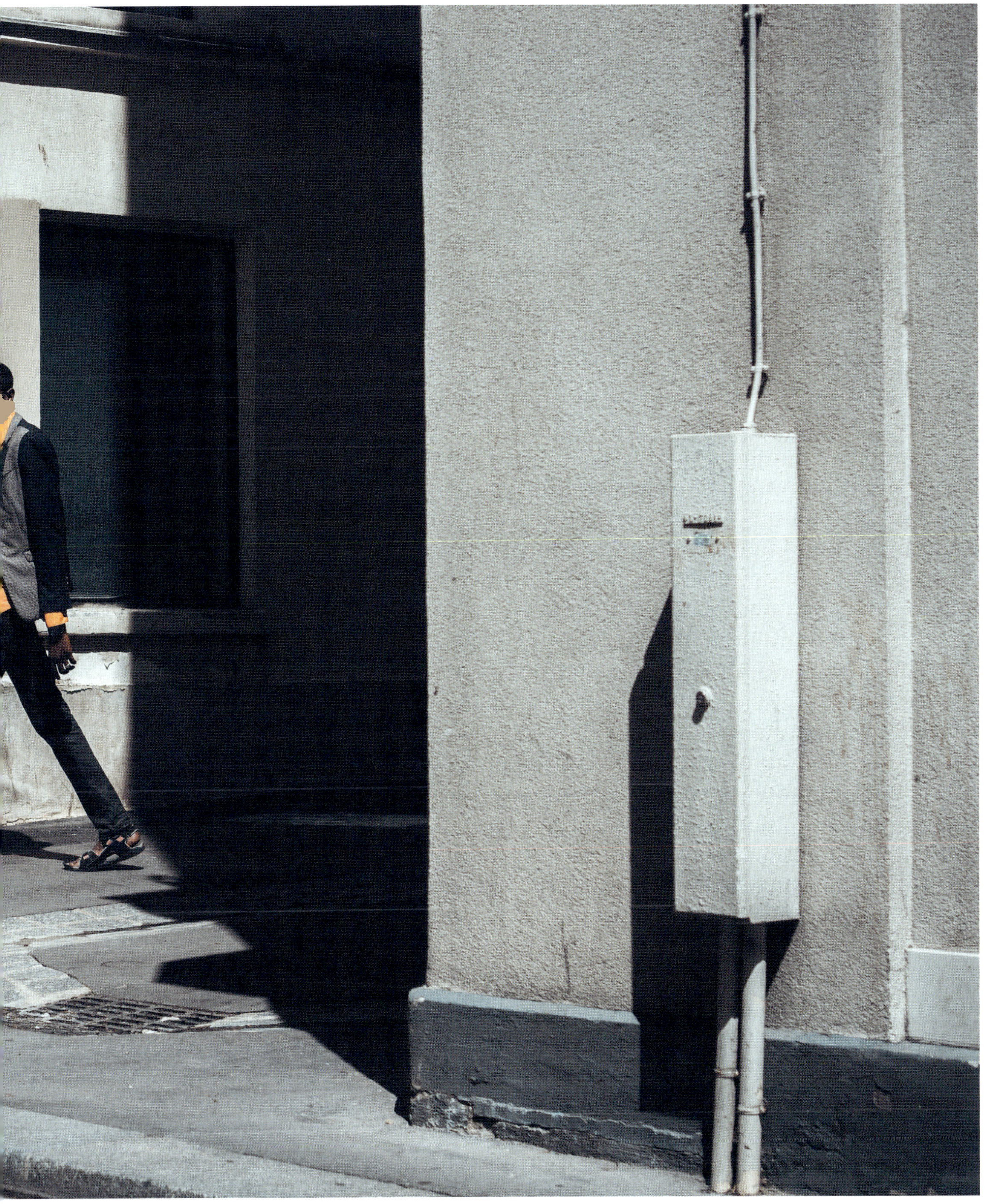

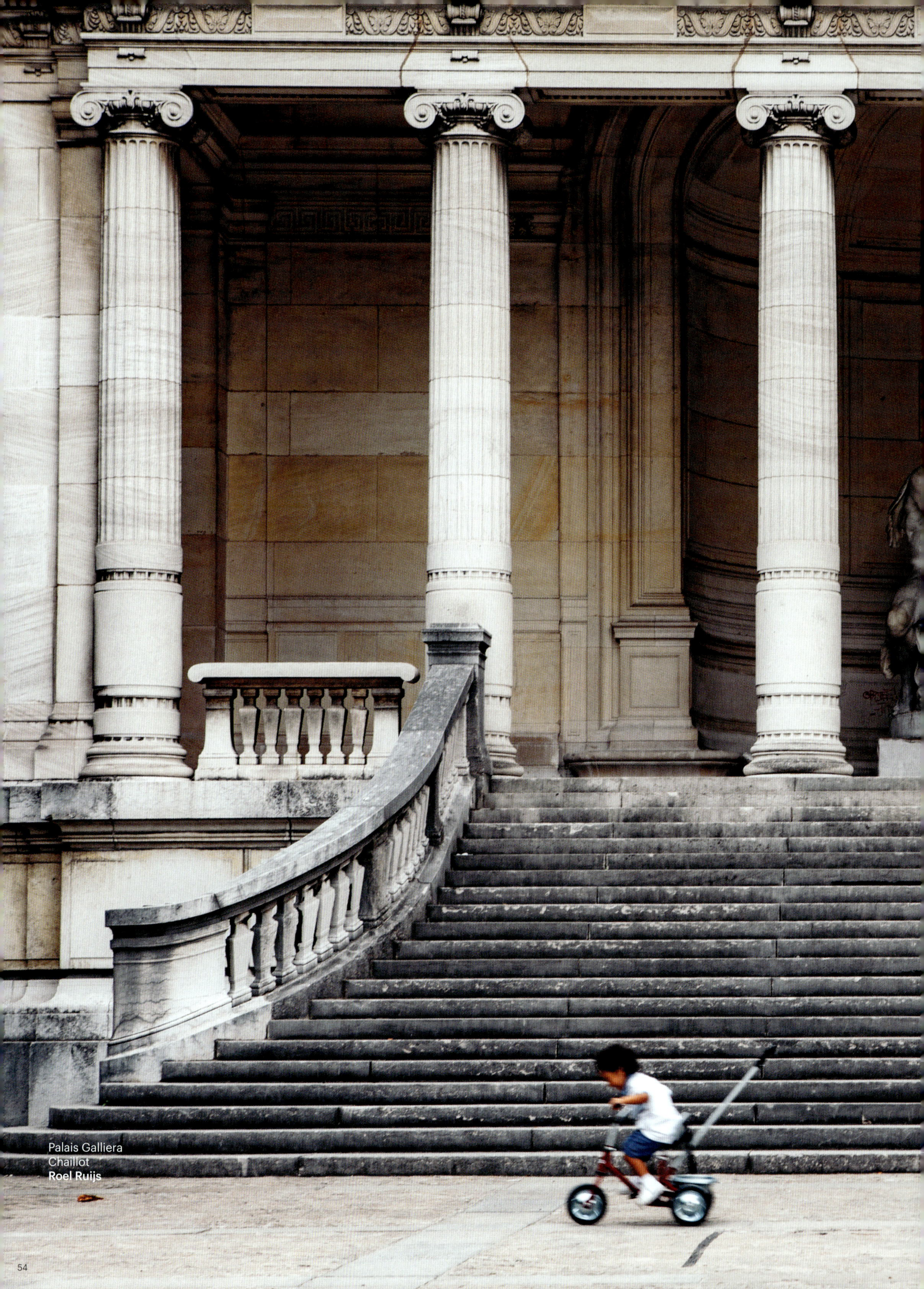

Palais Galliera
Chaillot
Roel Ruijs

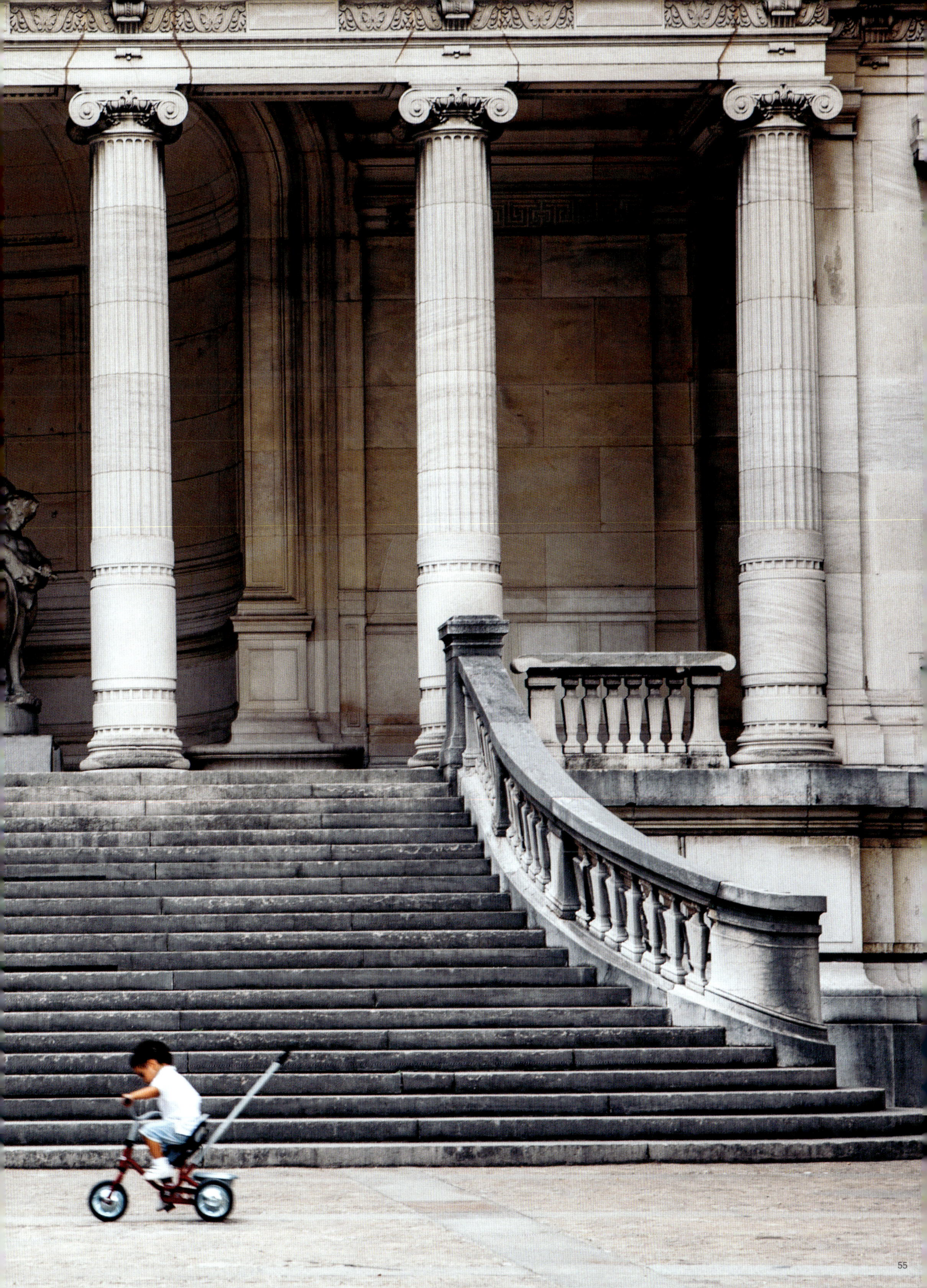

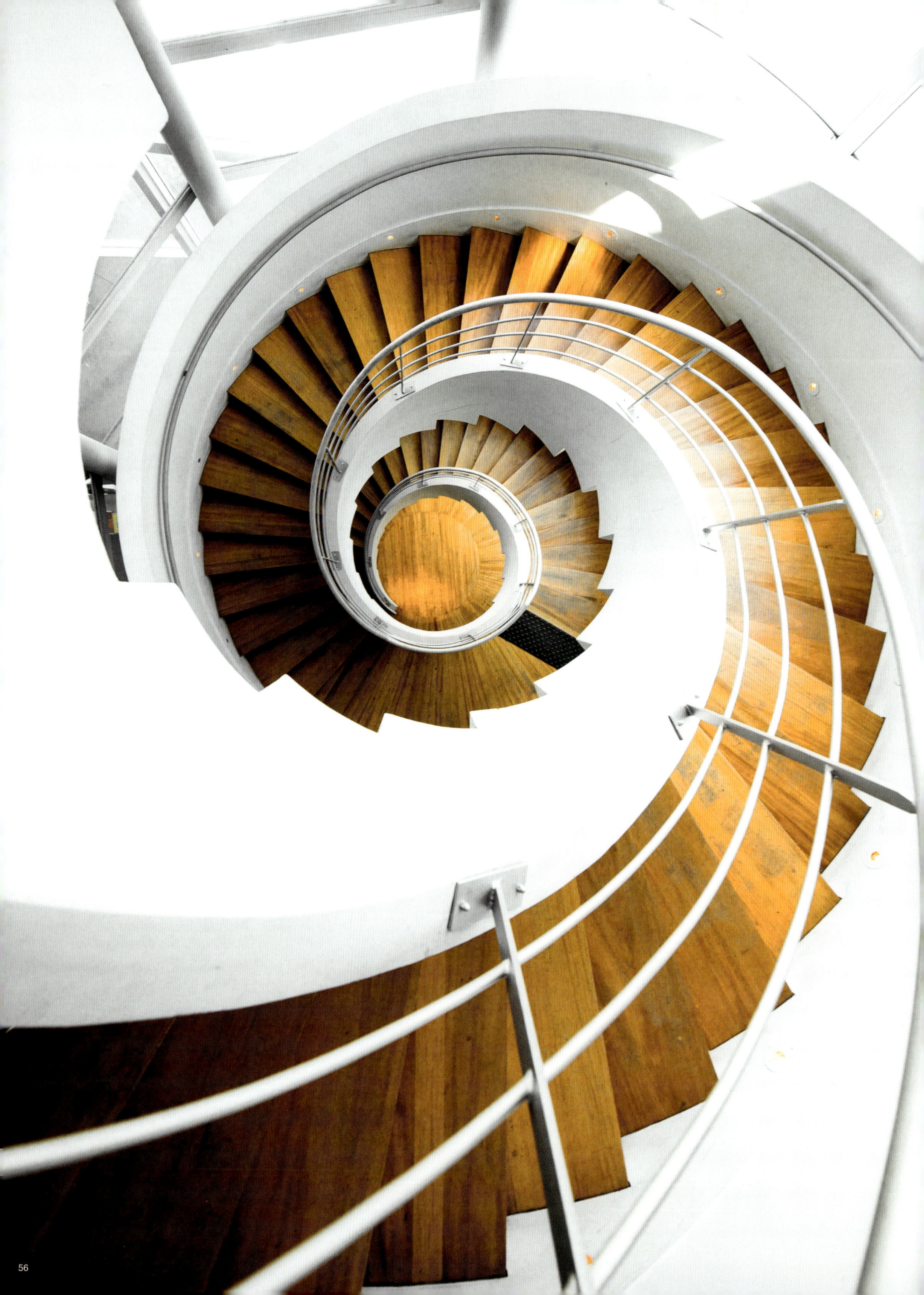

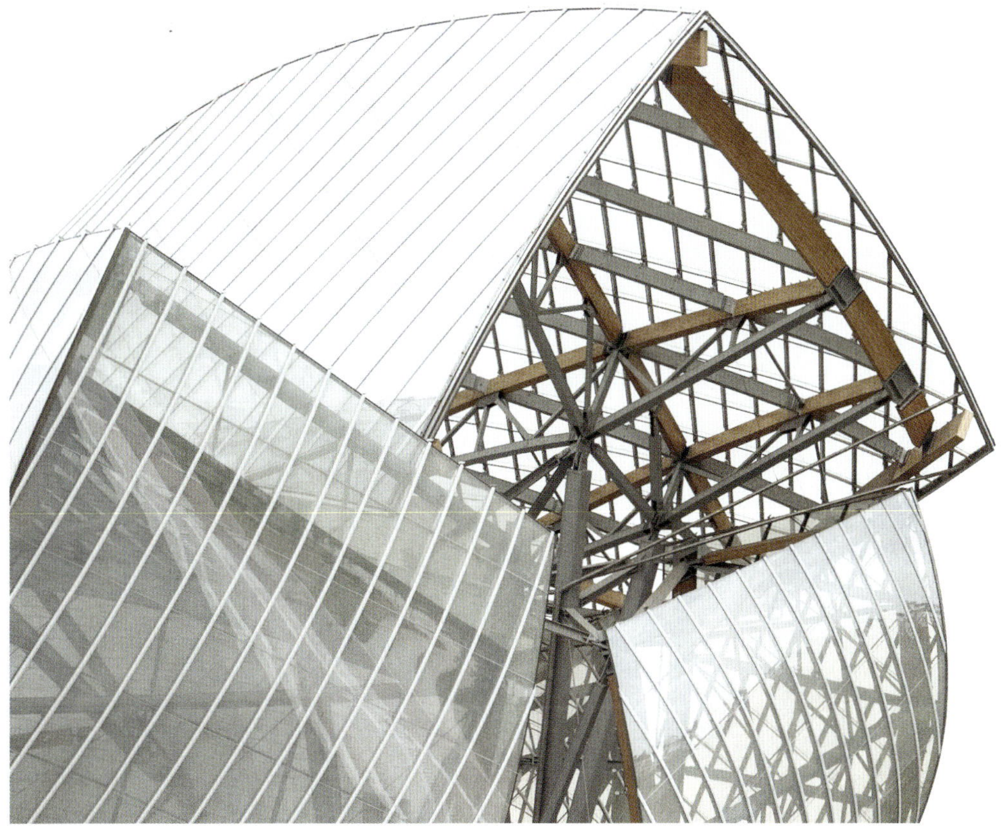

Médiathèque Jean-Pierre Melville
← **Sulay Kelly**

Fondation Louis Vuitton
16e Arrondissement
Raul Cabrera

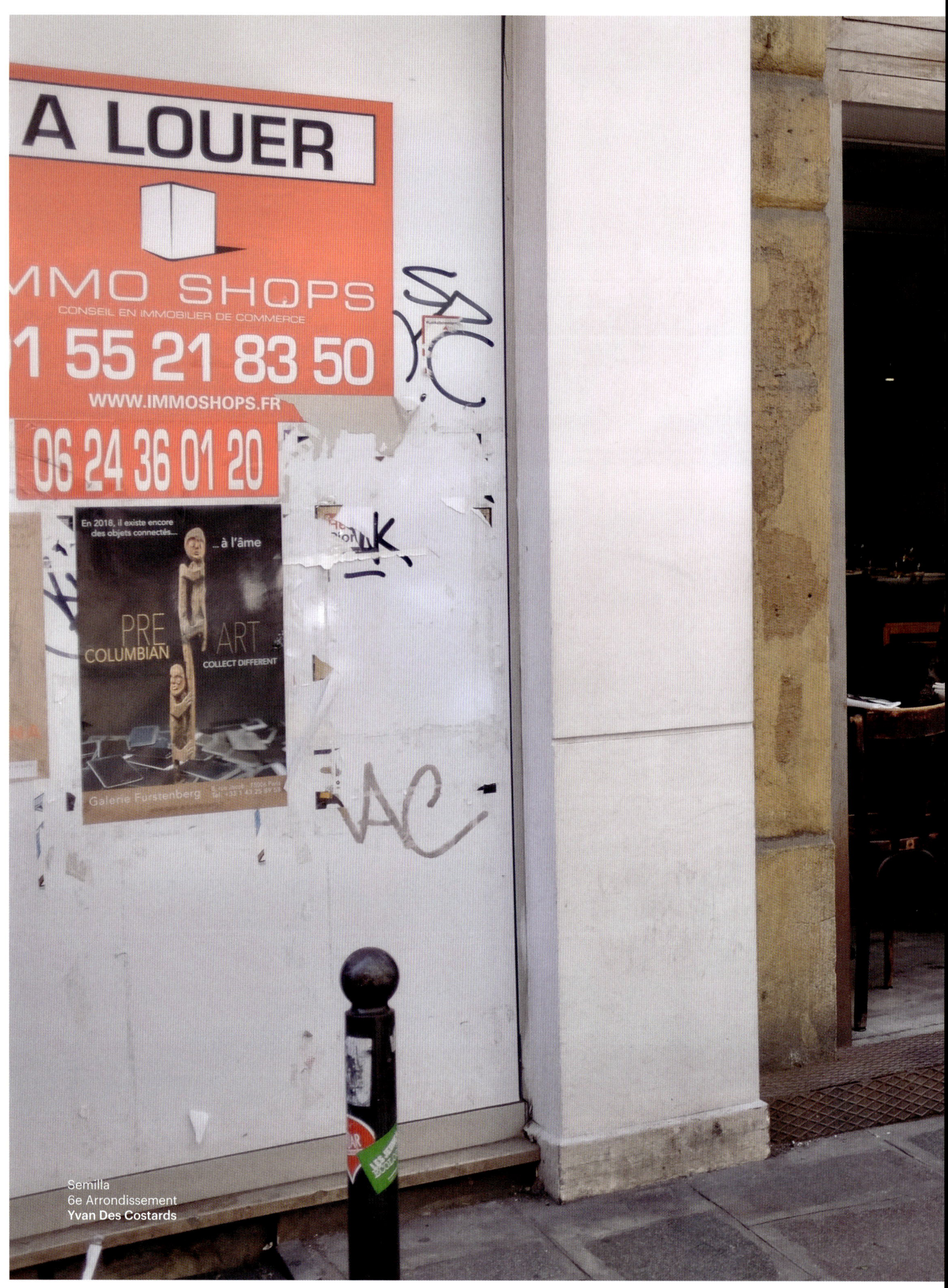

Semilla
6e Arrondissement
Yvan Des Costards

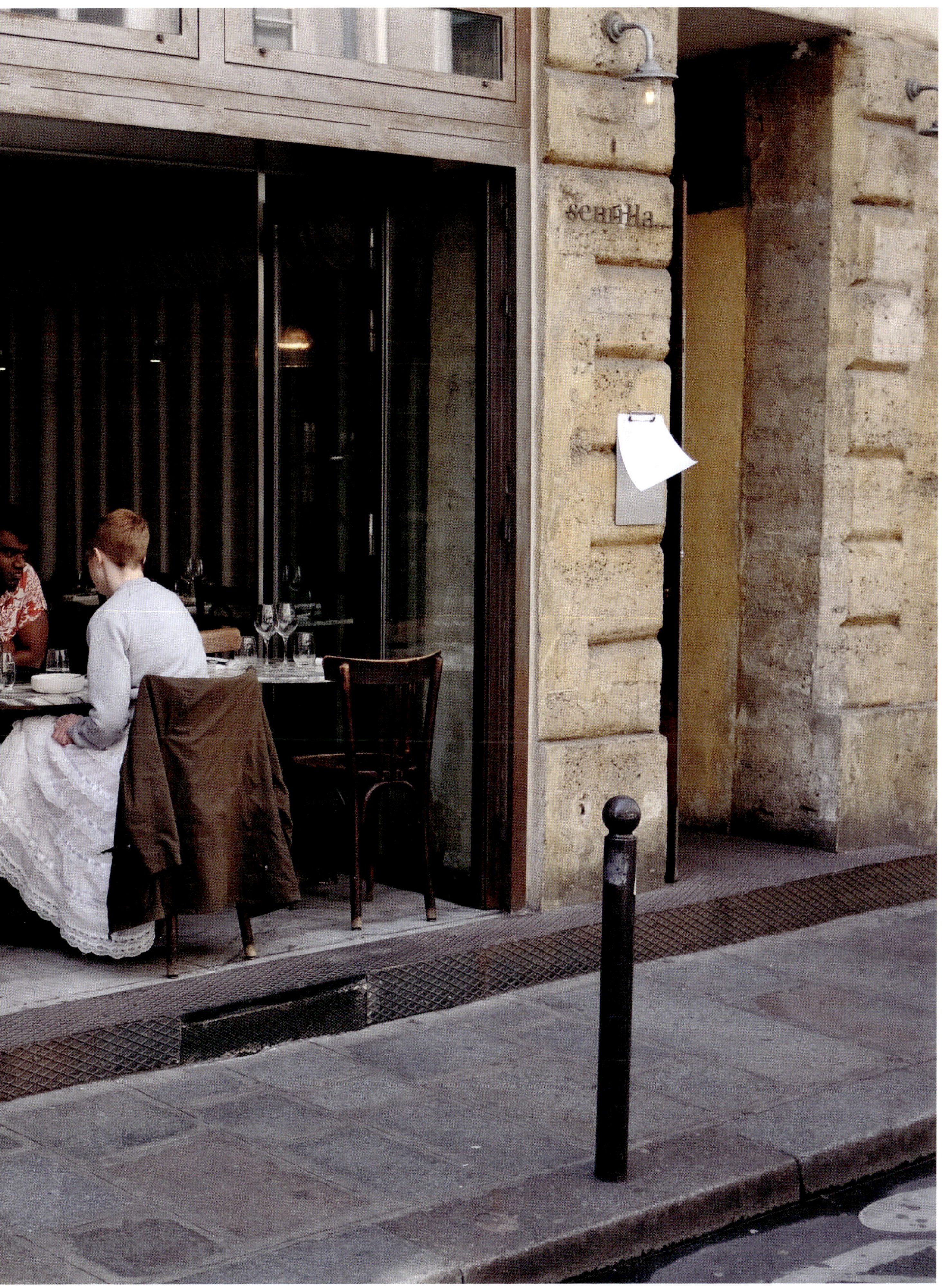

I like my images to be soothing to the eye. It's satisfying to look at something harmonious.

—Guillaume Dutreix

Saint-Ouen
Seine-Saint-Denis
Olivier Morisse

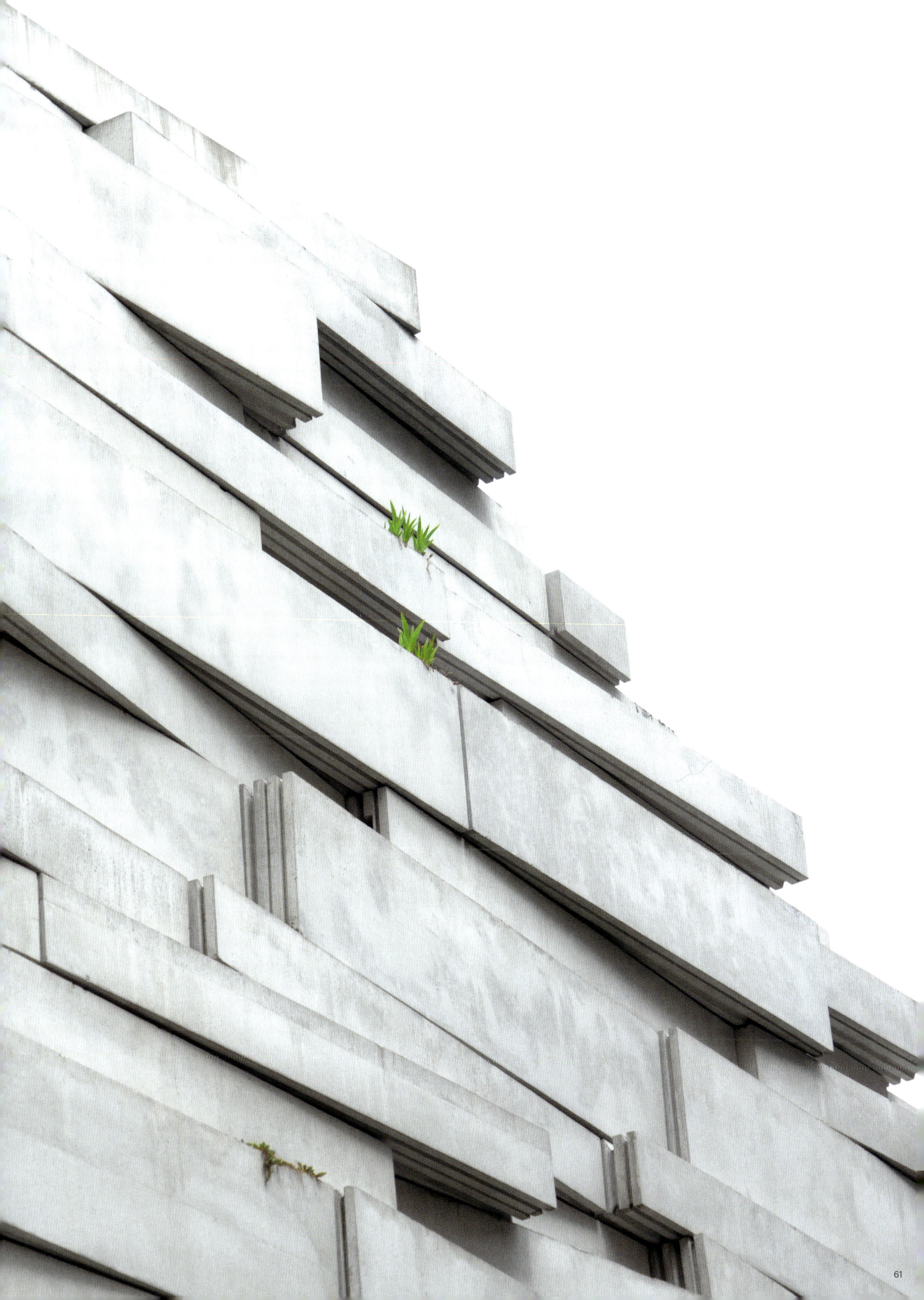

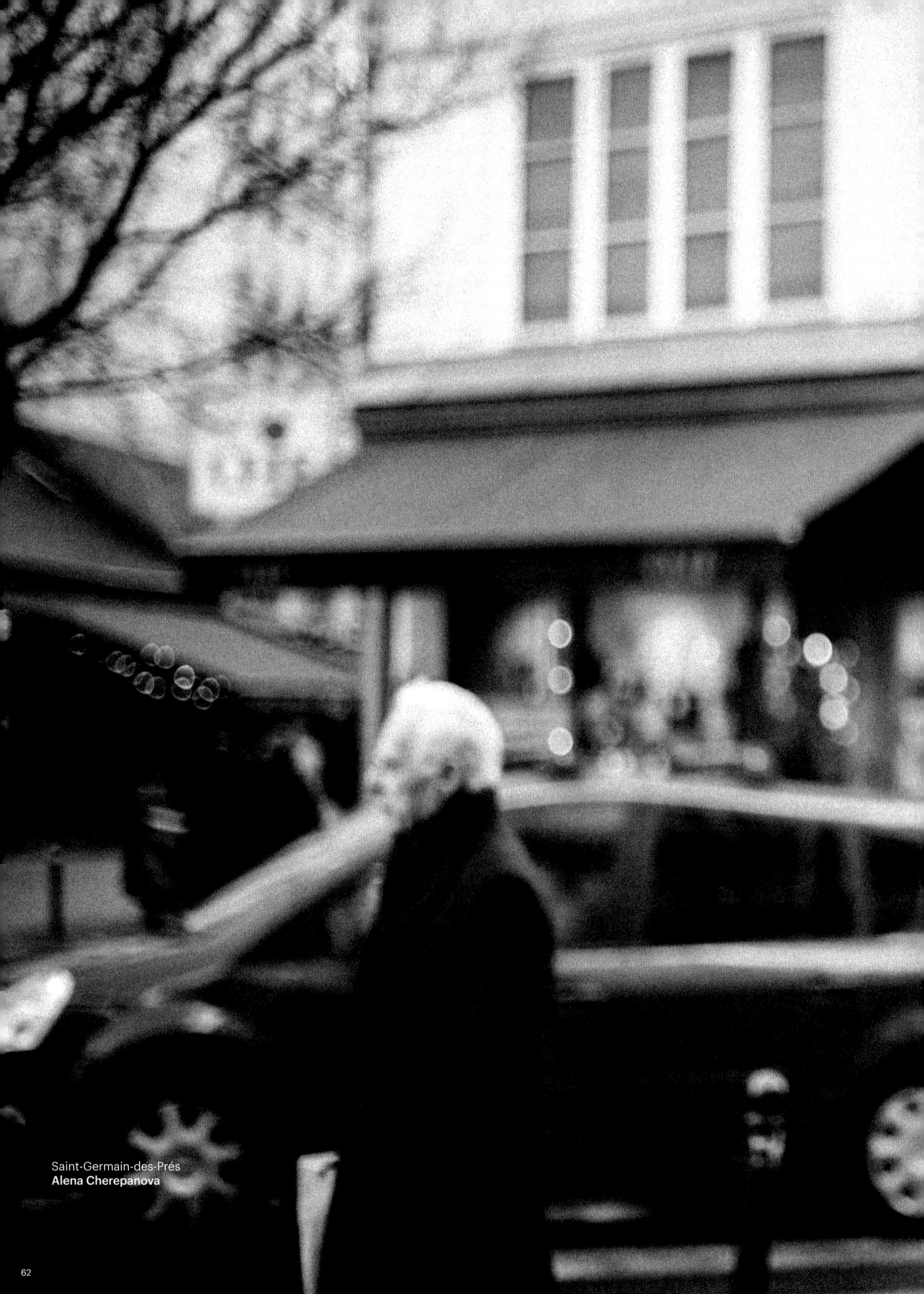

Saint-Germain-des-Prés
Alena Cherepanova

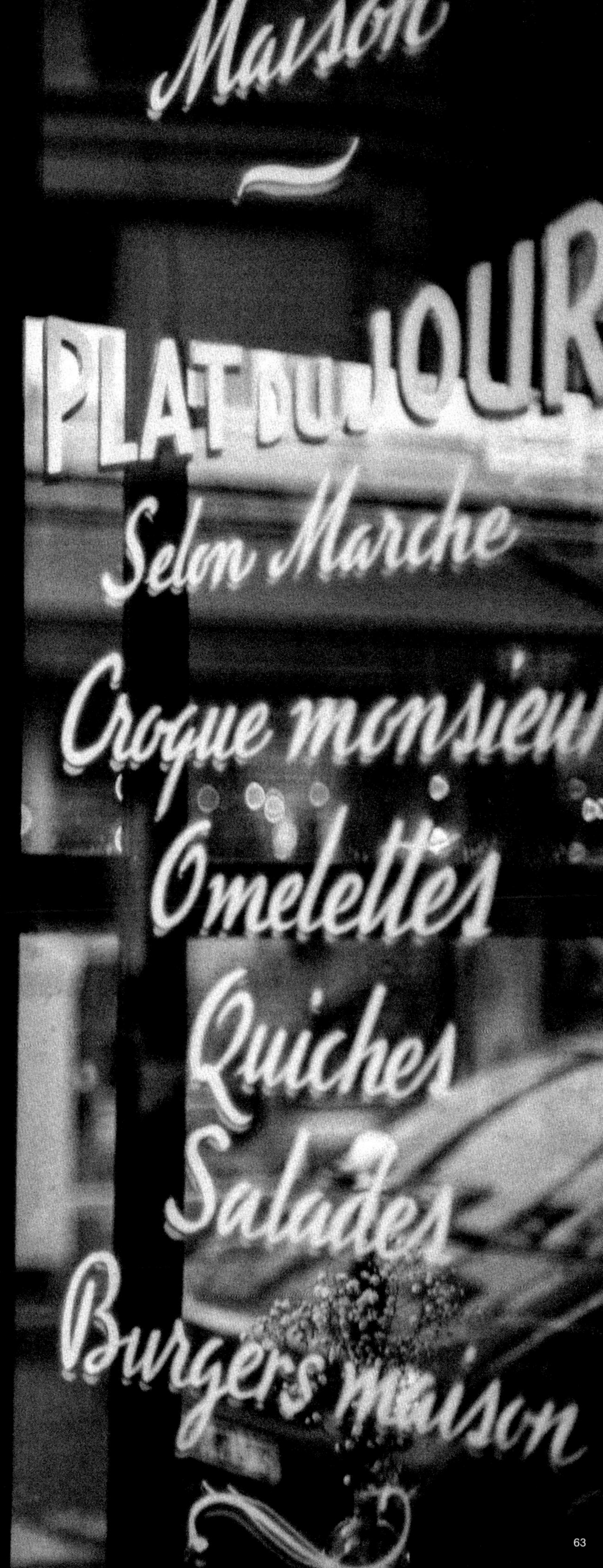
& Assiette Brunch
CRÈME GLACÉE
& Sorbets
(Une glace à Paris)
Meilleur ouvrier de France
THÉS · CAFÉS
Chocolat à l'ancienne
Maison
PLAT DU JOUR
Selon Marche
Omelettes
Quiches
Salades
Burgers maison

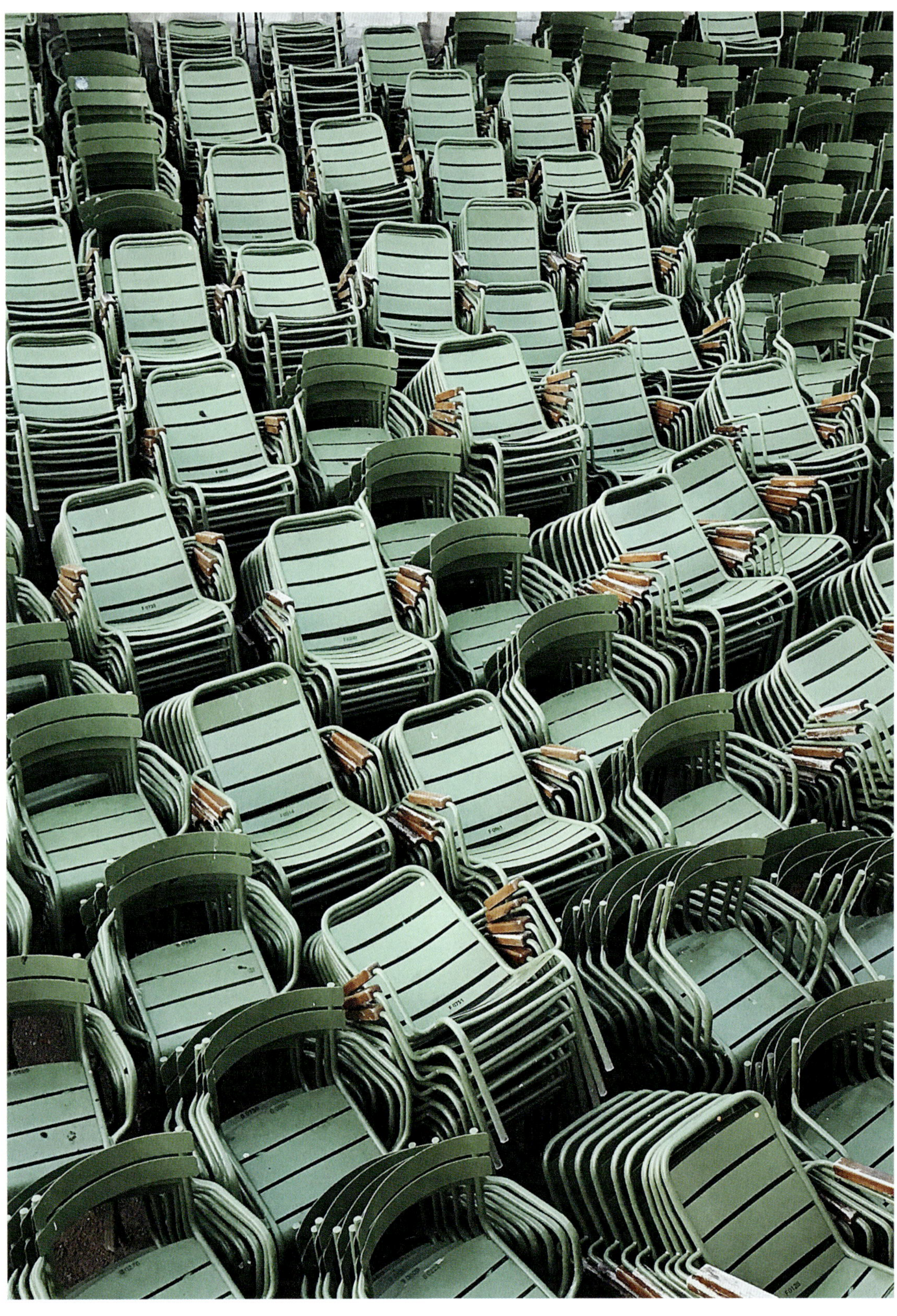

Jardin du Luxembourg chairs
6e Arrondissement
Laurent Dassencourt

Rue Oberkampf
11e Arrondissement
Yvan Des Costards —

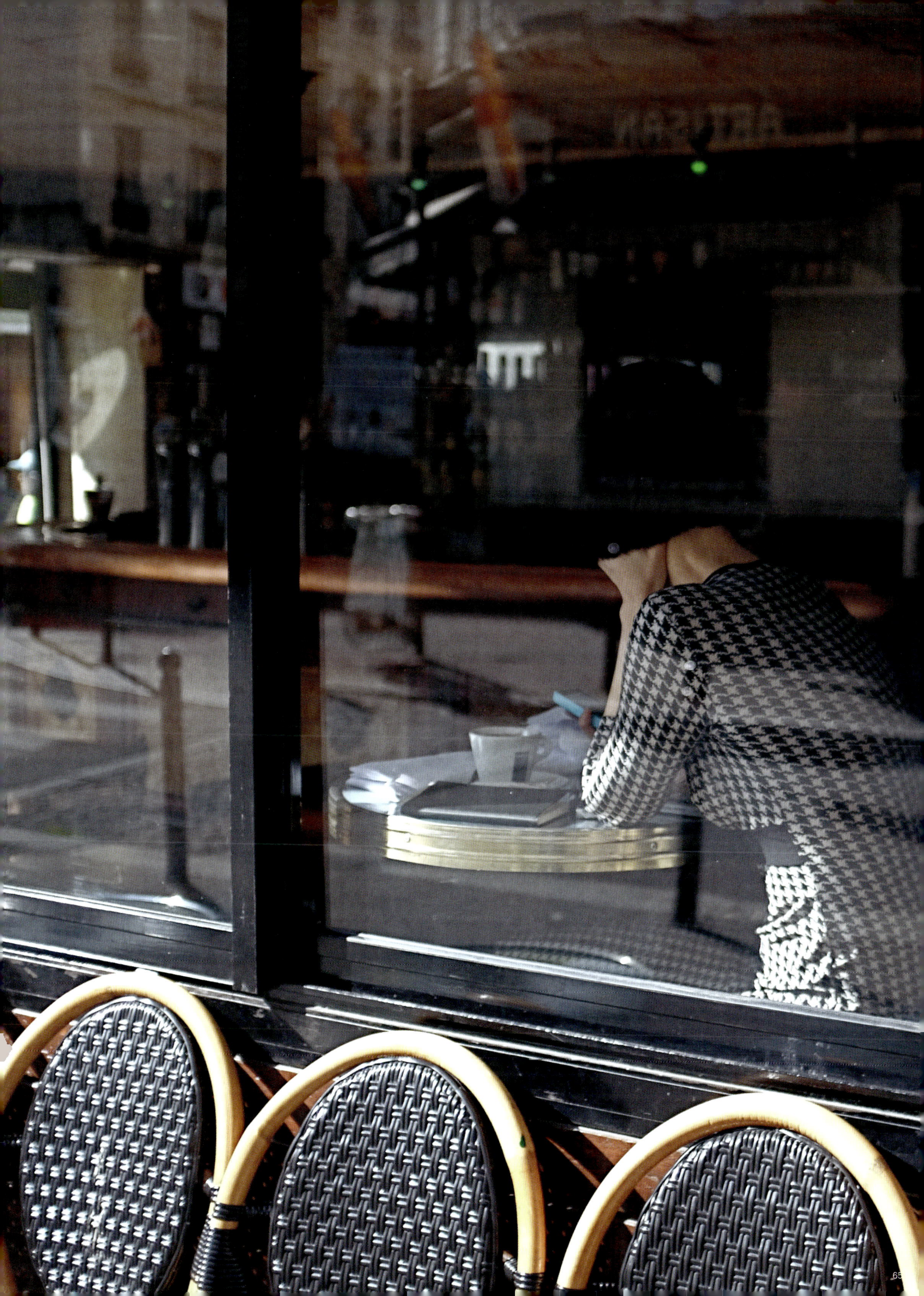

Eiffel Tower
7e Arrondissement
Maxime Roig

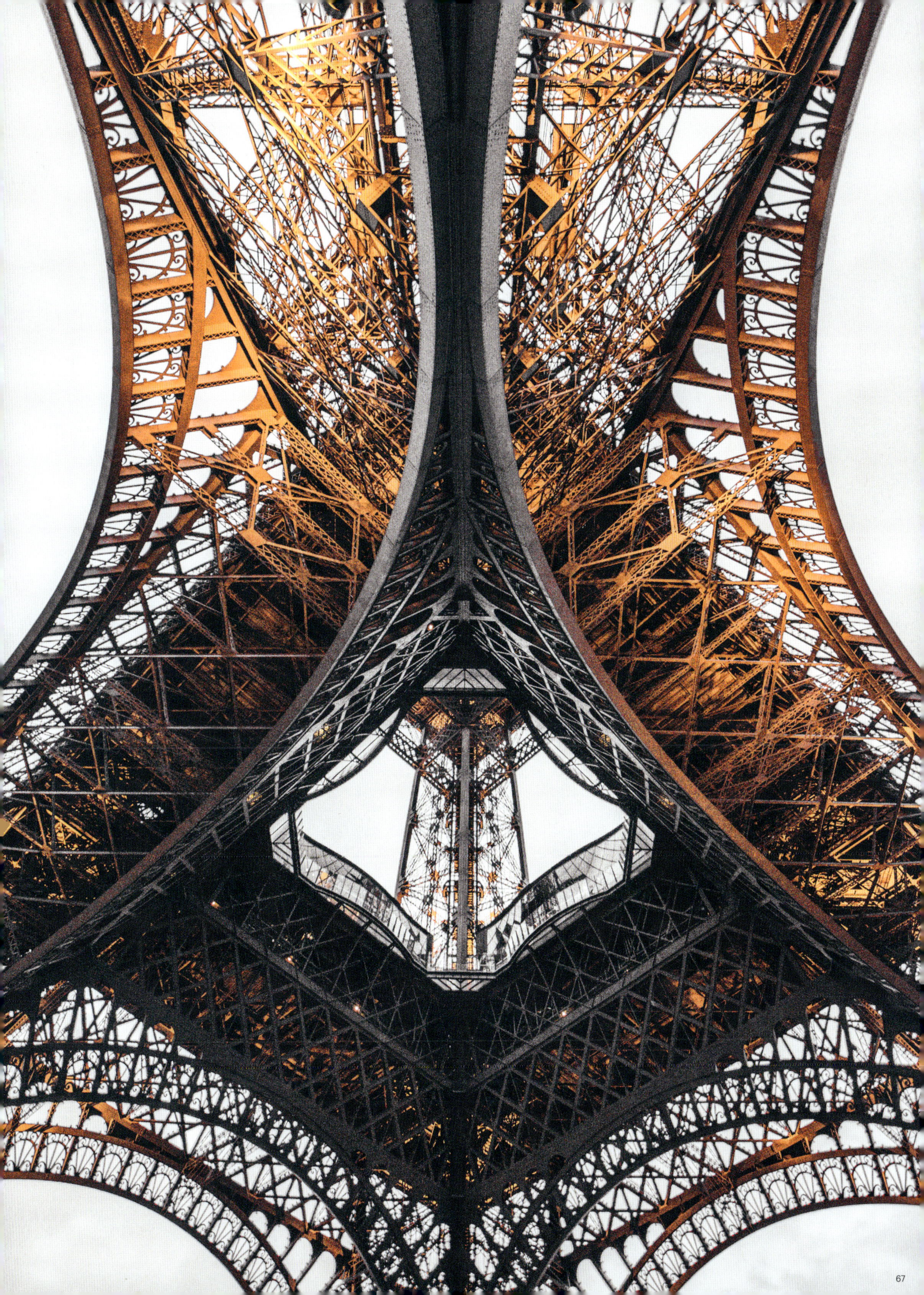

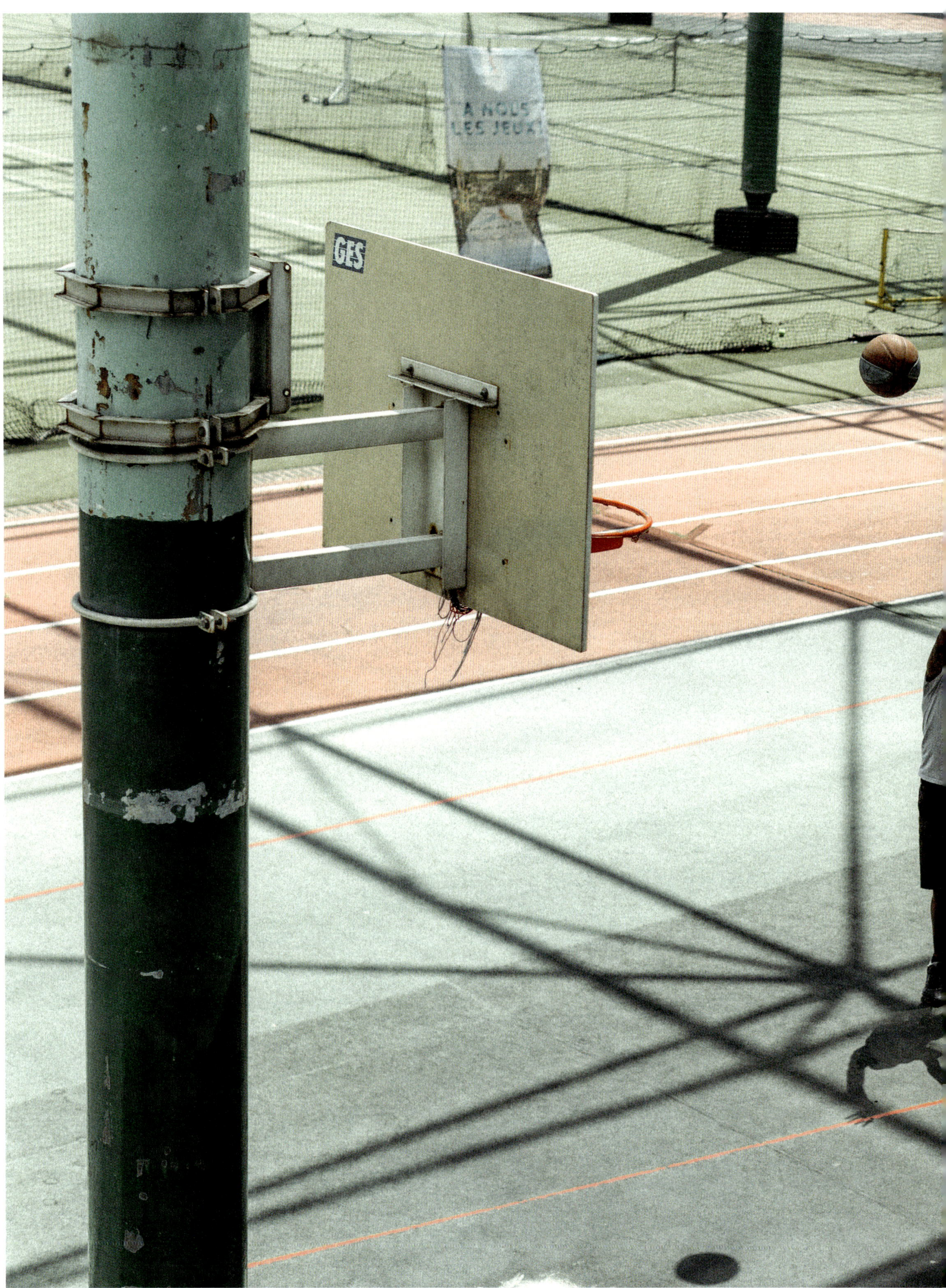
GES
A NOUS
LES JEUX

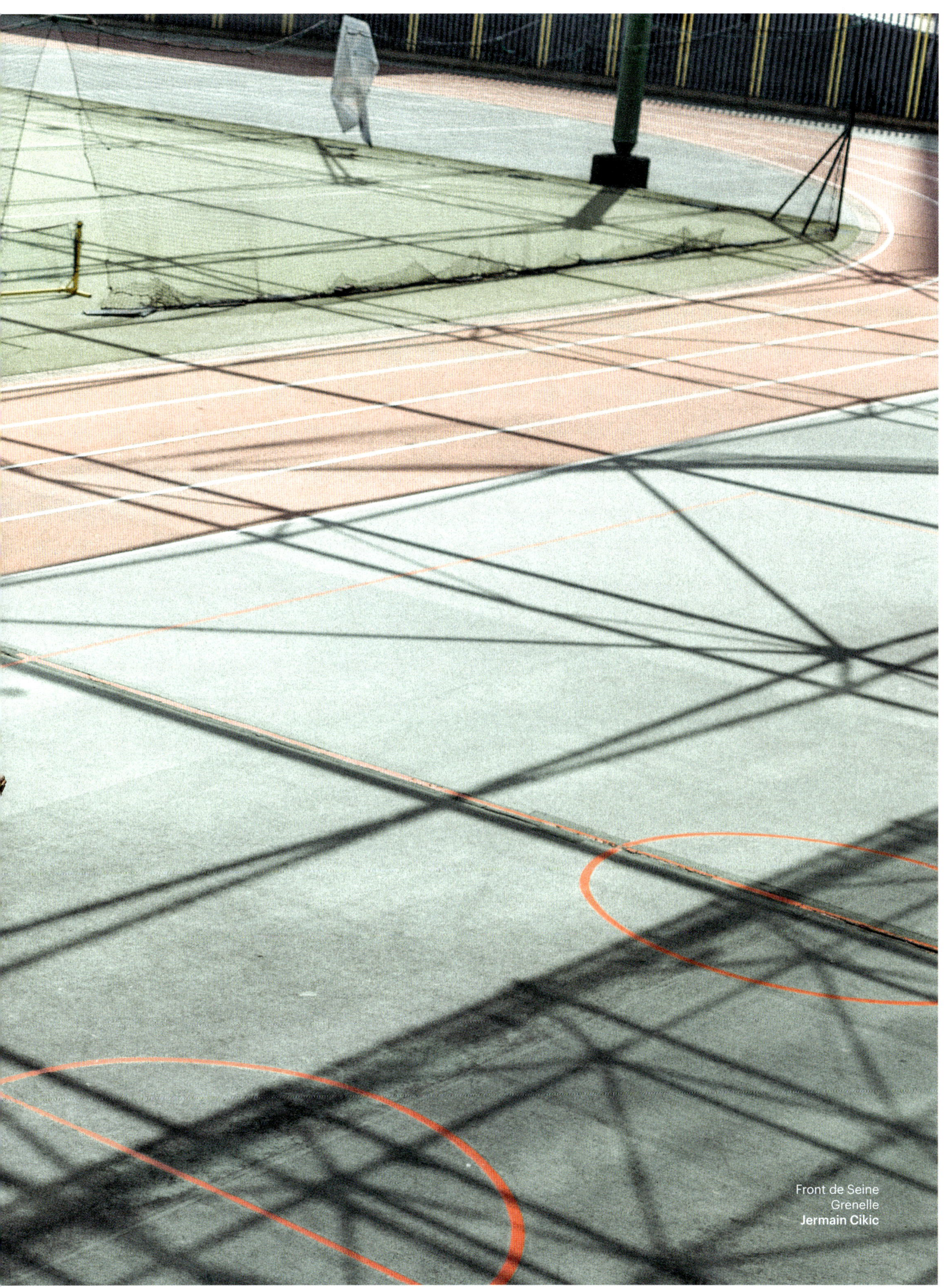

Front de Seine
Grenelle
Jermain Cikic

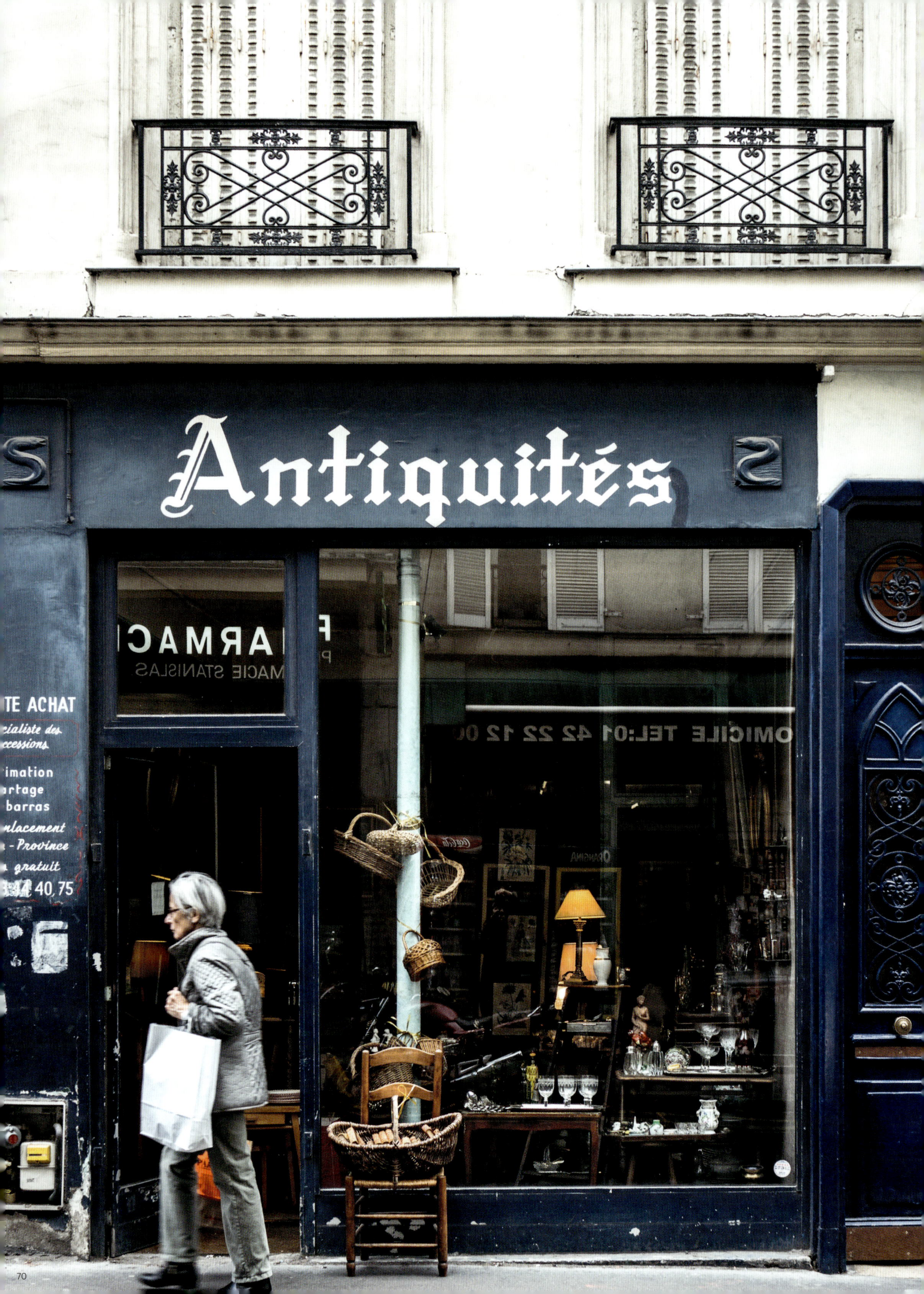
Antiquités
TE ACHAT
imation
artage
barras
-Province
gratuit
44 40 75

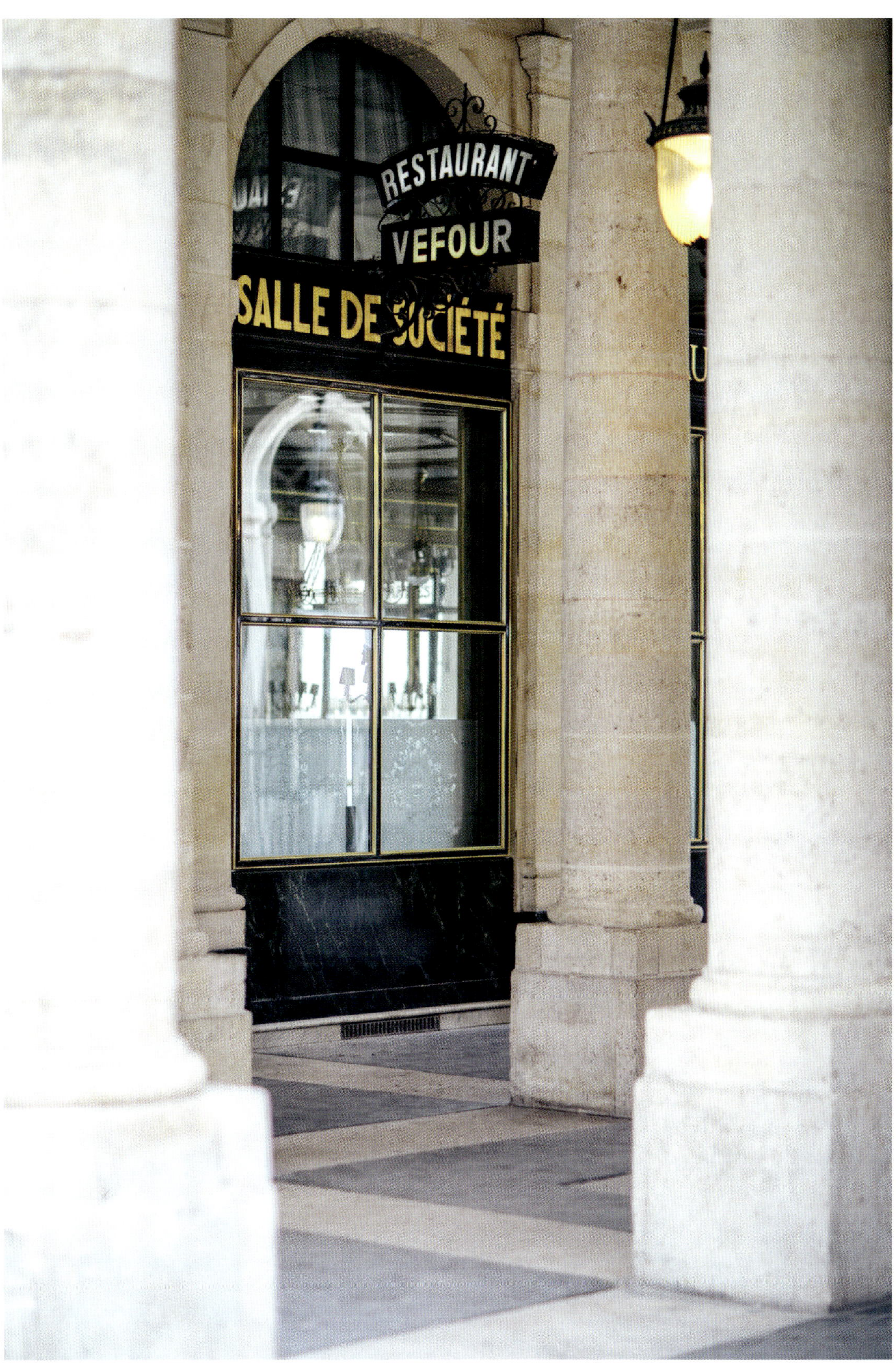

← Notre-Dame-des-Champs
Joann Pai

Le Grand Vefour
Palais-Royal
Roel Ruijs

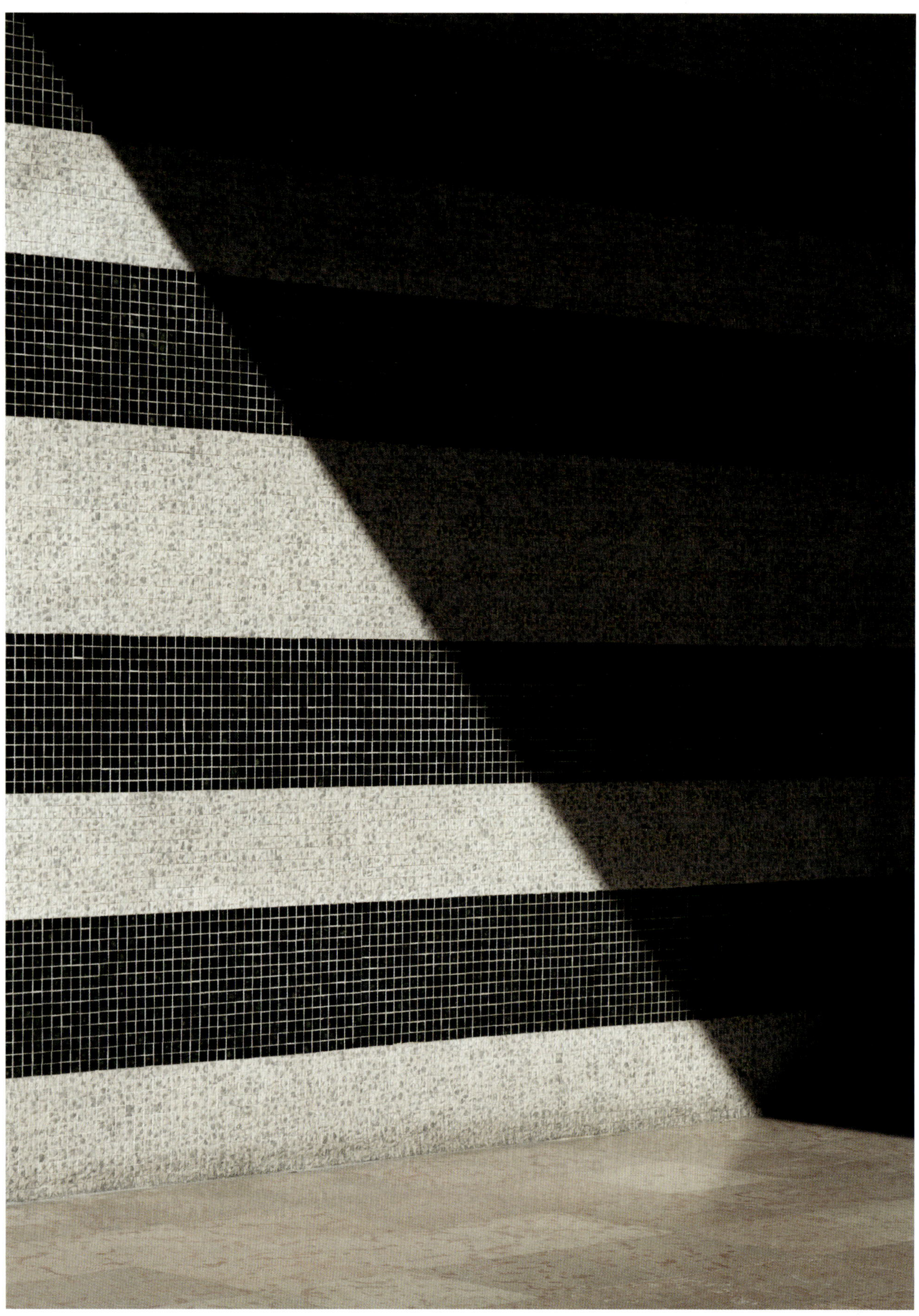

13e Arrondissement
Dariusz Jasak

Pont d'Iéna
7e Arrondissement
Hugo Michaudel →

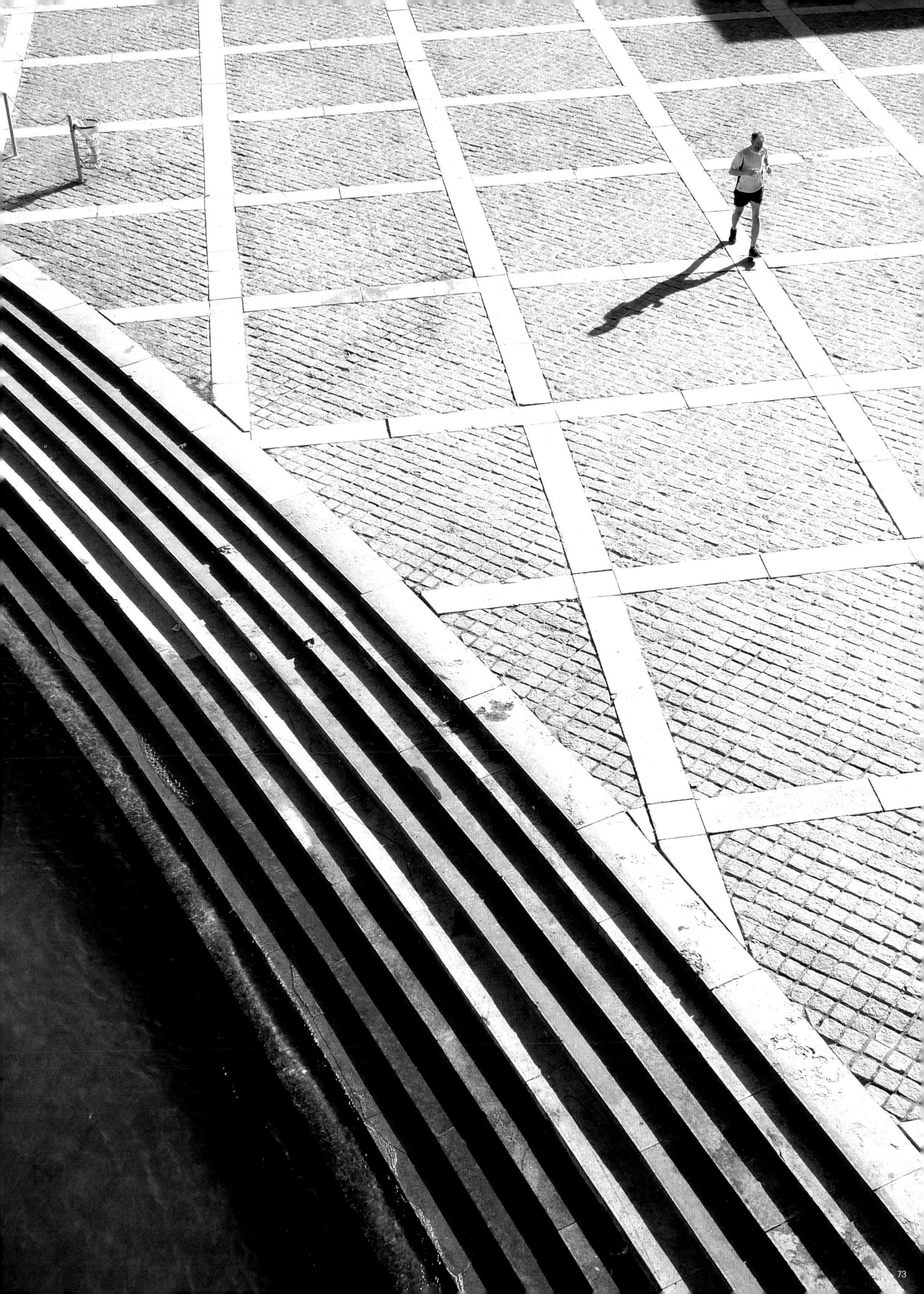

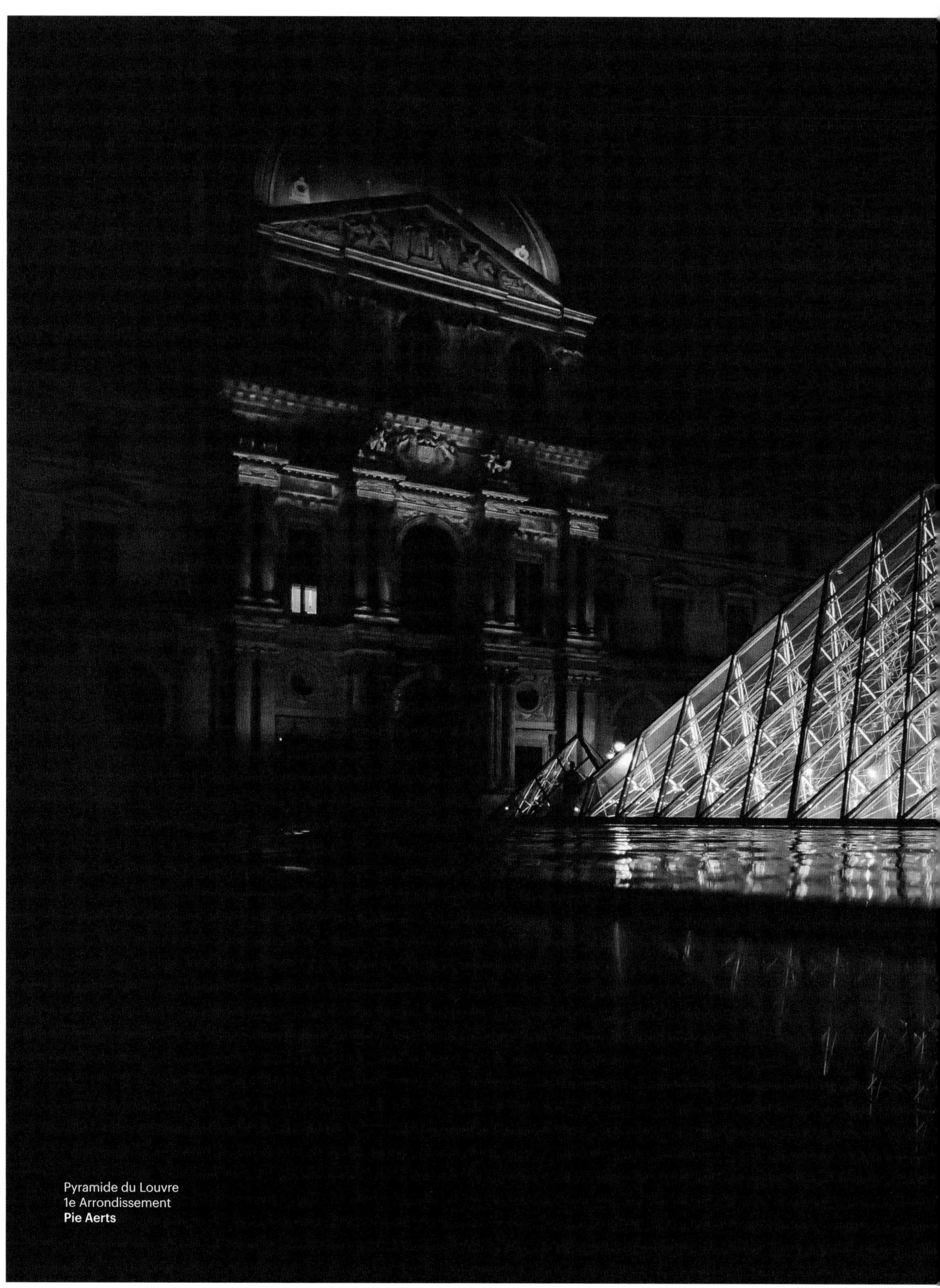

Pyramide du Louvre
1e Arrondissement
Pie Aerts

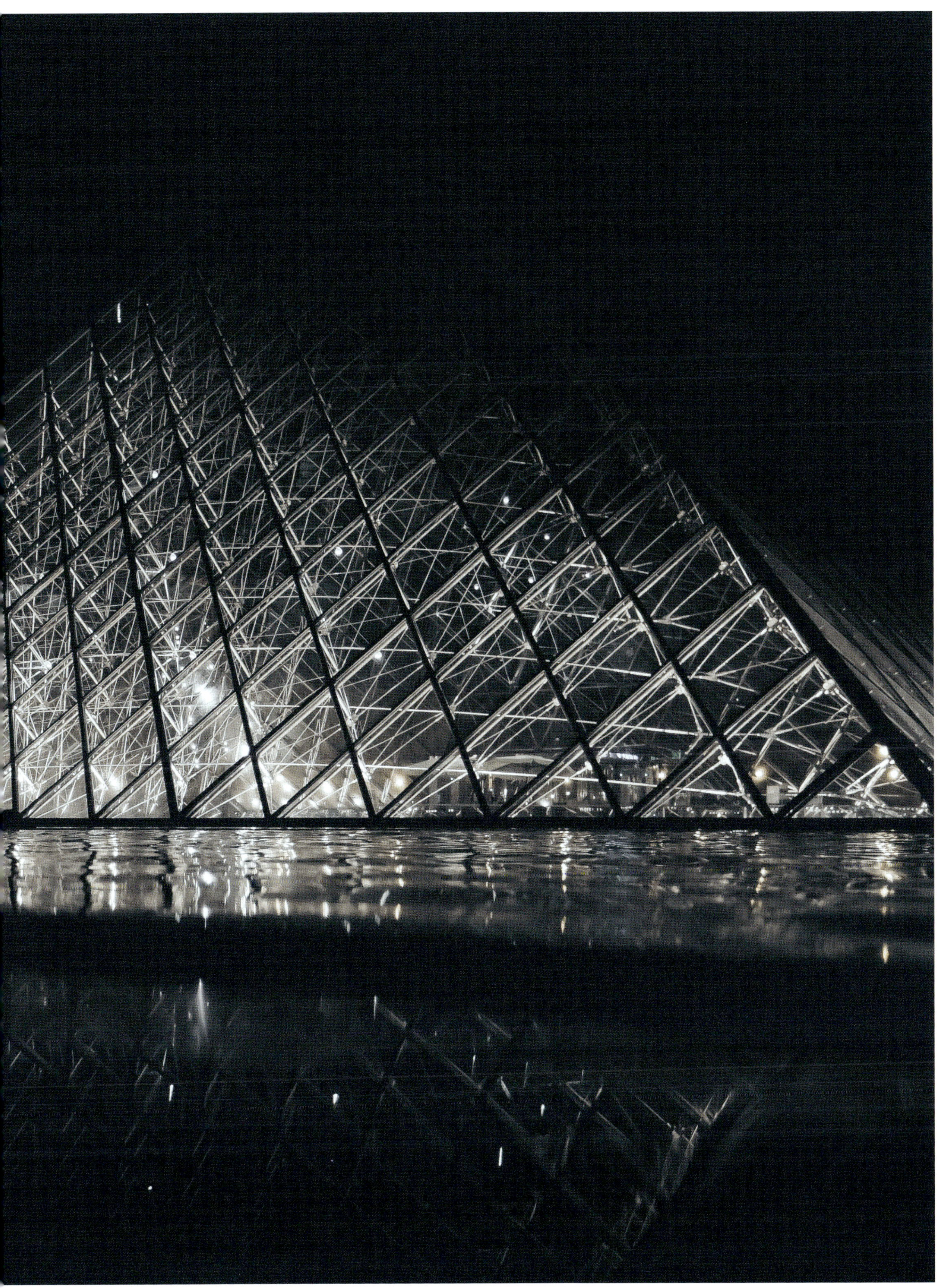

There will always be new angles, perspectives and takes to discover on this magnificent city.

—Joost Bastmeijer

Le Carrousel de la Tour Eiffel
7e Arrondissement
Romain Figuiere

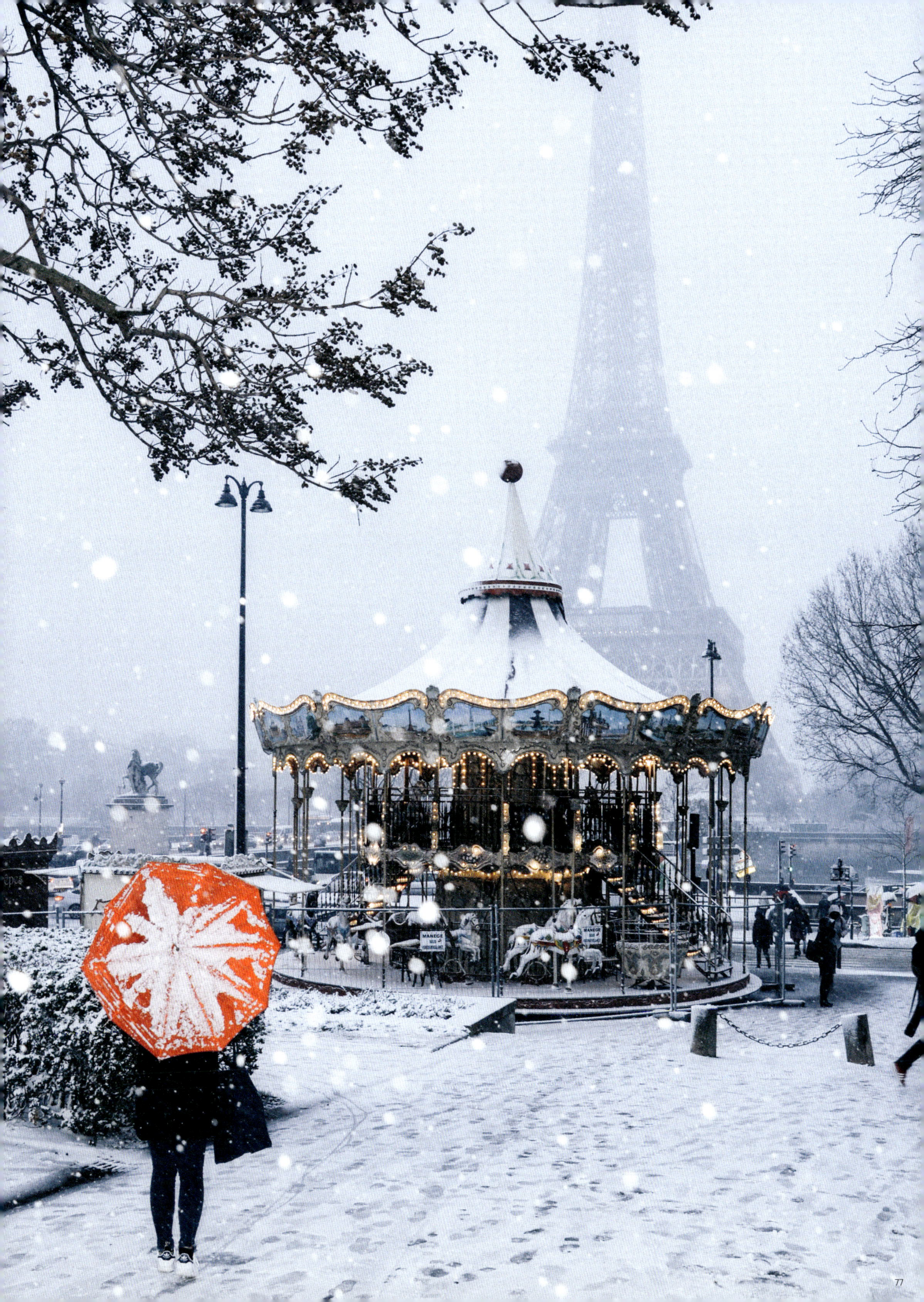

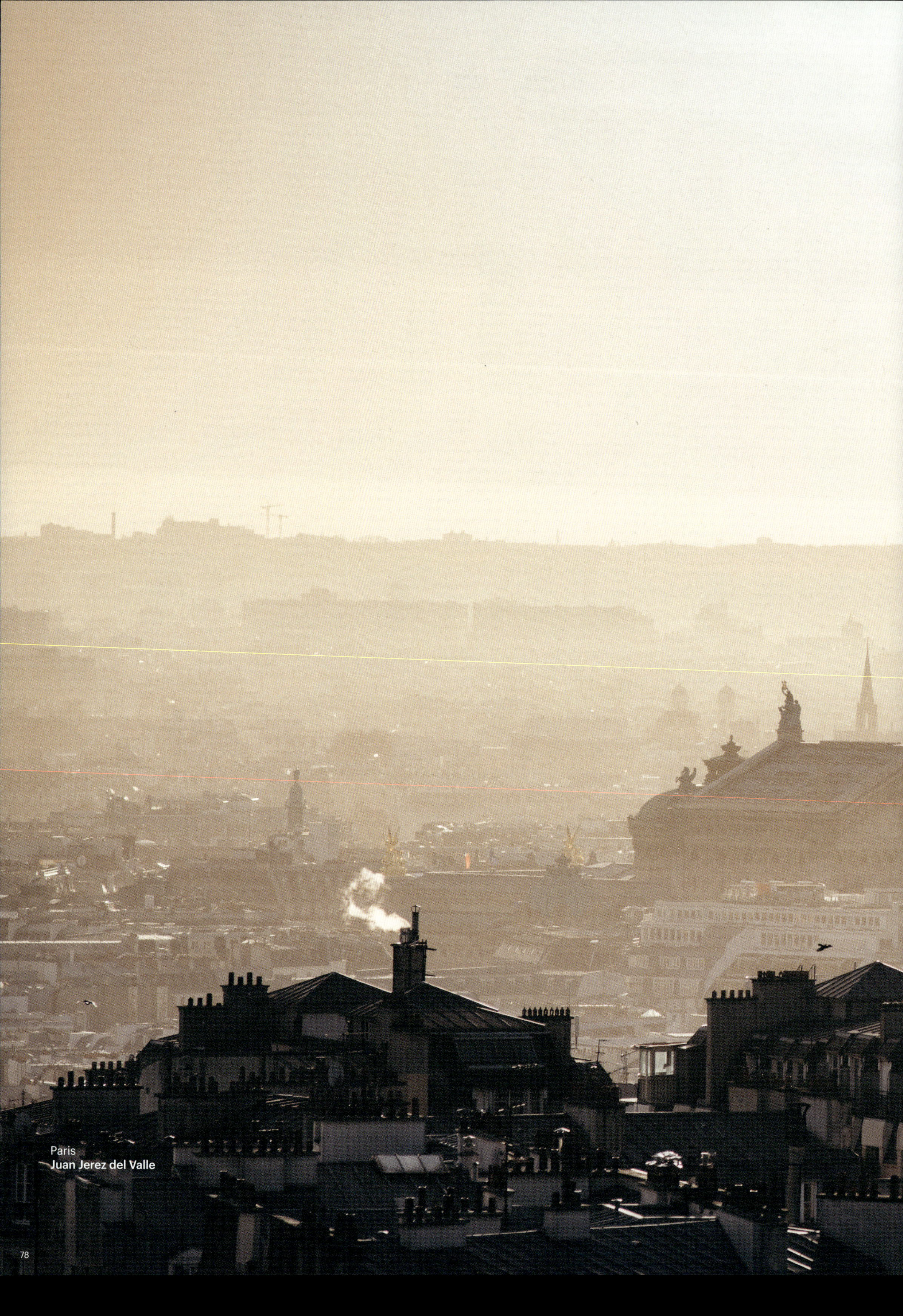

Paris
Juan Jerez del Valle

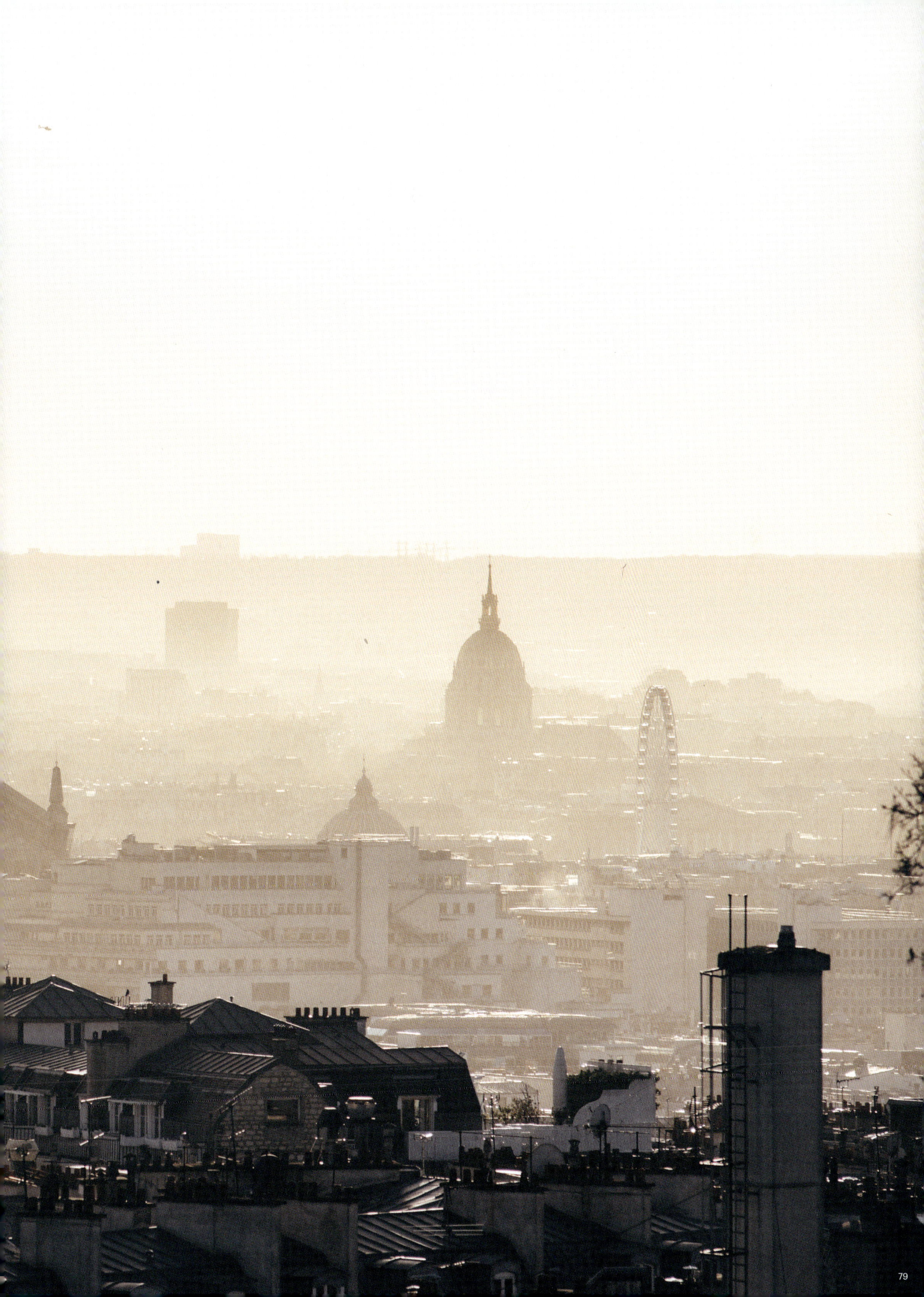

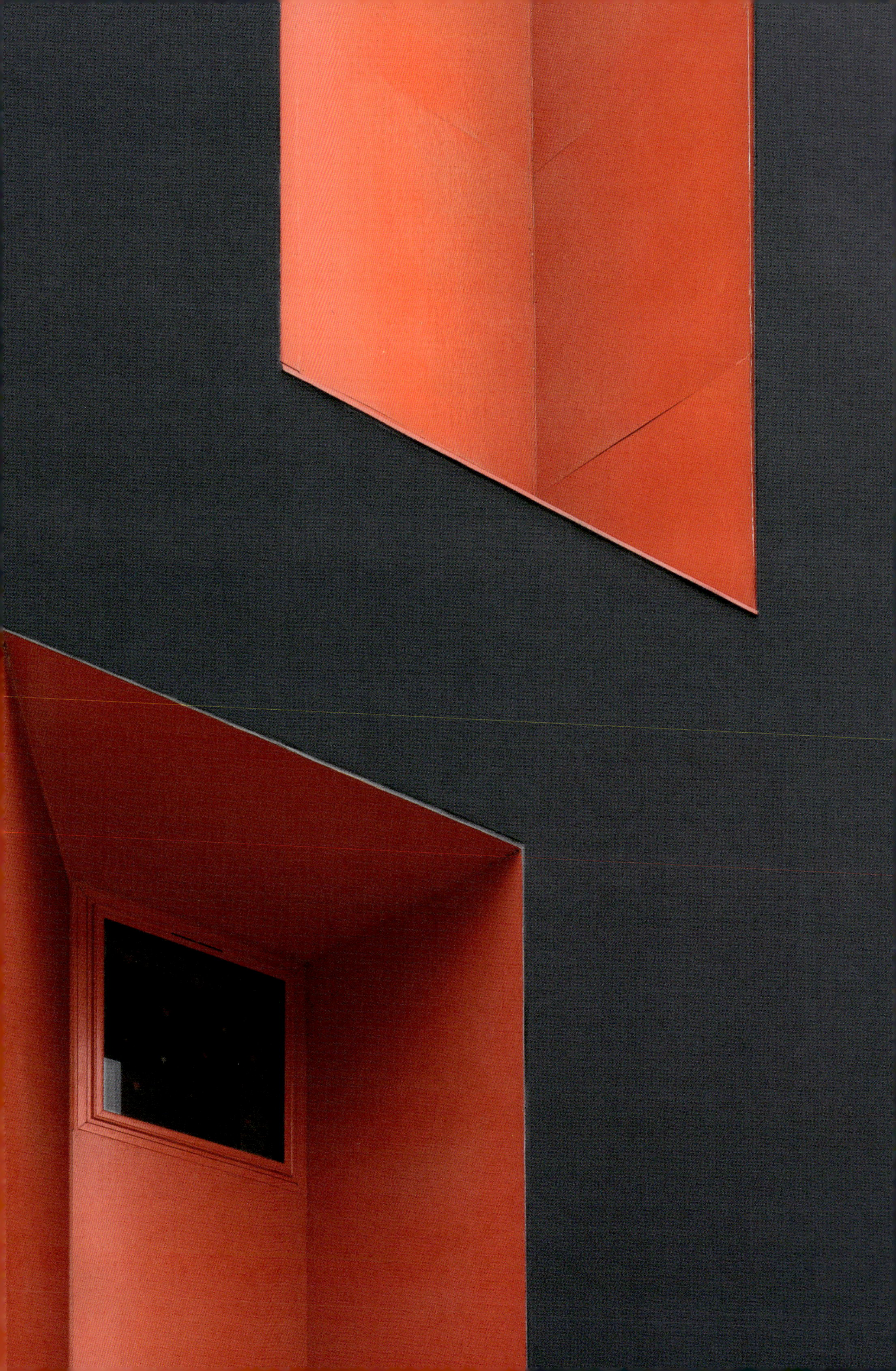

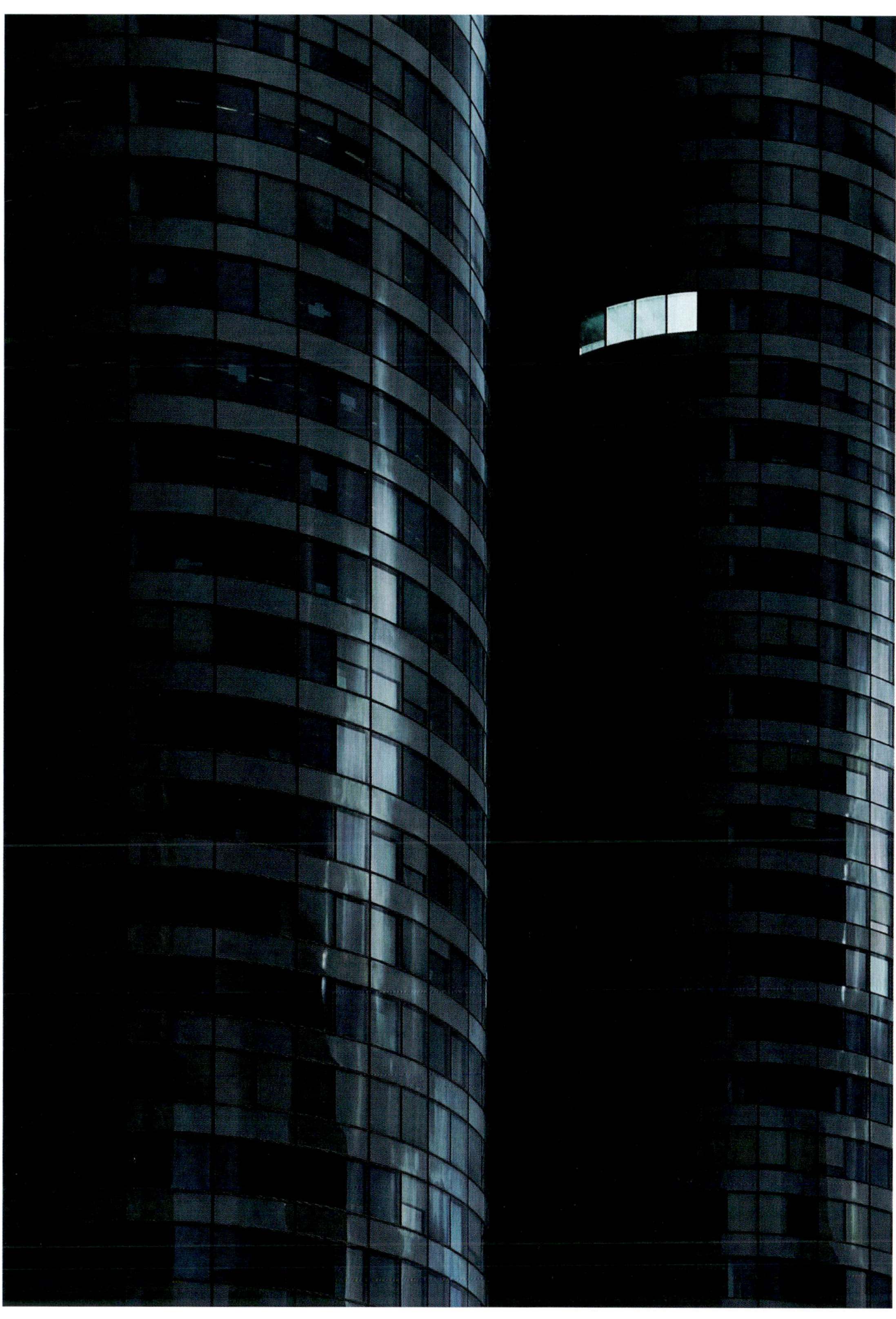

Saint-Ouen
Seine-Saint-Denis
– **Olivier Morisse**

Saint-Ouen
Seine-Saint-Denis
Olivier Morisse

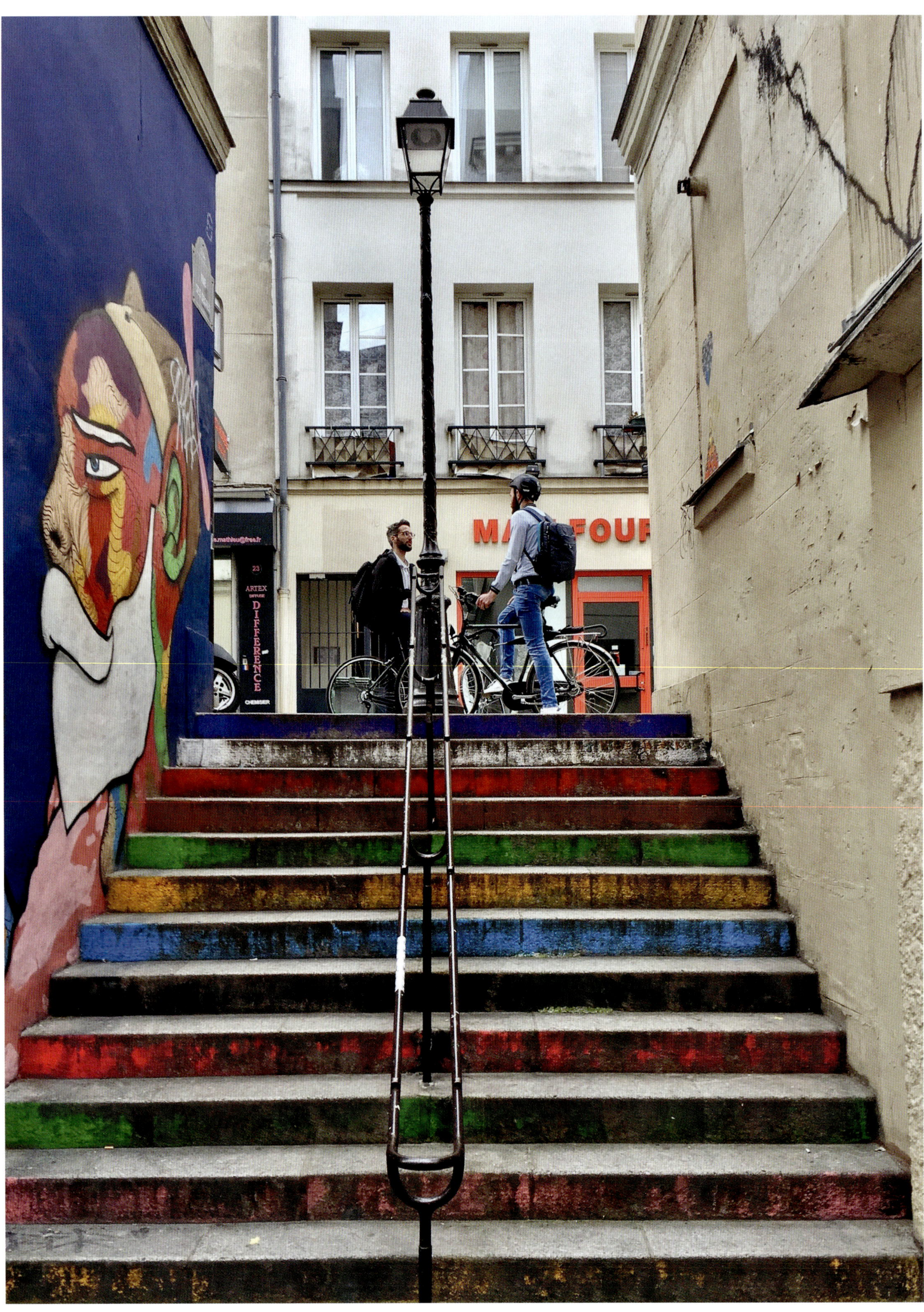
MA FOUR
23
ARTEX
DIFFERENCE
CHEMISIER

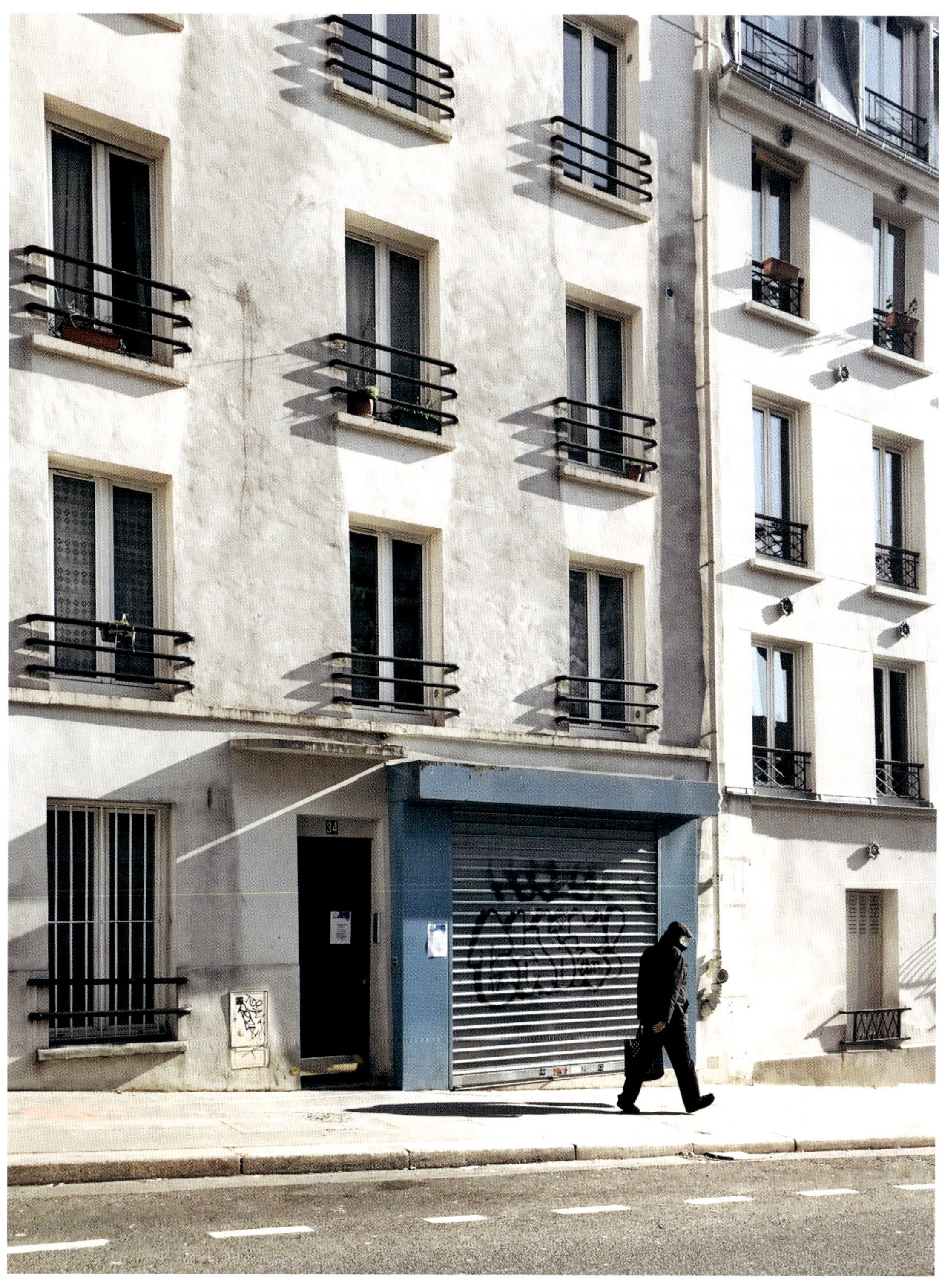

Rue de Cléry
10e Arrondissement
– **Willem Evers**

Rue Pradier
Buttes Chaumont
Laurent Dassencourt

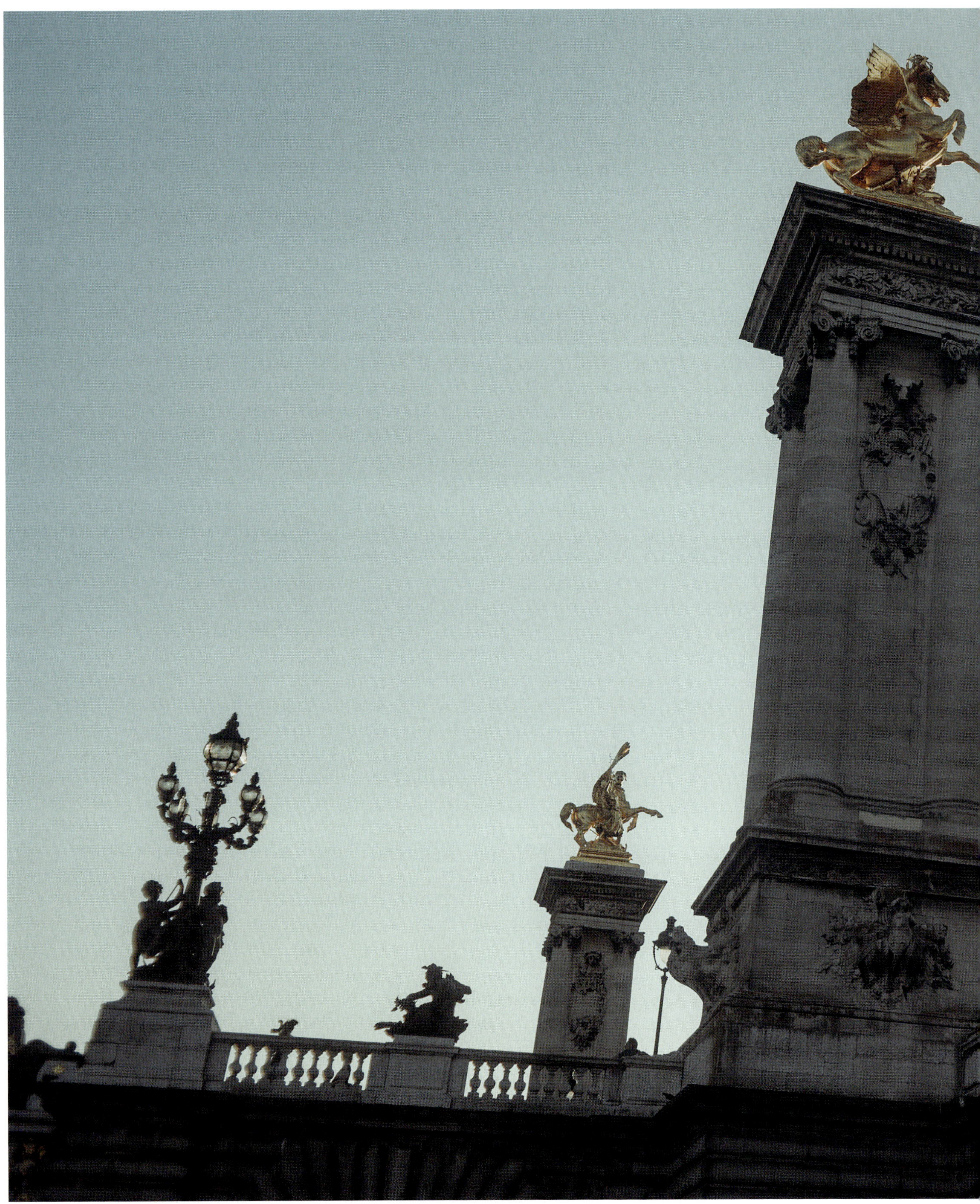

Pont Alexandre III
Seine River
Stijn Hoekstra

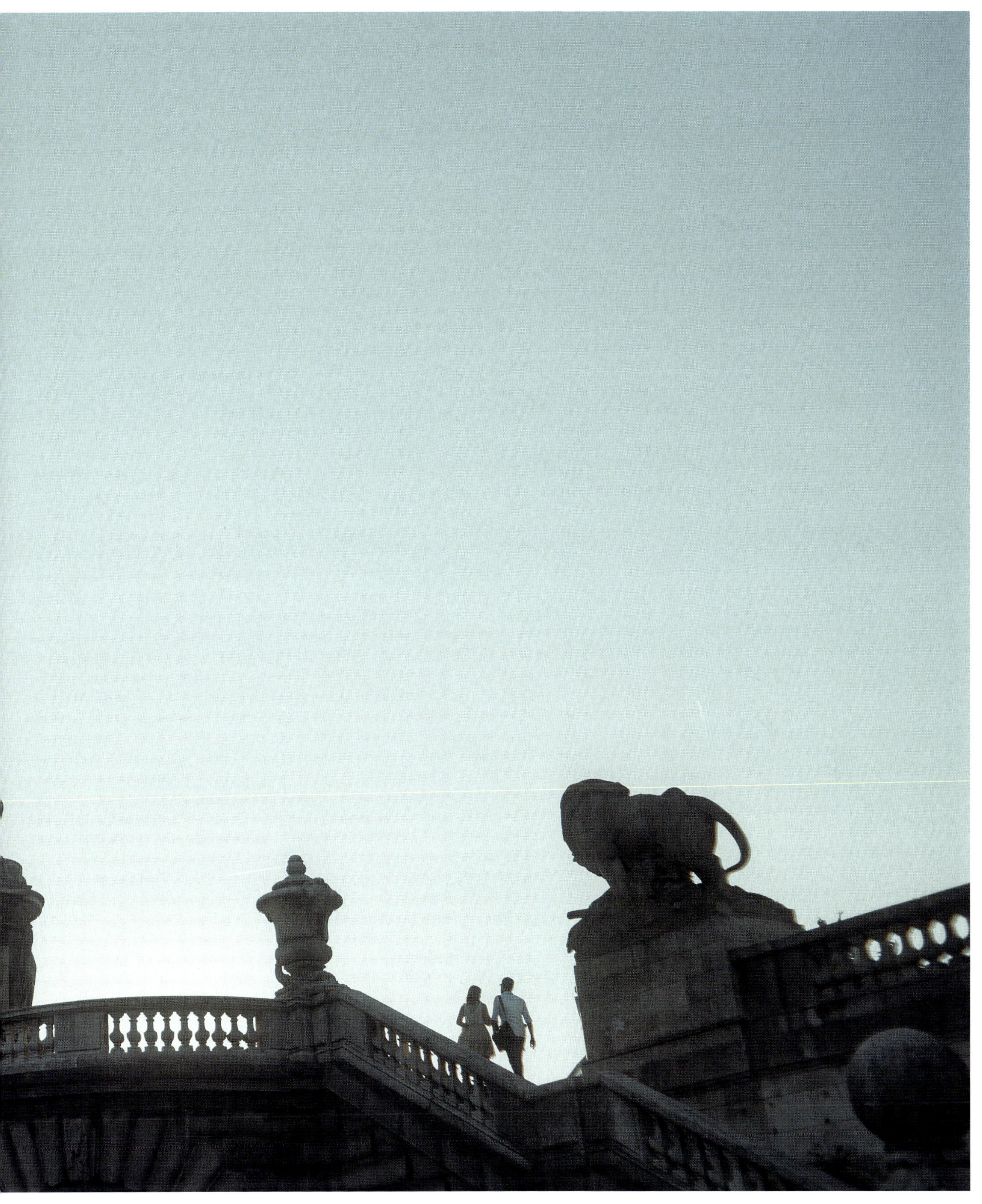

Laetitia Modine

hometown Nantes & Bordeaux, France
IG handle @laetitiamodine

"There still are numerous Parisian places I have yet to discover, although I get to know the city bit by bit on my short visits." Living between the less busy French cities of Nantes and Bordeaux, photographer and web designer Laetitia Modine hates the omnipresence of cars in Paris and the polluted air and noise they bring with them. "But there are also a lot of nice parts — the quiet streets that are lined with greenery, the areas removed from the urban hustle and bustle." It's amid this "countryside in the city" that Laetitia feels the greatest connection. "I have always loved open and deserted spaces, tranquility and nature, and this greatly influences my shots. I like to contemplate and immerse myself. This is probably the reason why my style is often described as contemplative. I try to share and express the emotions that I feel when I observe a touching scene. To share its beauty, its atmosphere, and its serenity." When you take a look at Laetitia's Instagram feed or at her pictures in this book, it's easy to see that she also enjoys Paris's modern architecture. While most people visit the historical parts of the city with its countless landmarks, Laetitia ventures to the city's more modern quarters, including La Défense. "The business districts of Paris are often very photogenic," she says. "On each visit, I keep discovering new parts of the city in a state of renewal. I love being able to vary my style with architectural lines."

„Es gibt noch immer eine Menge Orte in Paris zu entdecken, obwohl ich die Stadt bei meinen kurzen Besuchen Stück für Stück besser kennenlerne." Die Fotografin und Web-Designerin Laetitia Modine wohnt zwischen den weniger hektischen französischen Städten Nantes und Bordeaux. An Paris hasst sie die Omnipräsenz der Autos und die damit verbundene Luftverschmutzung und den Lärm. „Aber es gibt auch viele schöne Orte – die ruhigen Straßen mit den Bäumen, die Viertel abseits des hektischen Treibens der Stadt." Mit diesen Rückzugsorten in der Stadt fühlt sich Laetitia am meisten verbunden. „Ich habe schon immer offene und verlassene Orte geliebt, Ruhe und Natur, und das hat großen Einfluss auf meine Bilder. Dann stehe ich einfach staunend da und tauche in die Umgebung ein. Wahrscheinlich bezeichnet man deswegen meinen Stil oft als kontemplativ. Ich versuche, anderen meine Gefühle beim Betrachten einer bewegenden Szene mitzuteilen und sie zum Ausdruck zu bringen, die Schönheit, die Atmosphäre und die Gelassenheit." Der Blick auf ihre Instagram-Bilder oder auf die Bilder in diesem Buch zeigt deutlich, dass sie an Paris auch die moderne Architektur liebt. Während die meisten Besucher die historischen Teile der Stadt mit den zahllosen Sehenswürdigkeiten besichtigen, setzt sich Laetitia mit den modernen Vierteln der Stadt wie zum Beispiel der Défense auseinander. „Die Geschäftsviertel der Stadt sind oft sehr fotogen", meint sie. „Bei jedem meiner Besuche entdecke ich neue Teile der Stadt, die sich im Umbau befinden. Ich liebe es, meinen Stil an die Gegebenheiten der Architektur anpassen zu können."

« Nombreux sont les lieux que j'ai encore à découvrir à Paris, que j'apprends pourtant à connaître, quartier par quartier, au cours de mes brèves visites ». Vivant entre les villes plus paisibles de Nantes et de Bordeaux, Laetitia Modine déteste l'omniprésence des voitures, la pollution et le bruit que celles-ci génèrent à Paris. « Mais il y a aussi tant d'aspects agréables – ces rues tranquilles, bordées d'arbres, ces quartiers situés loin du tohu-bohu urbain ». C'est au milieu de cette « campagne dans la ville » que la photographe et web designer se sent la plus proche de Paris. « J'ai toujours aimé les lieux ouverts et déserts, la sérénité et la nature, et cela influence nettement mes images. J'aime contempler, et m'immerger. C'est probablement la raison pour laquelle mon style est souvent considéré comme contemplatif. Je tente de partager et d'exprimer les émotions que j'éprouve lorsque j'observe une scène émouvante. De communiquer sa beauté, son atmosphère, sa sérénité ». Que l'on parcourt son compte Instagram ou les photographies présentées ici, nul ne doute que Laetitia Modine n'aime également l'architecture moderne de Paris. Alors que les quartiers historiques de la capitale, avec ses innombrables édifices ou monuments incontournables, attirent la plupart des visiteurs, Laetitia préfère s'aventurer dans des zones plus modernes, à l'exemple de la Défense. « Les quartiers d'affaires parisiens sont souvent très photogéniques, affirme la photographe. A chacune de mes visites, je continue à découvrir des lieux nouveaux, dans une ville en rénovation. J'aime pouvoir varier mon style grâce aux lignes architecturales ».

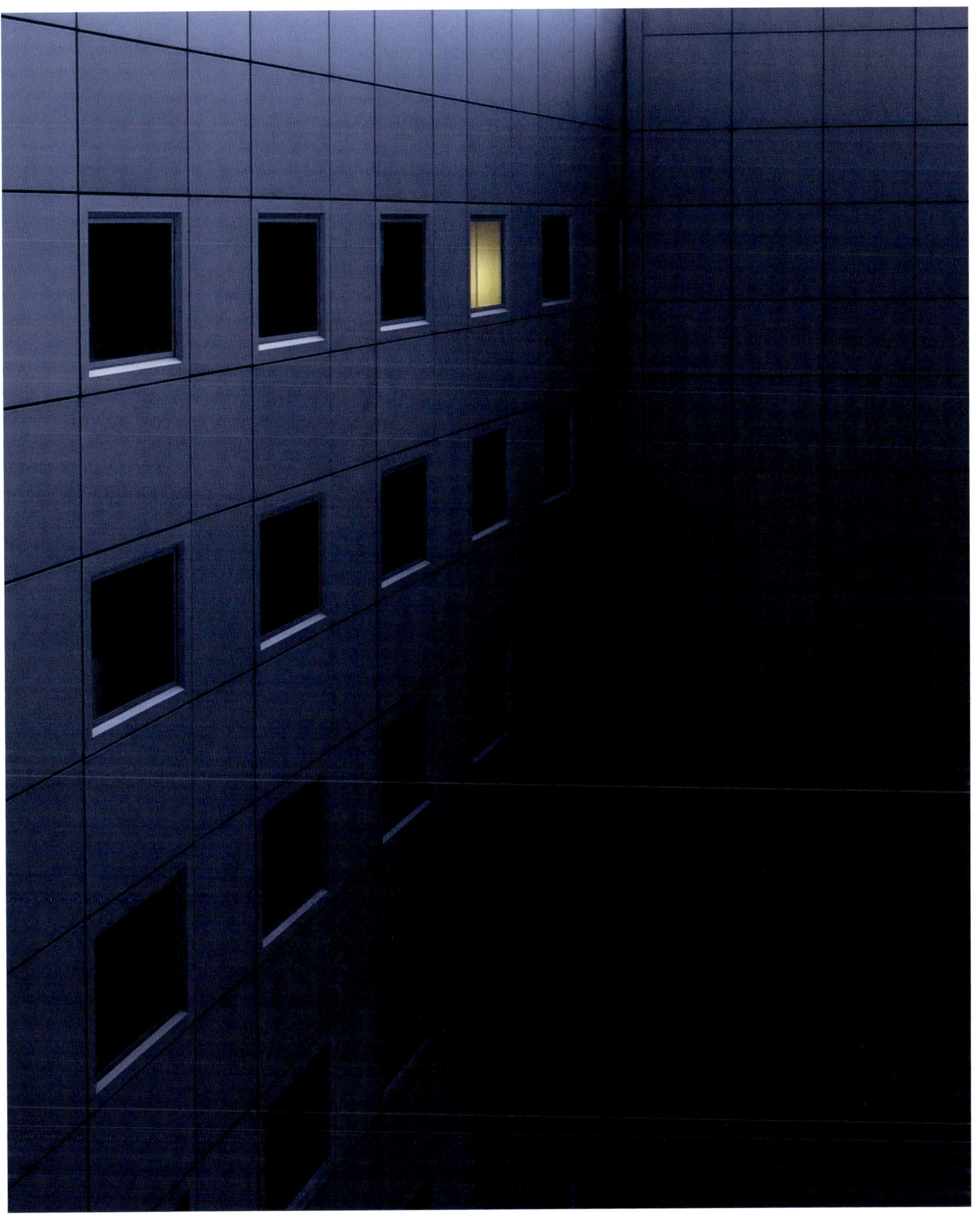

Pacific
La Défense
Laetitia Modine

4e Arrondissement
Romain Figuiere

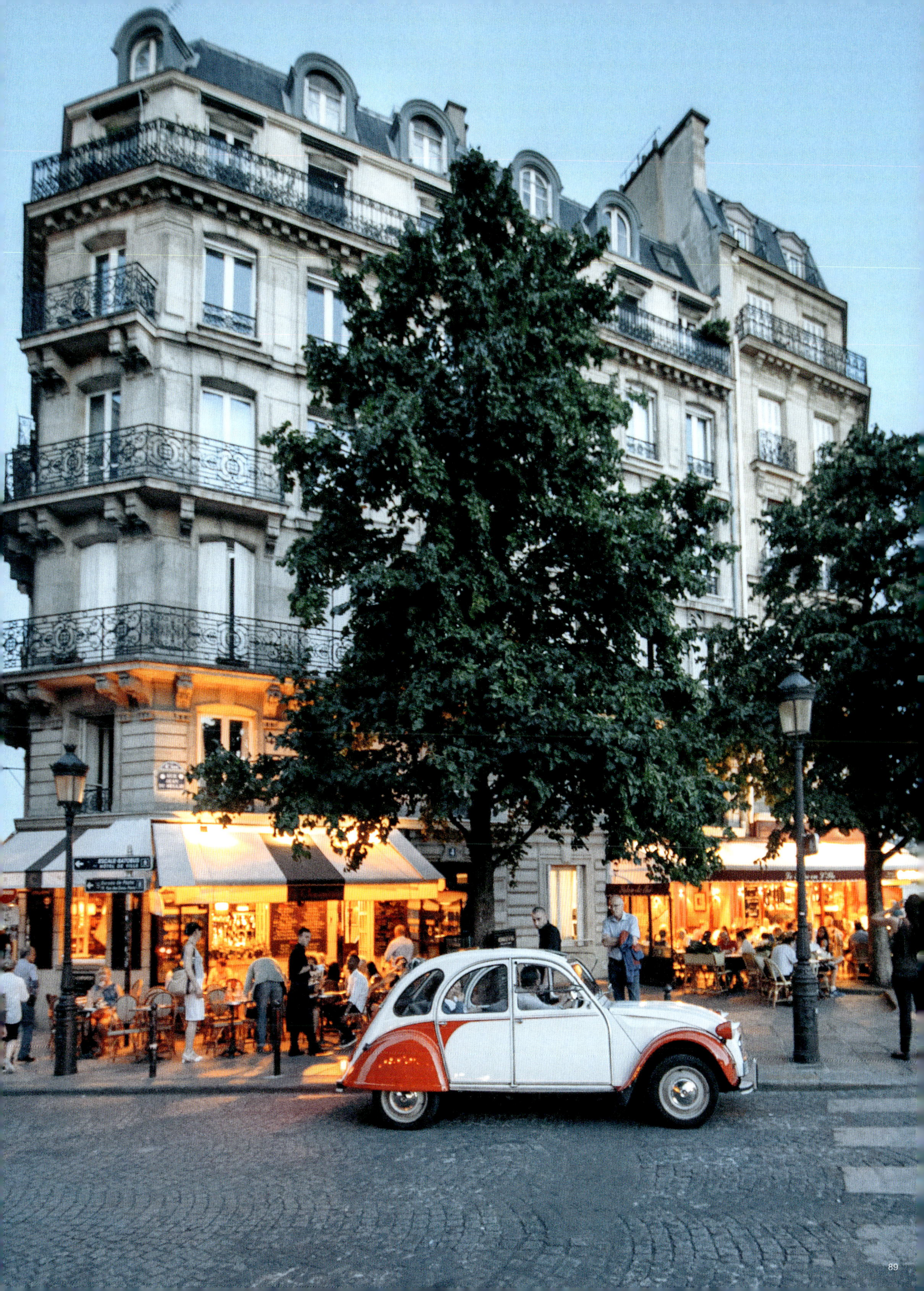

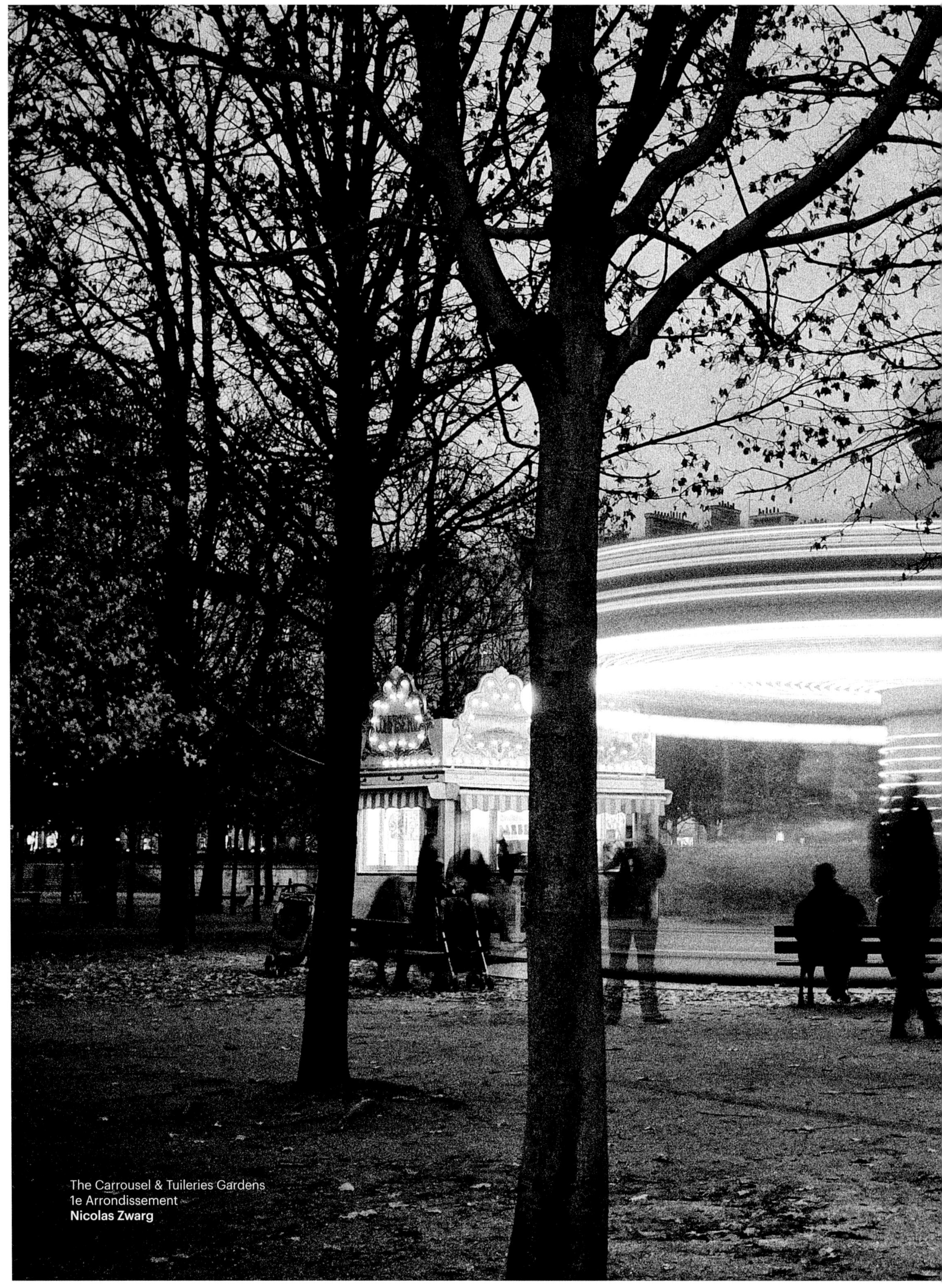

The Carrousel & Tuileries Gardens
1e Arrondissement
Nicolas Zwarg

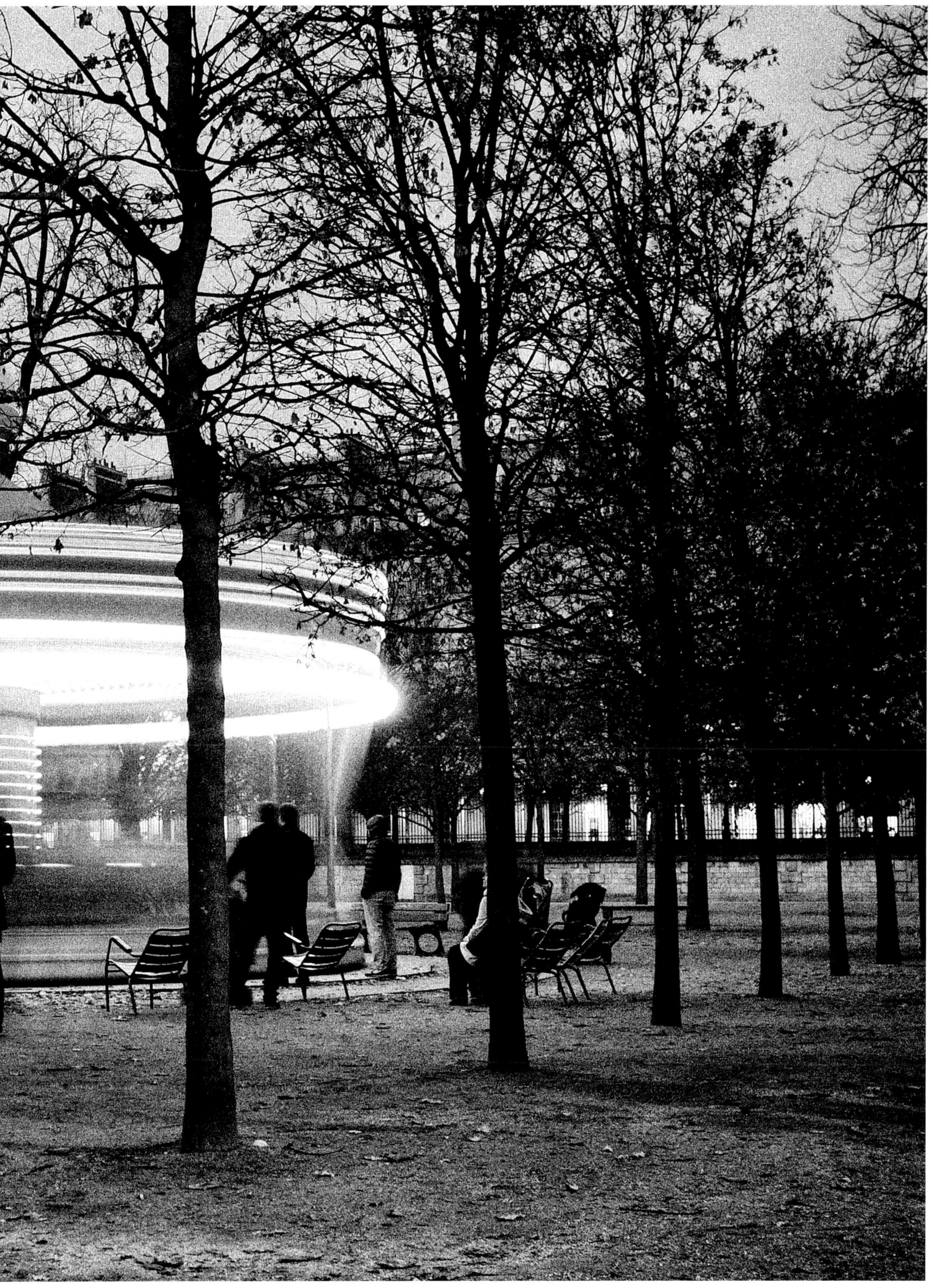

I just want to share the beauty that is sometimes found right there in the ordinary situation.

—Erica Gonzalez

Montmartre
Stéphanie Le Lay →

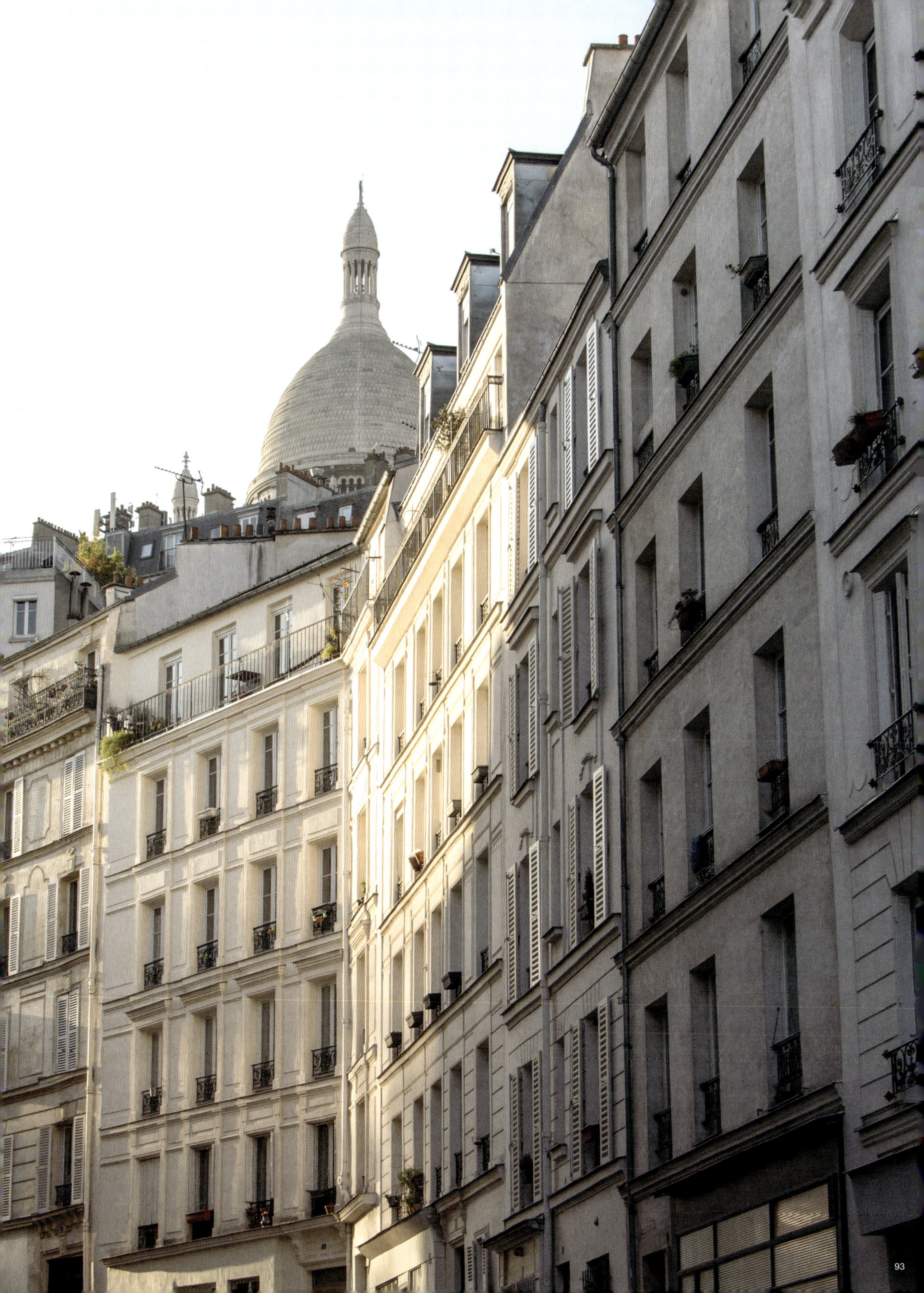

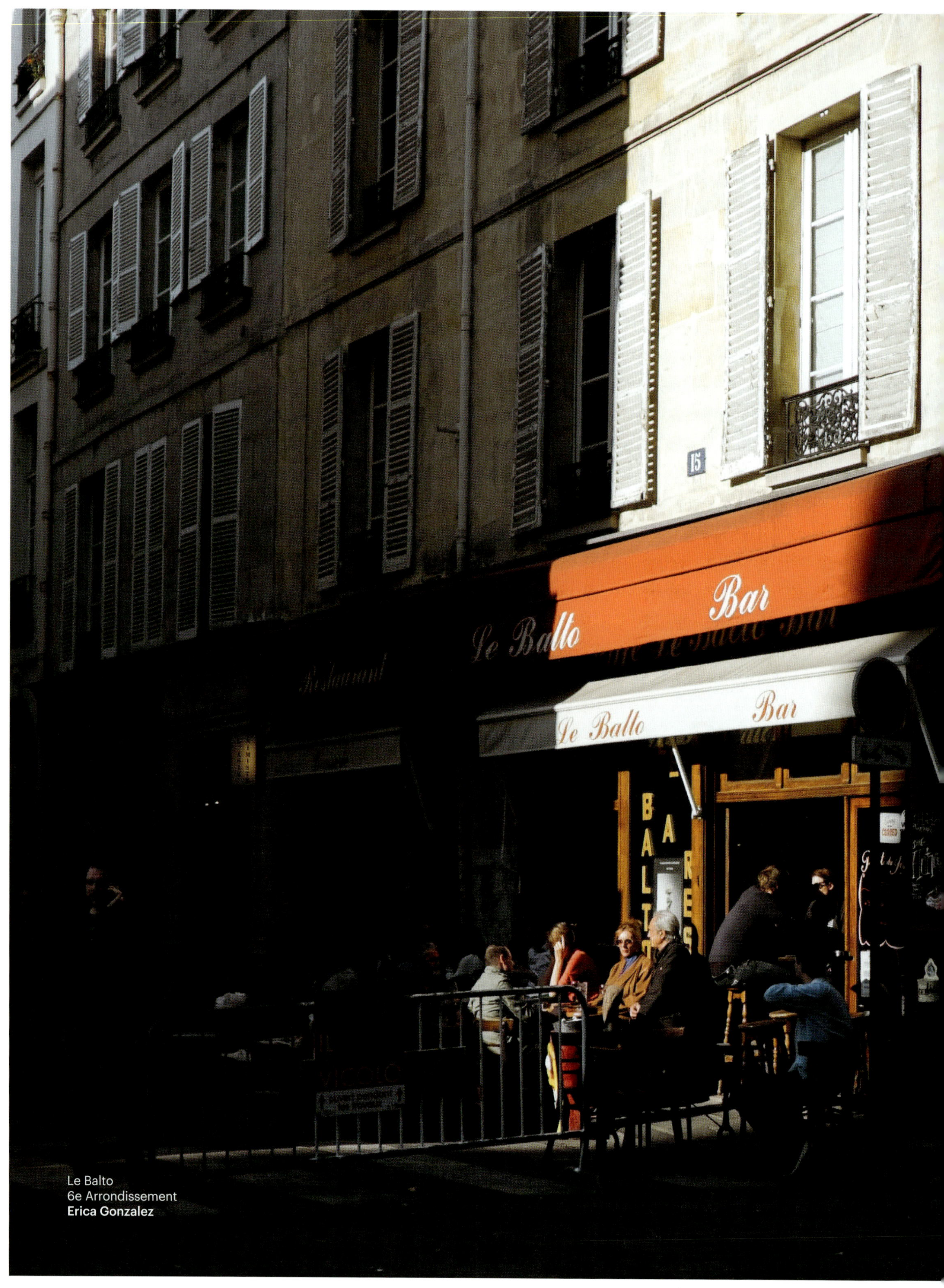

Le Balto
6e Arrondissement
Erica Gonzalez

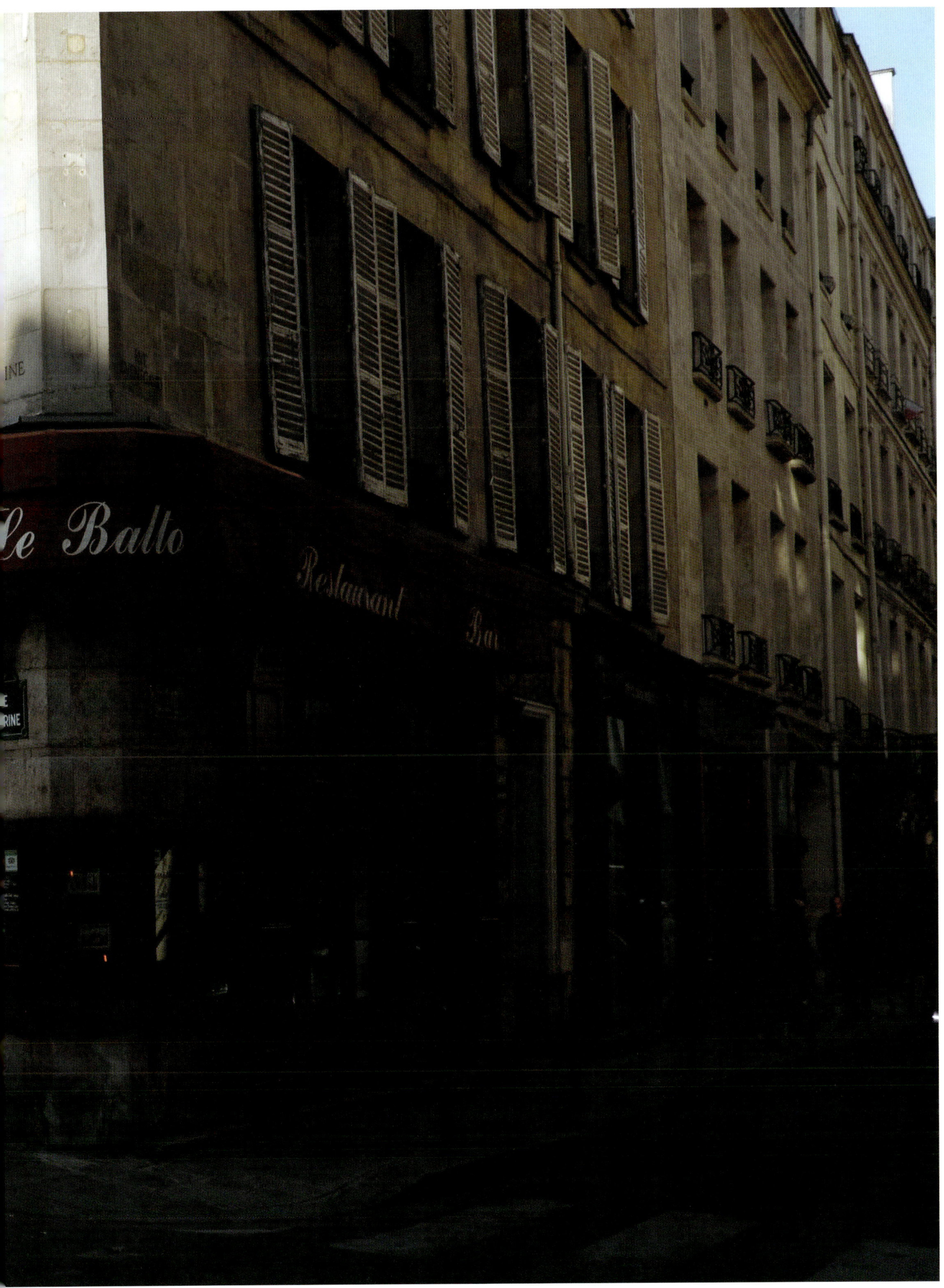
Le Balto
Restaurant
Bar

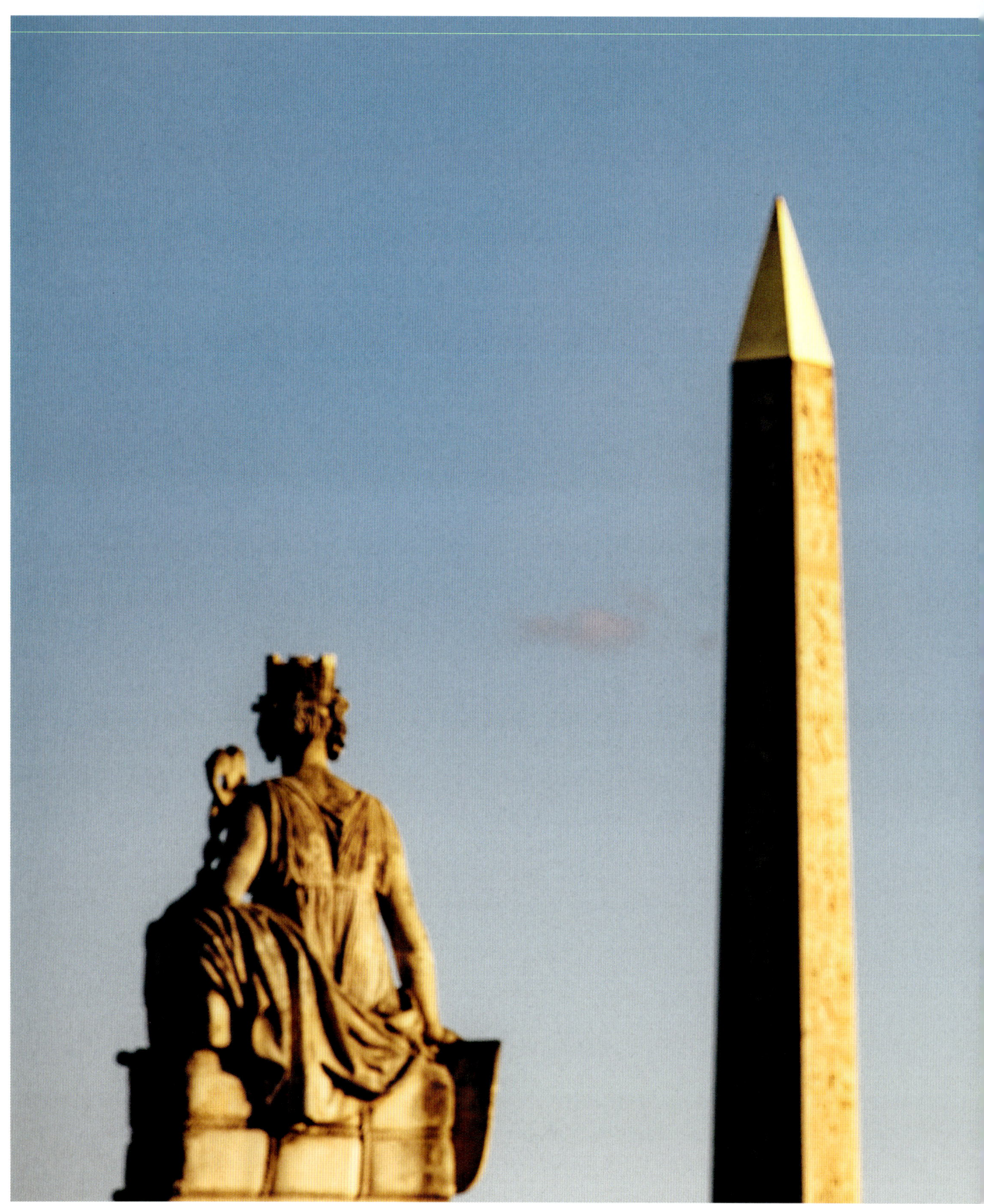

Obélisque de Louxor
7e Arrondissement
Roel Ruijs

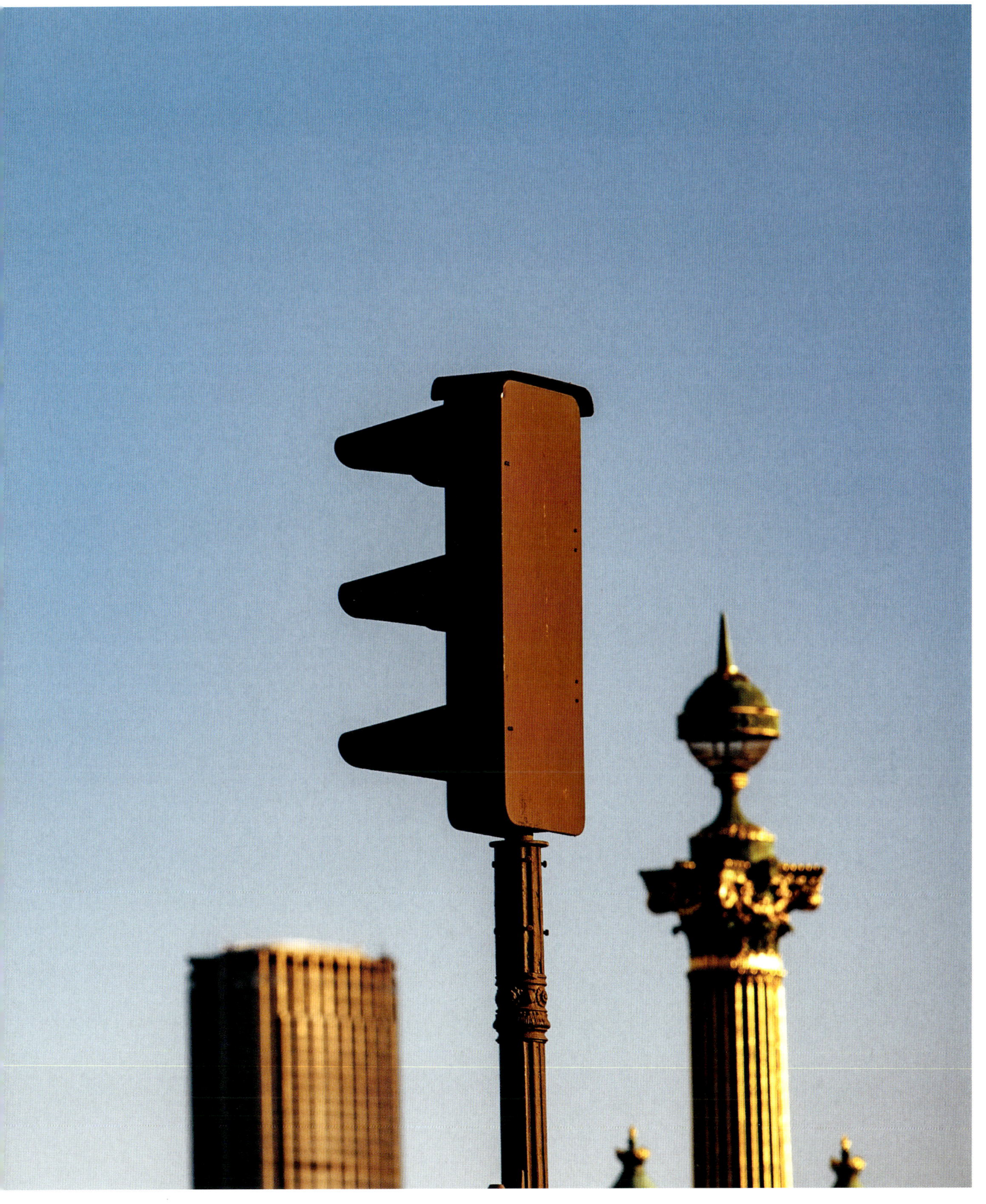

Gare de Lyon
12e Arrondissement
Barry Glassman

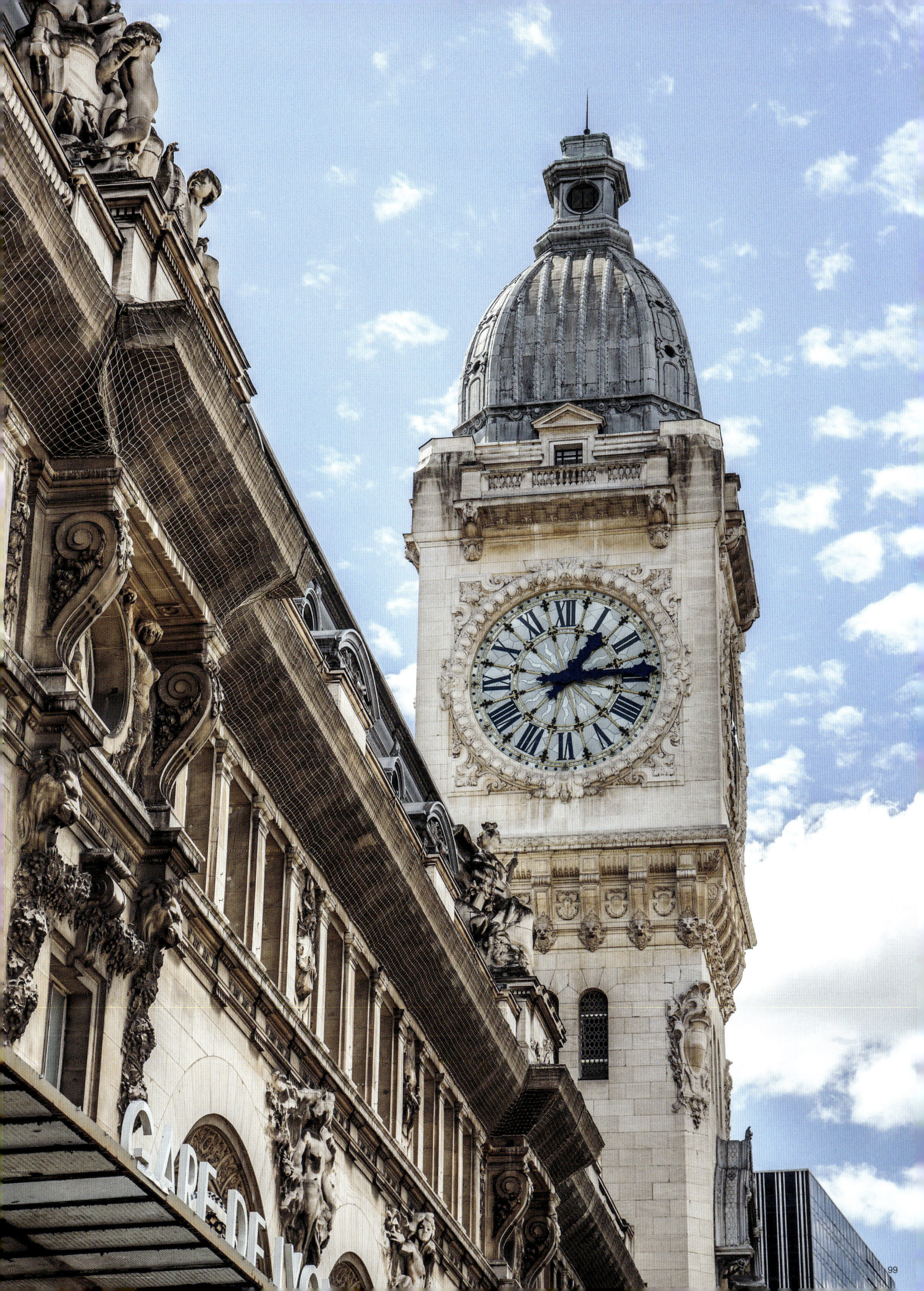
GARE DE LY

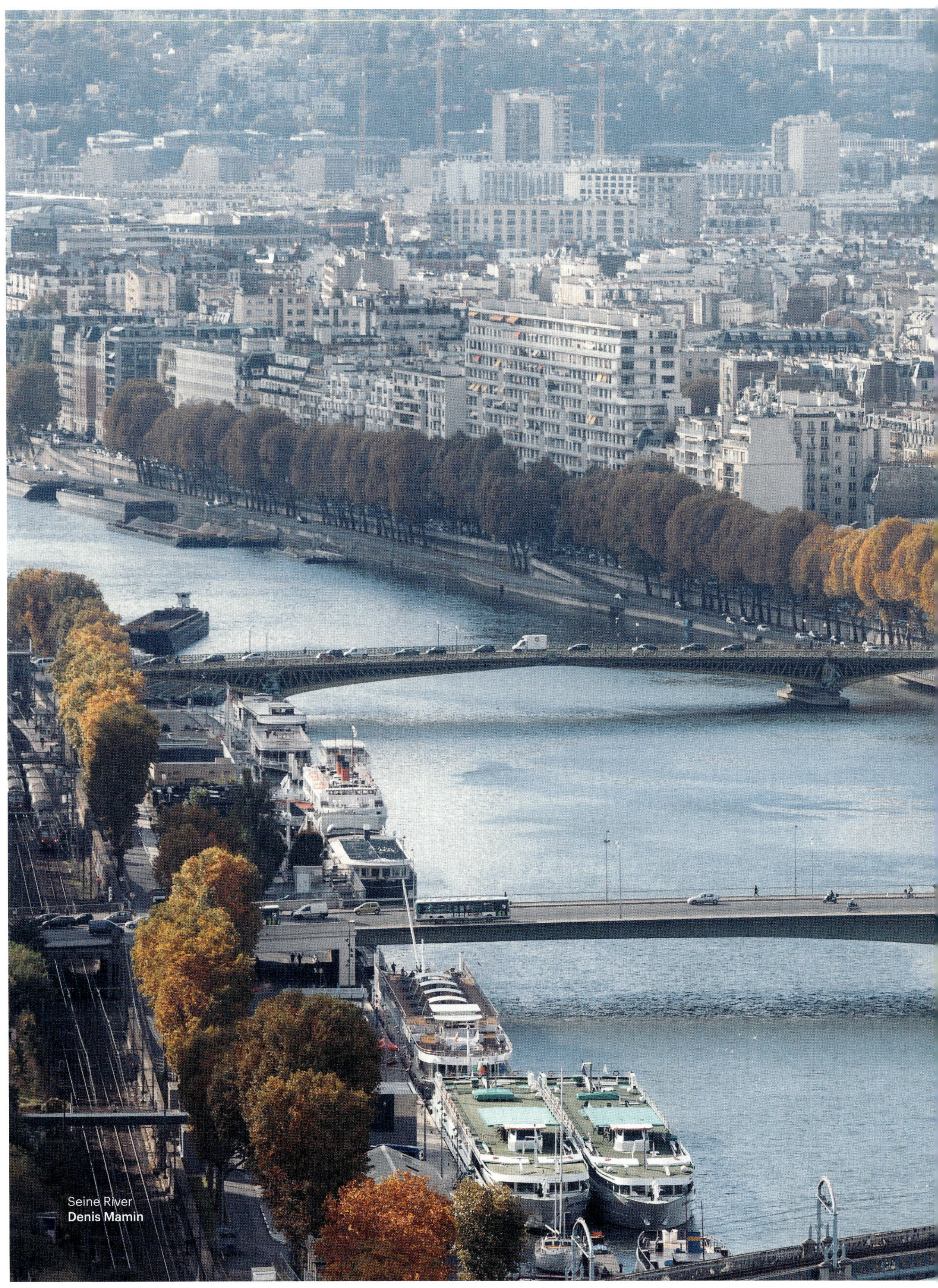
Seine River
Denis Mamin

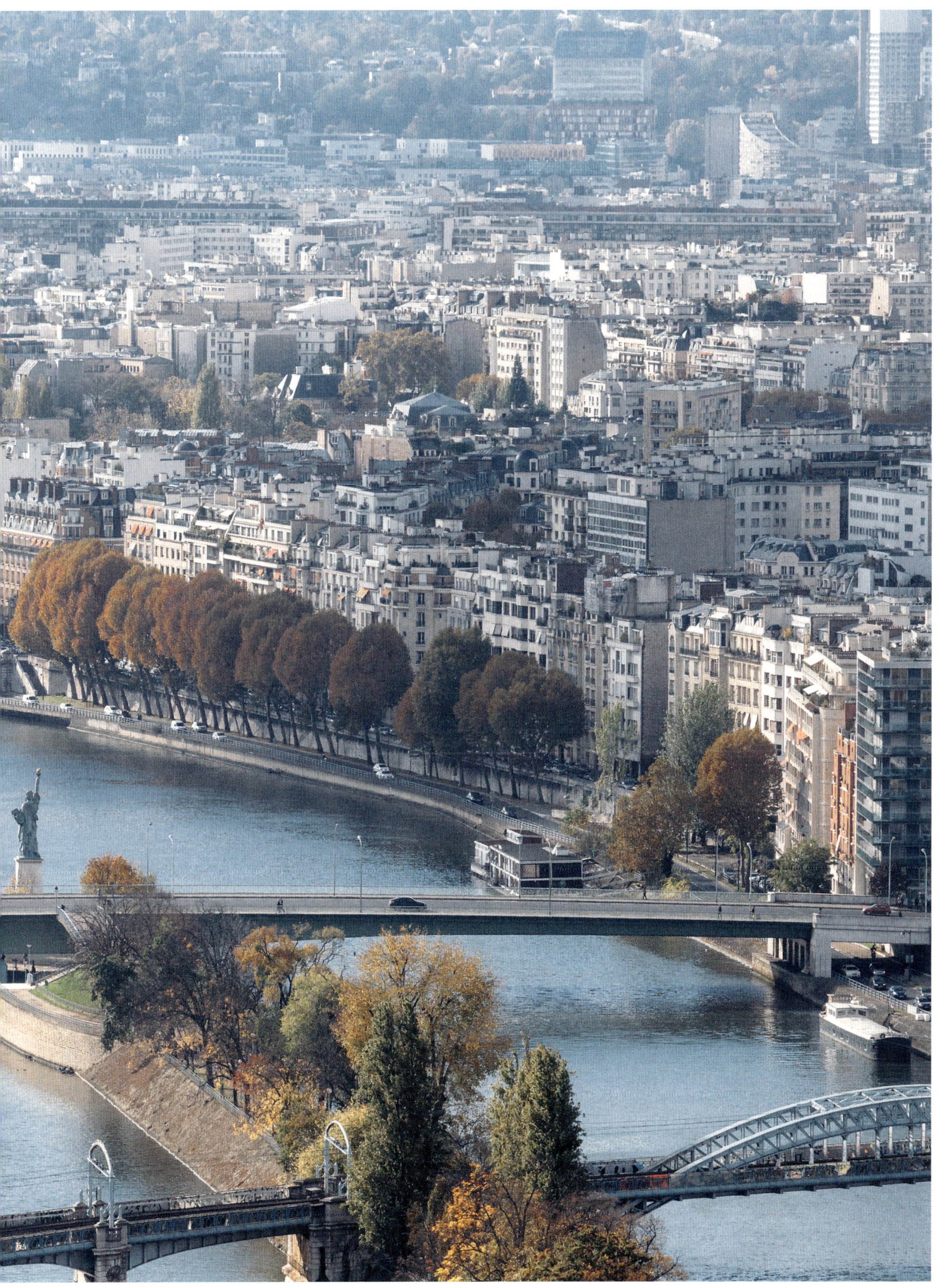

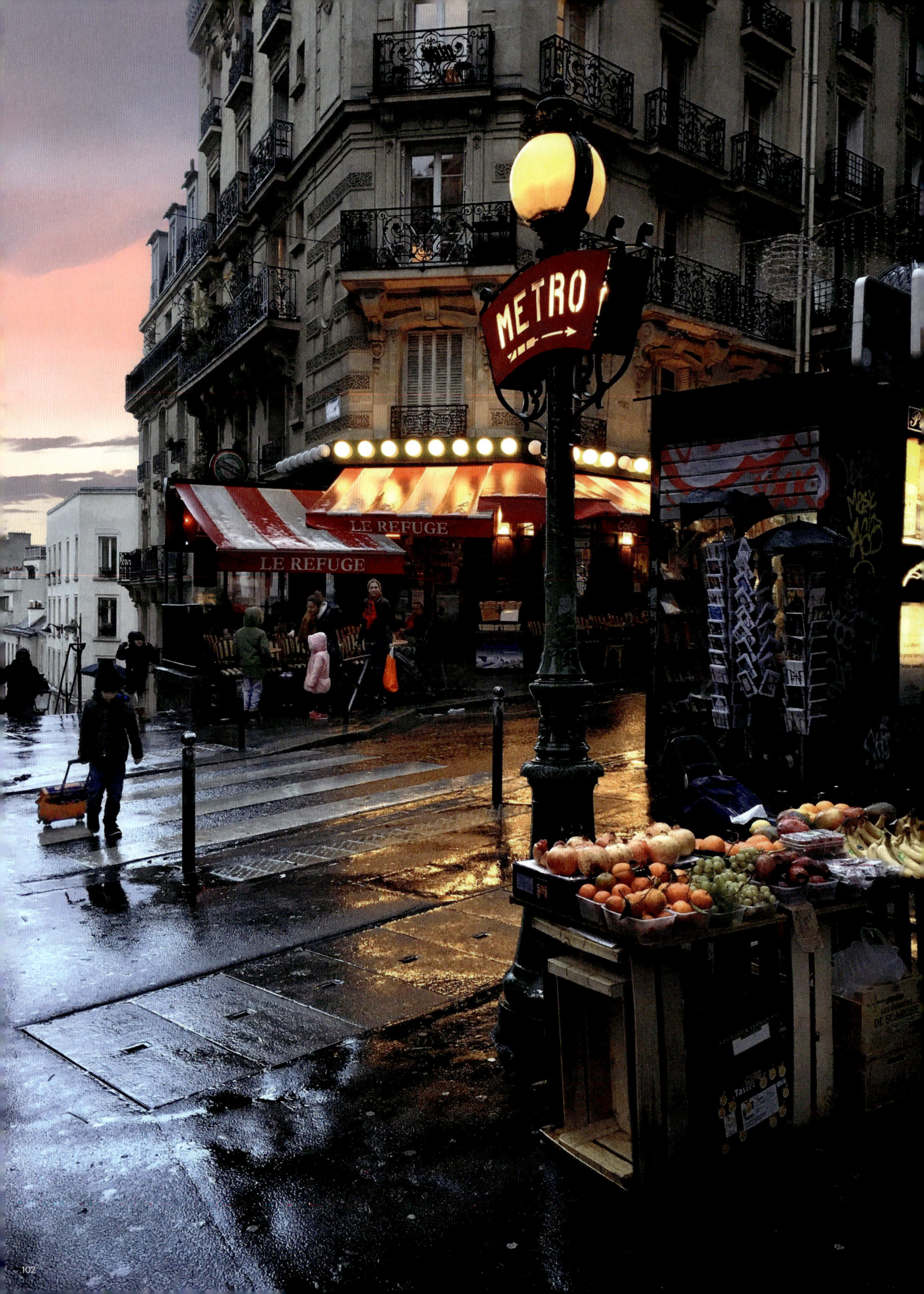
METRO
LE REFUGE
LE REFUGE

People from all over the world live here and use the subway to commute to their jobs in the city.

—Joost Bastmeijer

Le Refuge
Clignancourt
Willem Evers

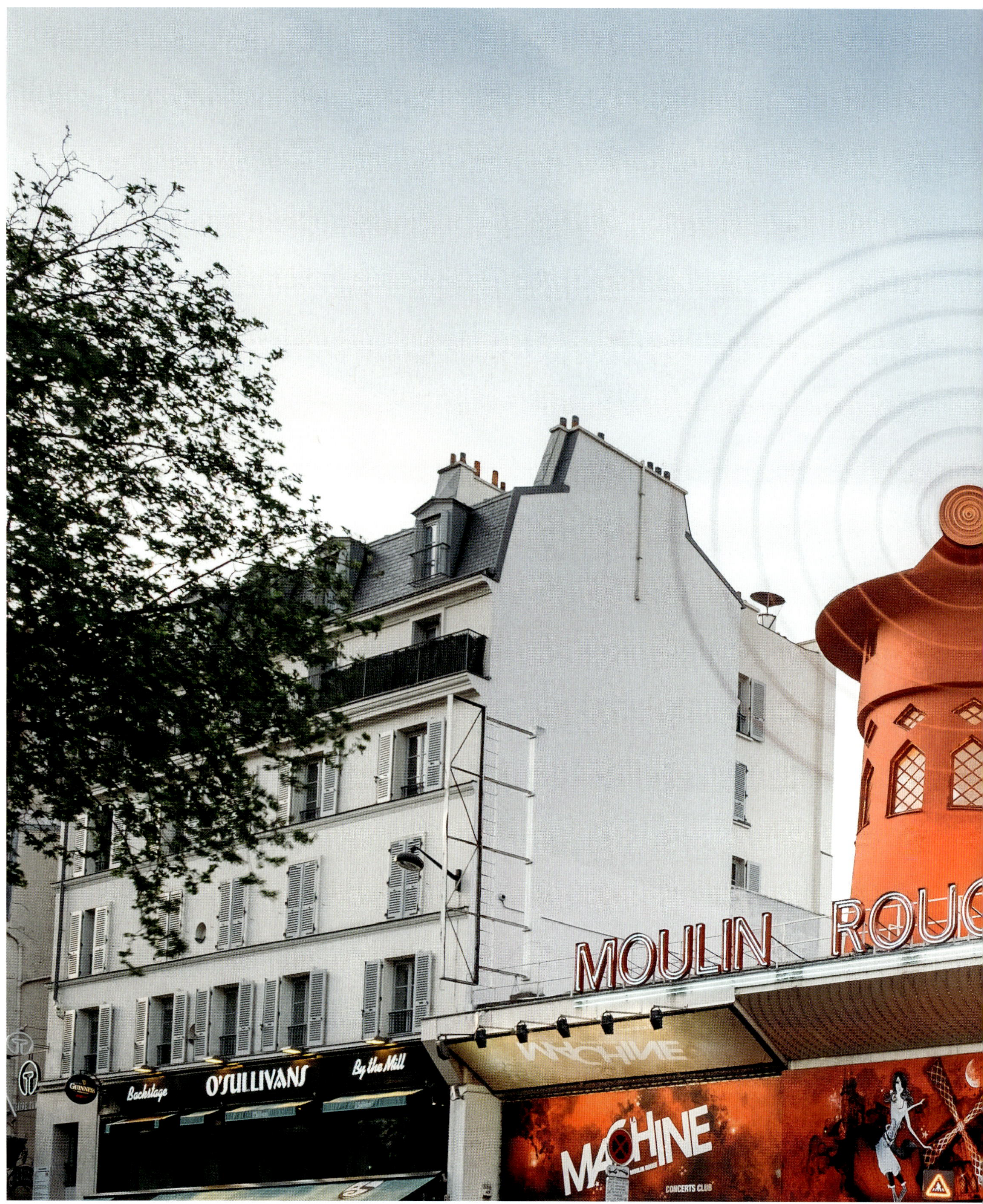

Moulin Rouge
Pigalle
Laurent Dassencourt

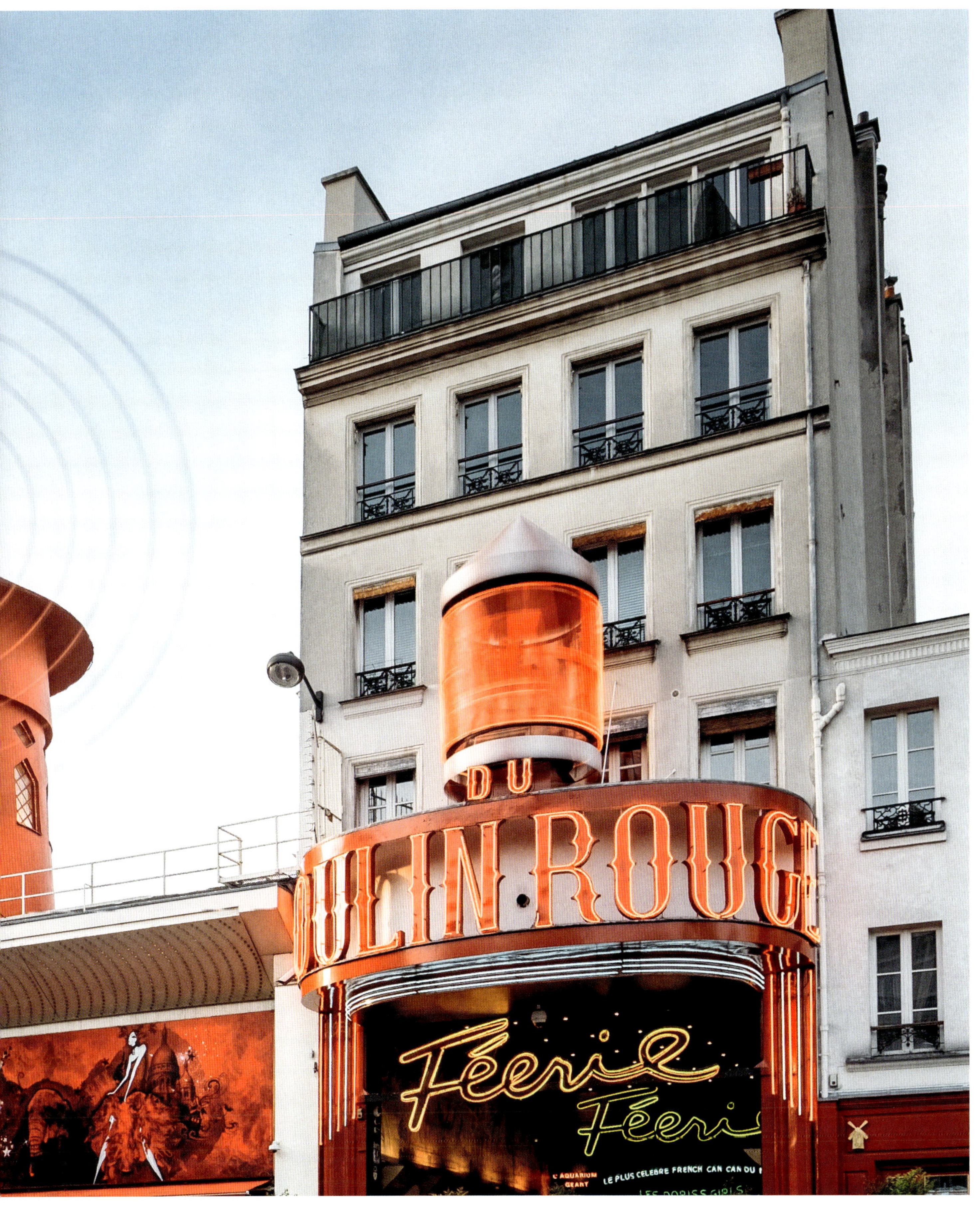
DU
OULIN ROUGE
Féerie
L'AQUARIUM GEANT
LE PLUS CELEBRE FRENCH CAN CAN DU

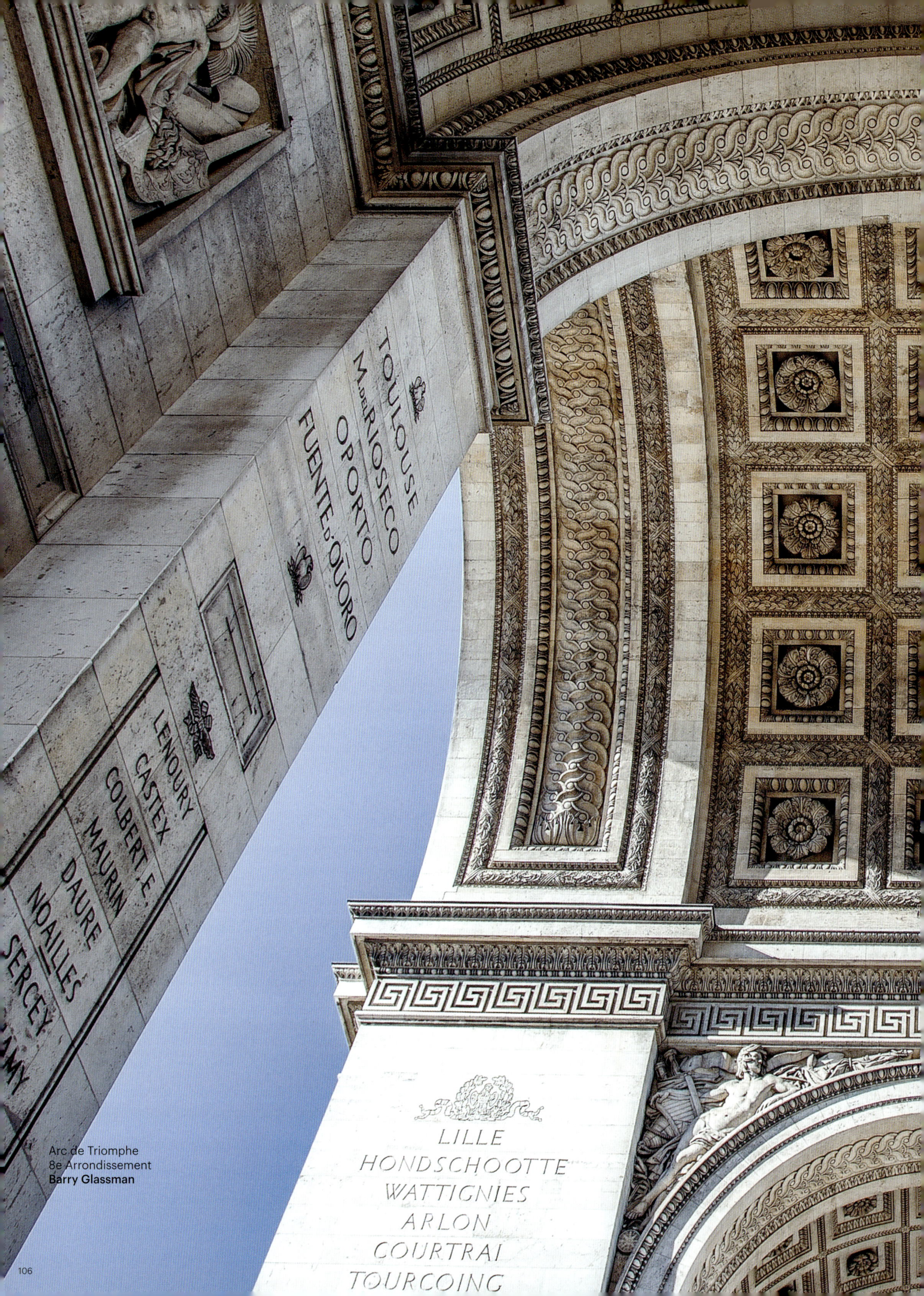

Arc de Triomphe
8e Arrondissement
Barry Glassman

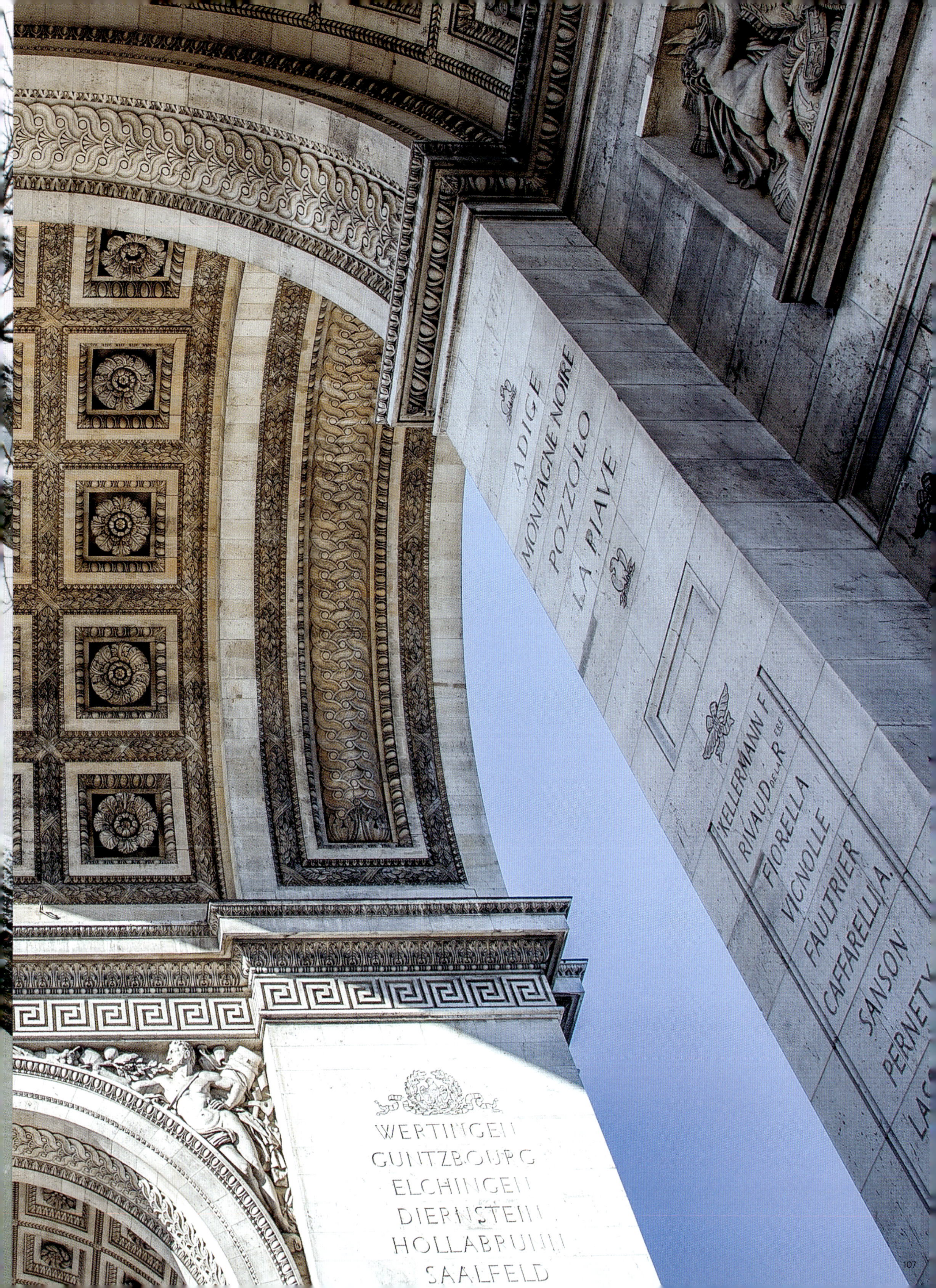
ADIGE
MONTAGNE NOIRE
POZZOLO
LA PIAVE
KELLERMANN F.
FIORELLA
VIGNOLLE
FAULTRIER
CAFFARELLI A.
SANSON
WERTINGEN
GUNTZBOURG
ELCHINGEN
DIERNSTEIN
HOLLABRUNN
SAALFELD

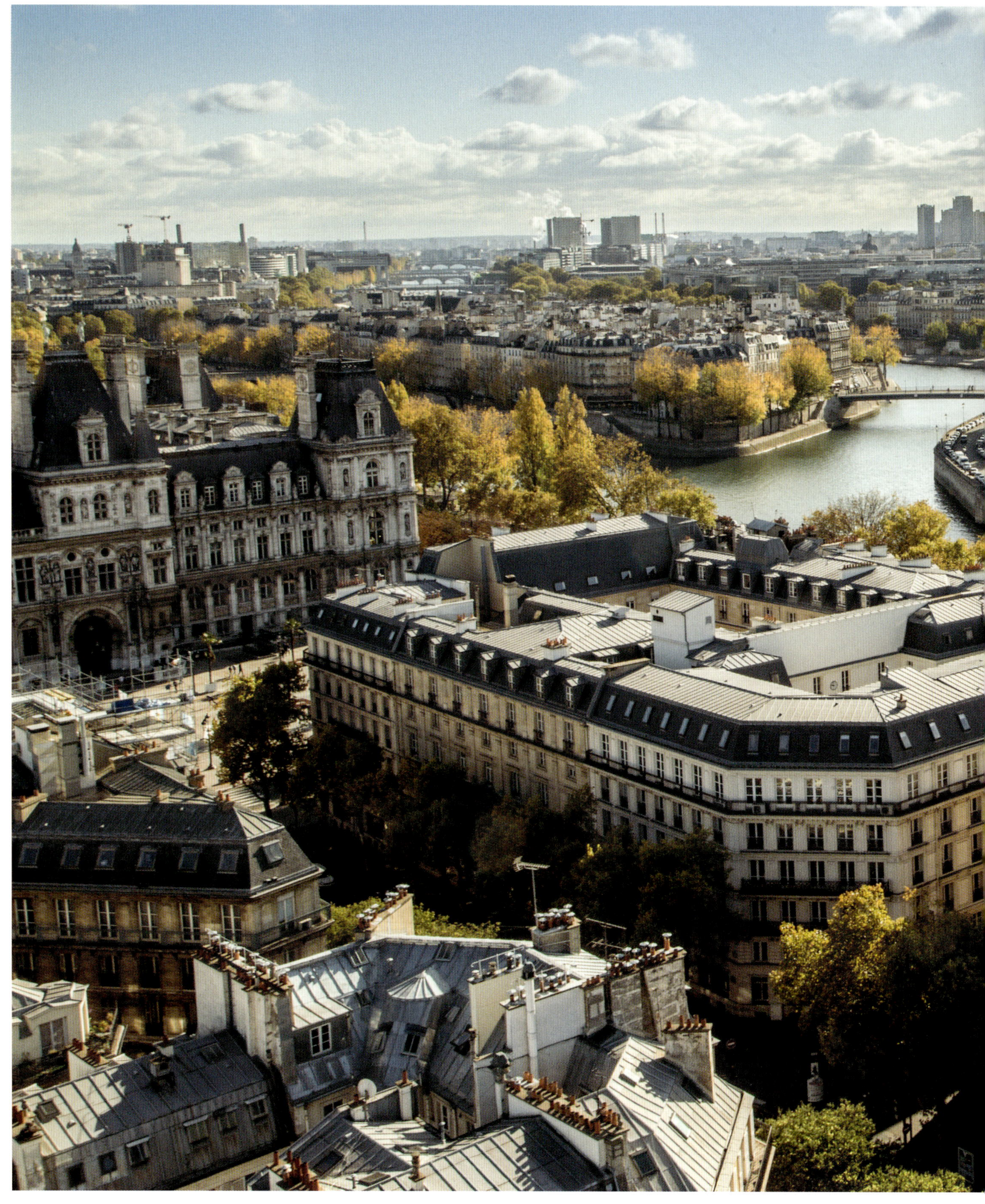

Île de la Cité
Baptiste Jayat

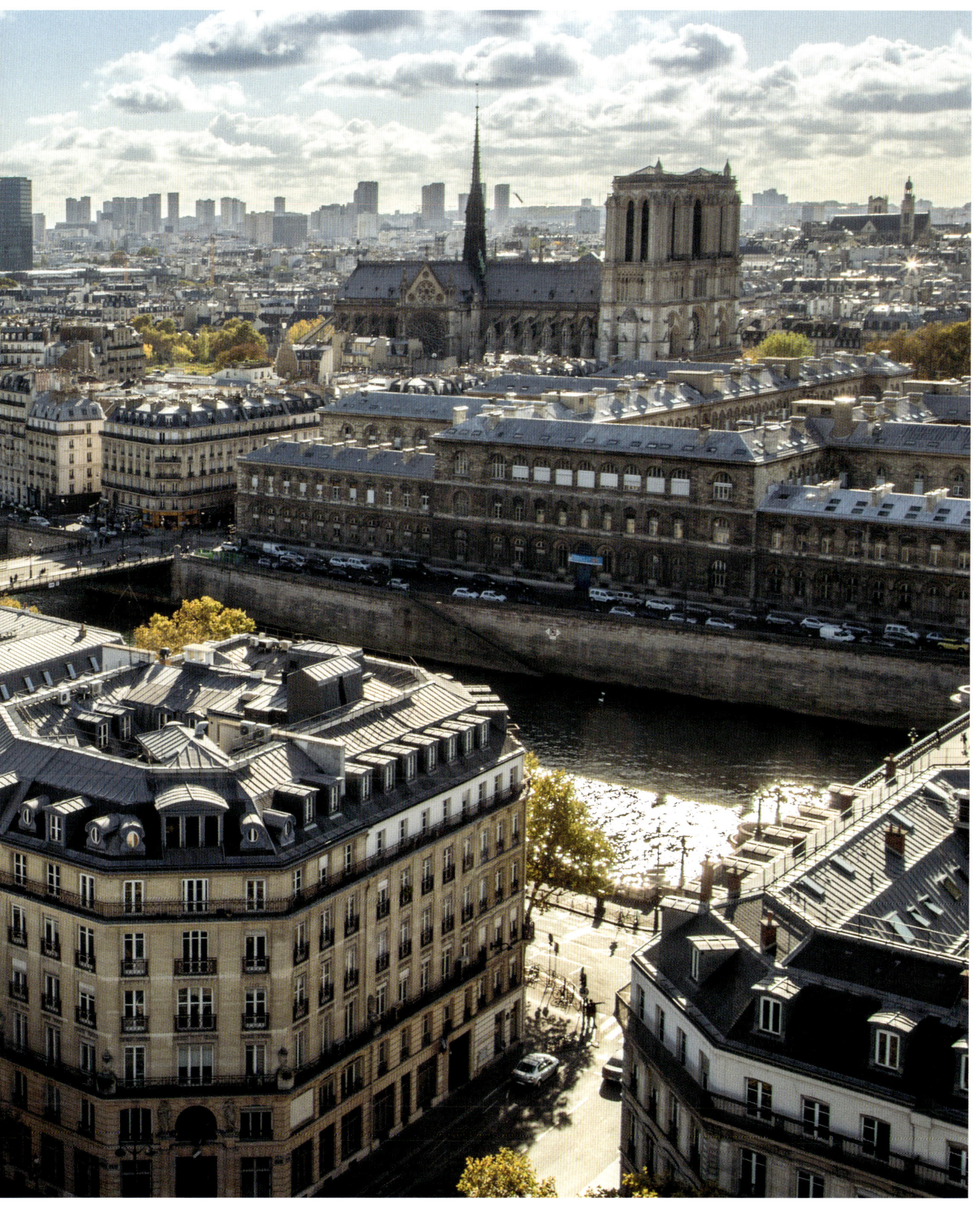

Halle Saguez
Saint-Denis
Olivier Morisse

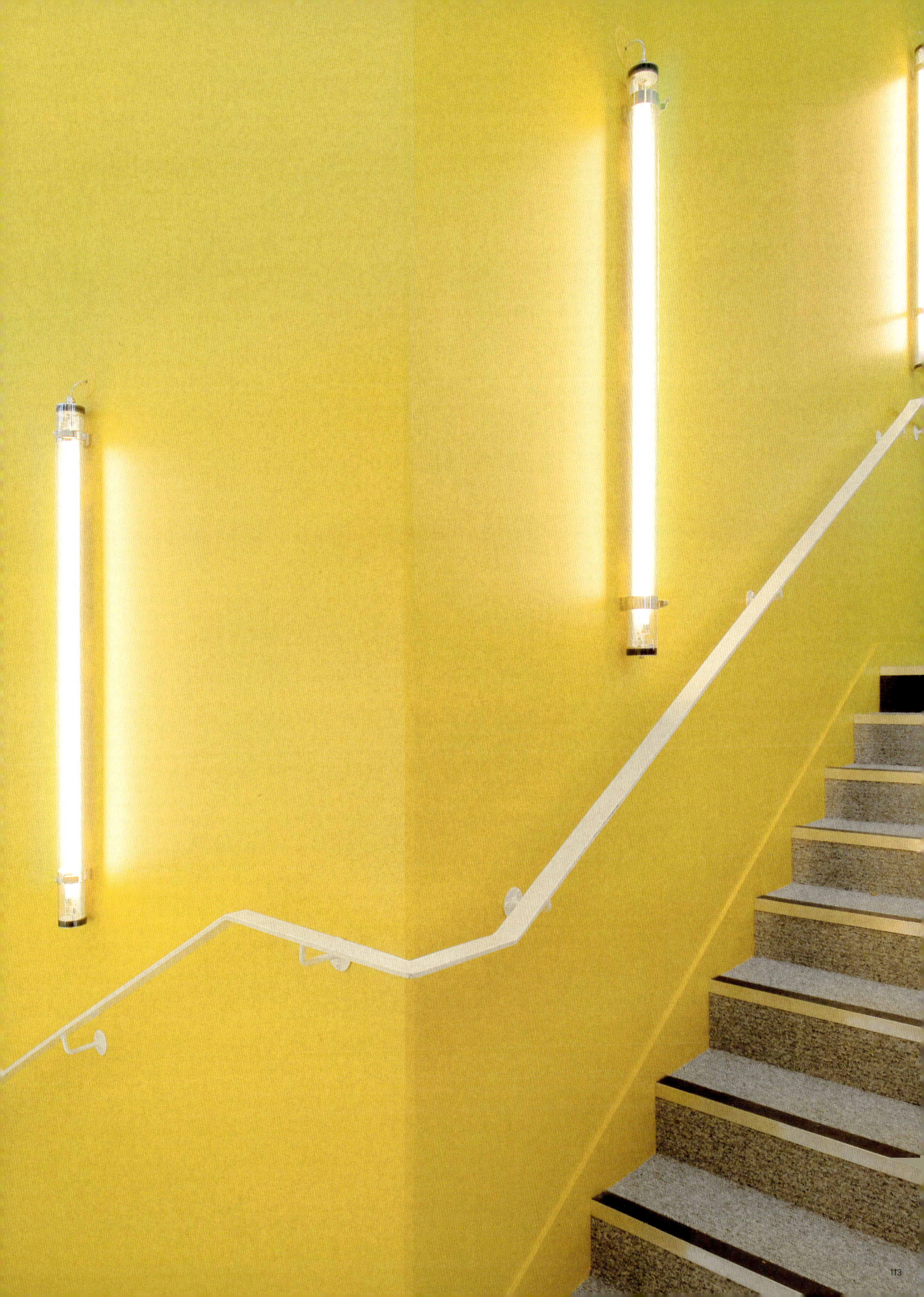

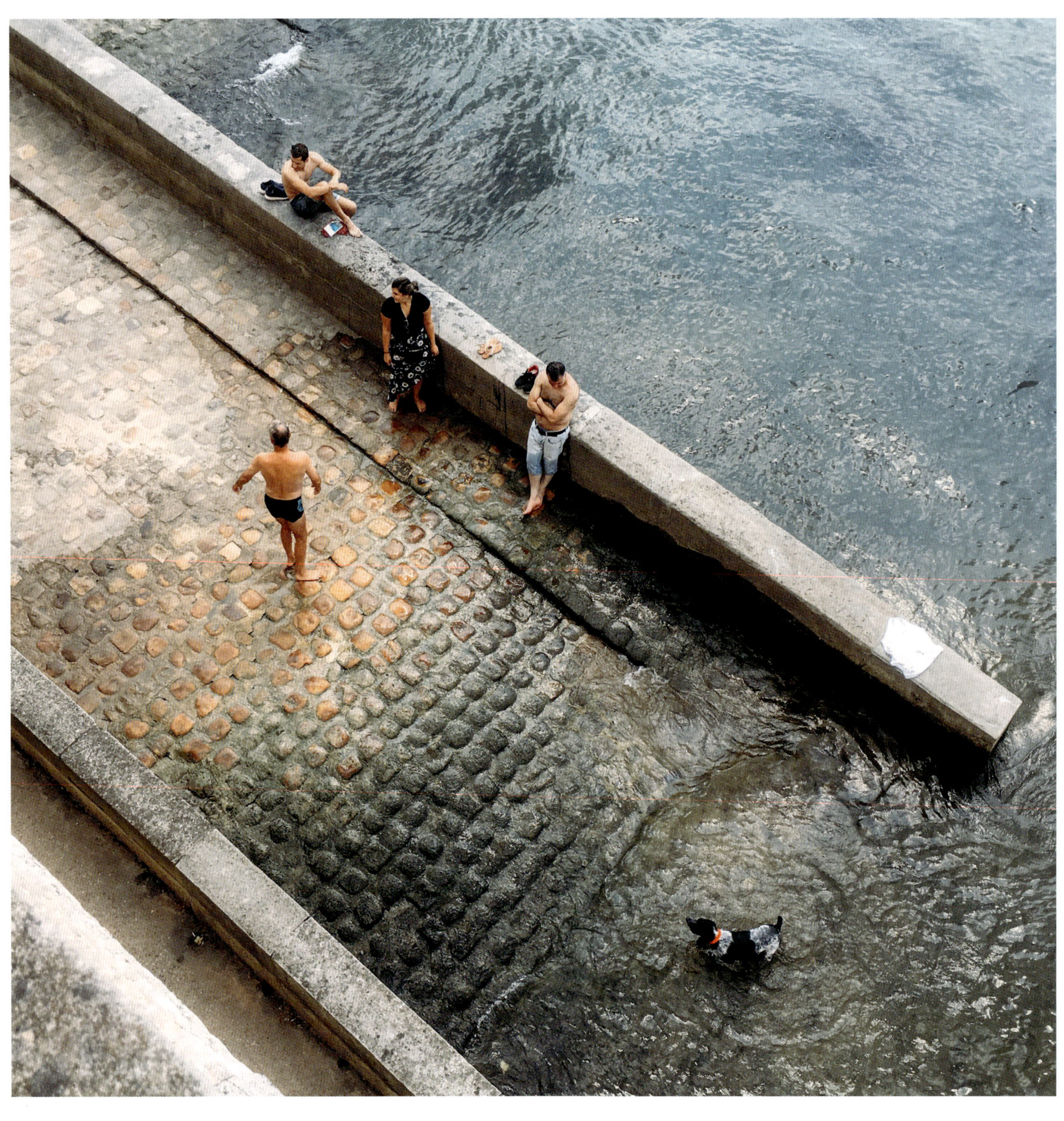

Seine River
Romain Figuiere

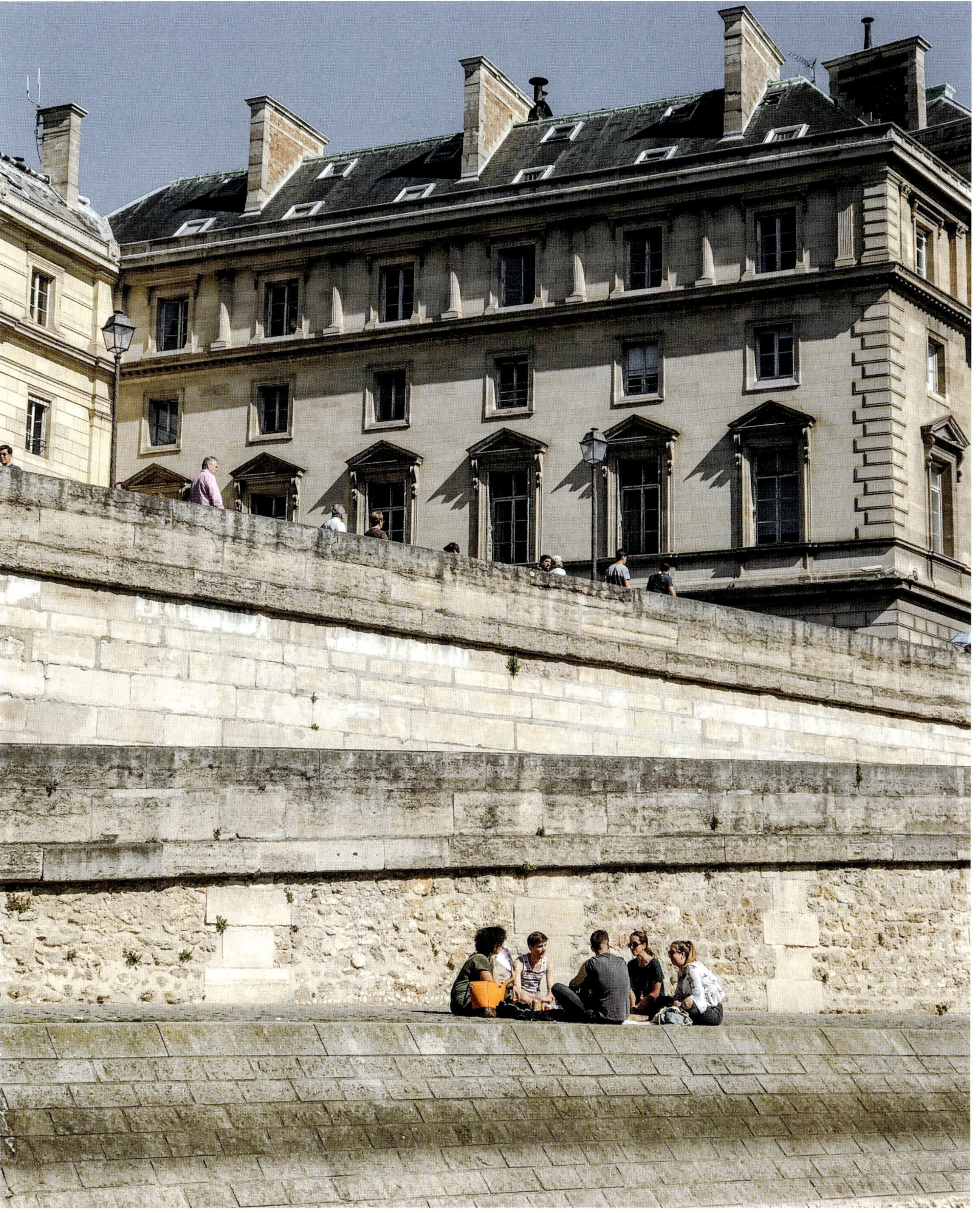

Seine River
Erica Gonzalez

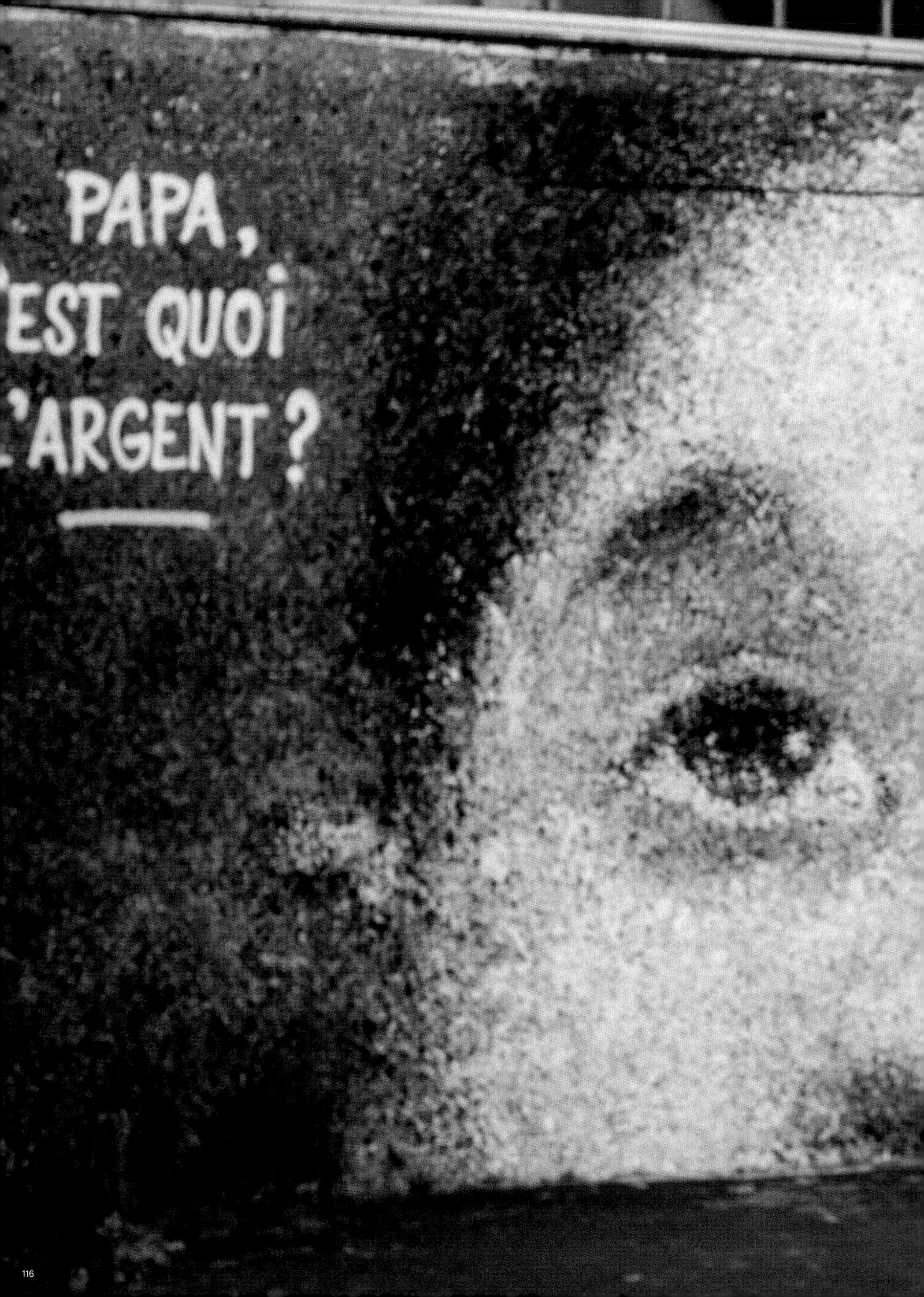

PAPA,
'EST QUOI
'ARGENT ?

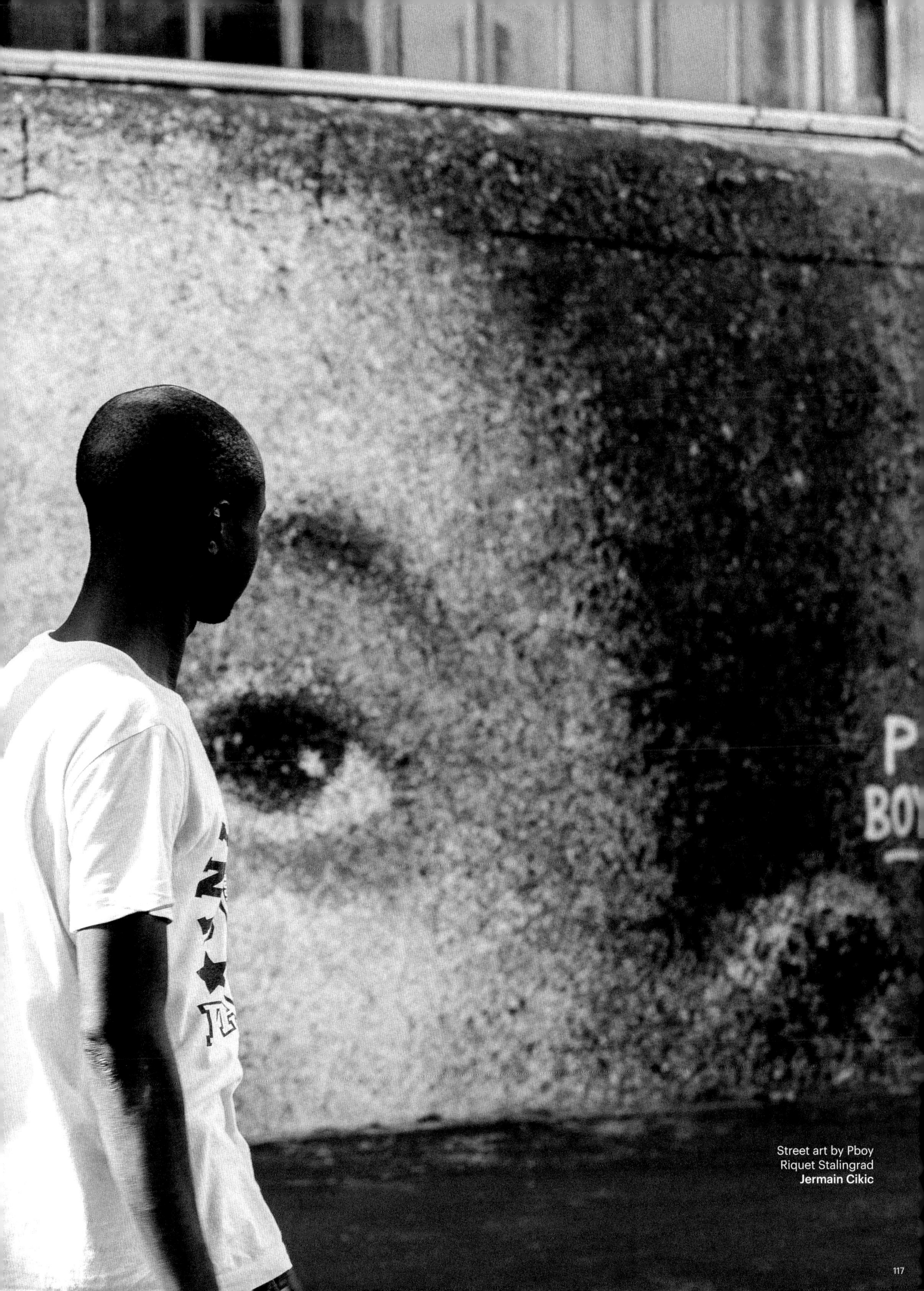

Street art by Pboy
Riquet Stalingrad
Jermain Cikic

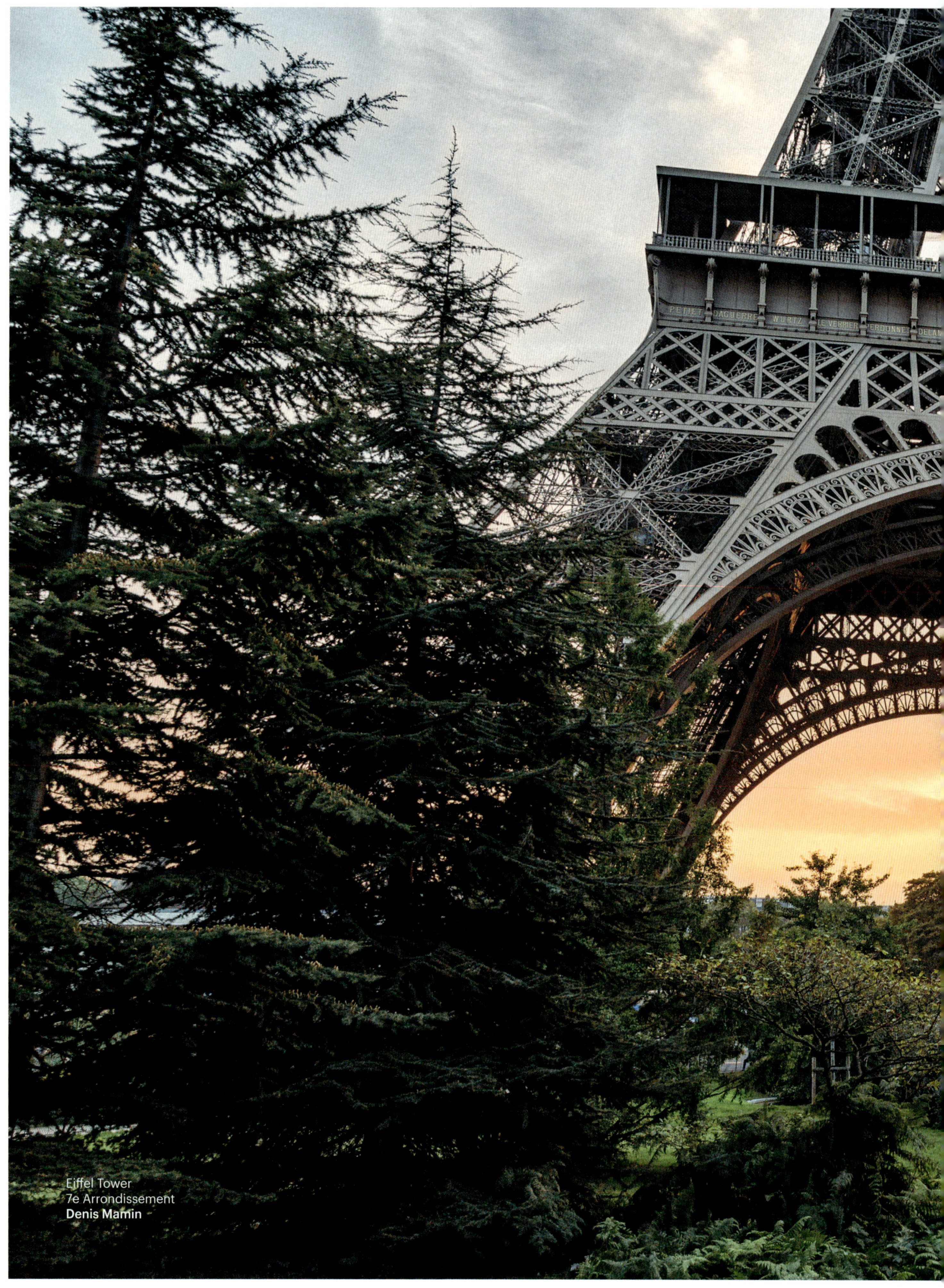

Eiffel Tower
7e Arrondissement
Denis Mamin

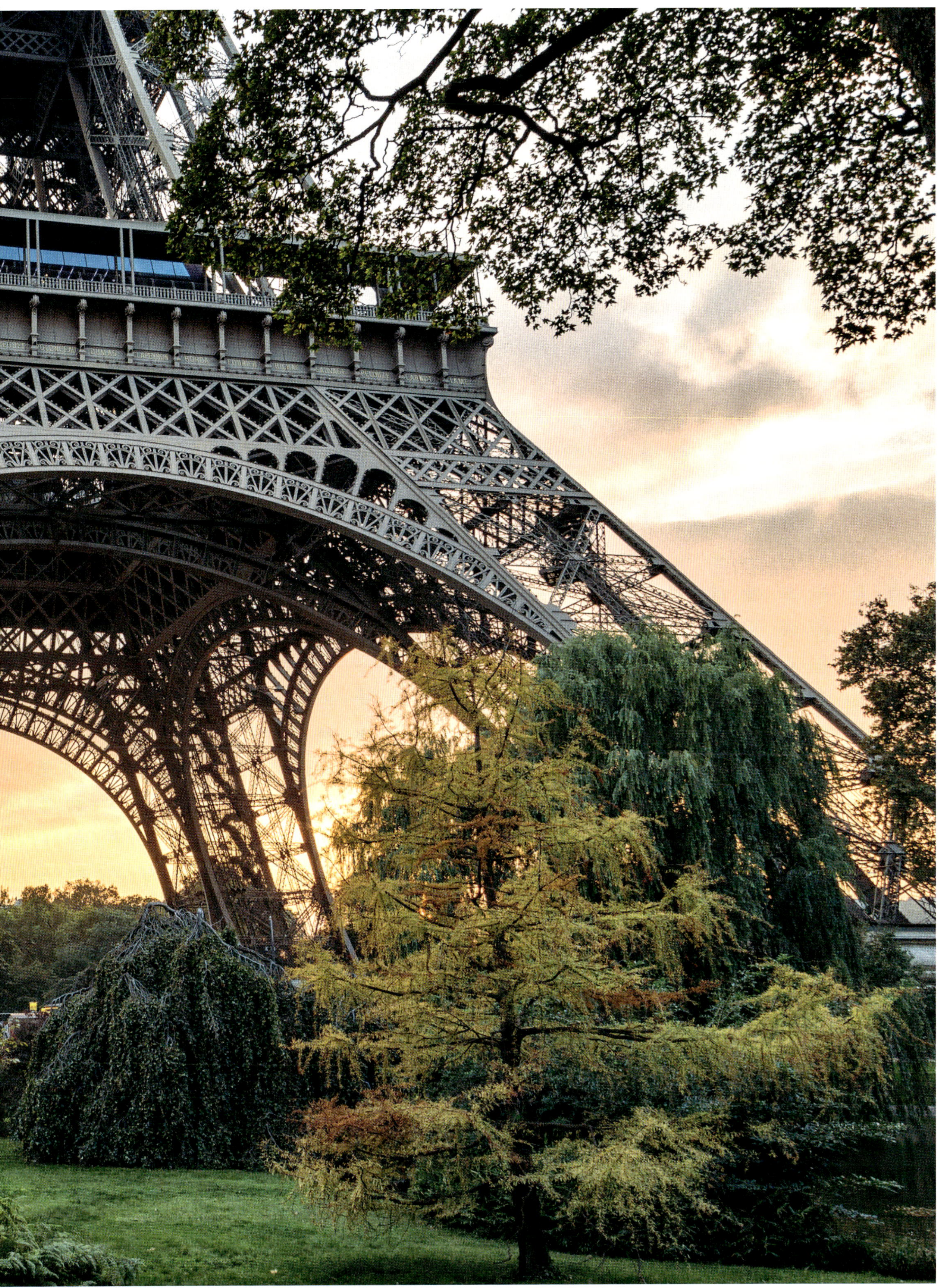

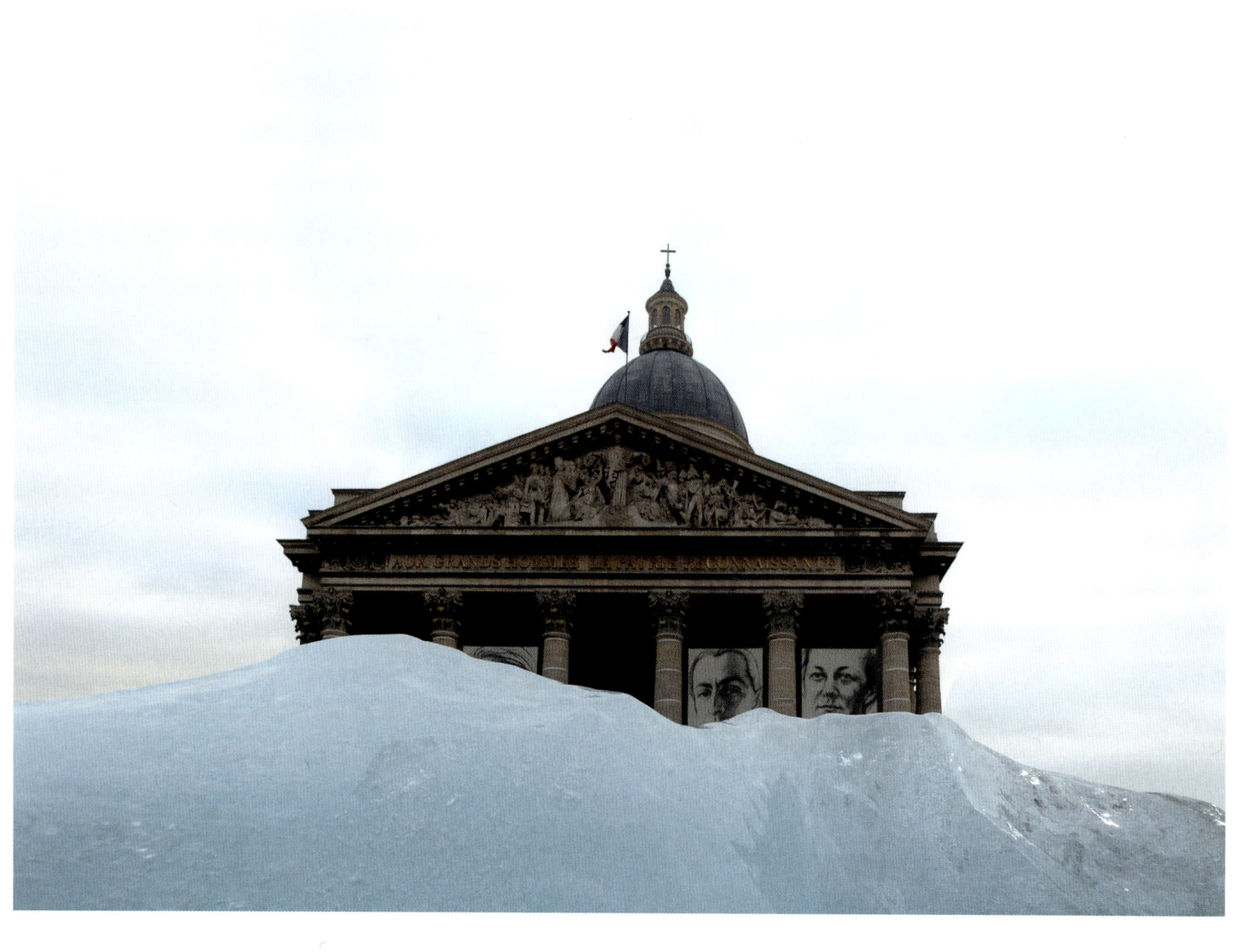

Panthéon
5e Arrondissement
Joseph Jabbour

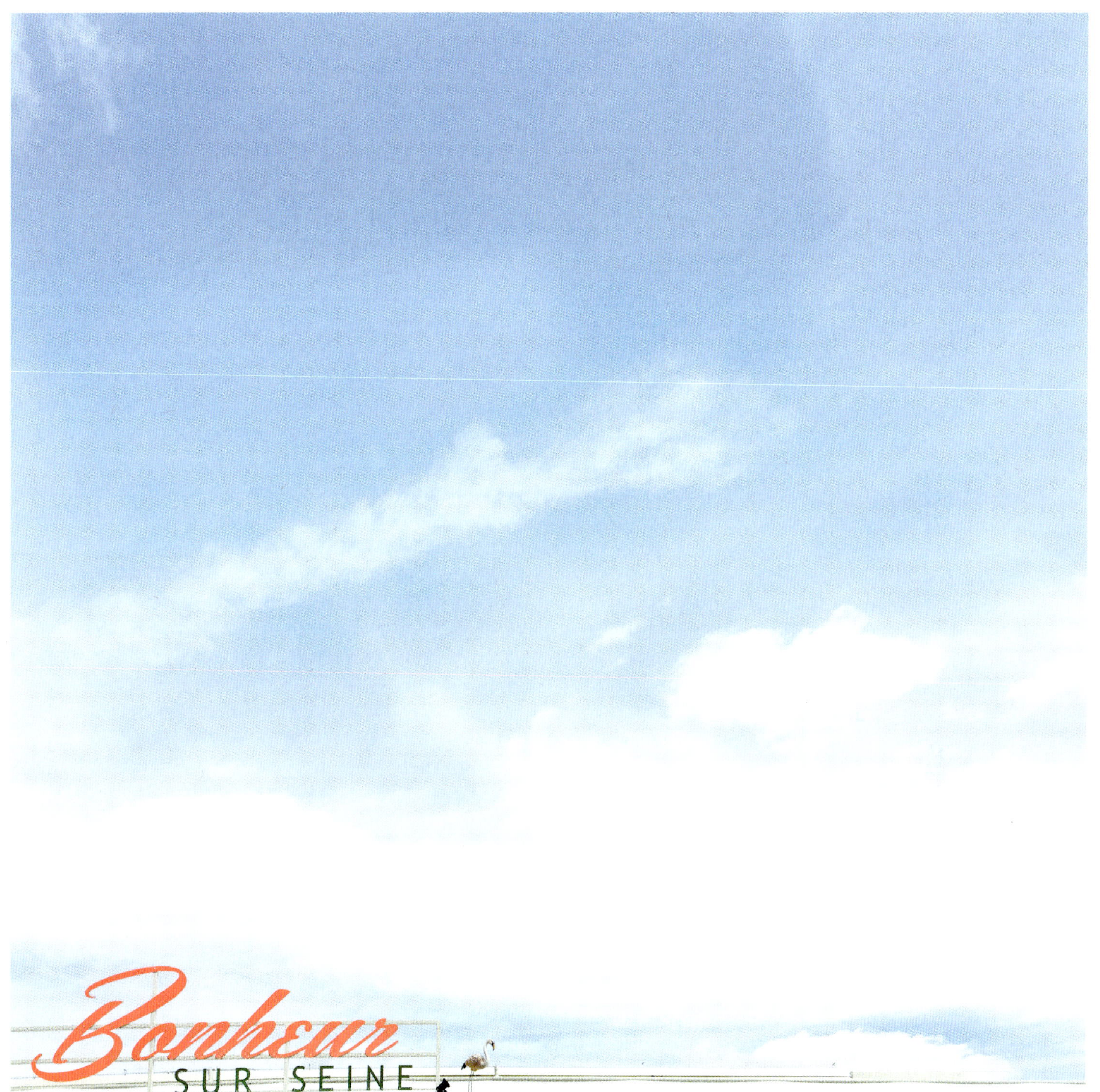

Rosa Bonheur sur Seine
Seine River
Joseph Jabbour

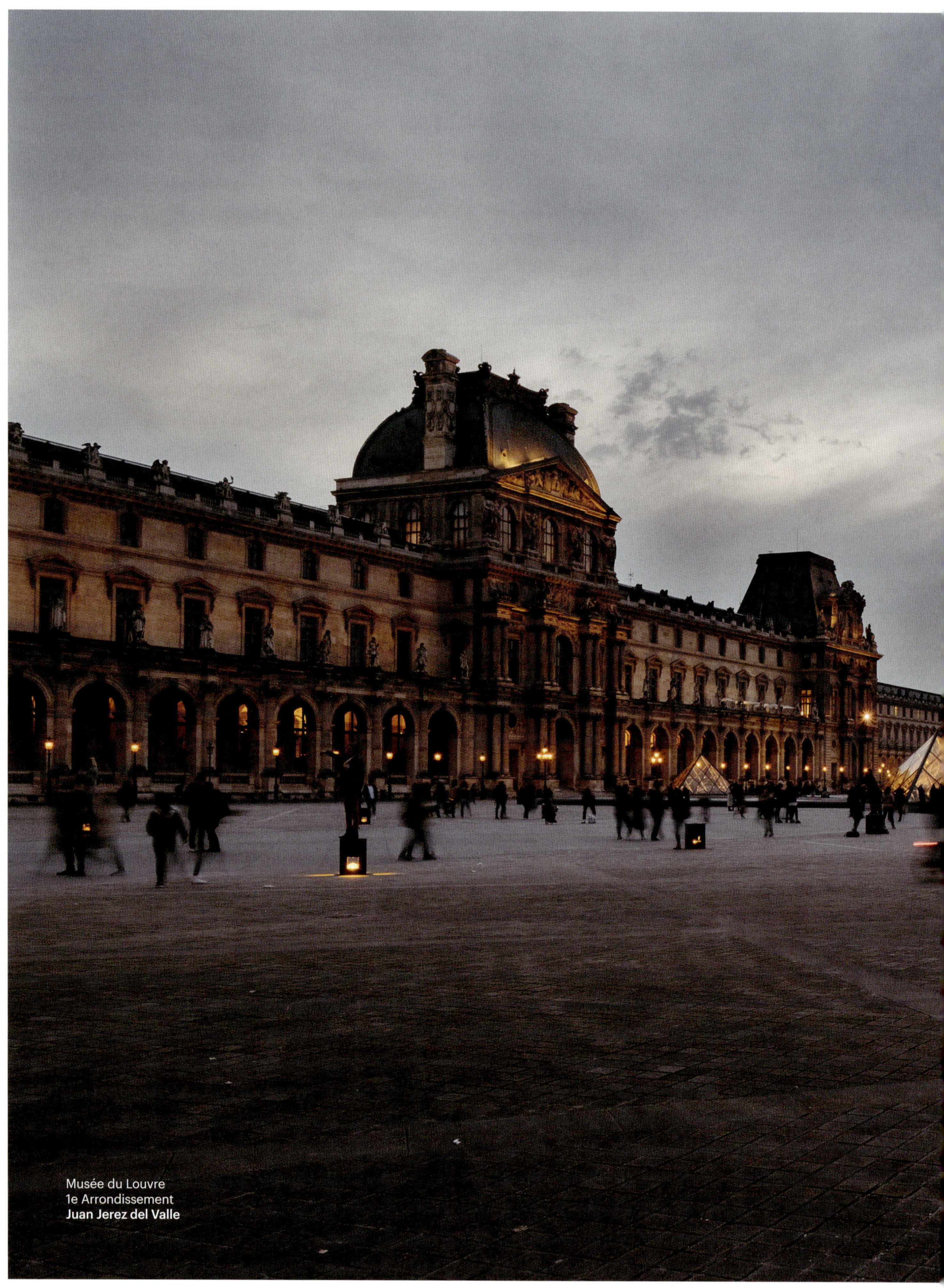

Musée du Louvre
1e Arrondissement
Juan Jerez del Valle

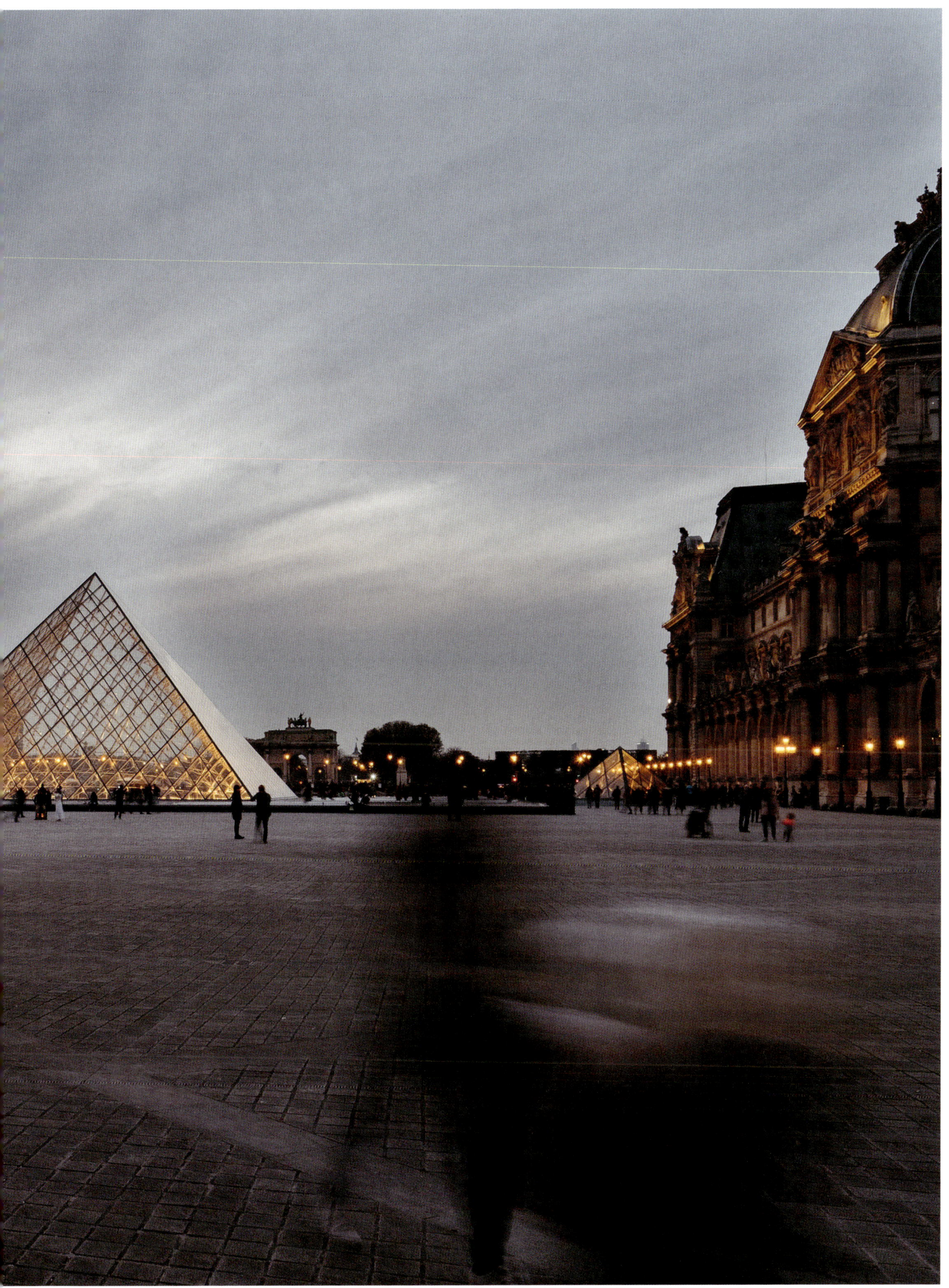

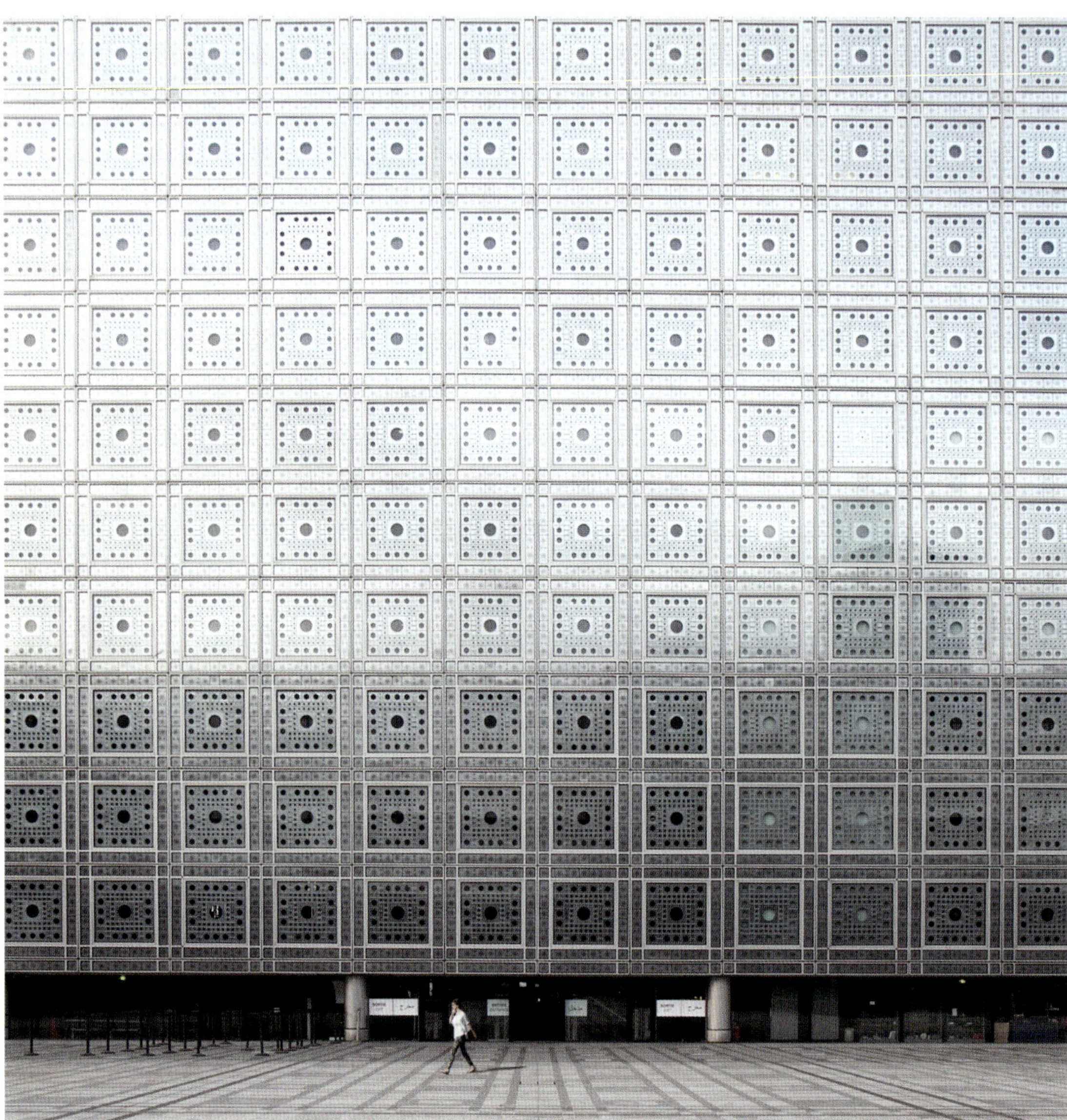

Institut du Monde Arabe
5e Arrondissement
Raul Cabrera

Front de Seine
Grenelle
Maxime Roig —

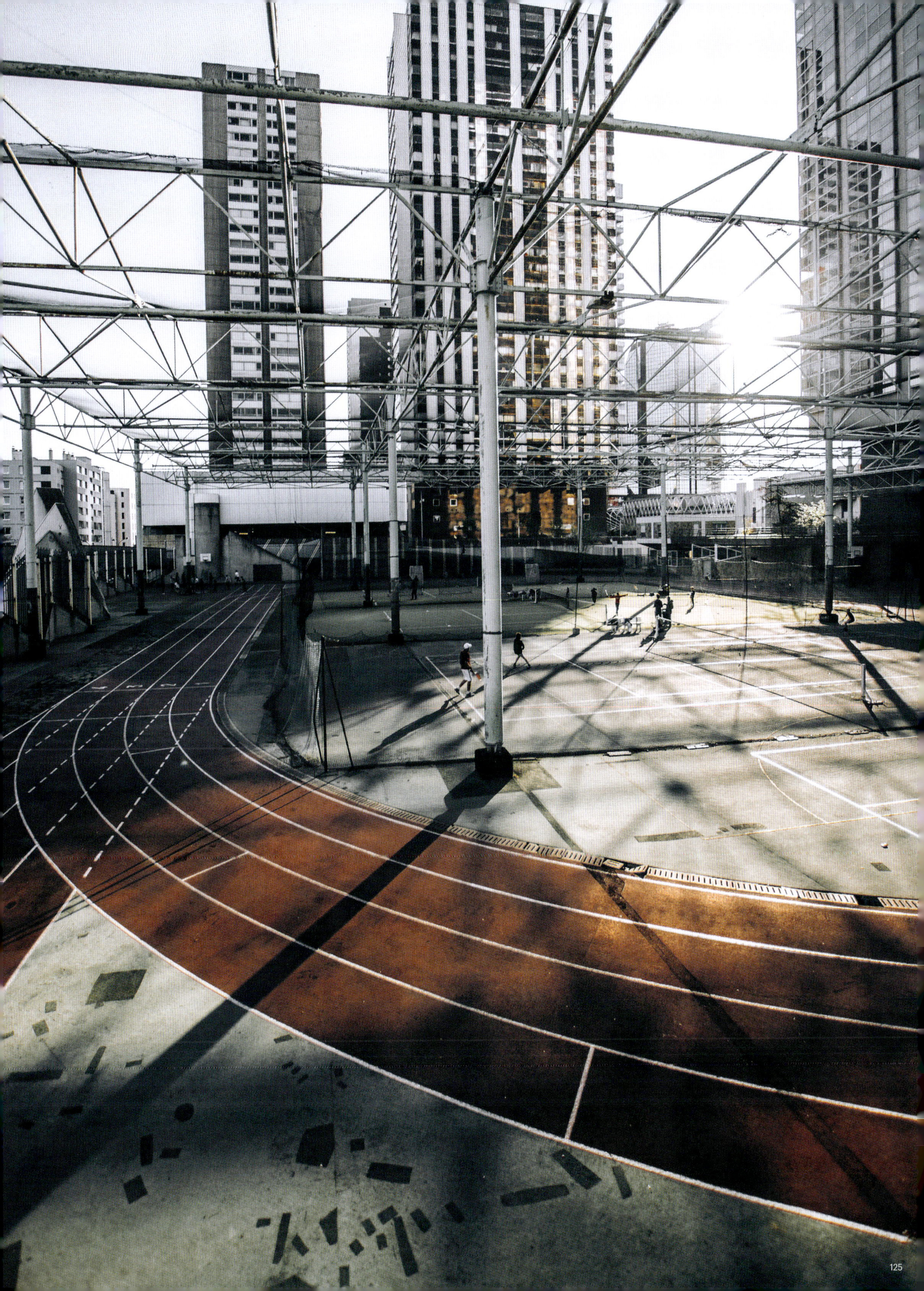

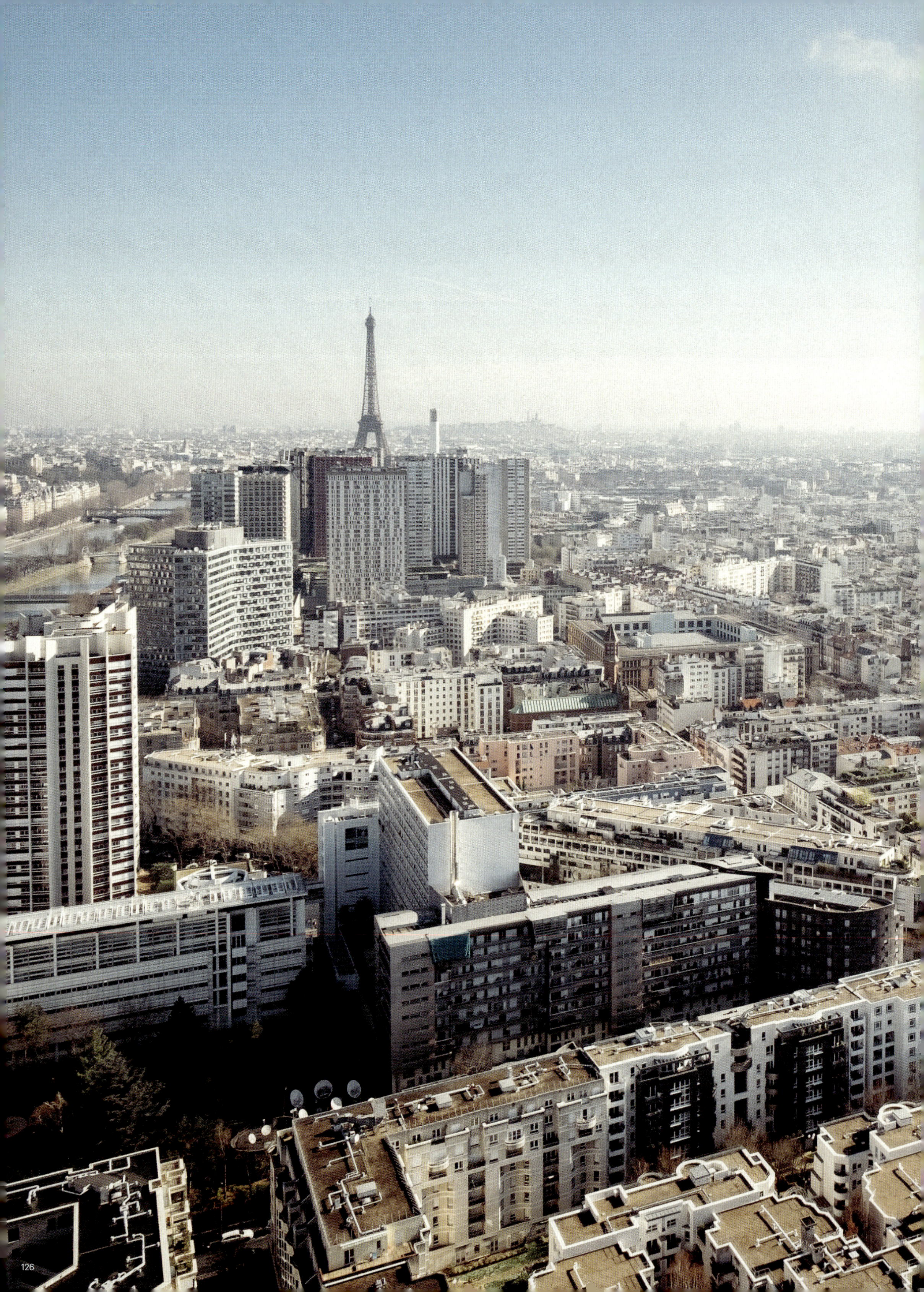

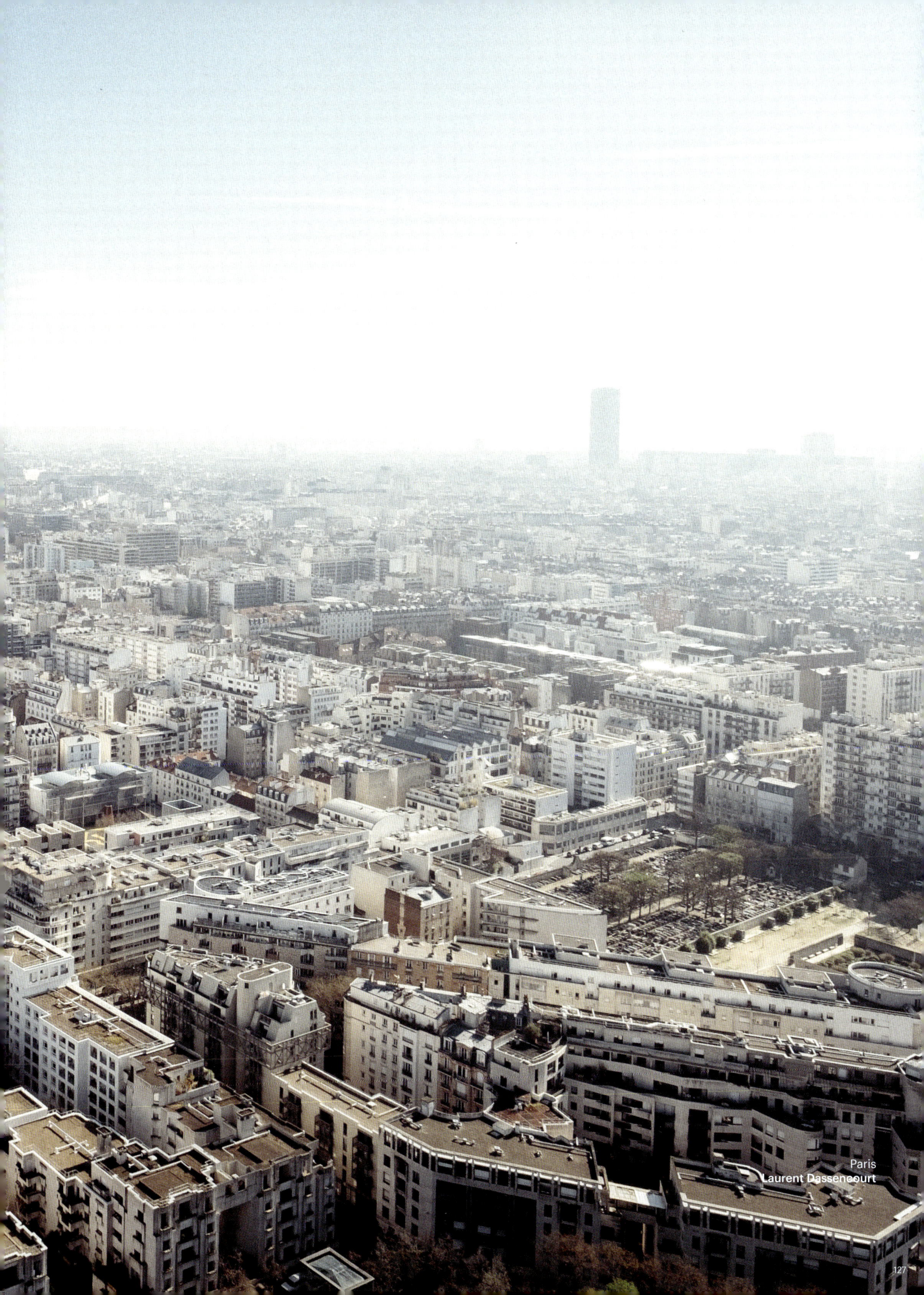

Paris
Laurent Dassencourt

Whenever I take a simple walk in the historical center, the architecture always reminds me how unique this city actually is.

—Guillaume Dutreix

Odette
5e Arrondissement
Joann Pai

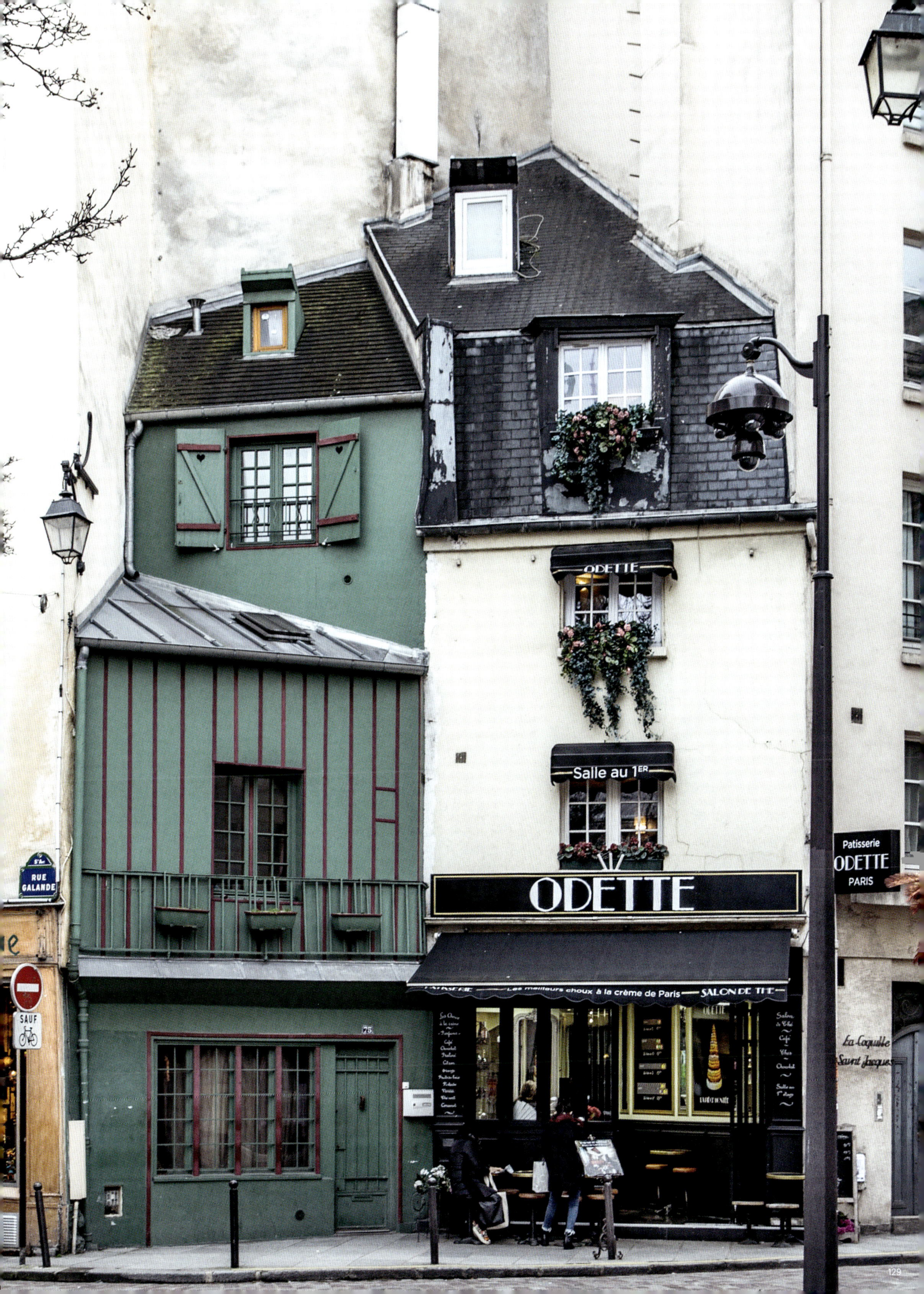
ODETTE
Salle au 1ER
Patisserie
ODETTE
PARIS
RUE
GALANDE
ODETTE
SAUF
Les meilleurs choux à la crème de Paris
SALON DE THE
La Coquille
Saint Jacques

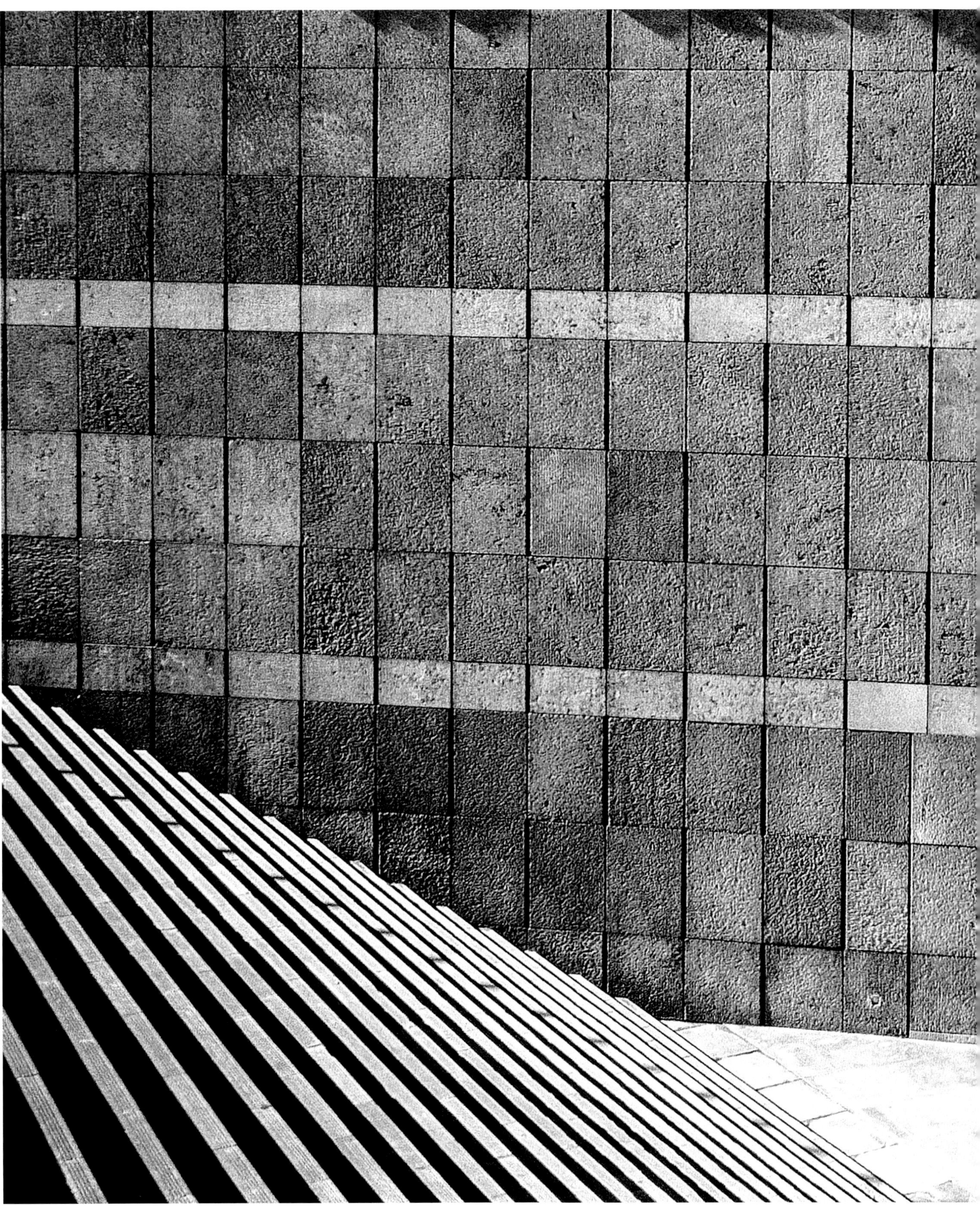

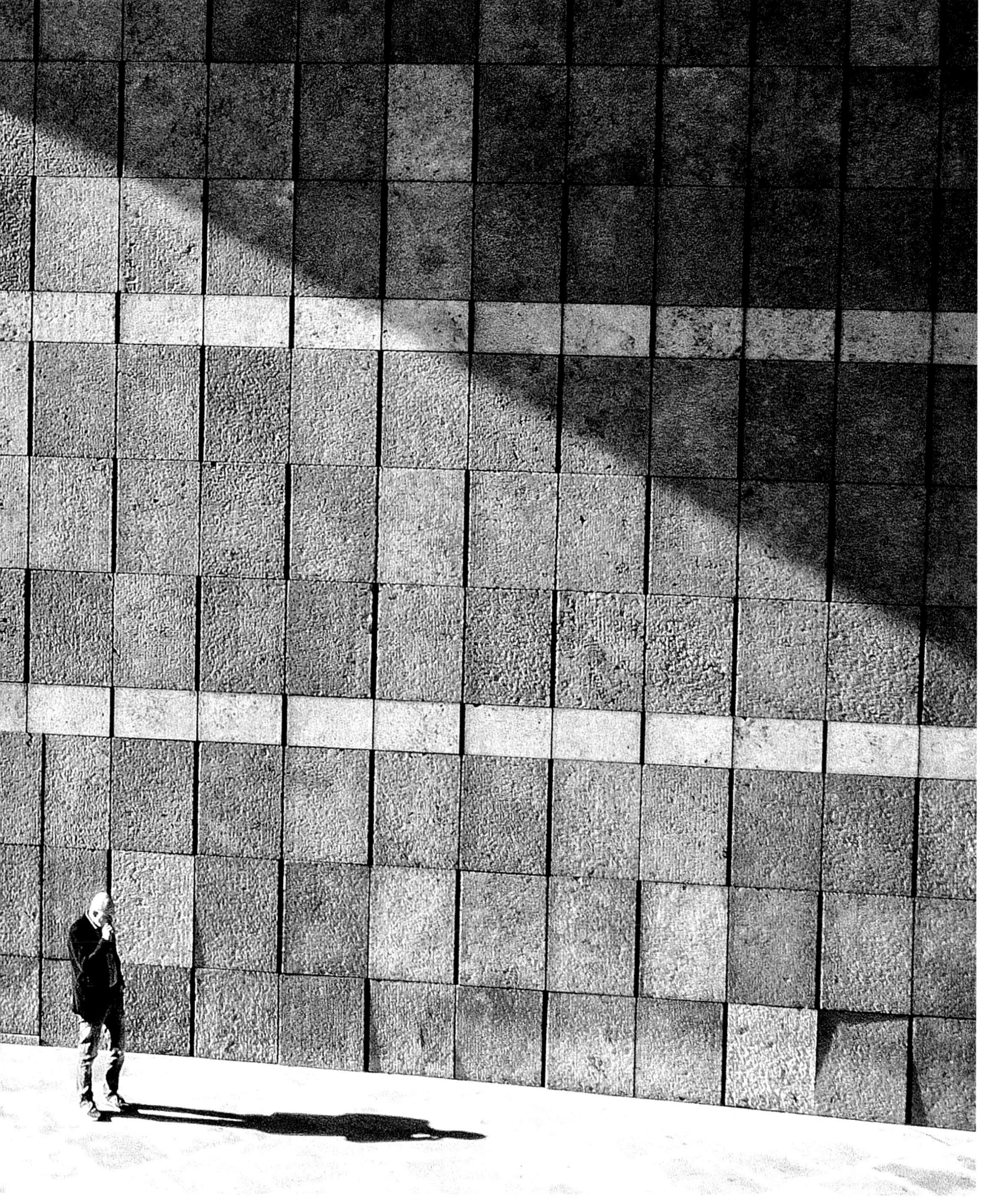

La Défense
Nicolas Zwarg

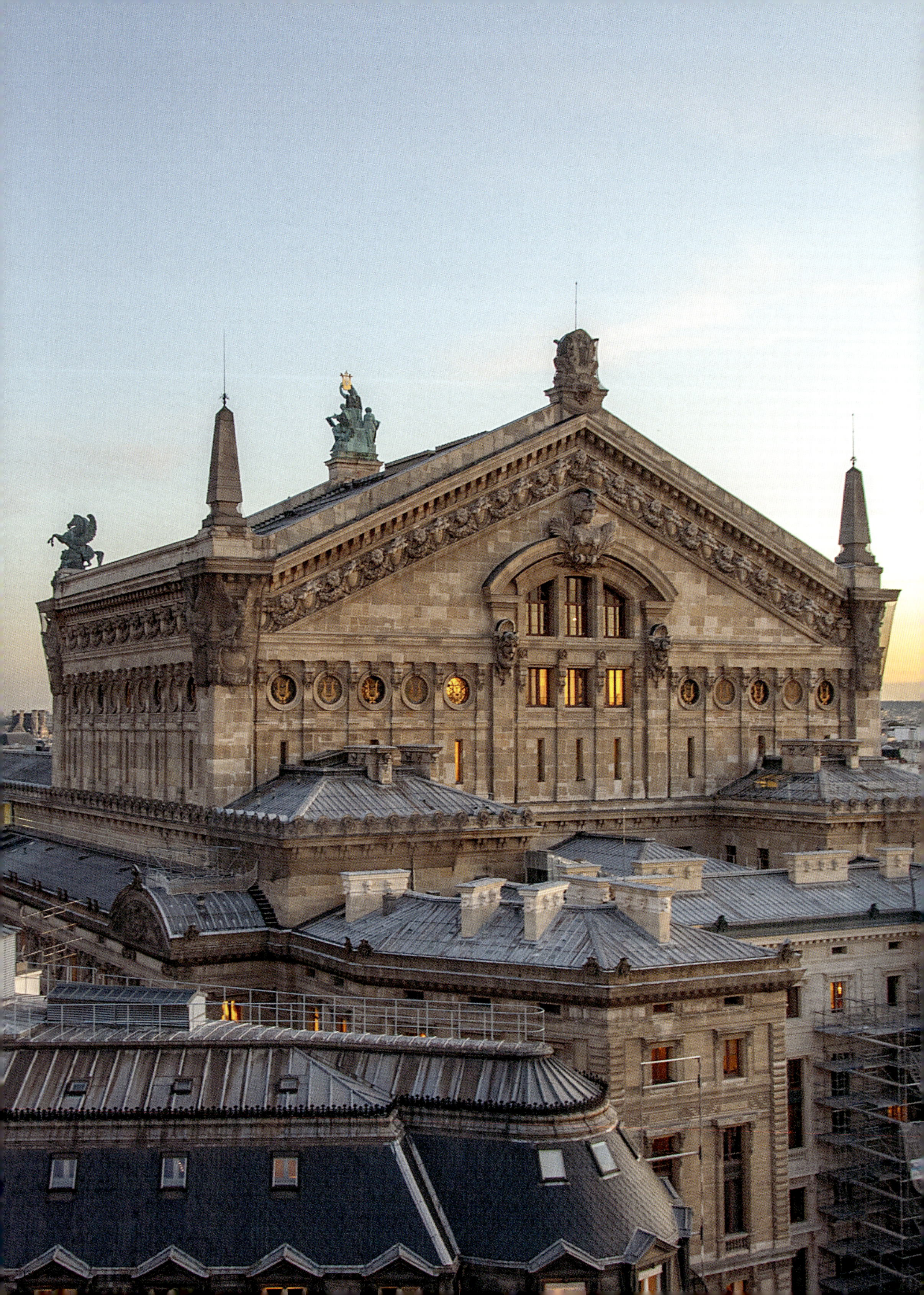

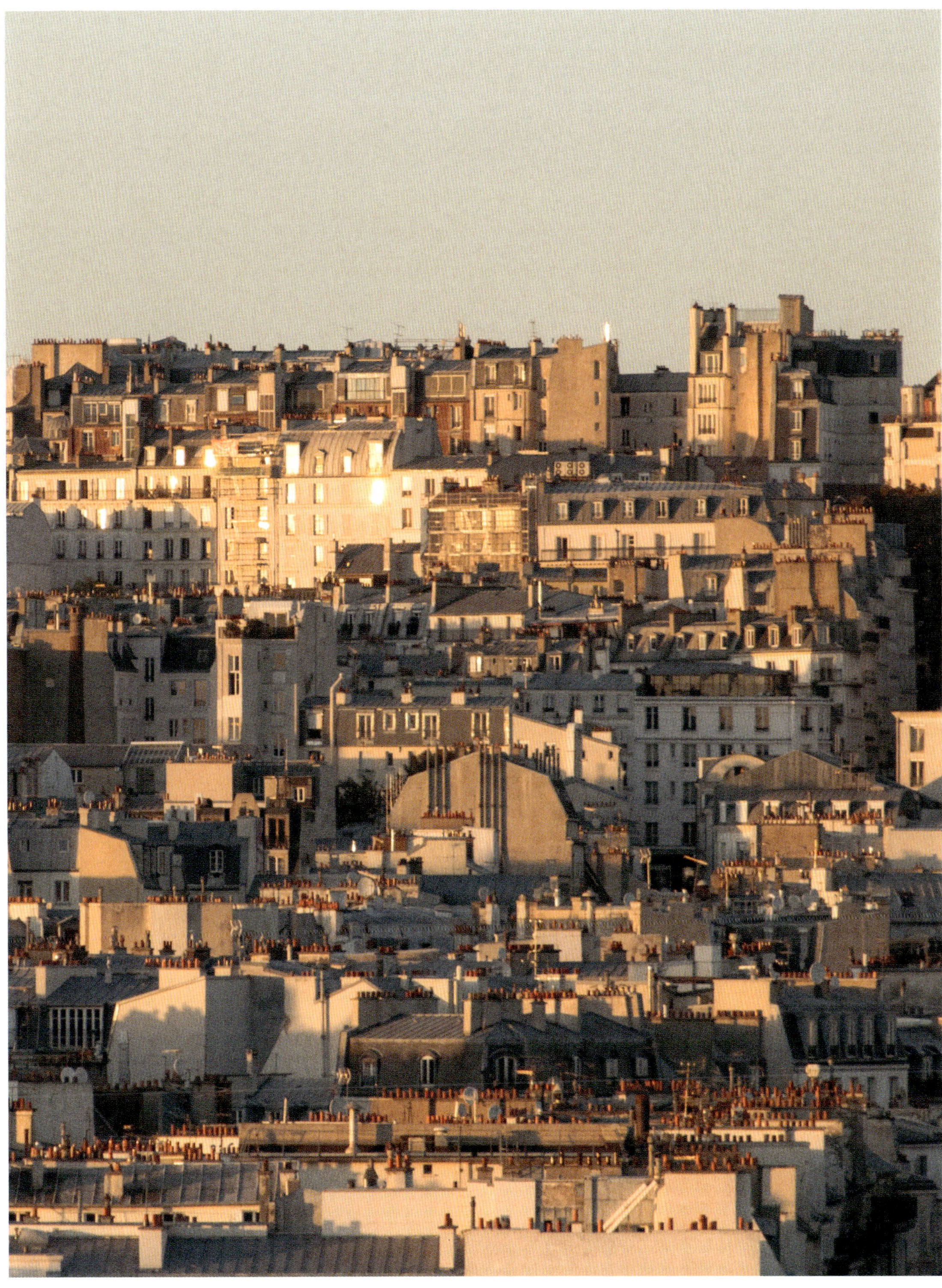

Palais Garnier, Opéra National de Paris
9e Arrondissement
← **Stéphanie Le Lay**

Paris
Stéphanie Le Lay

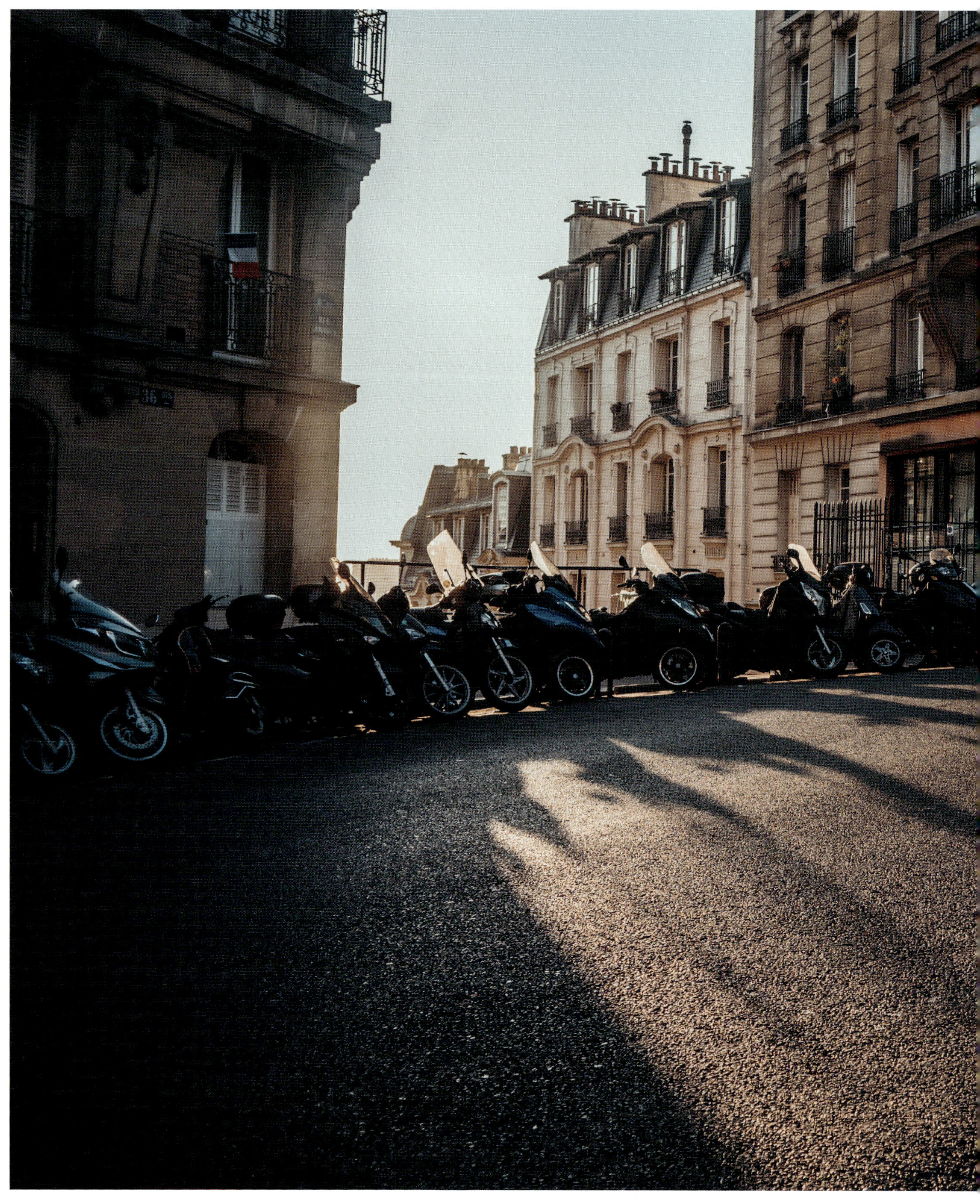

Clignancourt
Stijn Hoekstra

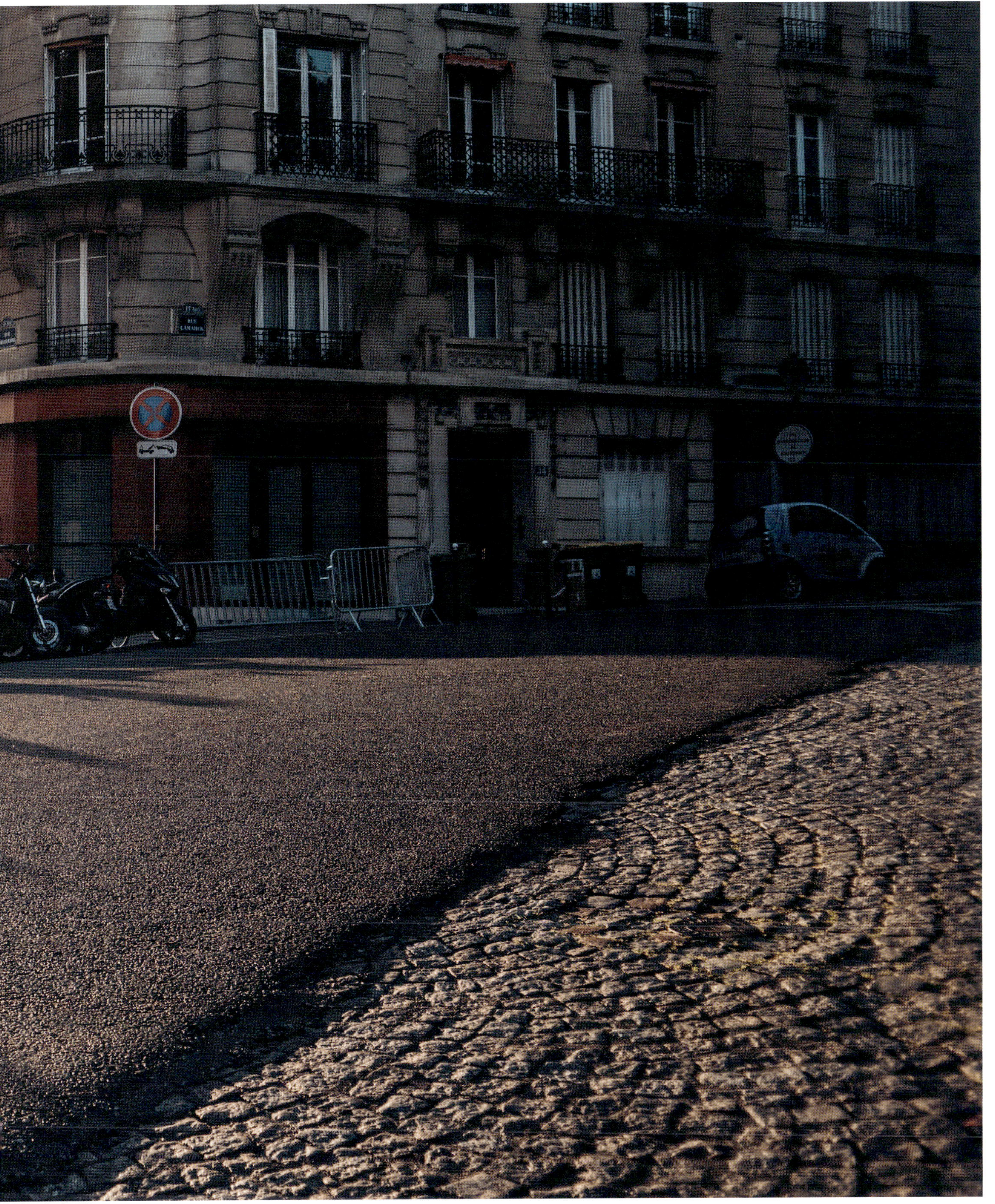
RUE
LAMARCK

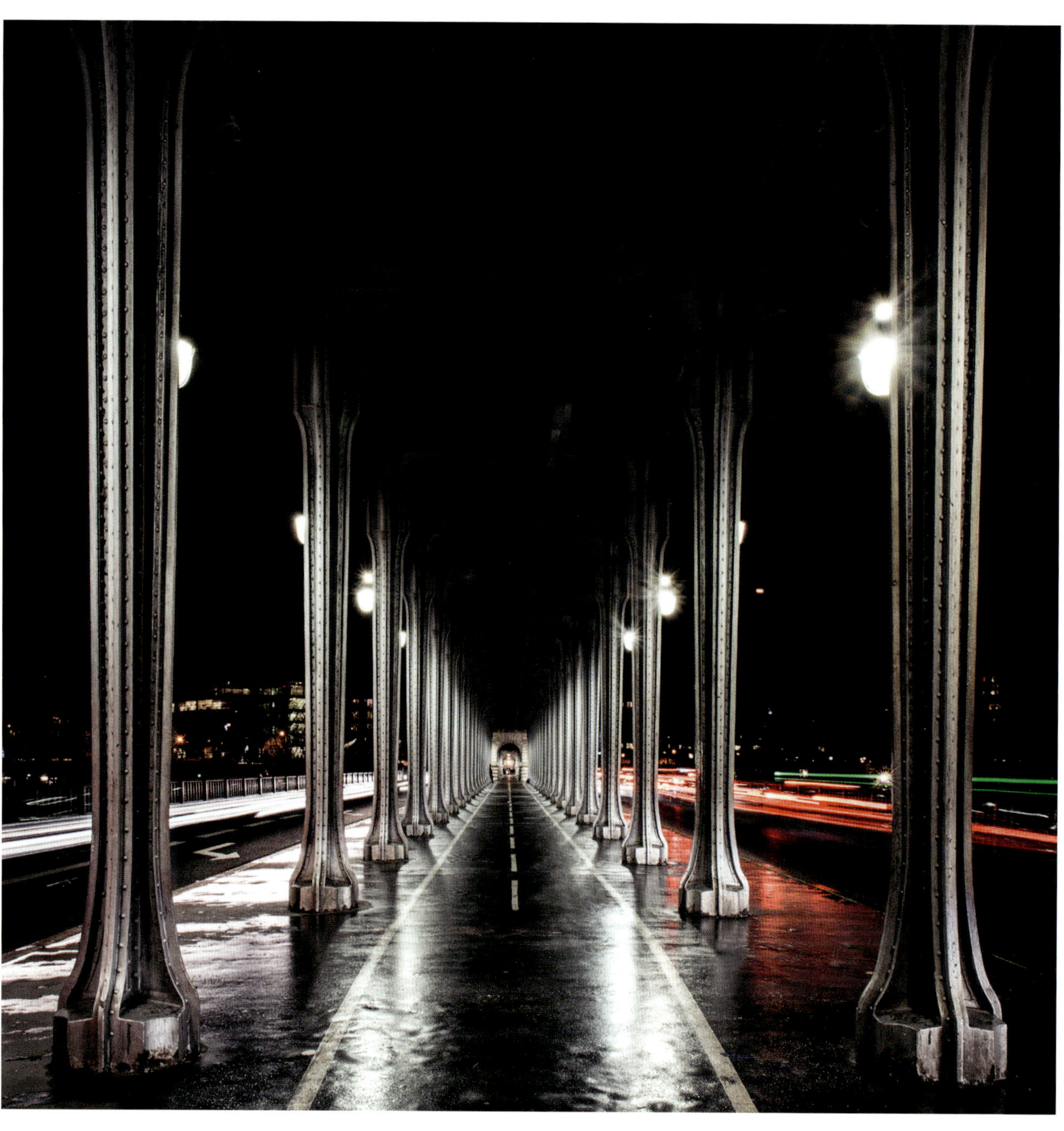

Pont de Bir-Hakeim
Seine River
Guillaume Dutreix

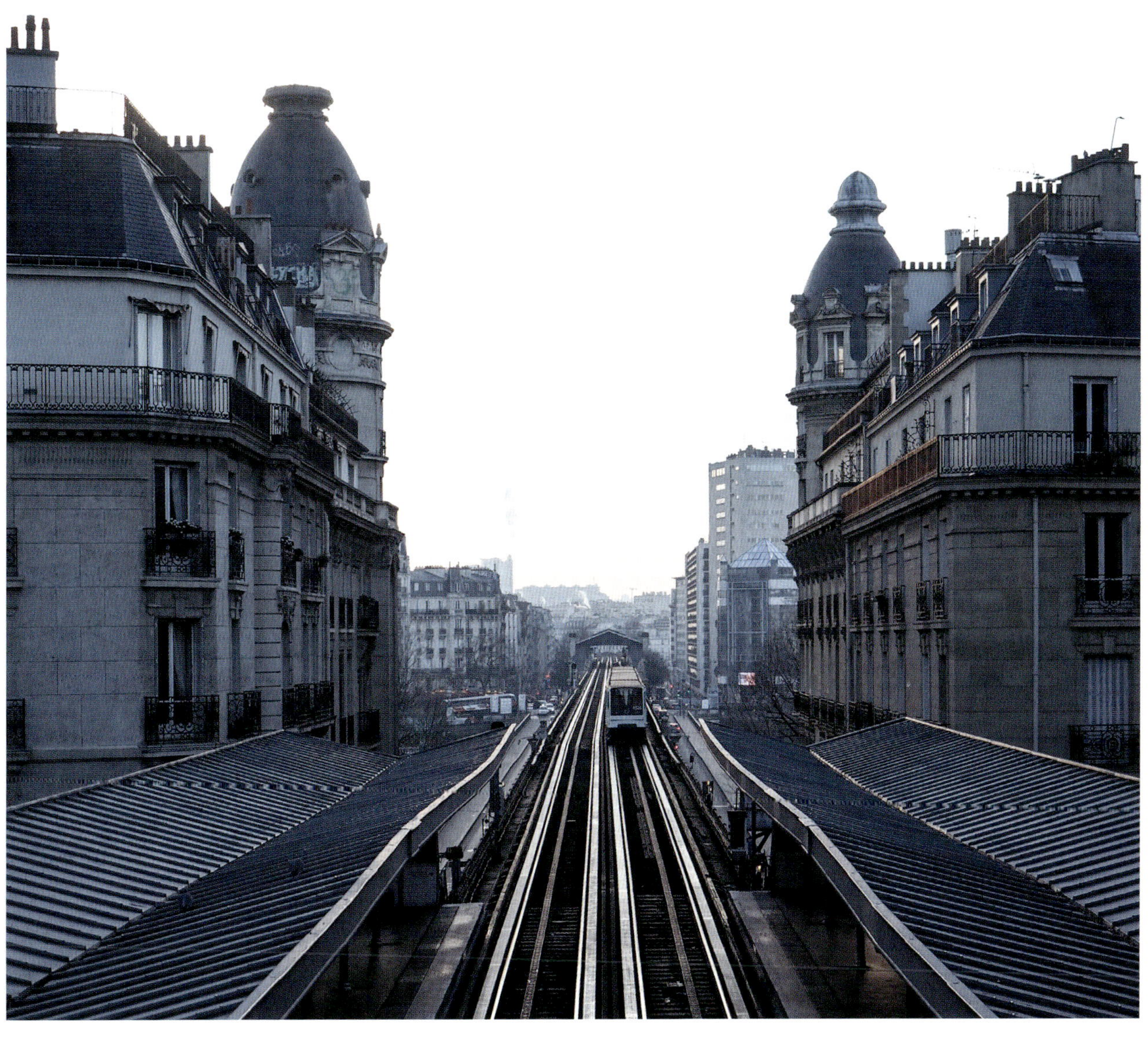

Passy Subway Station
16e arrondissement
Gérard Trang

Eiffel Tower
7e Arrondissement
Mikel van den Boogaard –

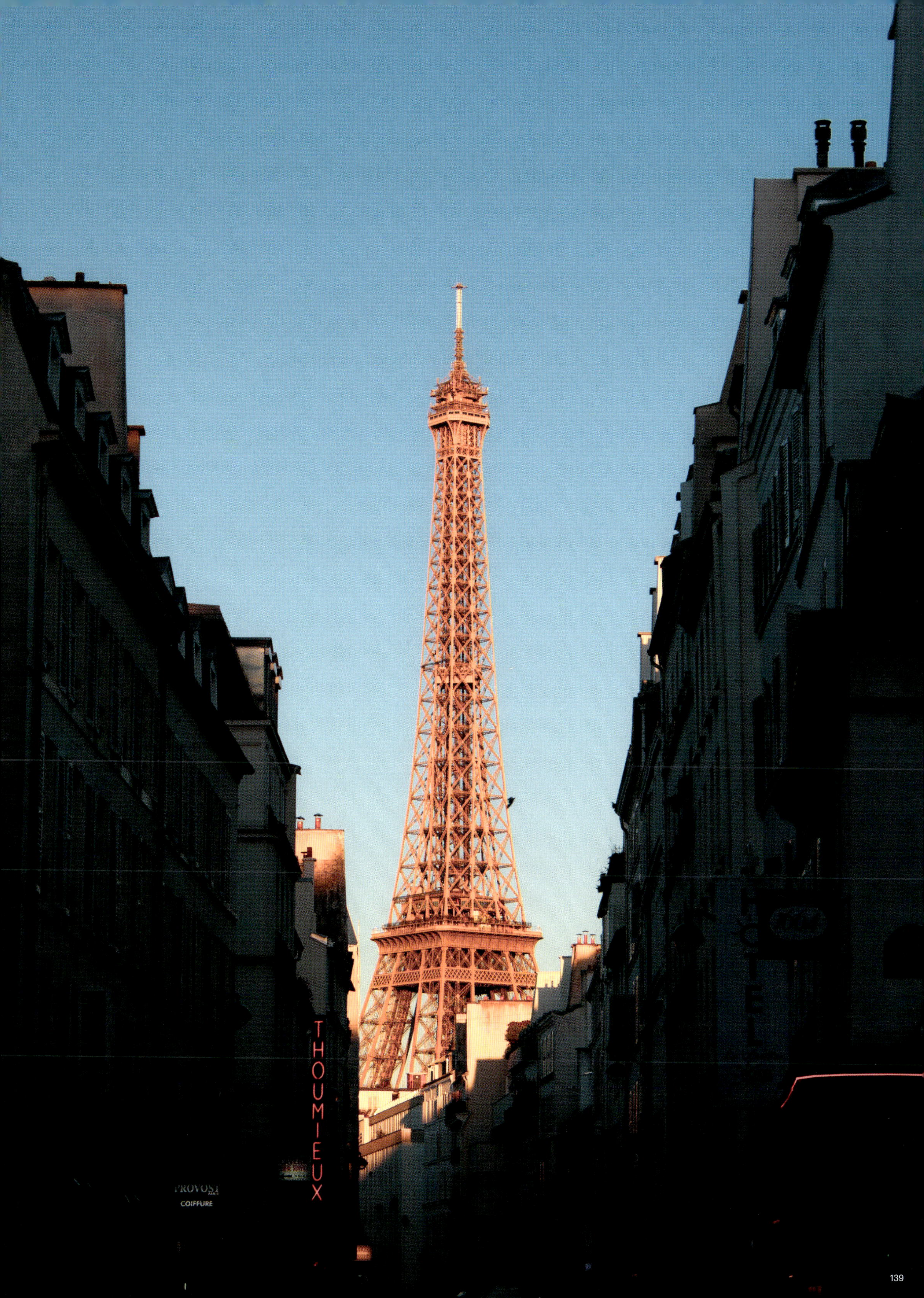
THOUMIEUX
PROVOST
COIFFURE
HOTEL

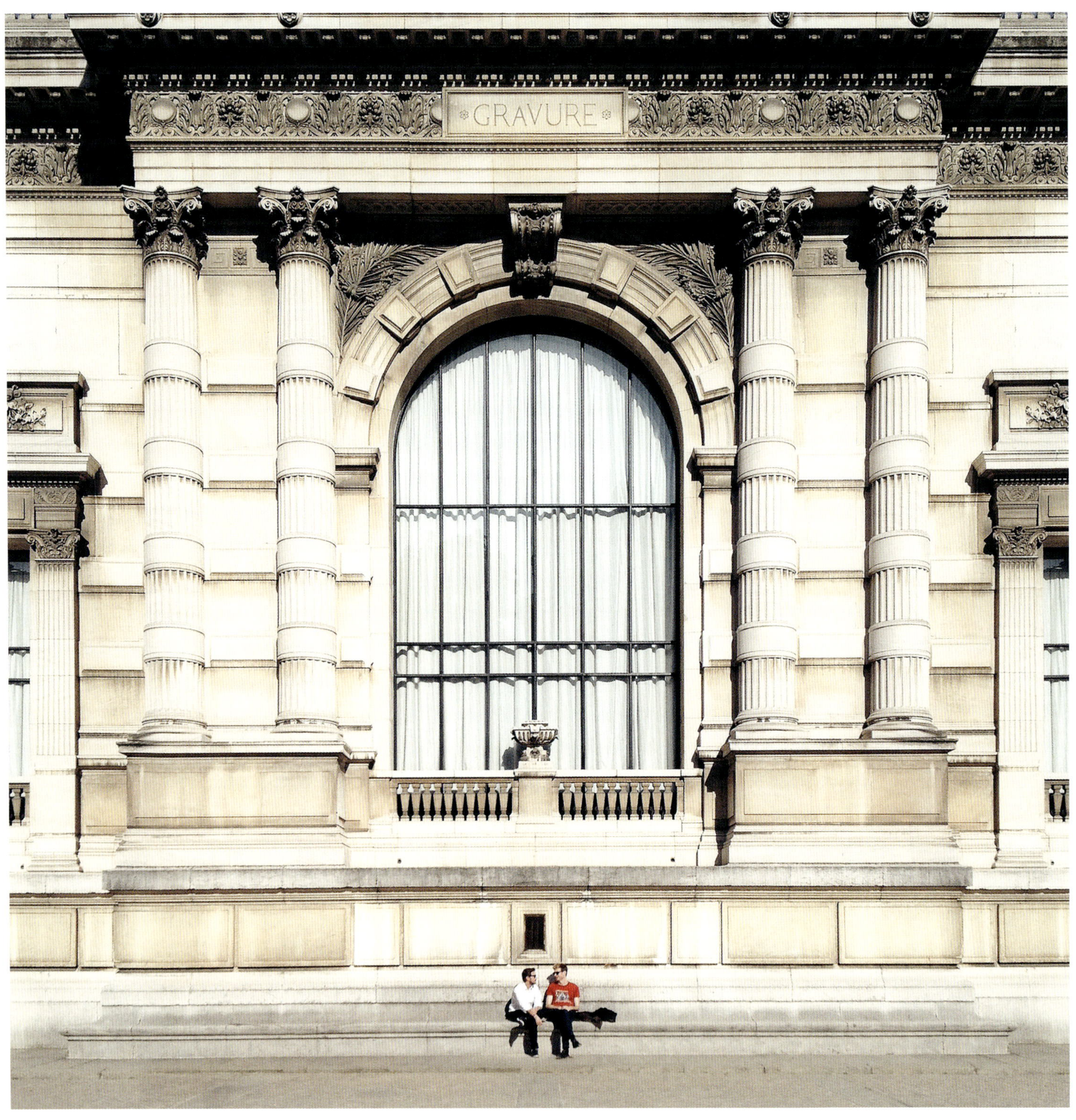

Palais Galliera
Chaillot
Raul Cabrera

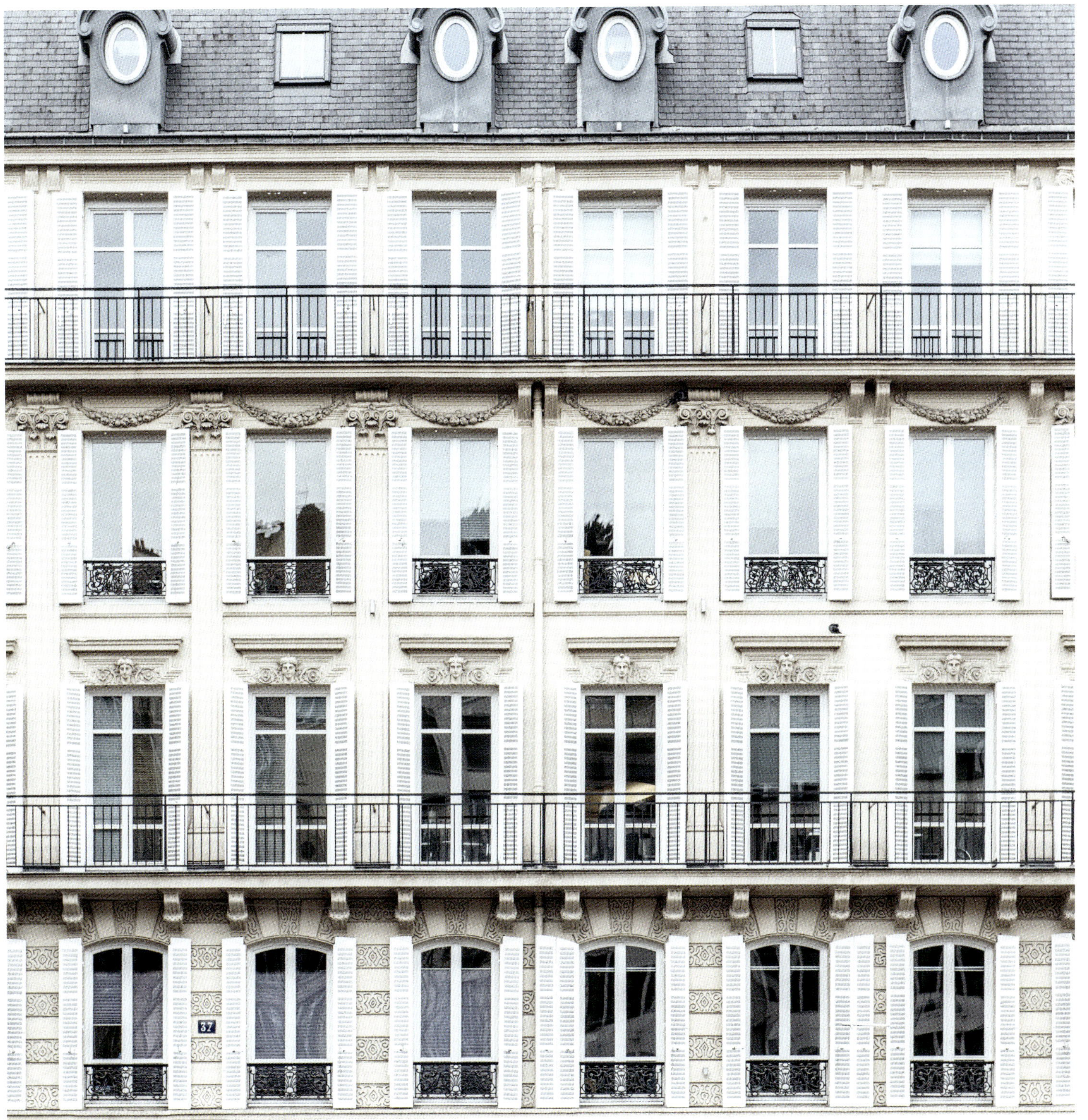

Paris
Raul Cabrera

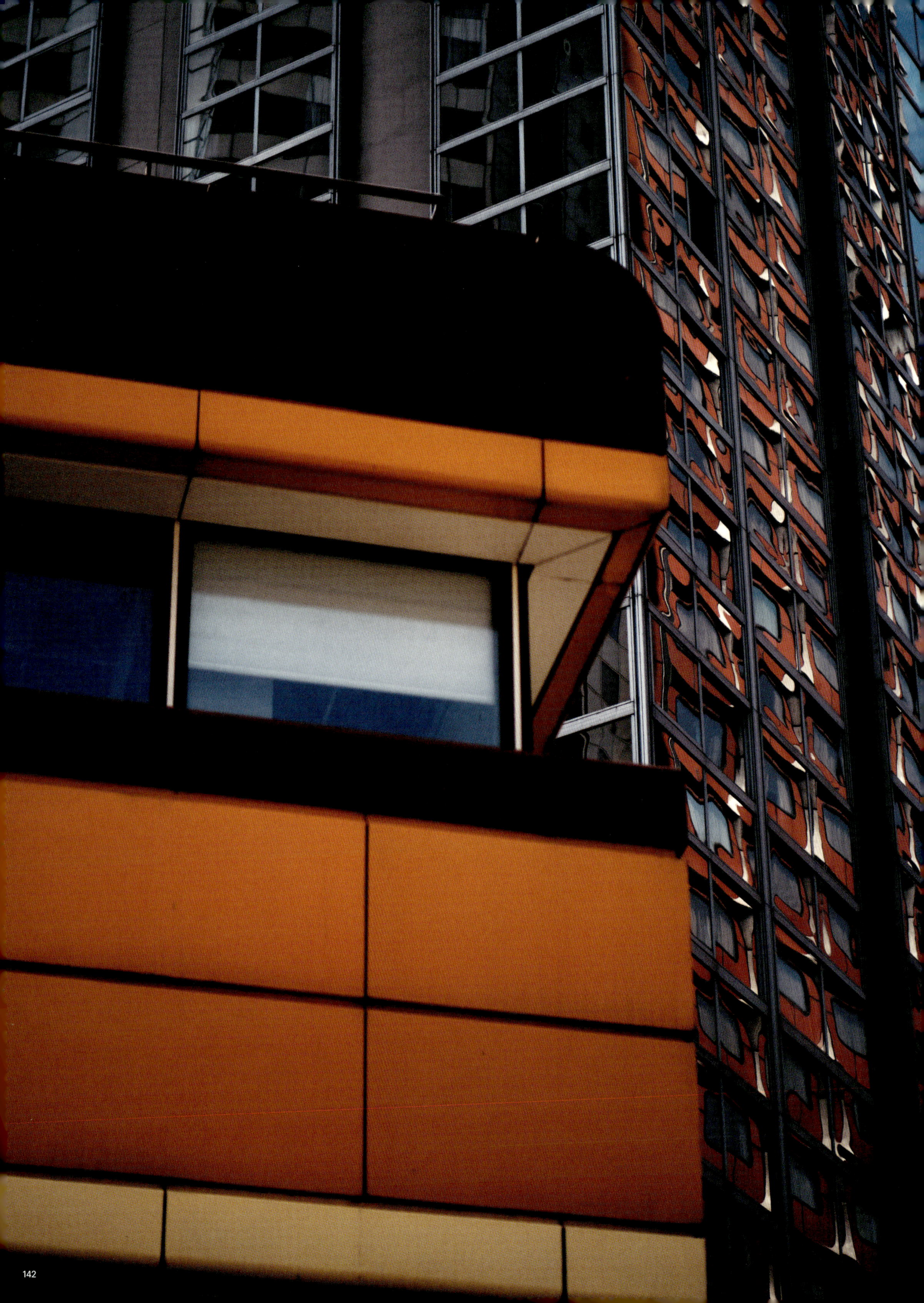

Grenelle
Willem Sizoo

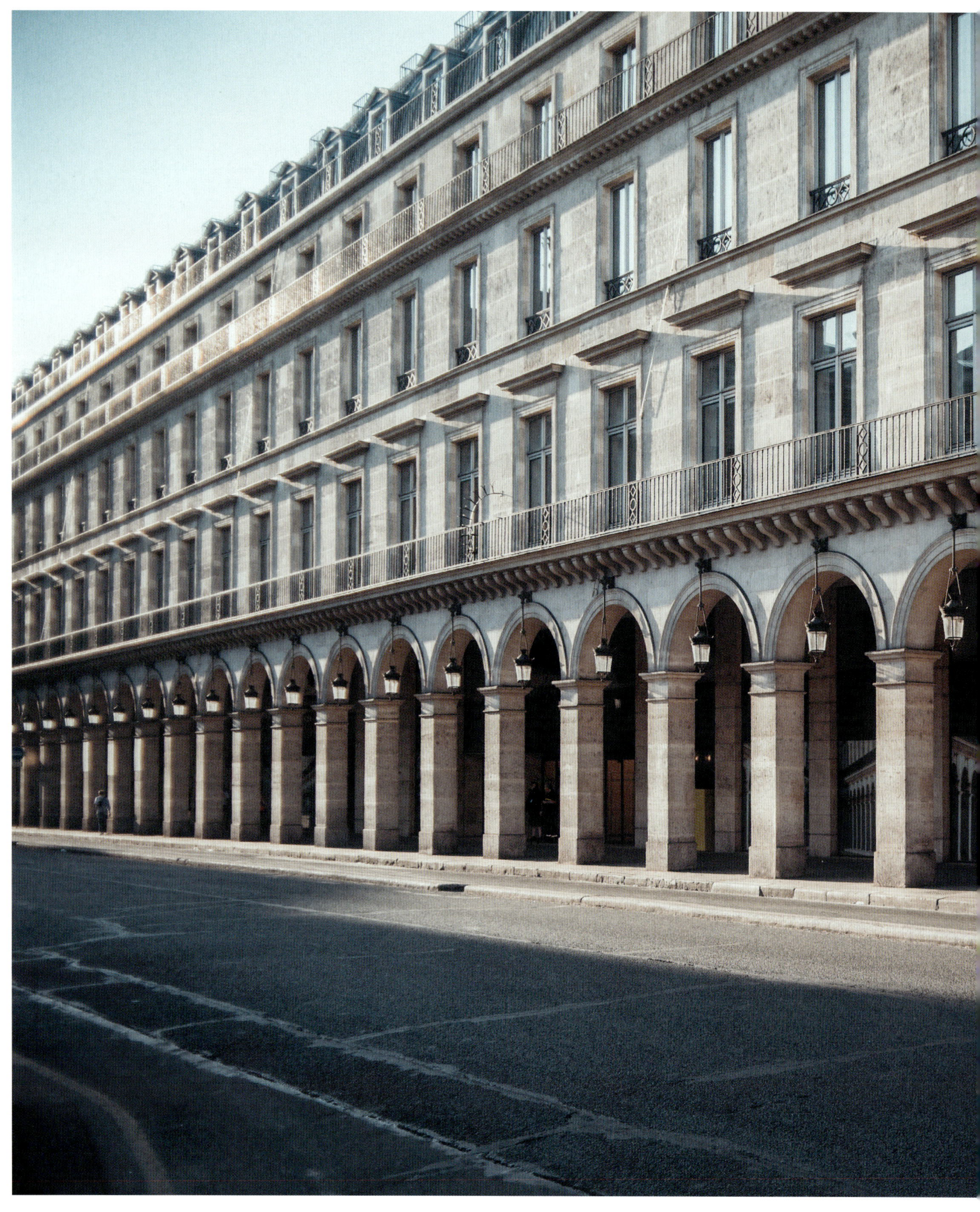

Rue de Rivoli
1e Arrondissement
Stijn Hoekstra

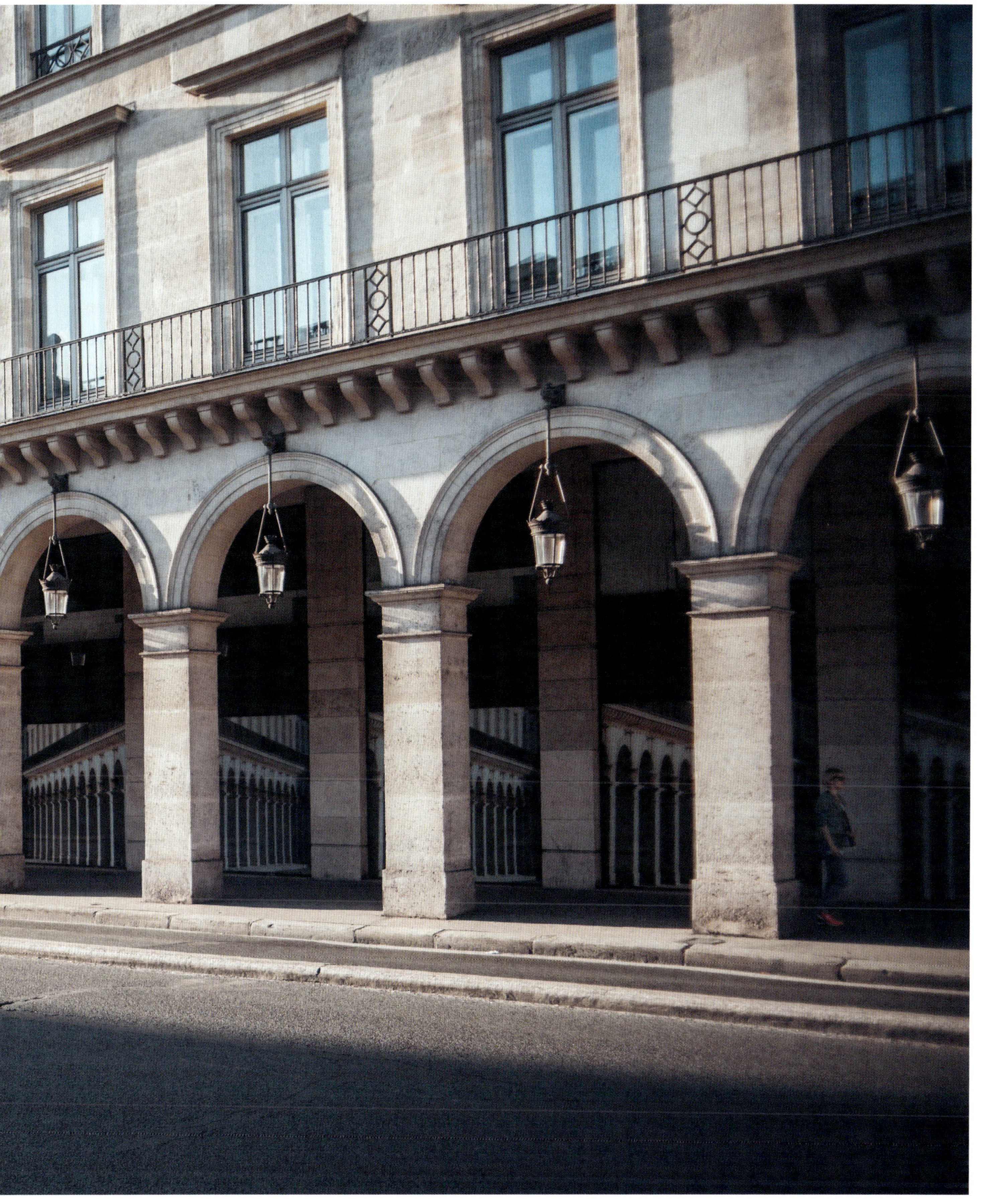

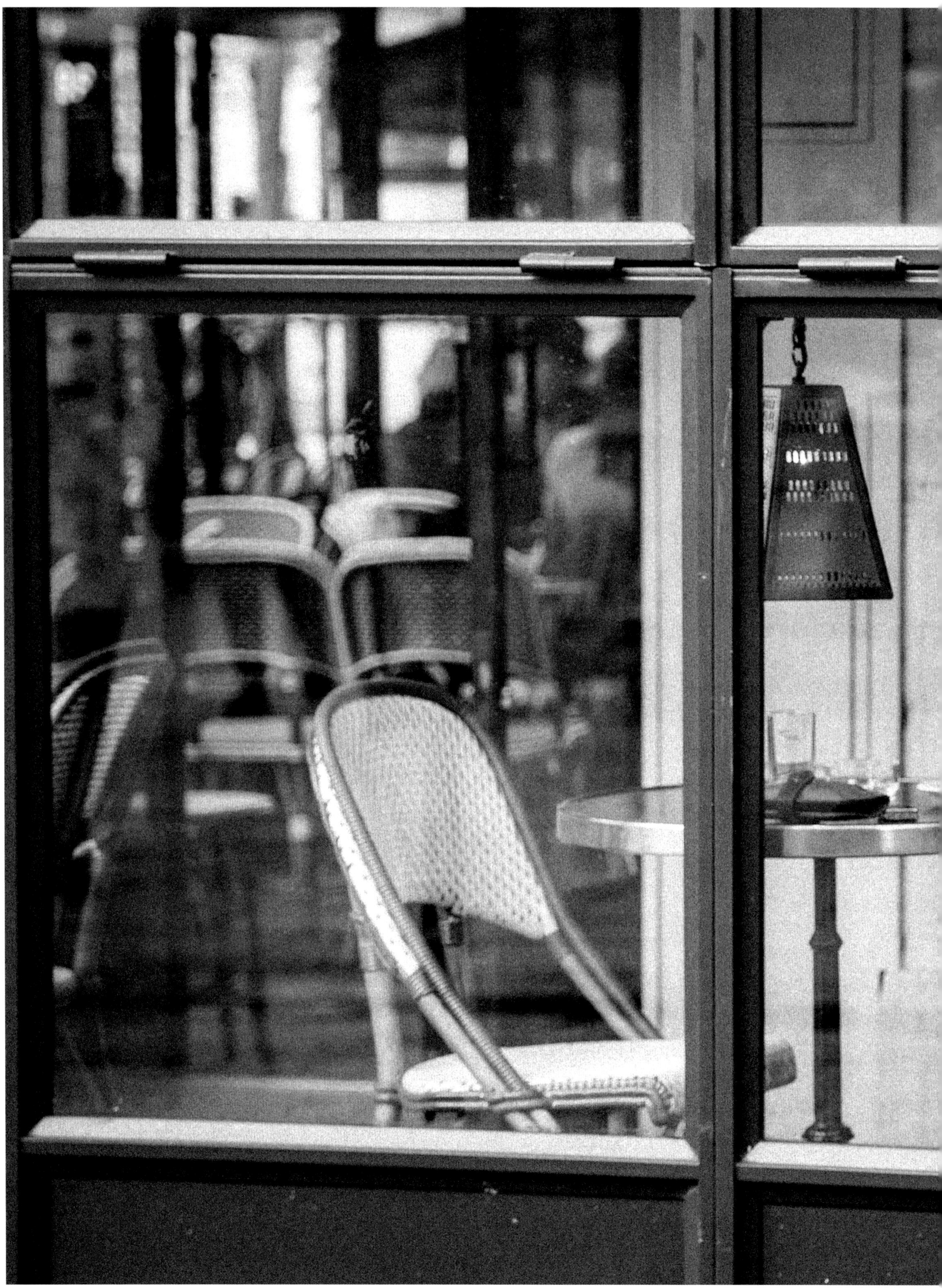

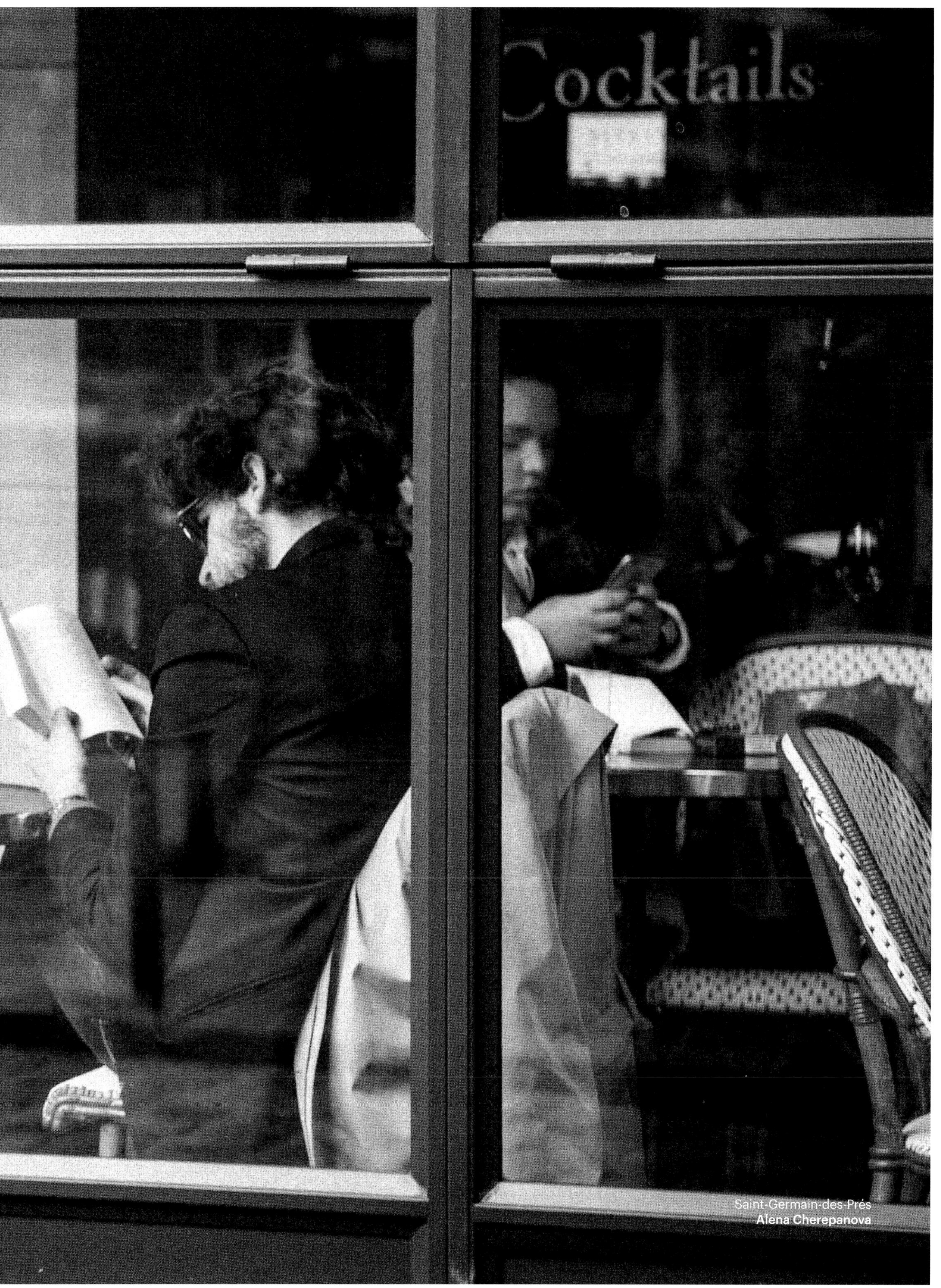

Saint-Germain-des-Prés
Alena Cherepanova

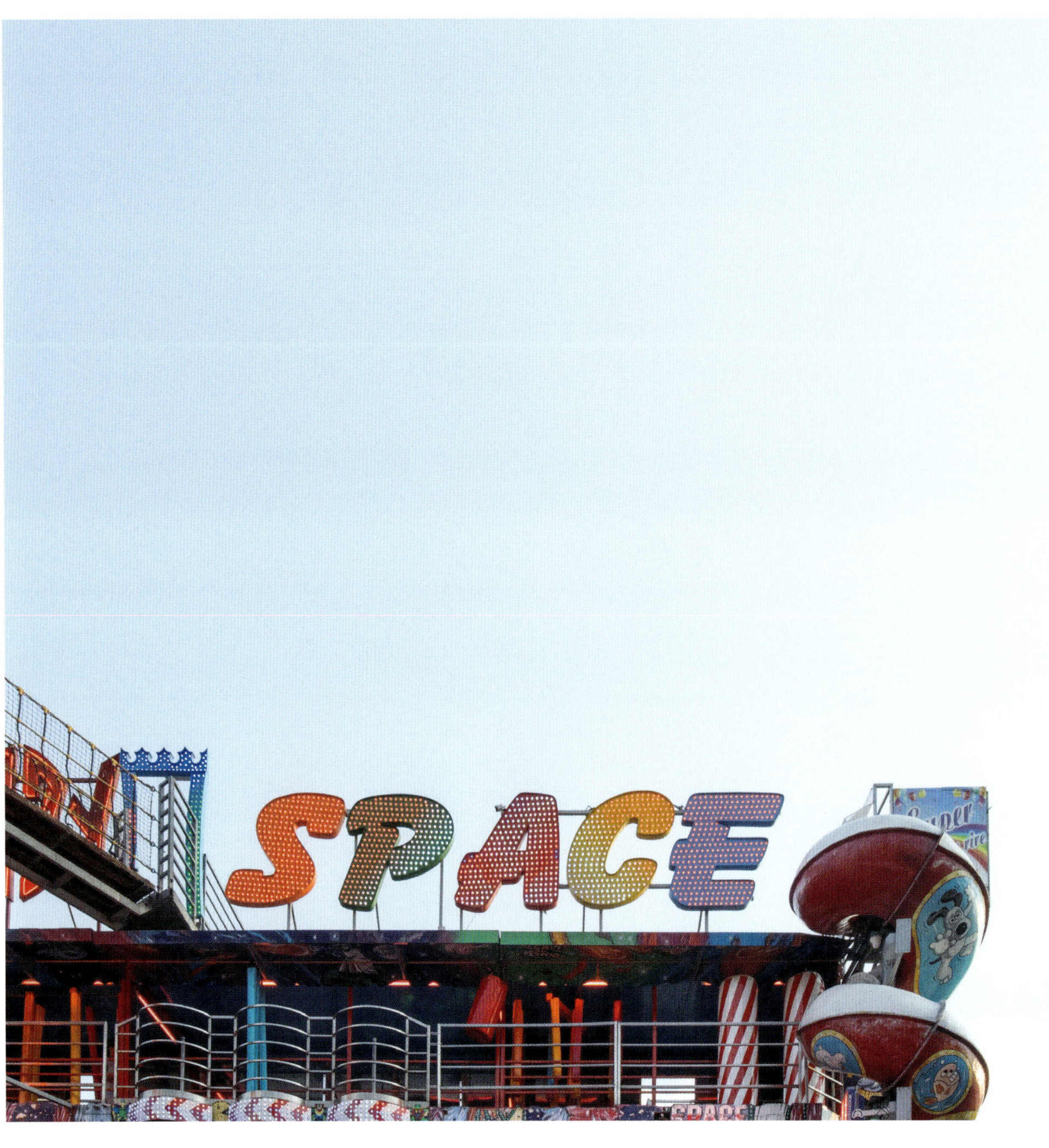

Fête des Tuileries
Jardin des Tuileries
Hugo Katsumi

Jussieu Campus
5e Arrondissement
Erica Gonzalez –

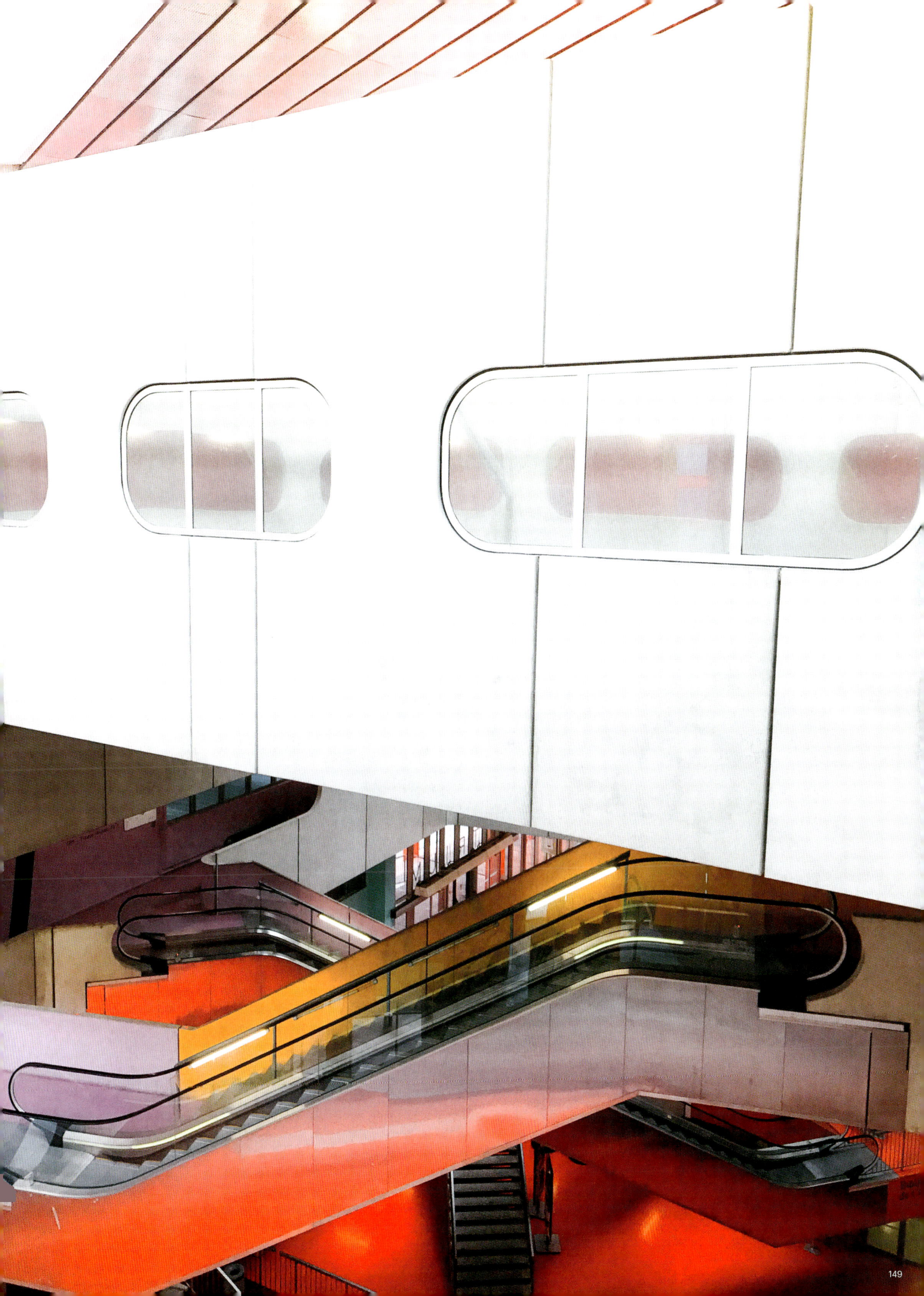

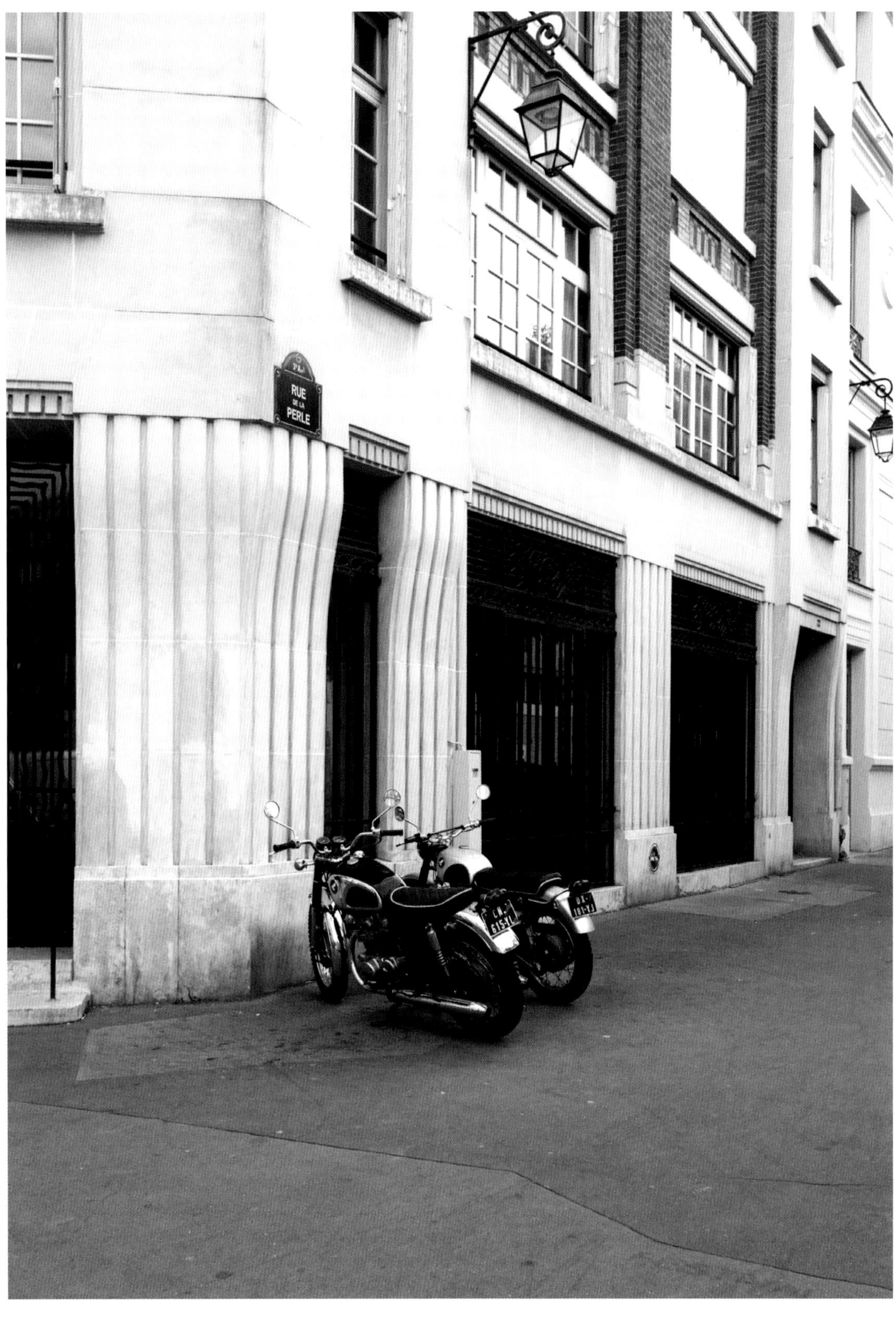

Rue de la Perle
Les Archives
Hugo Michaudel

Saint-Germain-des-Prés
Alena Cherepanova –

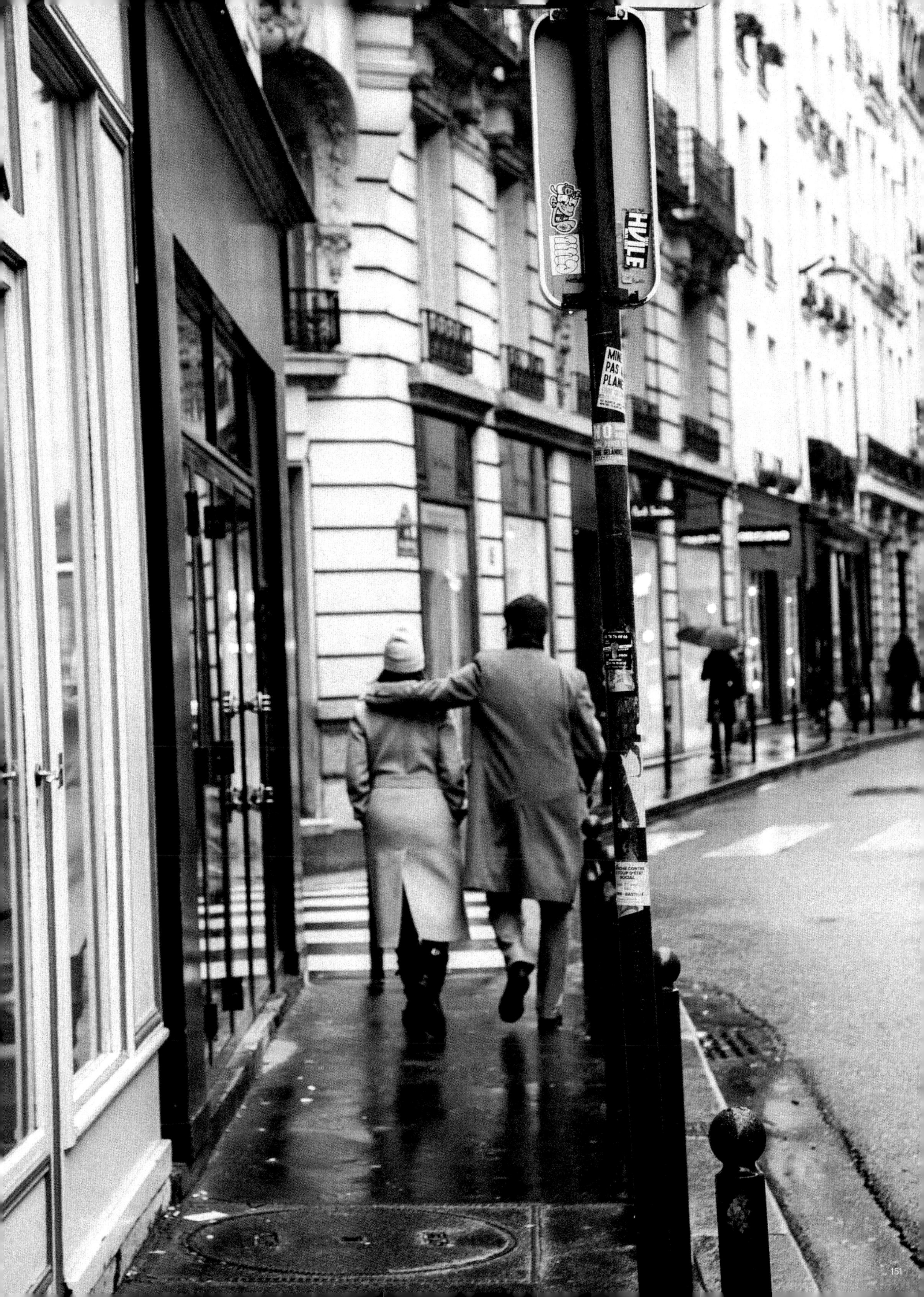
HVILE

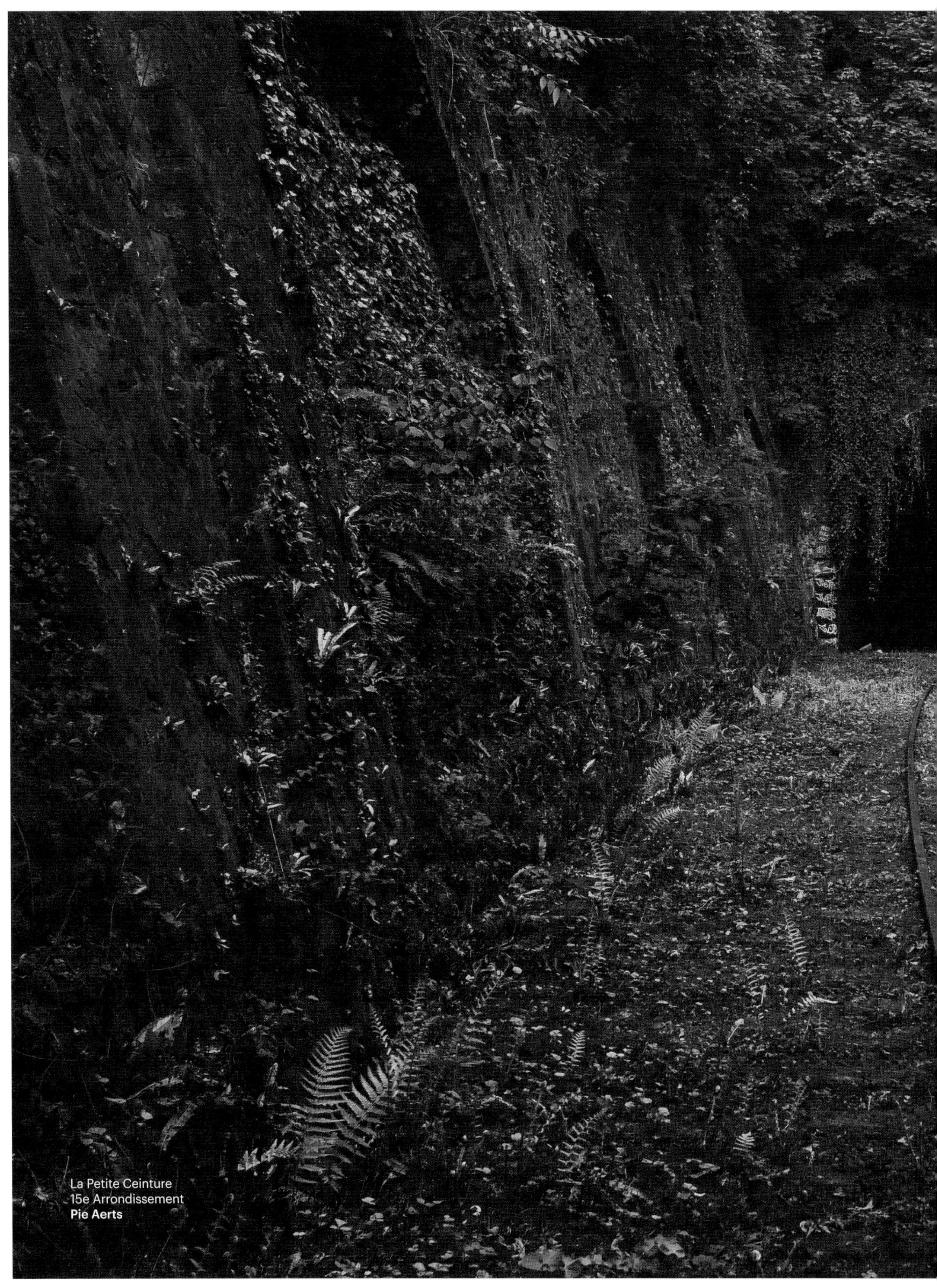
La Petite Ceinture
15e Arrondissement
Pie Aerts

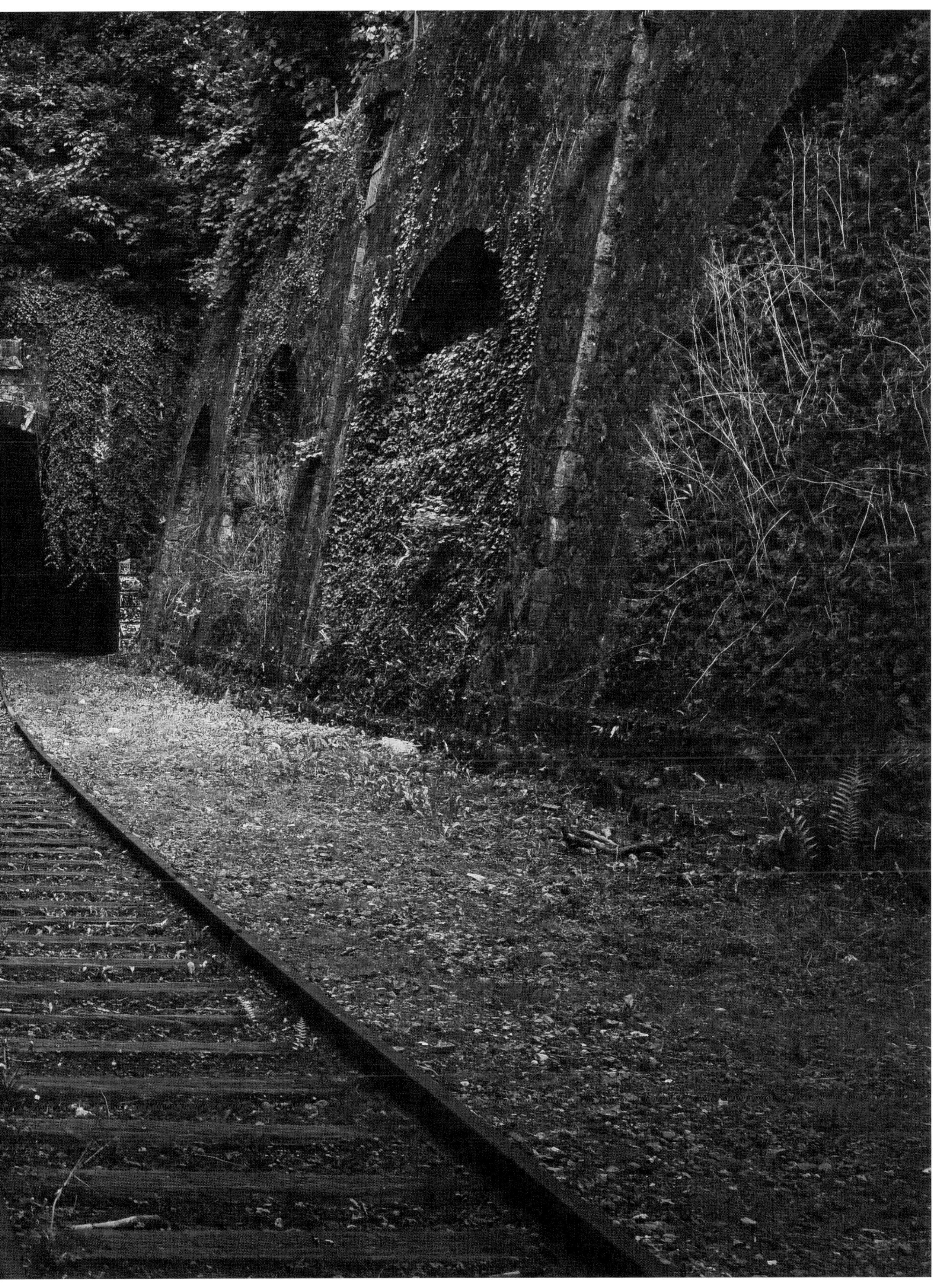

Sapeurs-Pompiers
Ivry-sur-Seine
Dariusz Jasak →

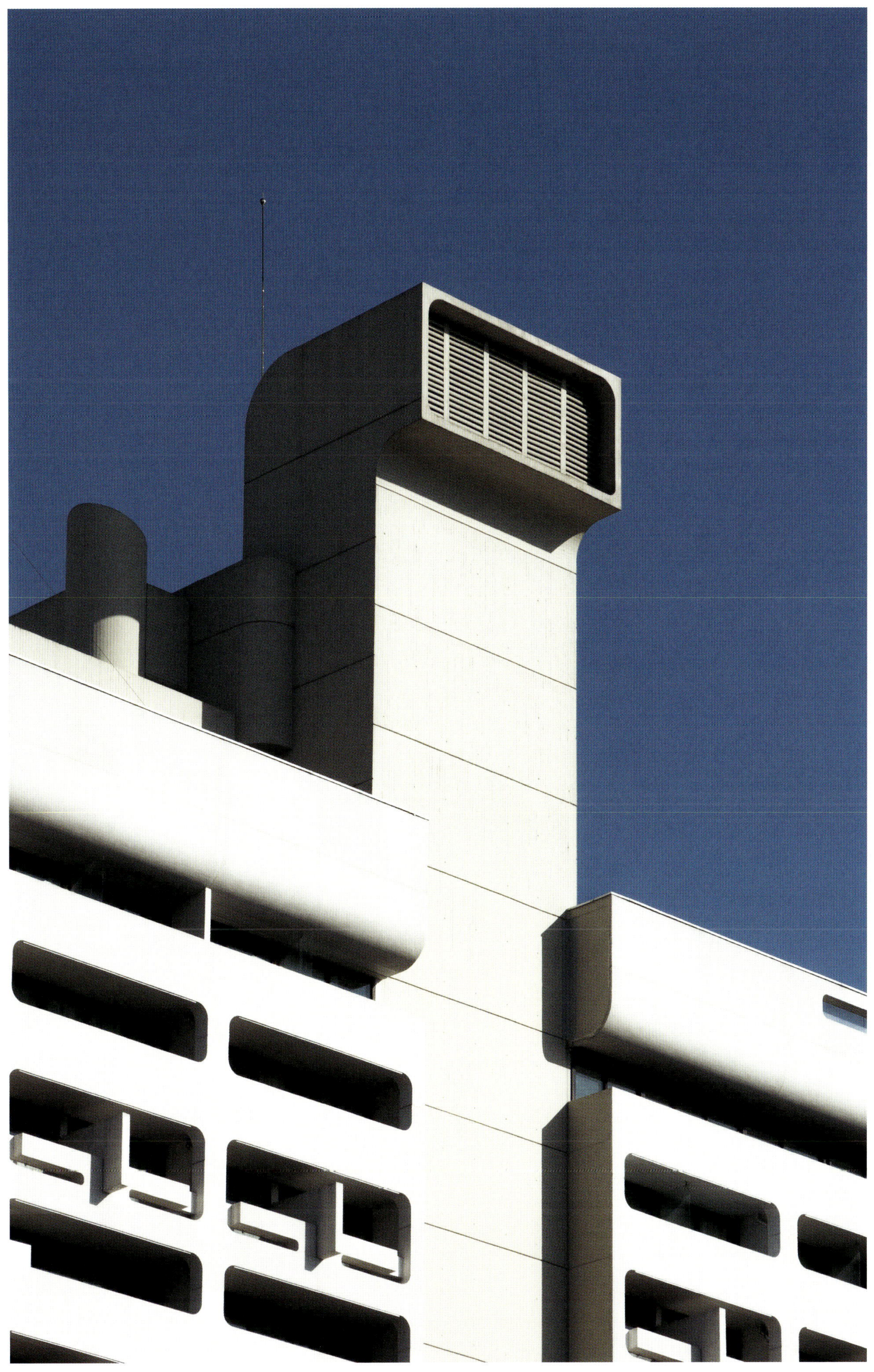

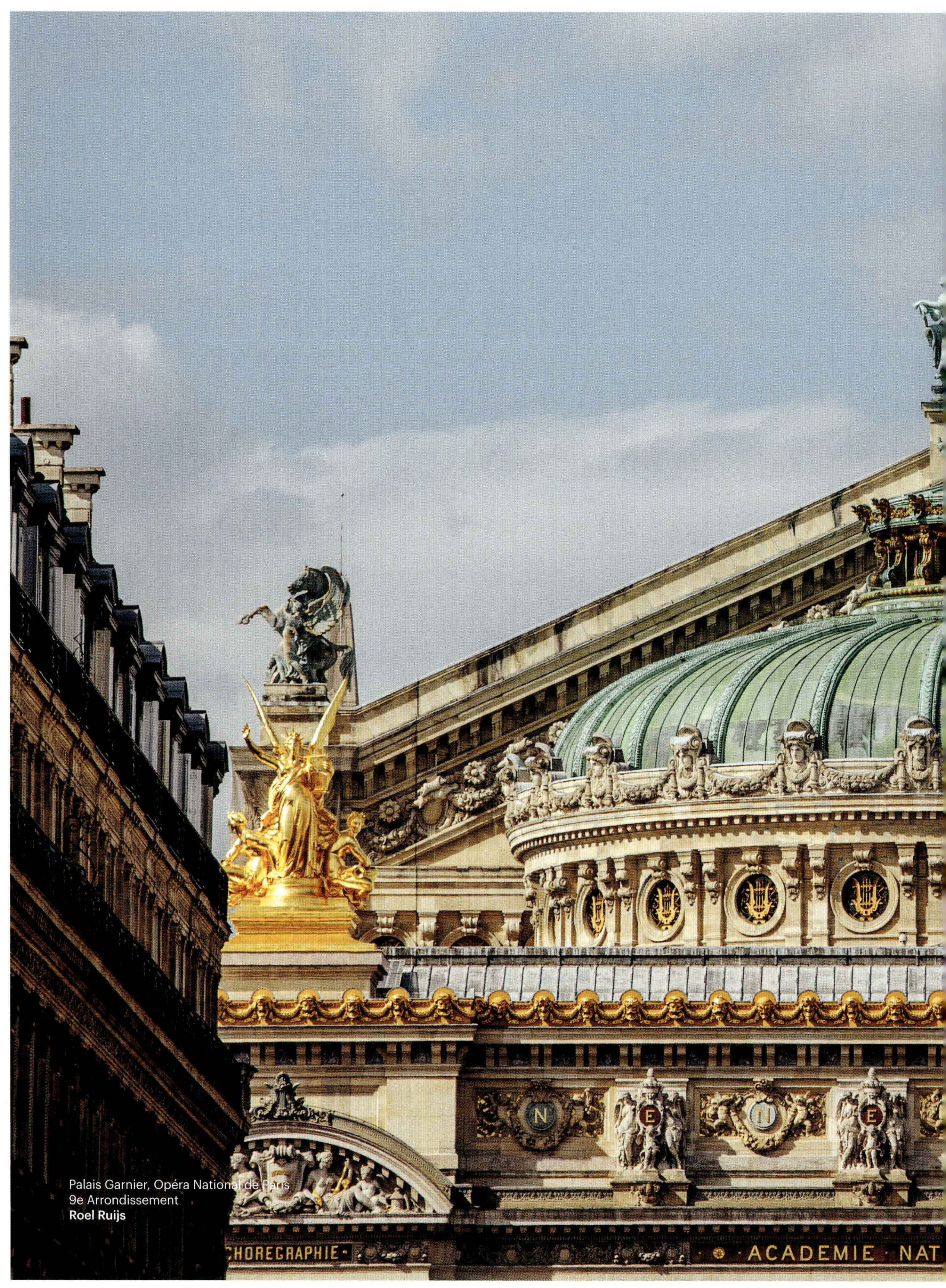

Palais Garnier, Opéra National de Paris
9e Arrondissement
Roel Ruijs

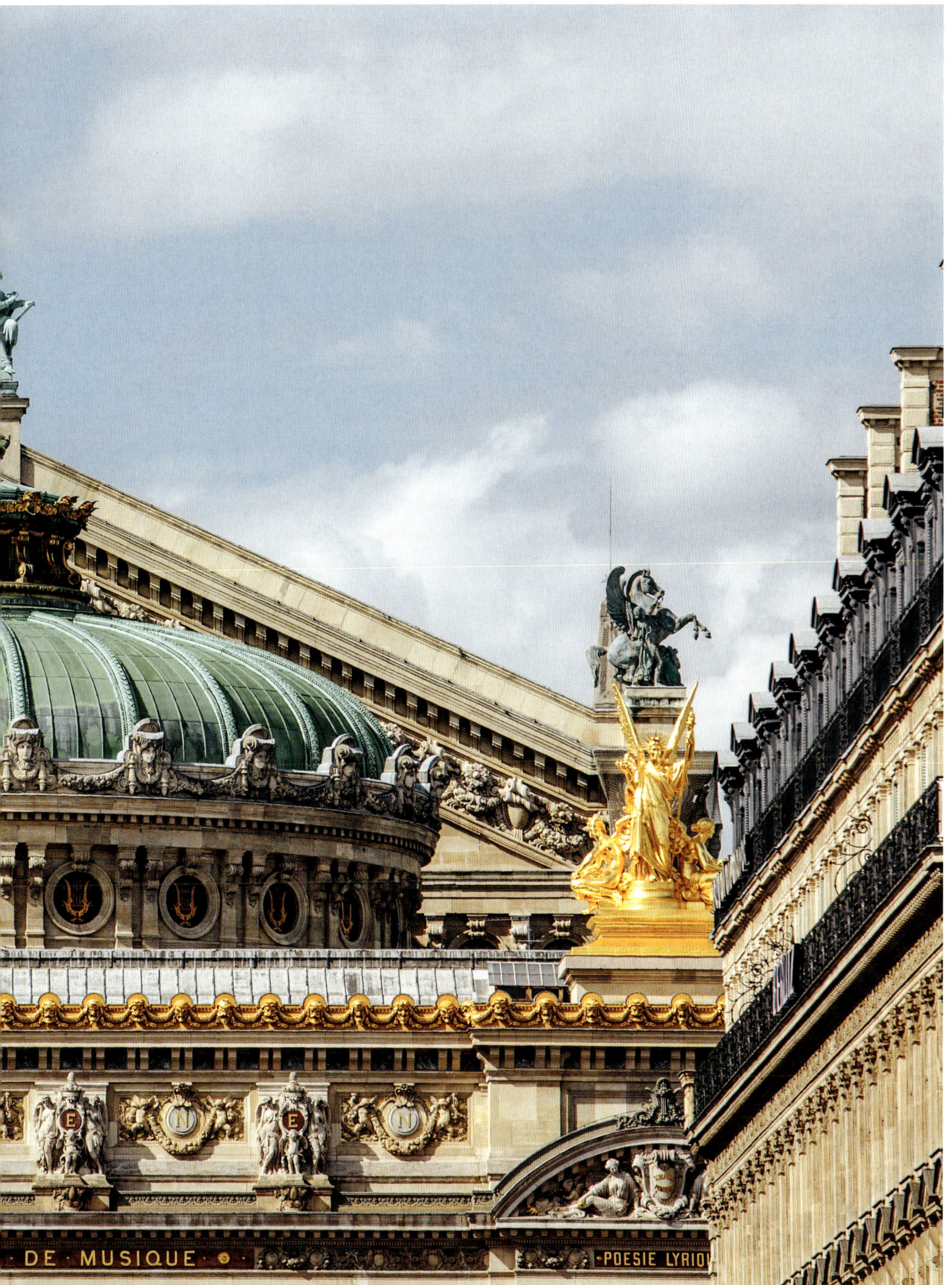
DE · MUSIQUE ·
· POESIE LYRIQ

Le Marais
Denis Mamin

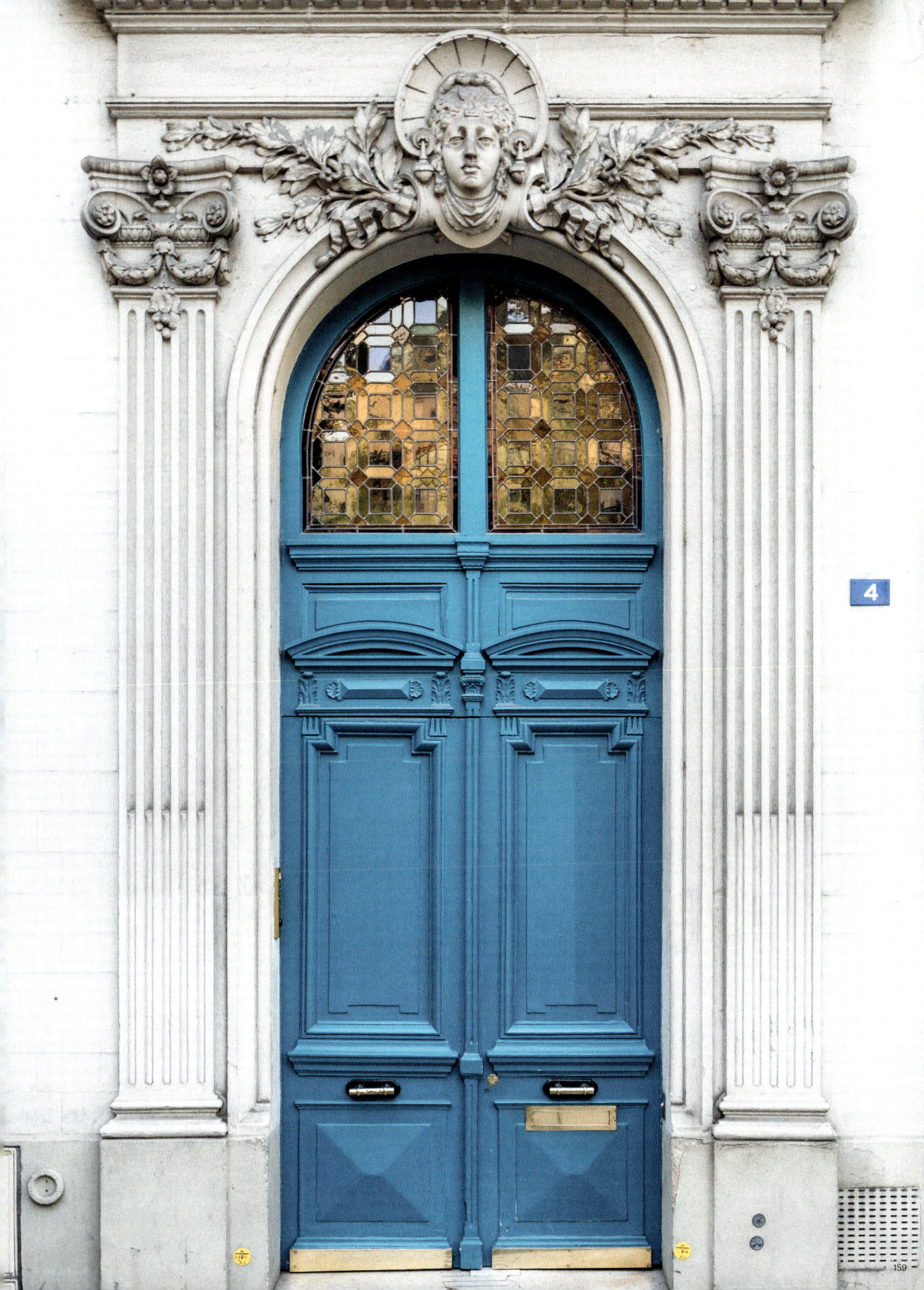
4

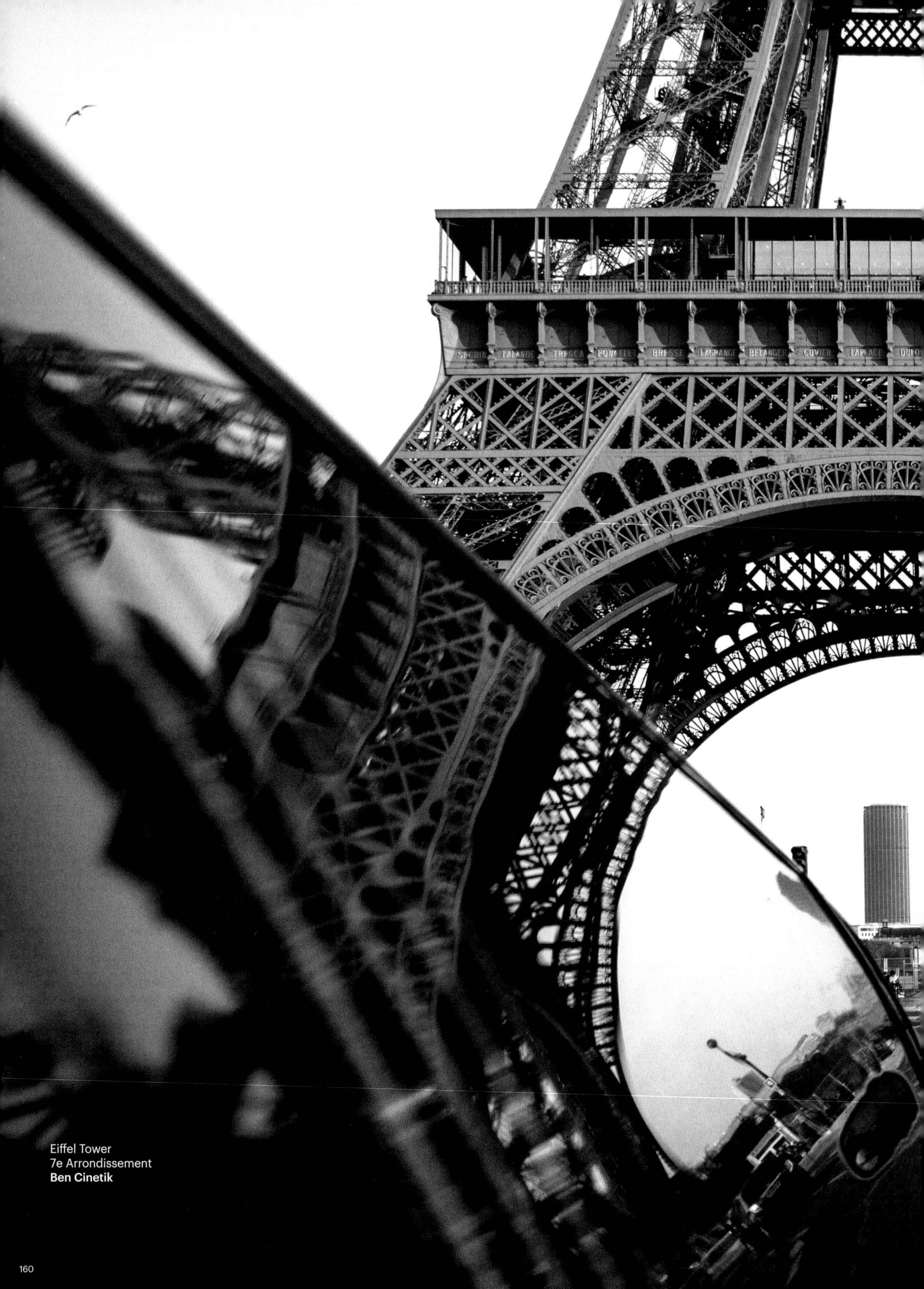

Eiffel Tower
7e Arrondissement
Ben Cinetik

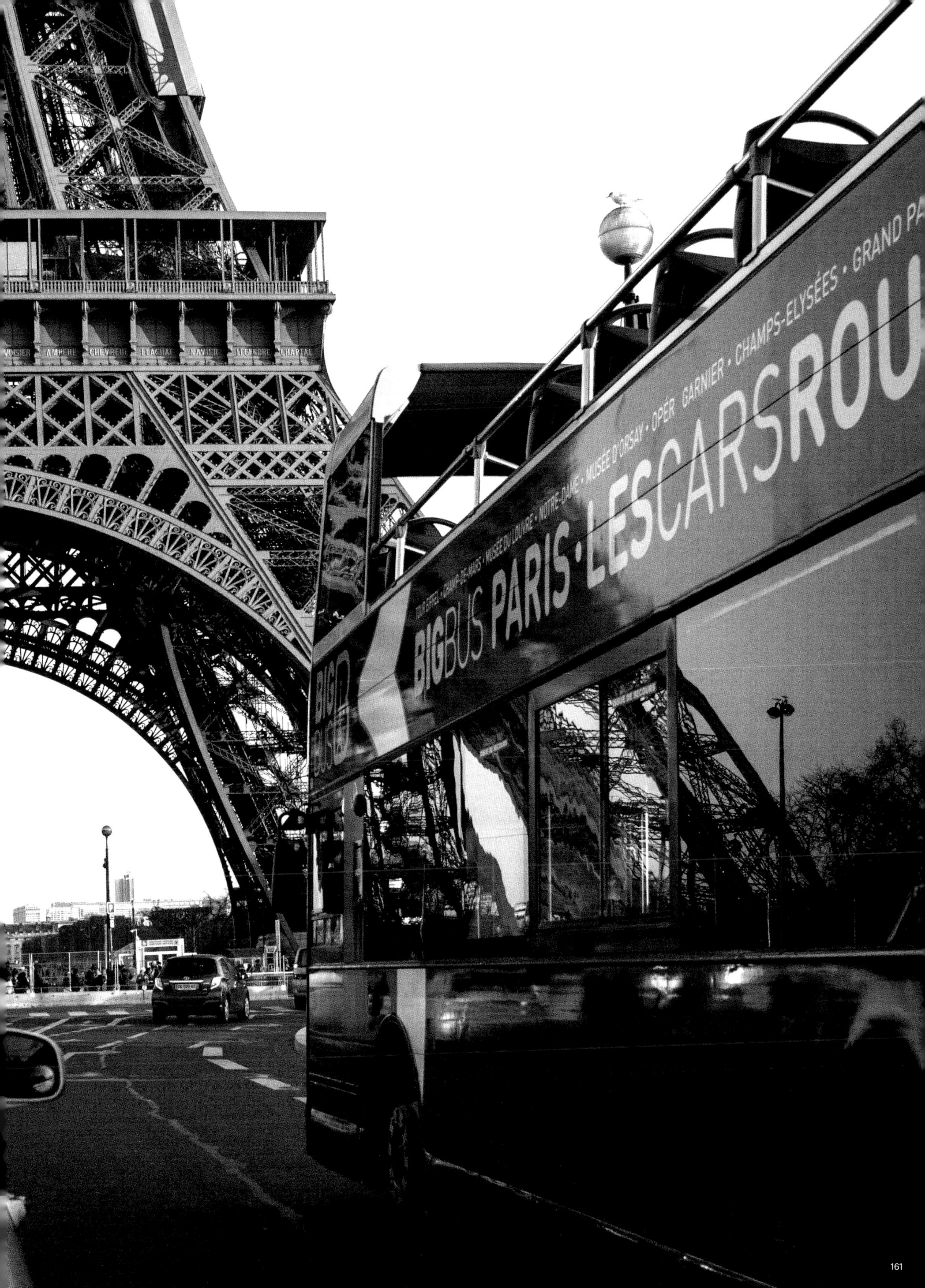
VOISIER AMPÈRE CHEVREUL FLACHAT NAVIER LEGENDRE CHAPTAL
TOUR EIFFEL • CHAMP-DE-MARS • MUSÉE DU LOUVRE • NOTRE-DAME • MUSÉE D'ORSAY • OPÉR GARNIER • CHAMPS-ELYSÉES • GRAND PA
BIGBUS PARIS • LESCARSROU

La Défense
Pie Aerts

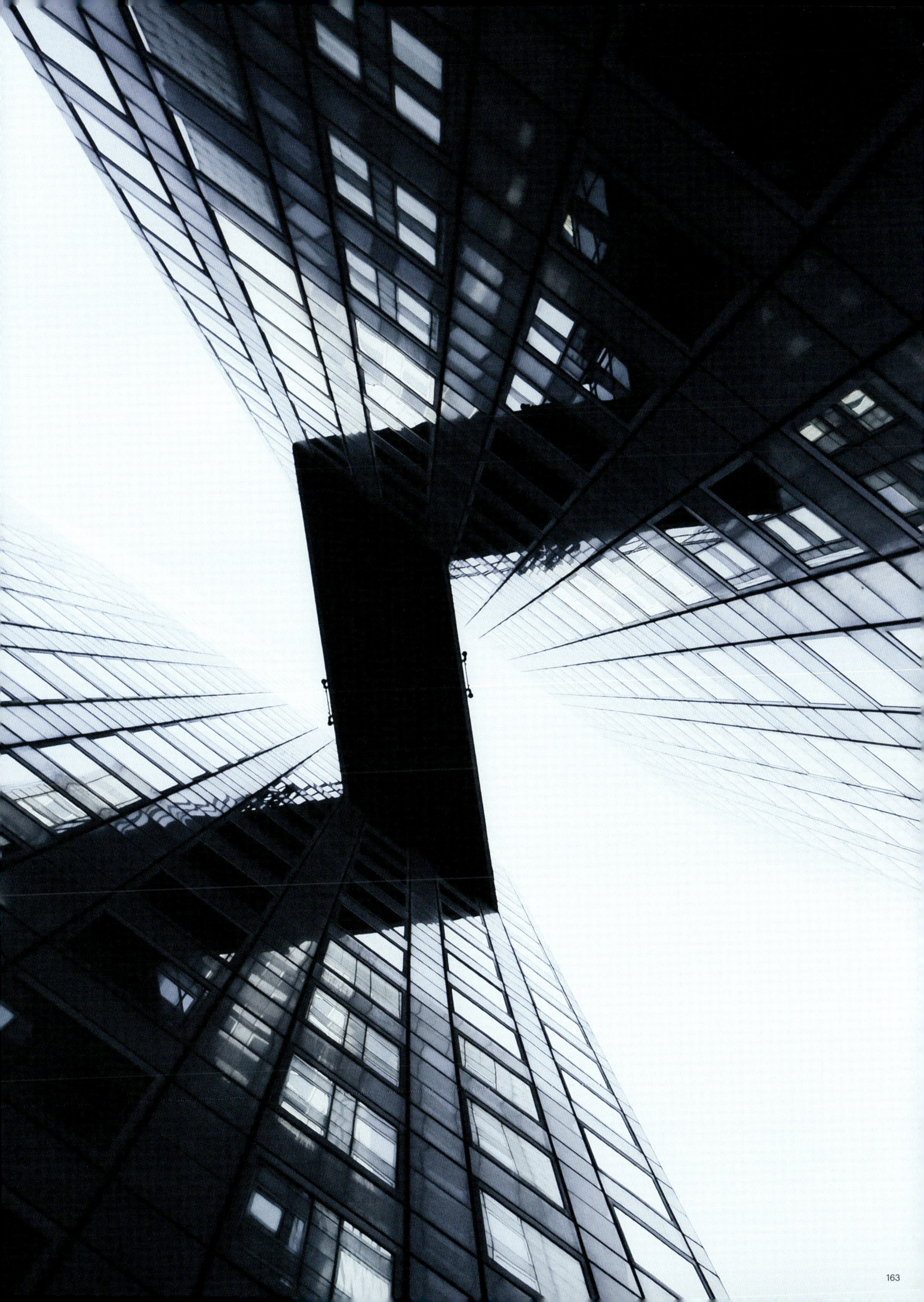

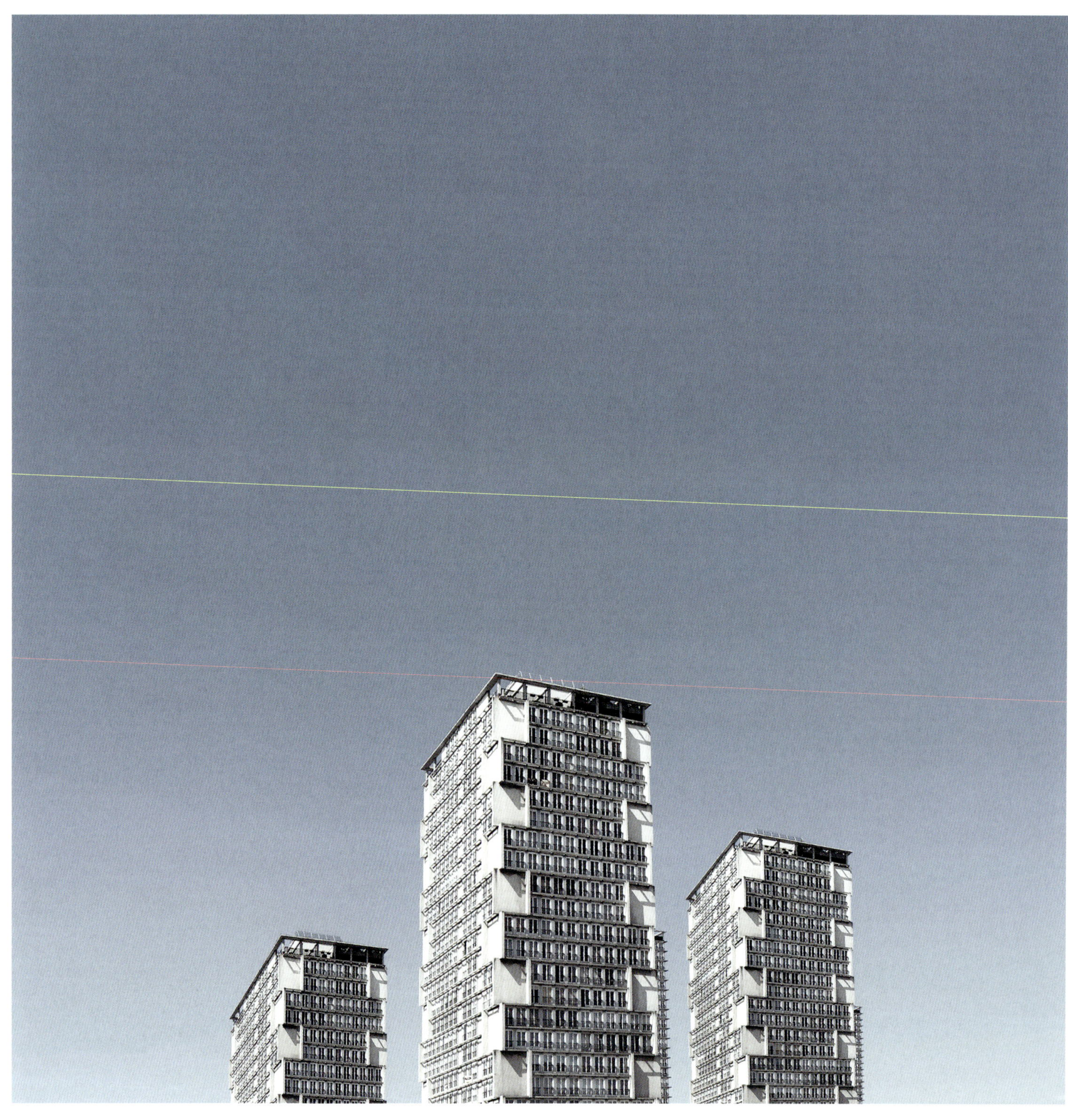

Créteil
Raul Cabrera

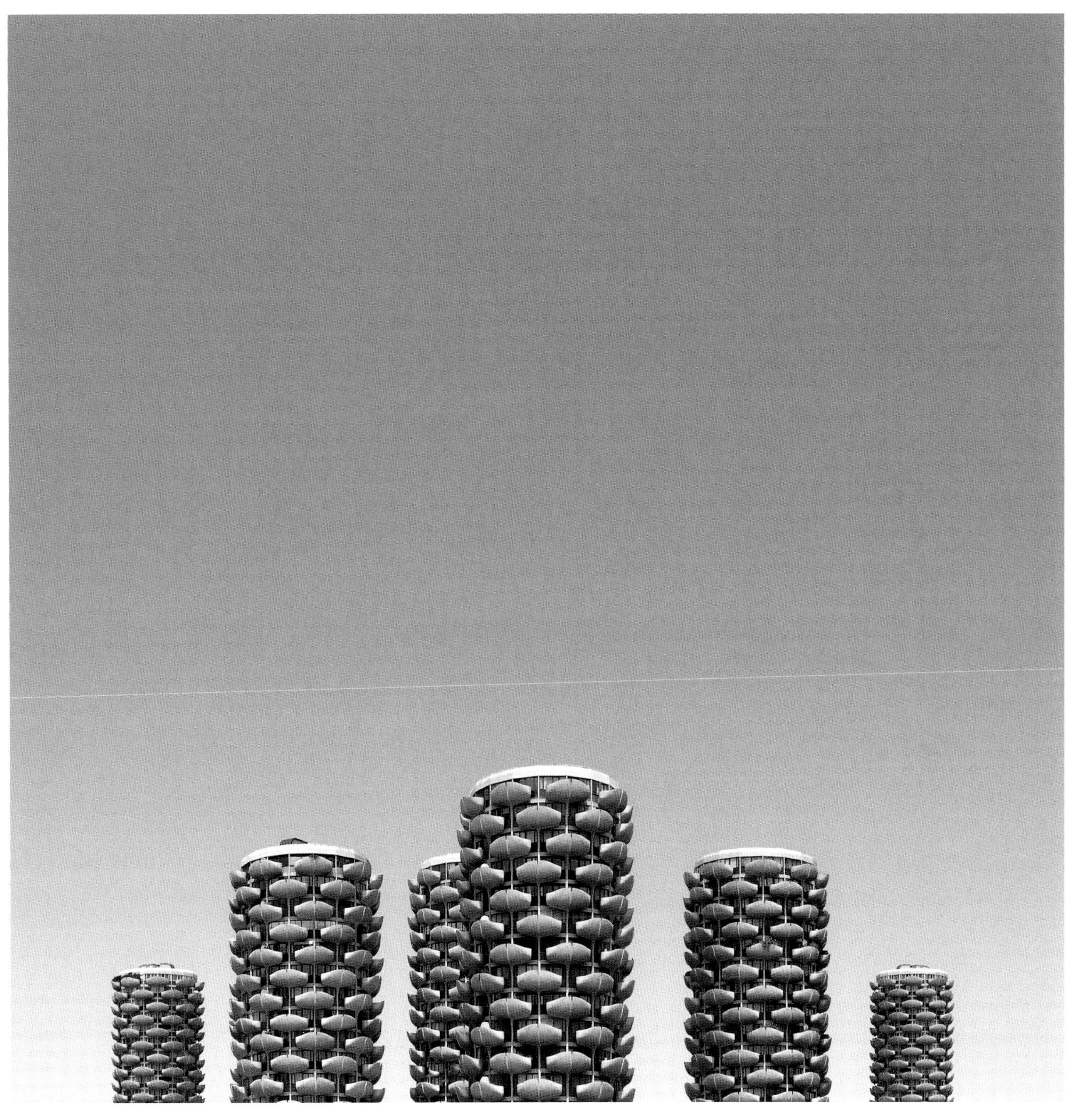

Créteil
Raul Cabrera

Librairie Loliée
6e Arrondissement
Sarah van Rij

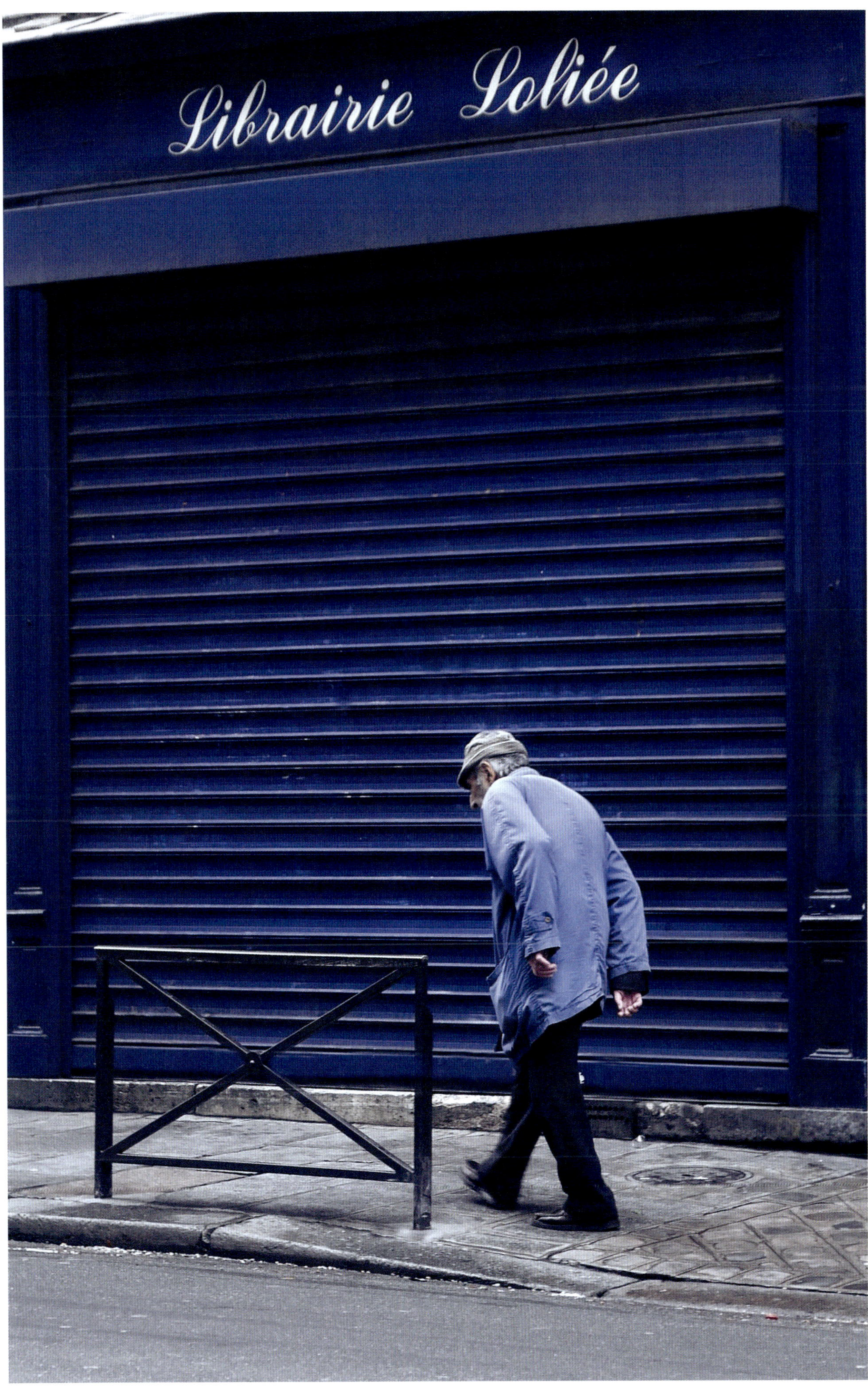
Librairie Loliée

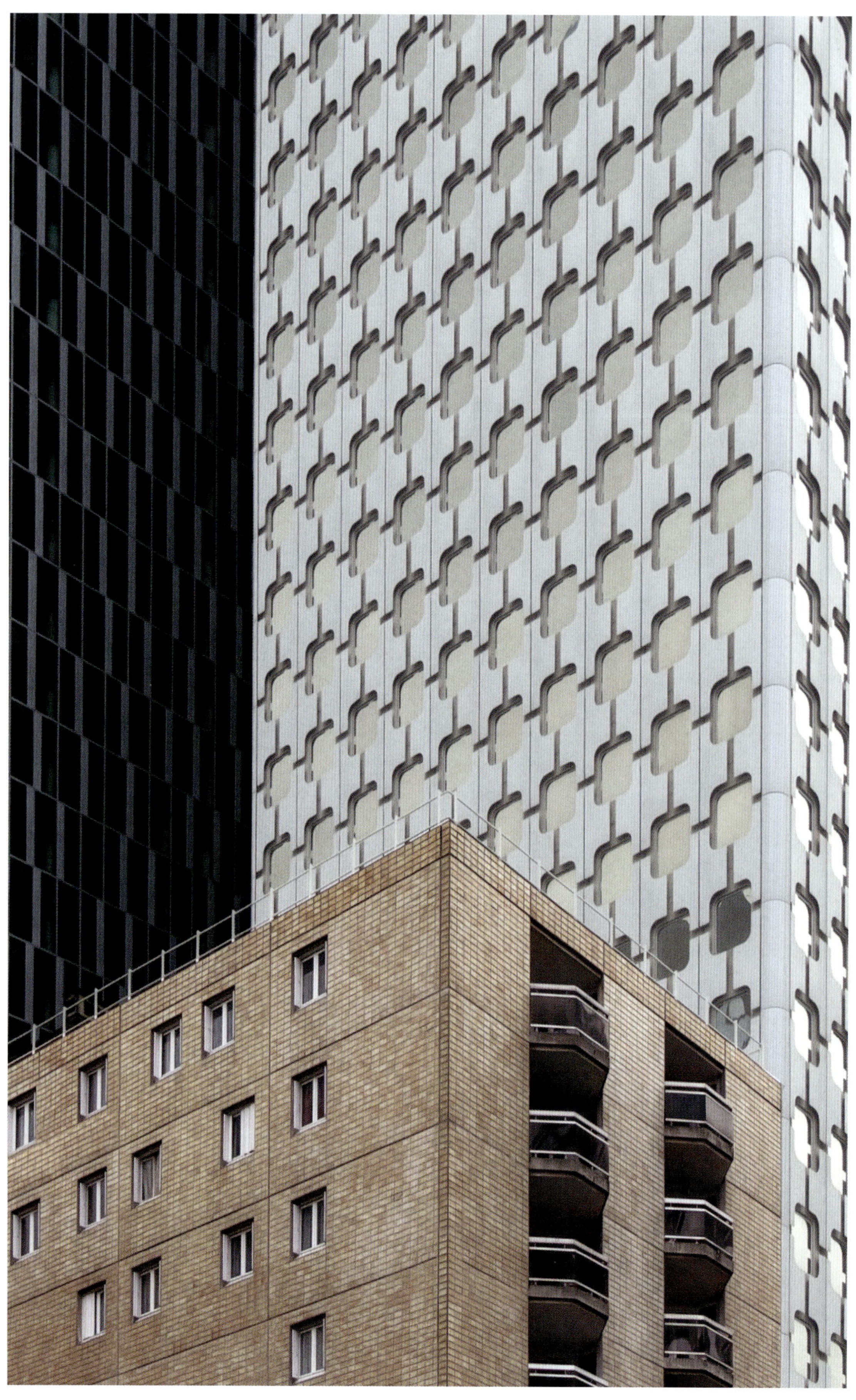

Ariane Tower
La Défense
Laetitia Modine

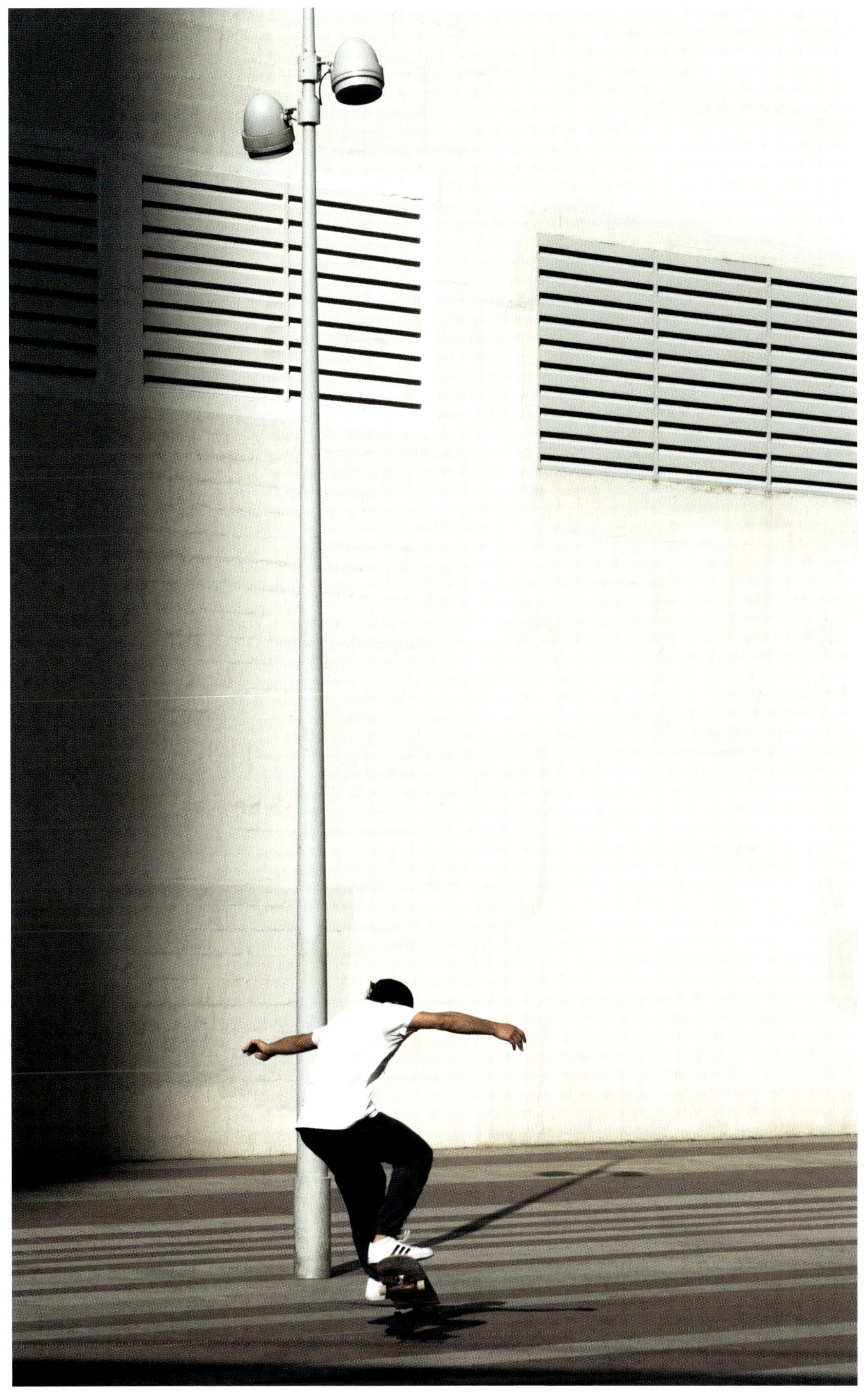

Grenelle
Dariusz Jasak

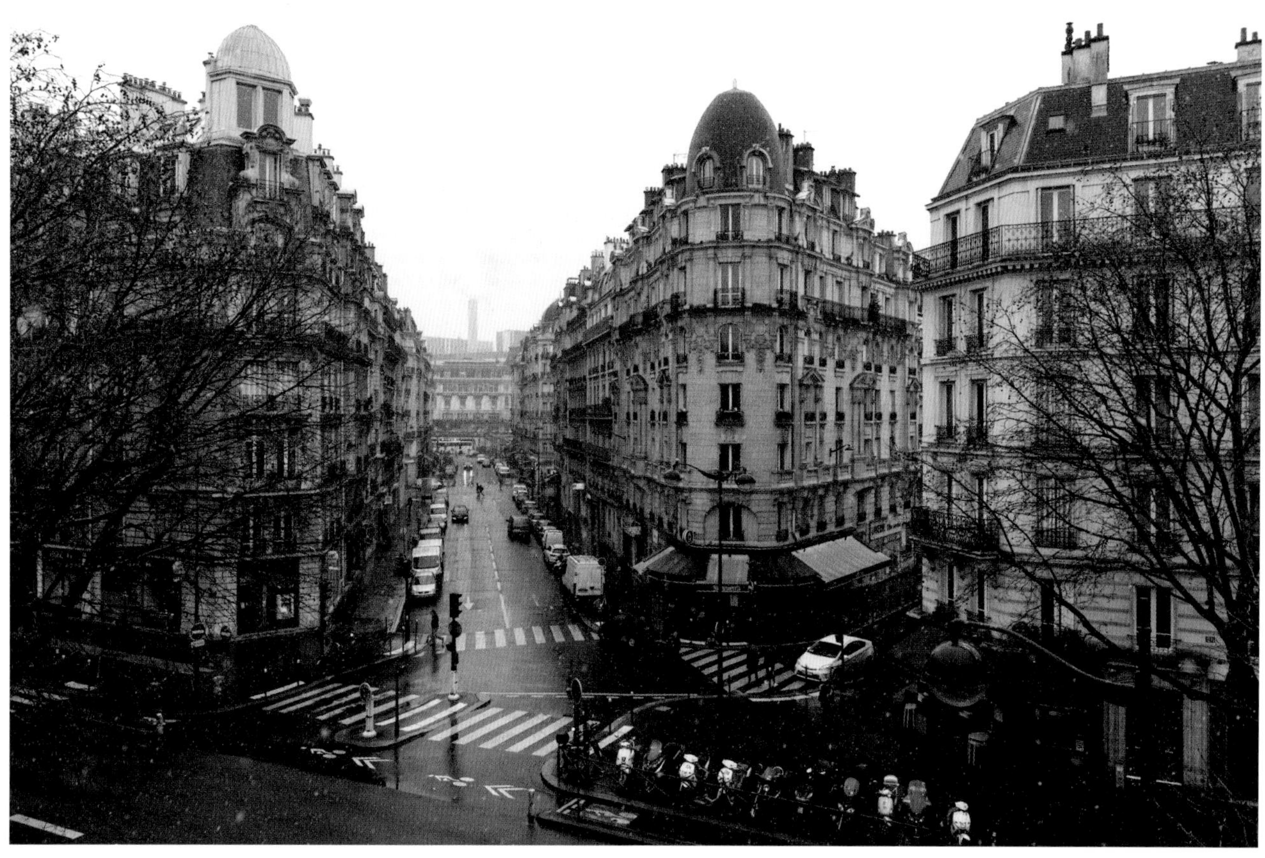

Avenue Daumesnil
12e Arrondissement
Juan Jerez del Valle

Rue de Turbigo
Le Marais
Hugo Michaudel →

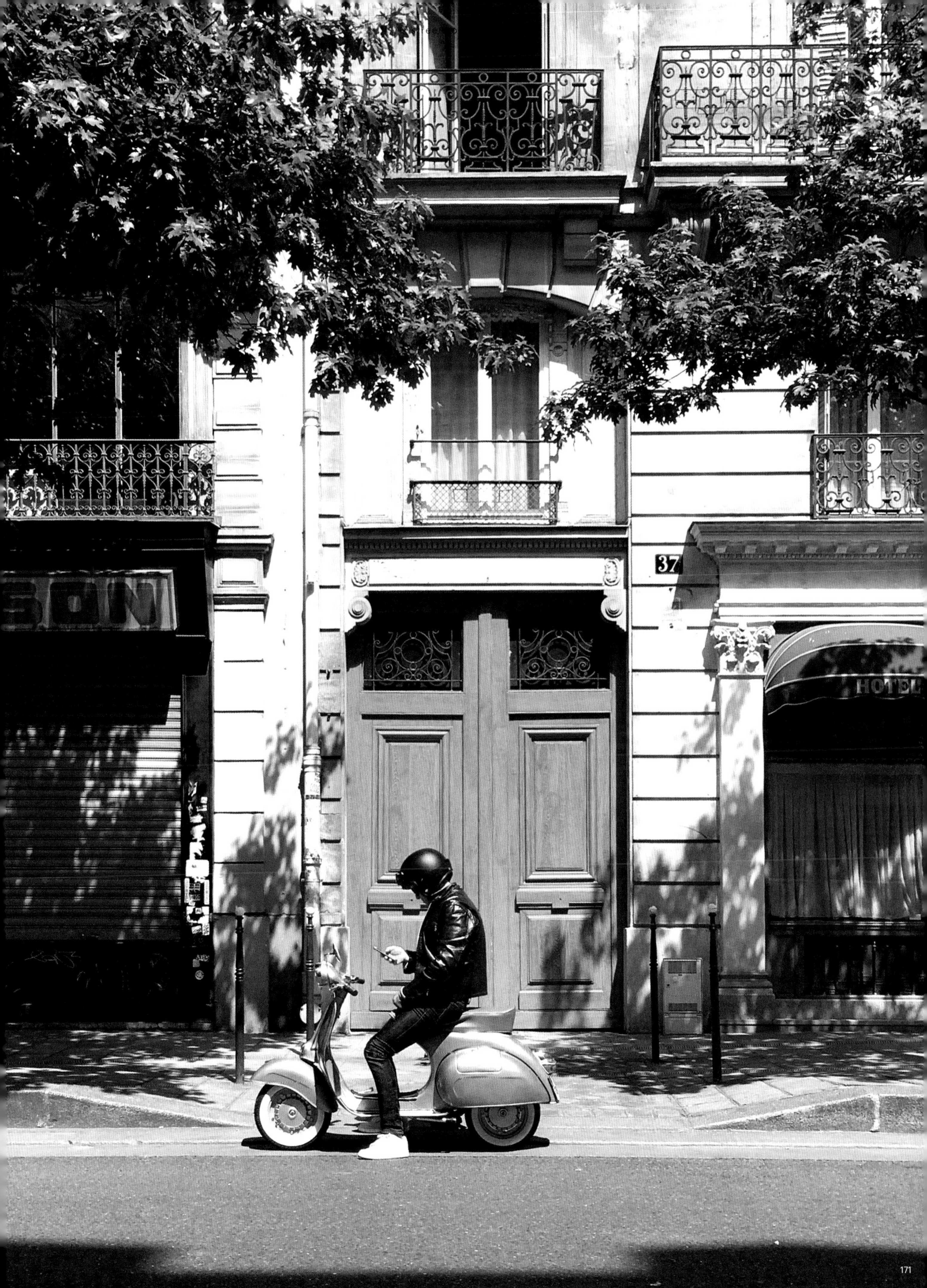
37

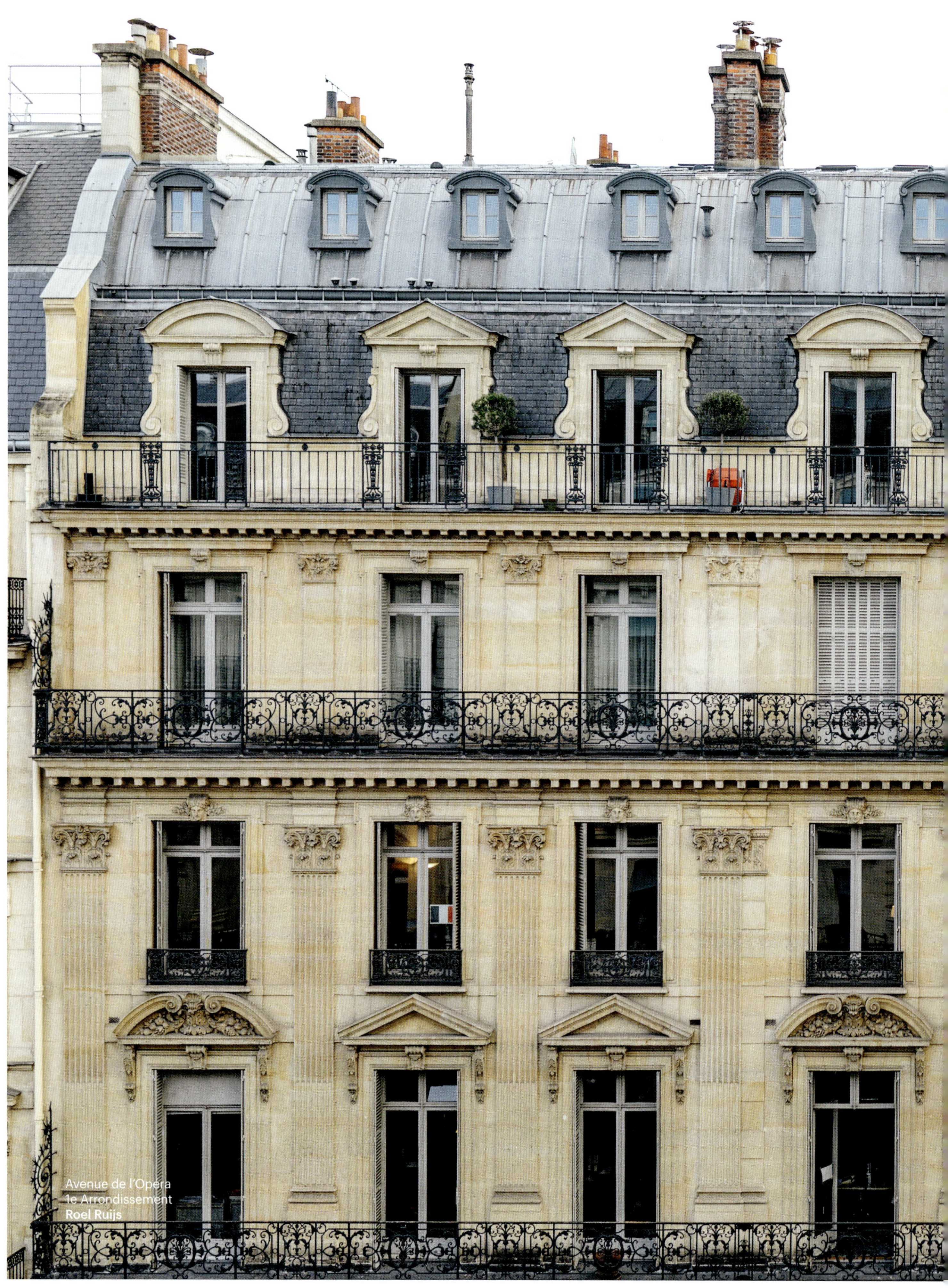

Avenue de l'Opéra
1e Arrondissement
Roel Ruijs

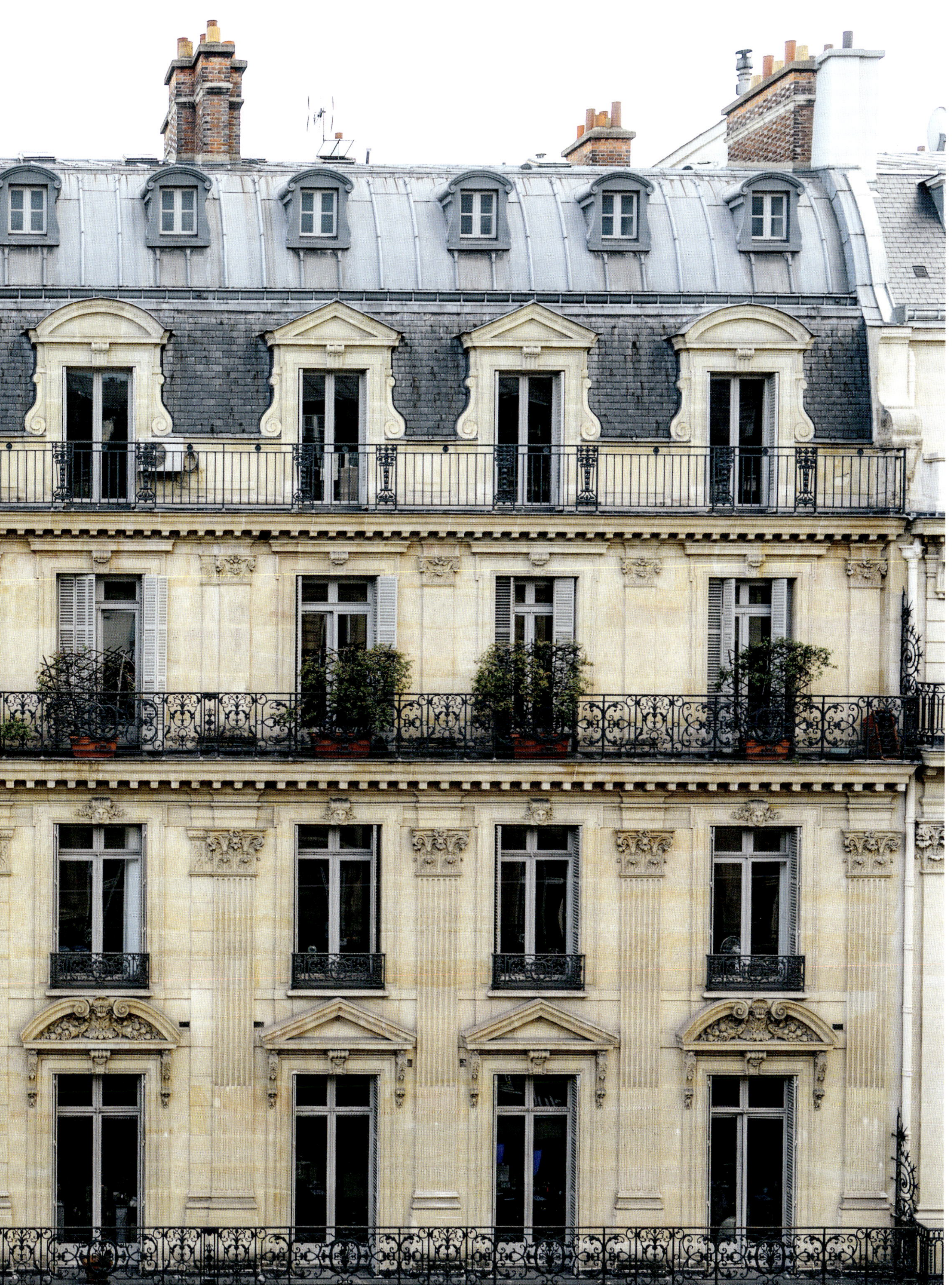

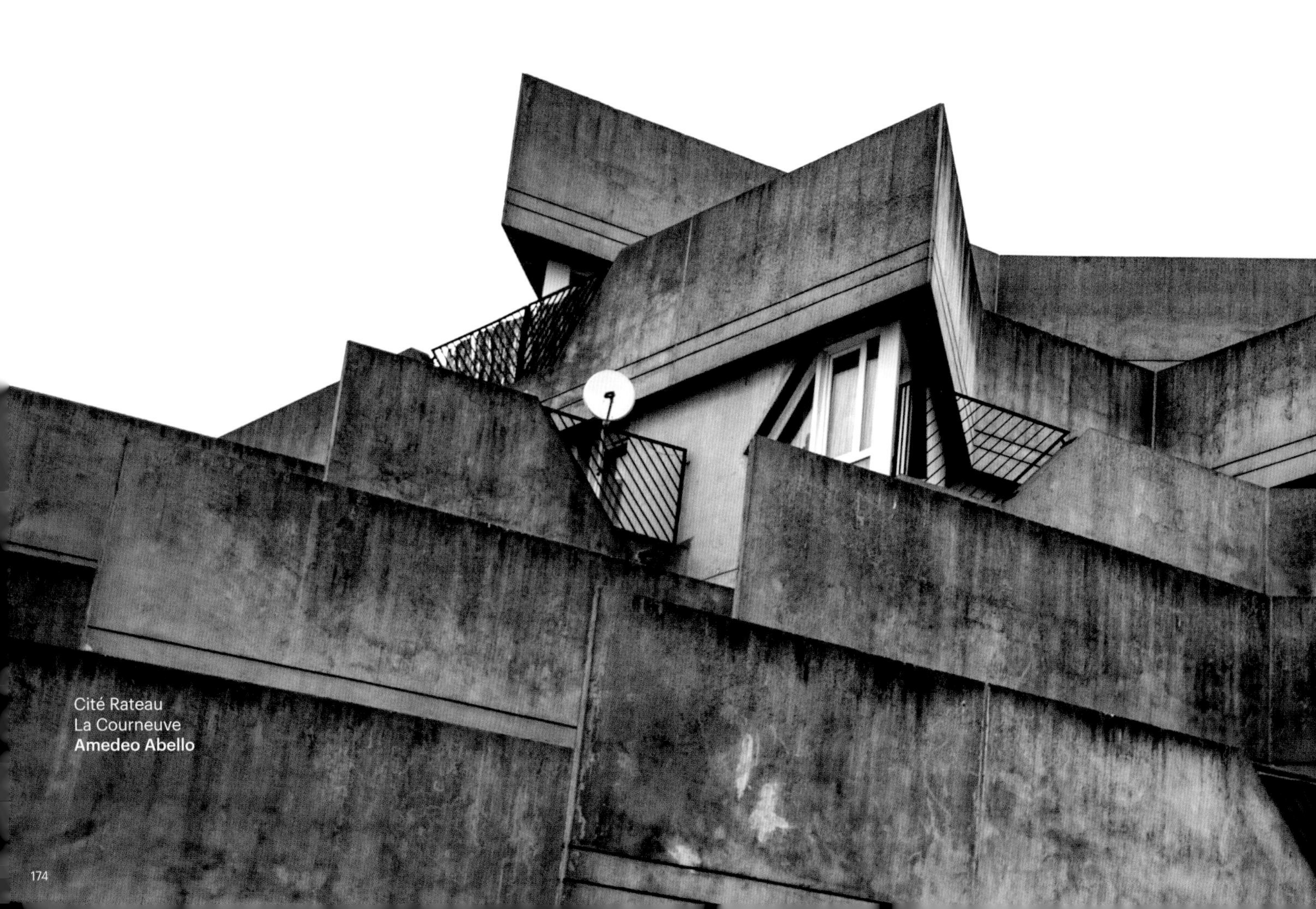

Cité Rateau
La Courneuve
Amedeo Abello

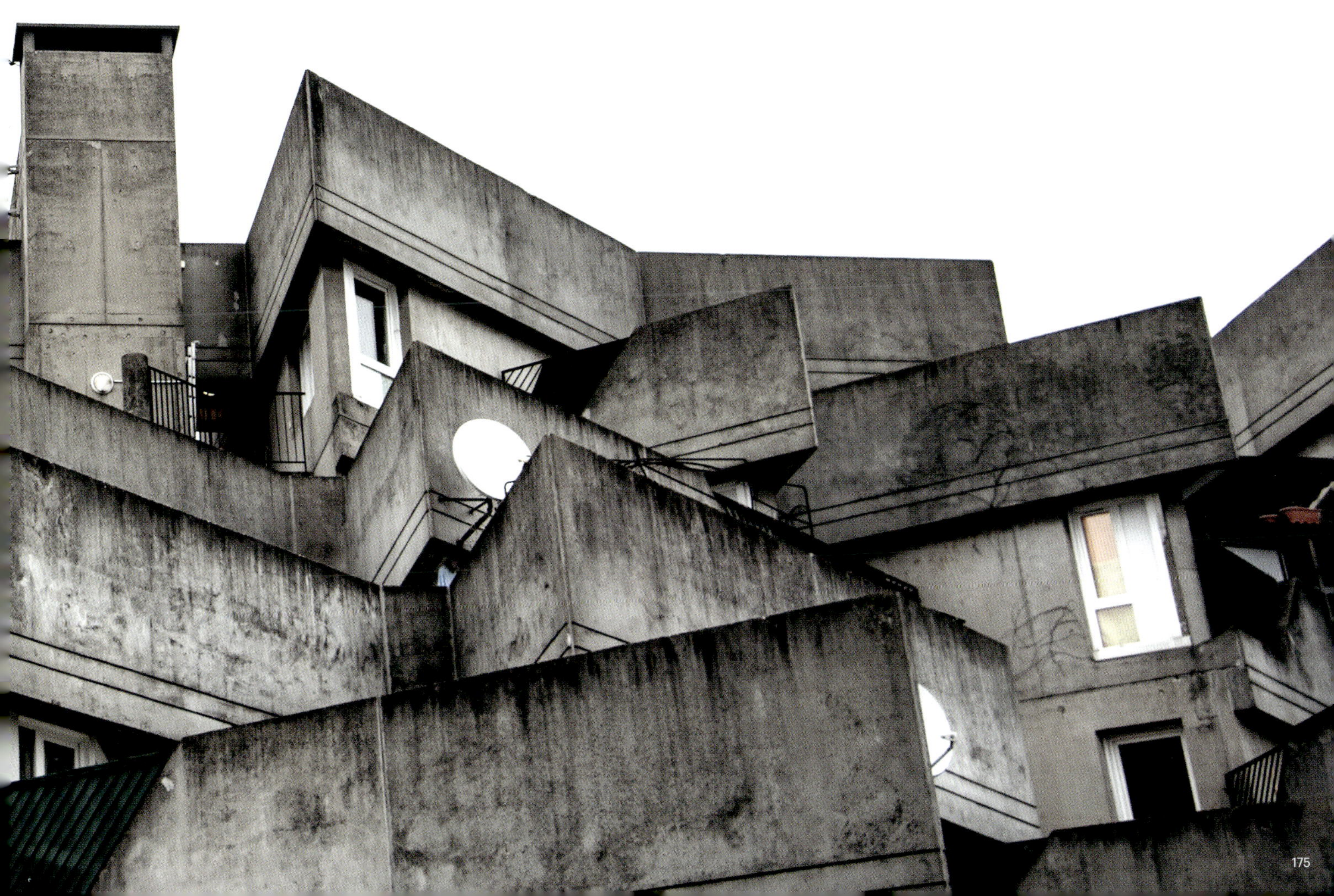

Basilique du Sacré-Cœur
Montmartre
Ben Cinetik →

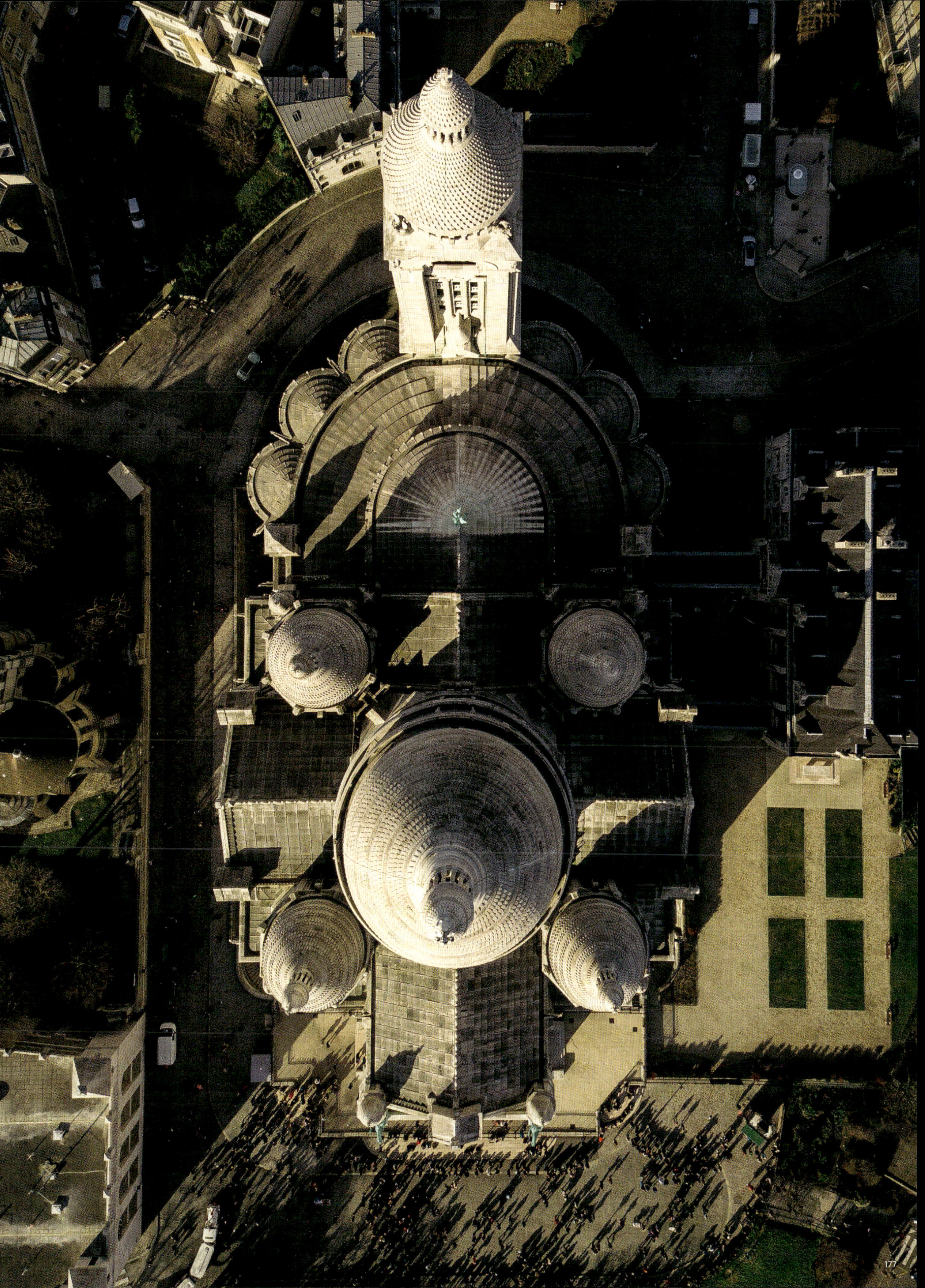

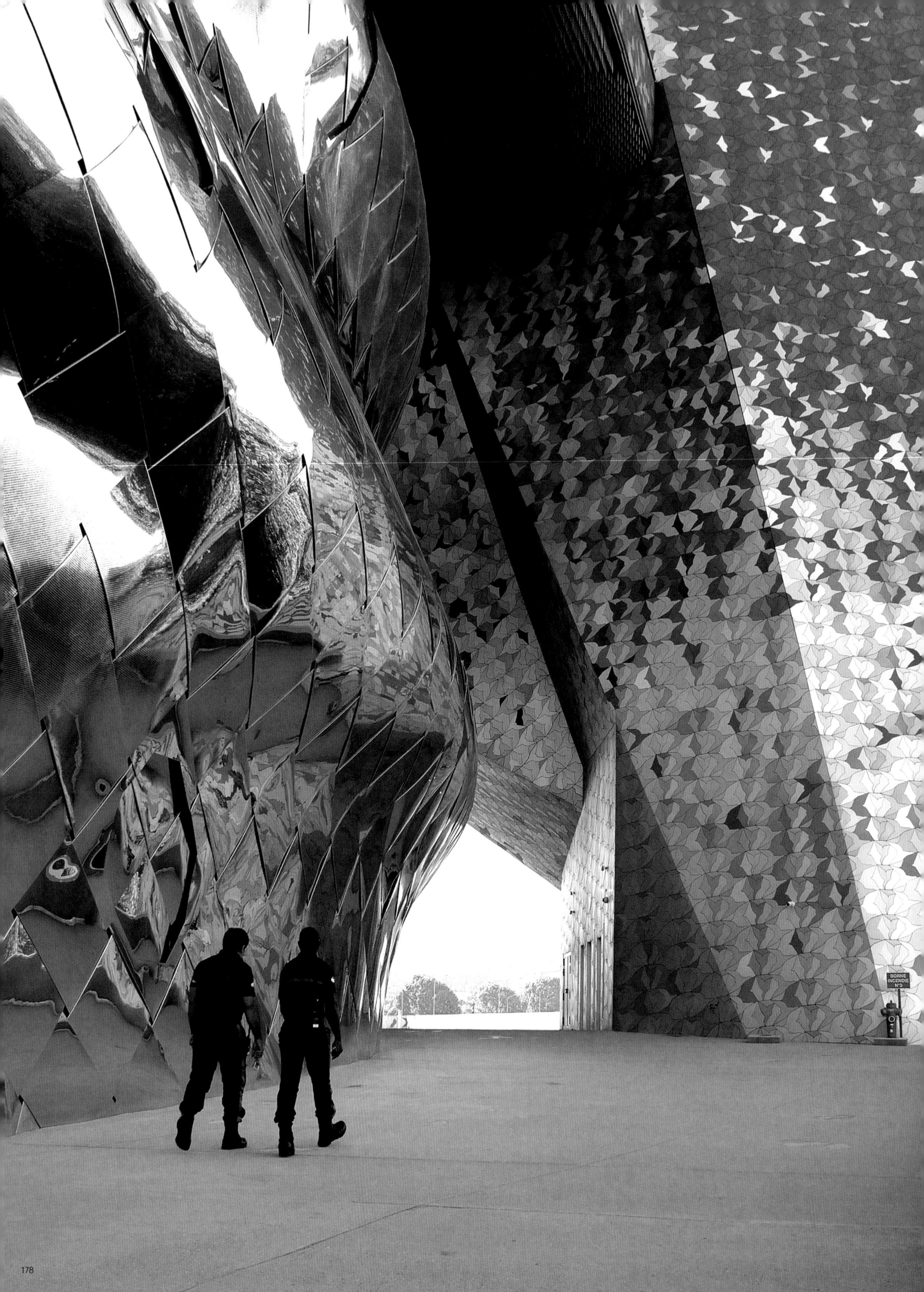
BORNE
INCENDIE
N°3

Philharmonie de Paris
Pont-de-Flandre
Hugo Michaudel

Juan Jerez del Valle

hometown Paris, France
IG handles @juanjerez

Andalusian photographer Juan Jerez del Valle was only supposed to spend a couple of weeks in Paris but developed a "kind of romantic" relationship with the City of Love over time. "We spend a lot of time together; sometimes I'm tired of her, but as soon as I leave her, I miss her terribly." To keep finding new angles on Paris, Juan has to leave town every once in a while. "Then I can come back with a fresh look—there's always a hidden Paris to discover. I often leave without any fixed goal, which allows me to follow my intuitions, an interesting individual, a particular light or the sound of a distant concert. In that manner, I have discovered many things." Juan also challenges himself by working with different lenses. "It's an interesting exercise; I walk into a certain area that I know well, but with a lens on my camera that I rarely use. It always allows me to get a new perspective on things." Juan started taking pictures in Rome, where he photographed a lot of ancient monuments as an educated architect and art historian. The city's buildings, baroque paintings, the dramatic light of Caravaggio all influenced his style: "In the scenes that I seek to photograph, I'm always looking to capture the same kind of light."

Der Fotograf Juan Jerez del Valle aus Andalusien wollte eigentlich nur ein paar Wochen in Paris bleiben. Mit der Zeit entwickelte er jedoch eine „Art romantische Beziehung" zu der Stadt der Liebe. „Wir verbringen viel Zeit miteinander, manchmal nervt sie mich, doch sobald ich sie verlasse, vermisse ich sie schrecklich." Um immer wieder neue Blickwinkel auf Paris zu finden, muss Juan dann und wann mal raus aus der Stadt. „Dann komme ich mit frischen Augen zurück – denn in Paris gibt es immer wieder Unbekanntes zu entdecken. Manchmal lasse ich mich treiben und folge einfach meiner Intuition, finde eine interessante Person hier, ein spezielles Licht dort oder höre die entfernten Klänge eines Konzerts. Auf diese Weise habe ich schon vieles entdeckt." Juan erprobt auch immer die Arbeit mit verschiedenen Objektiven. „Das ist eine interessante Übung; ich gehe in einen bestimmten Bezirk, den ich gut kenne, doch ausgerüstet mit einem Objektiv, das ich nur selten benutze. So bekomme ich dann eine neue Sicht auf die Dinge." Juan begann in Rom mit der Fotografie, wo er als ausgebildeter Architekt und Kunsthistoriker viele antike Denkmäler fotografierte. Die Gebäude in der City, die barocke Malerei, die Lichtdramatik von Caravaggio, all das beeinflusste seinen Stil: „Ich versuche bei allen Szenen, die ich fotografieren will, dasselbe Licht einzufangen."

Juan Jerez del Valle ne devait passer qu'une quinzaine de jours à Paris, mais au fil du temps, une sorte de relation « romantique » s'est établie entre le photographe andalou et la Ville de l'Amour. « Nous passons beaucoup de temps ensemble, parfois, elle me fatigue, mais dès que je la quitte, elle me manque terriblement ». Afin de continuer à découvrir de nouvelles perspectives, Juan s'éloigne régulièrement de la capitale française. « Alors, je reviens avec un regard neuf – il y a toujours un Paris caché à explorer. Je pars souvent sans but déterminé, ce qui me permet de suivre mes intuitions, une personne intéressante, une lumière singulière ou le son d'un concert au loin. J'ai, de cette façon, réalisé de nombreuses découvertes ». Juan se lance également des défis en travaillant avec des objectifs différents. « C'est un exercice intéressant ; je marche dans tel quartier, que je connais bien, mais avec un objectif que j'utilise rarement. Ce qui me permet chaque fois de découvrir des angles nouveaux ». C'est à Rome que Juan, tout à la fois architecte et historien d'art, se lance dans la photographie, capturant nombre de monuments anciens. Les édifices romains, la peinture baroque, ou encore, la théâtrale lumière des œuvres du Caravage influencent son style : « dans les scènes que je photographie, ce que je recherche, c'est chaque fois le même type de lumière ».

Place de la Concorde
8e Arrondissement
Juan Jerez del Valle

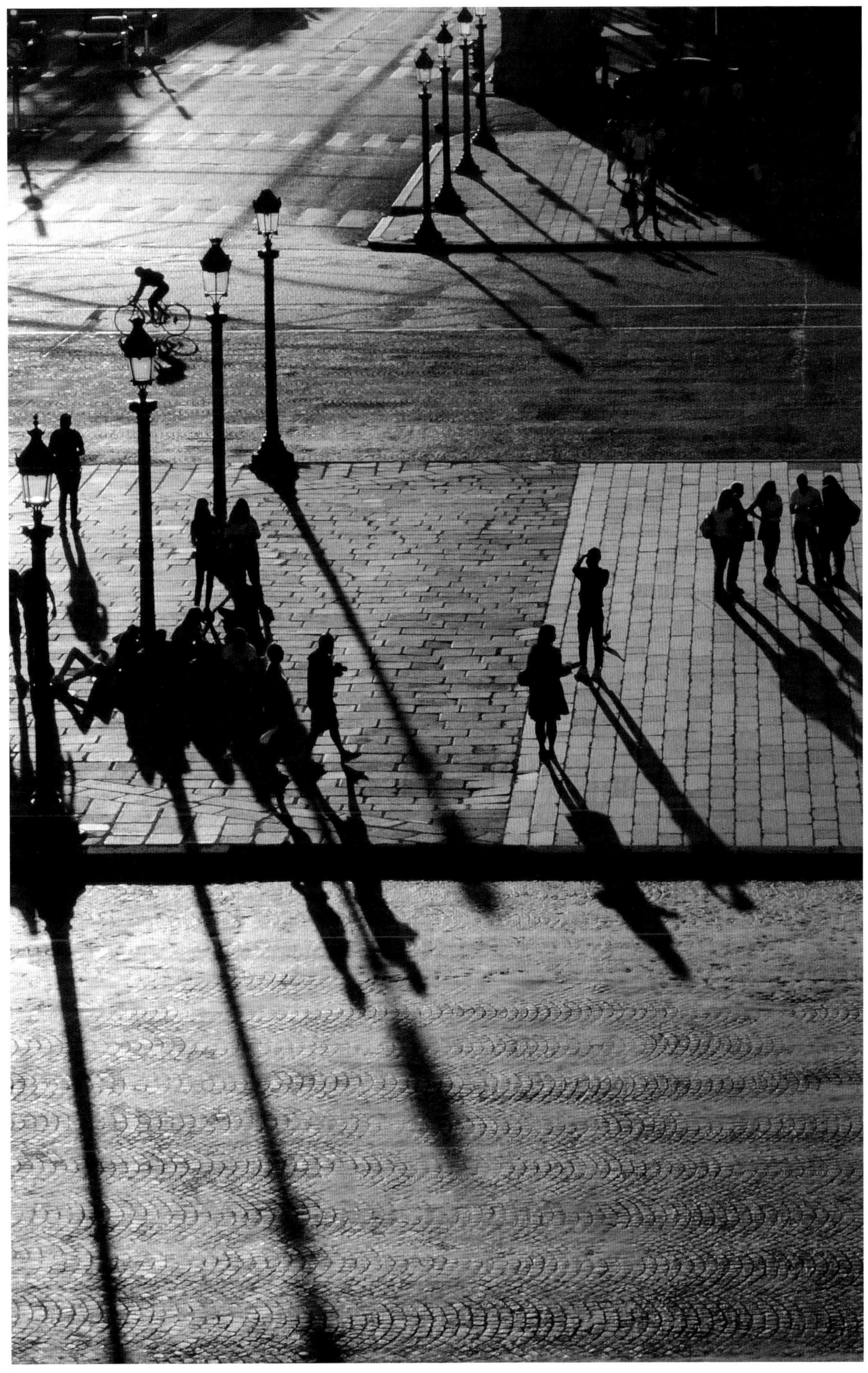

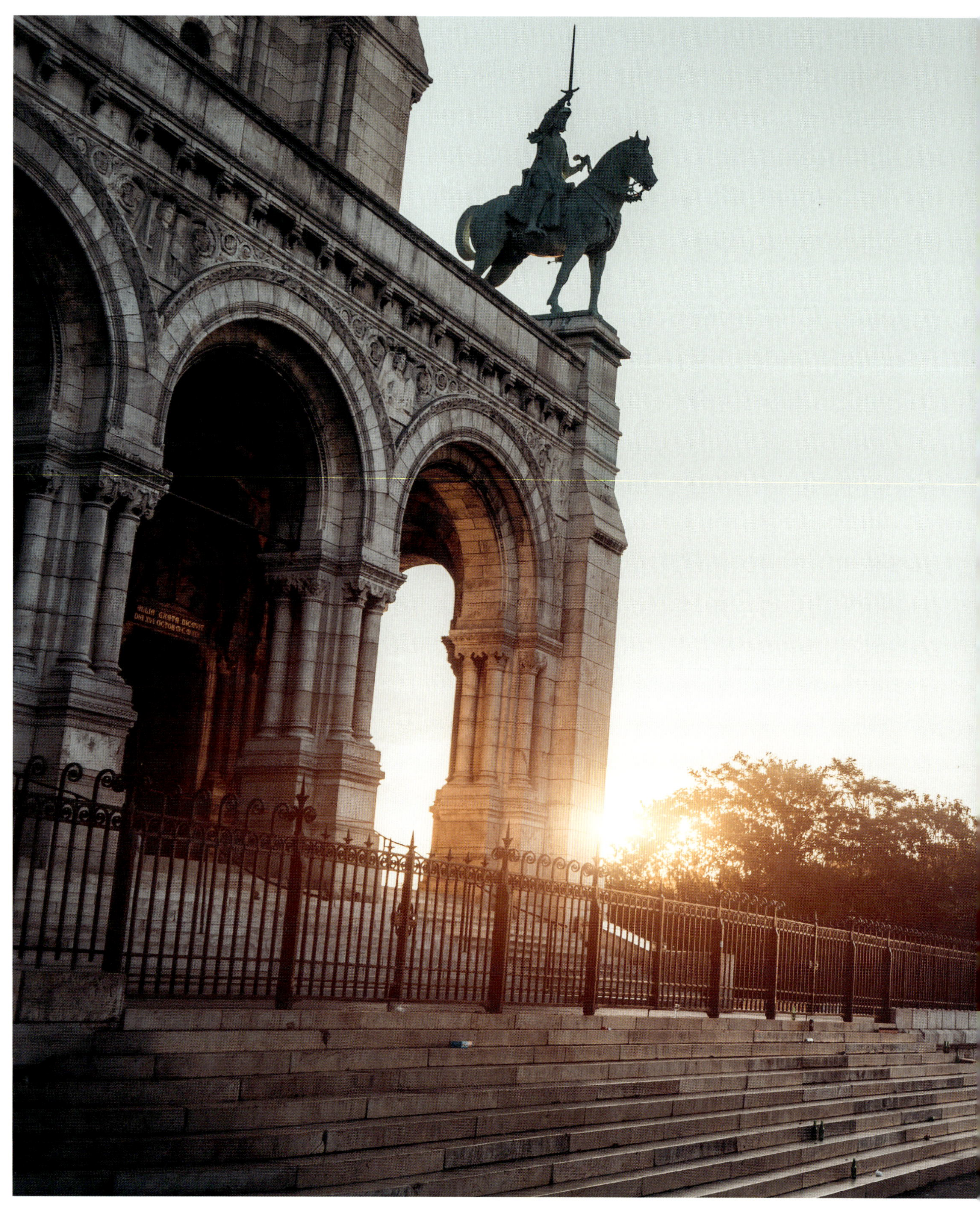

Basilique du Sacré-Cœur
Montmartre
Stijn Hoekstra

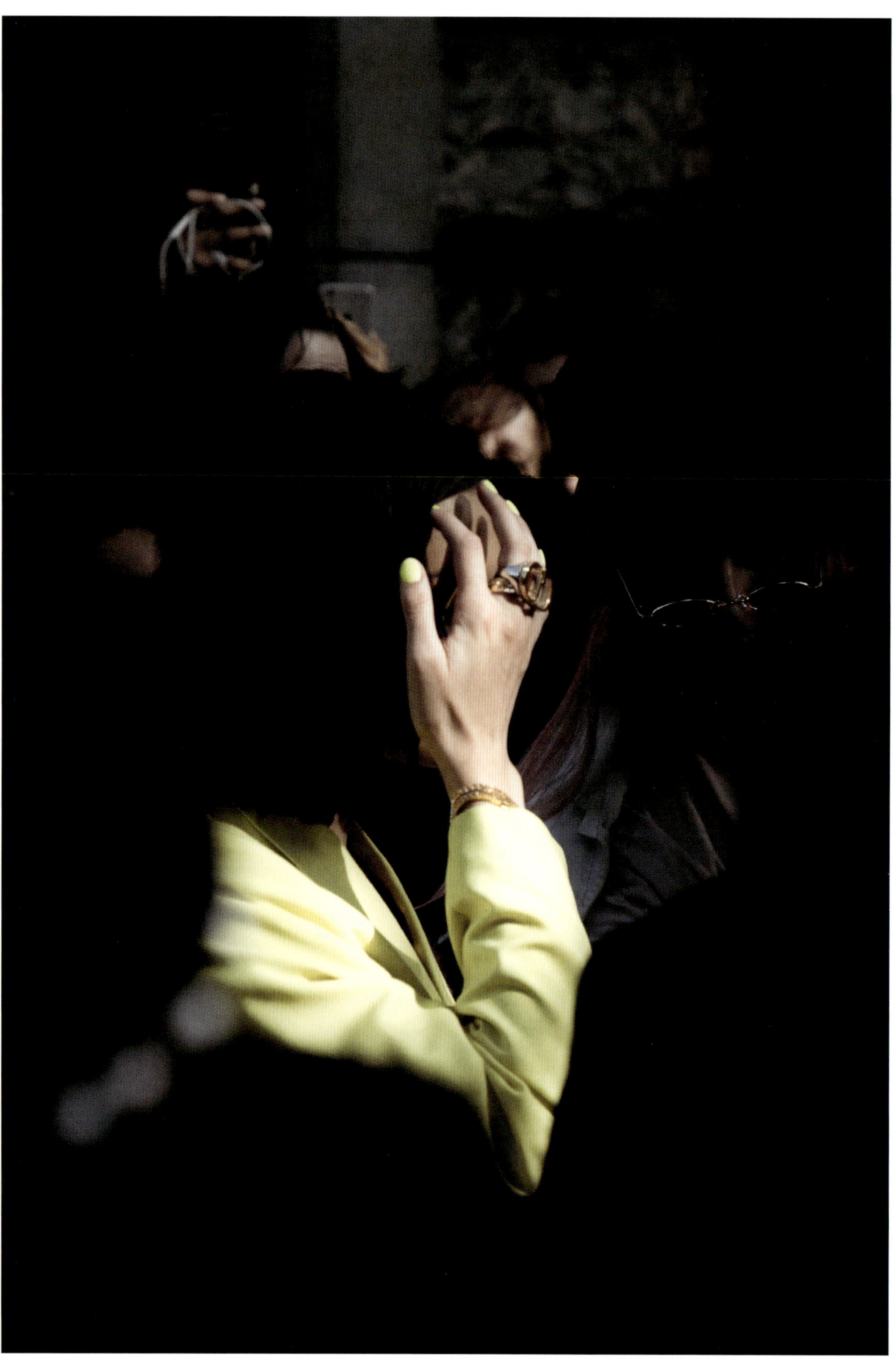

Garde Républicaine
4e Arrondissement
Dariusz Jasak

Place des Vosges
Le Marais
Erica Gonzalez →

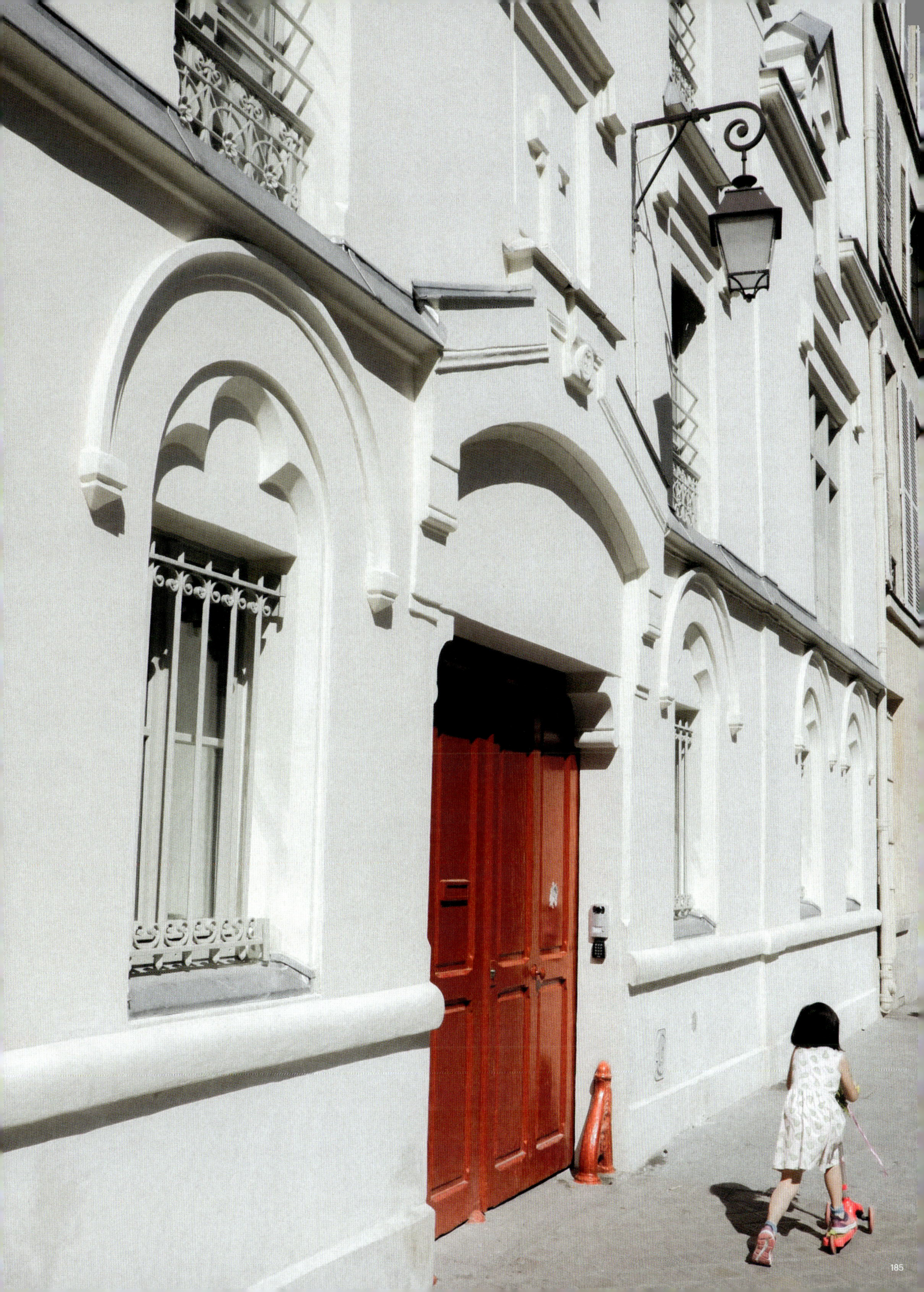

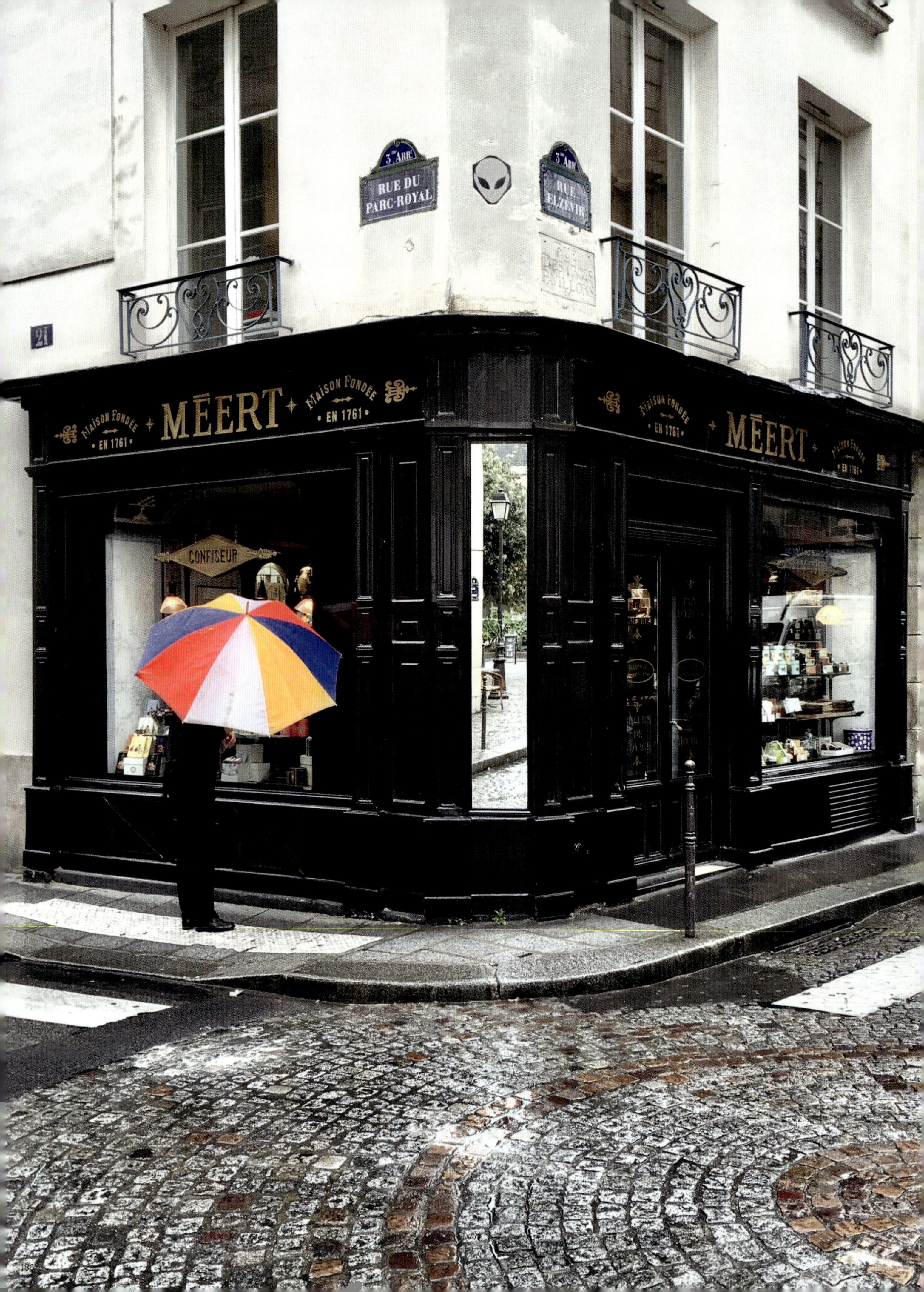
3e ARR.
RUE DU
PARC-ROYAL
3e ARR.
RUE
ELZEVIR
21
MEERT
Maison Fondée
EN 1761
CONFISEUR

I try to share and express the emotions that I feel when I observe a touching scene. To share its beauty, its atmosphere, and its serenity.

—Laetitia Modine

Méert
Le Marais
Willem Evers

Rue Poulbot
Montmartre
Romain Figuiere

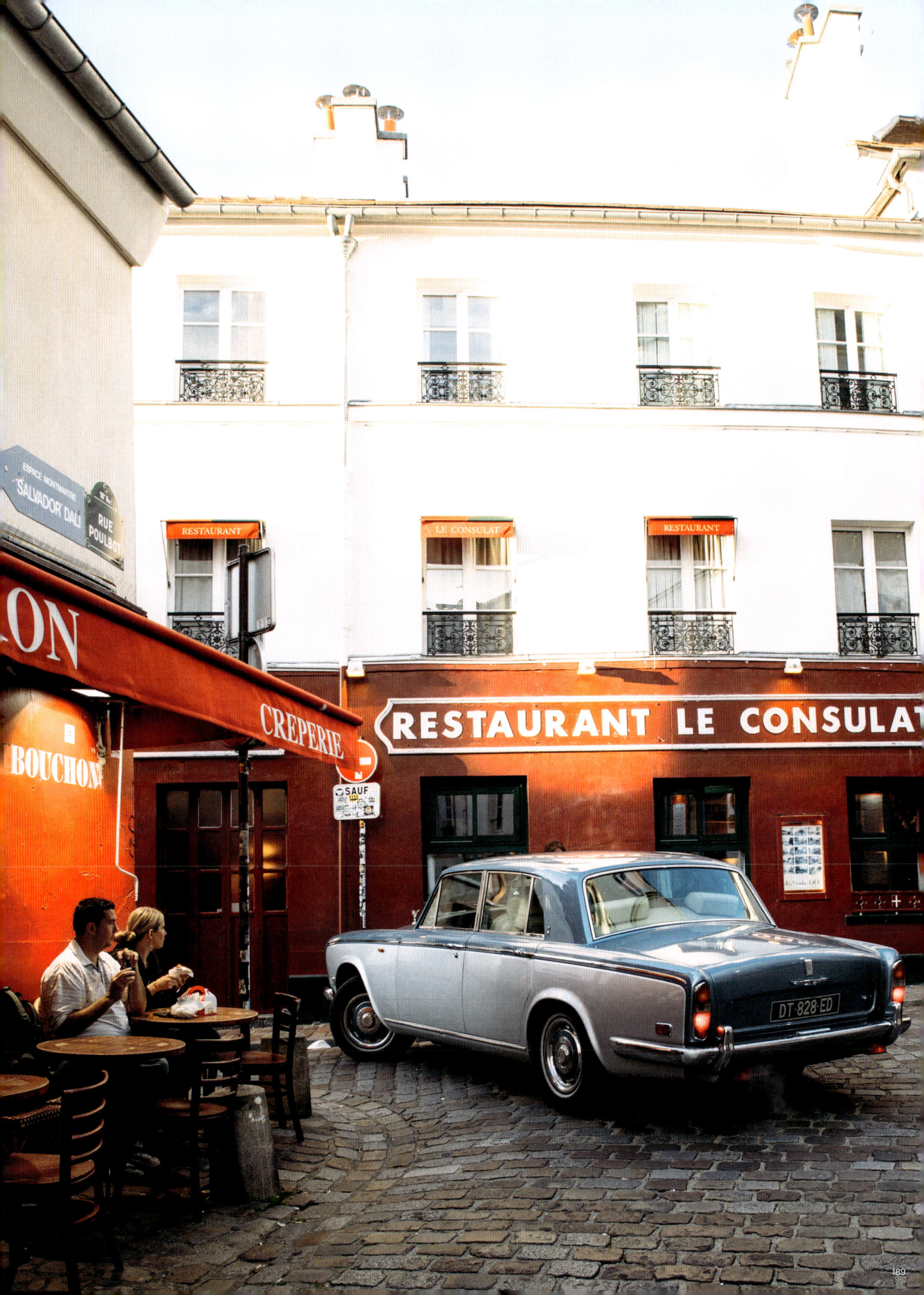
ESPACE MONTMARTRE
SALVADOR DALI
RUE POULBOT
RESTAURANT
LE CONSULAT
RESTAURANT
RESTAURANT LE CONSULAT
CREPERIE
BOUCHON
SAUF
DT-828-ED

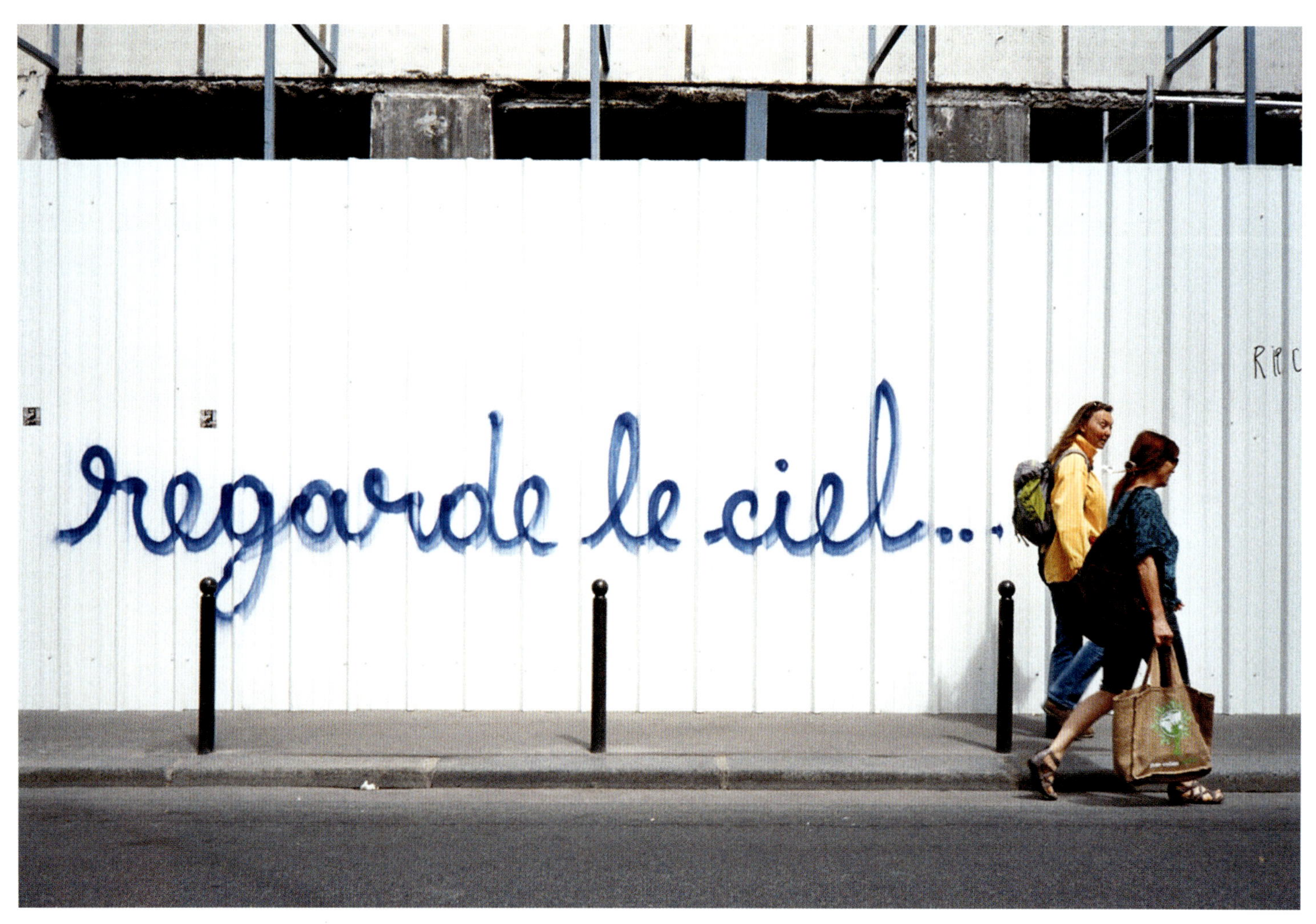

Rue Oberkampf
11e Arrondissement
IZBERG

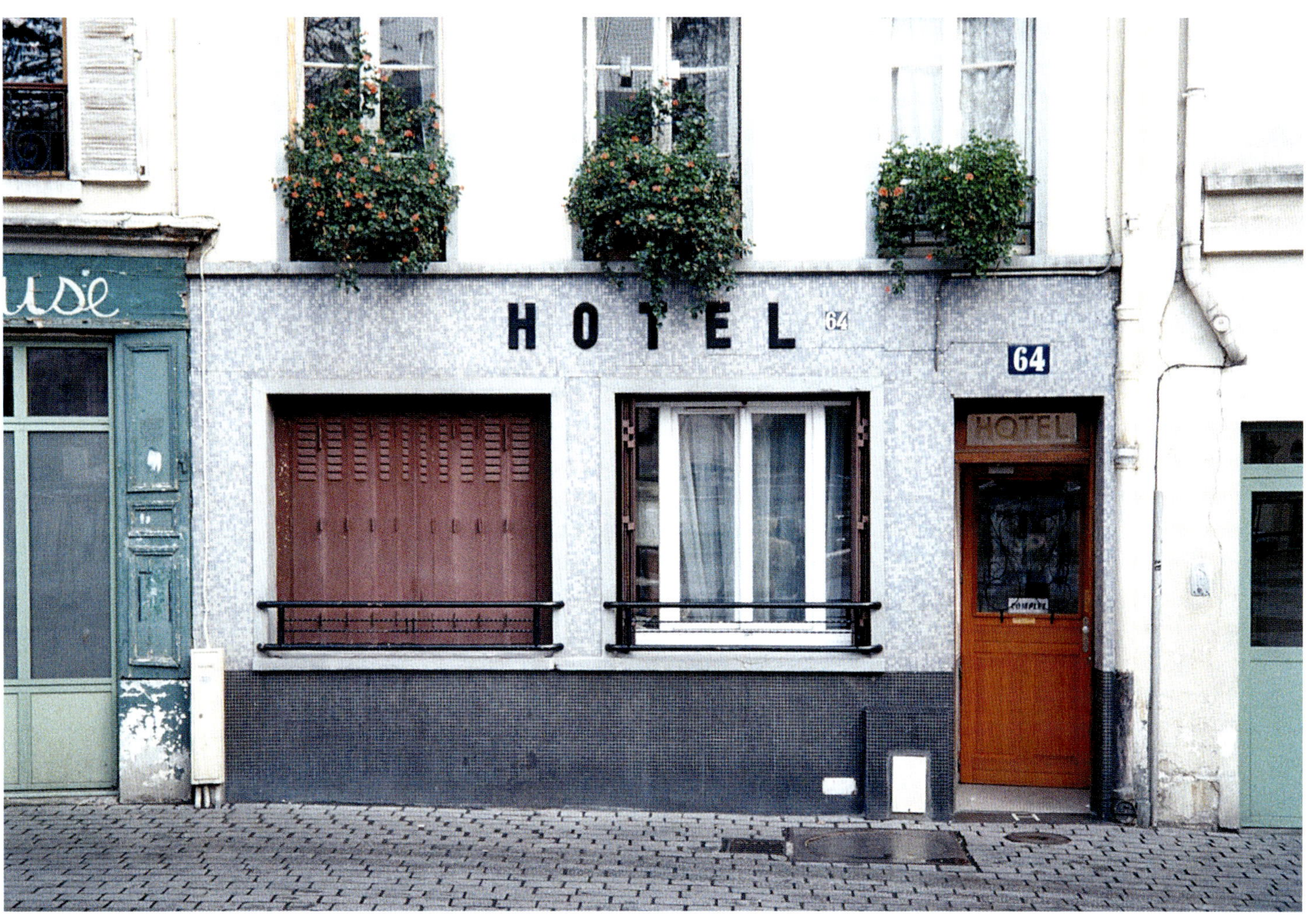

Place de la Reúnion
20e Arrondissement
IZBERG

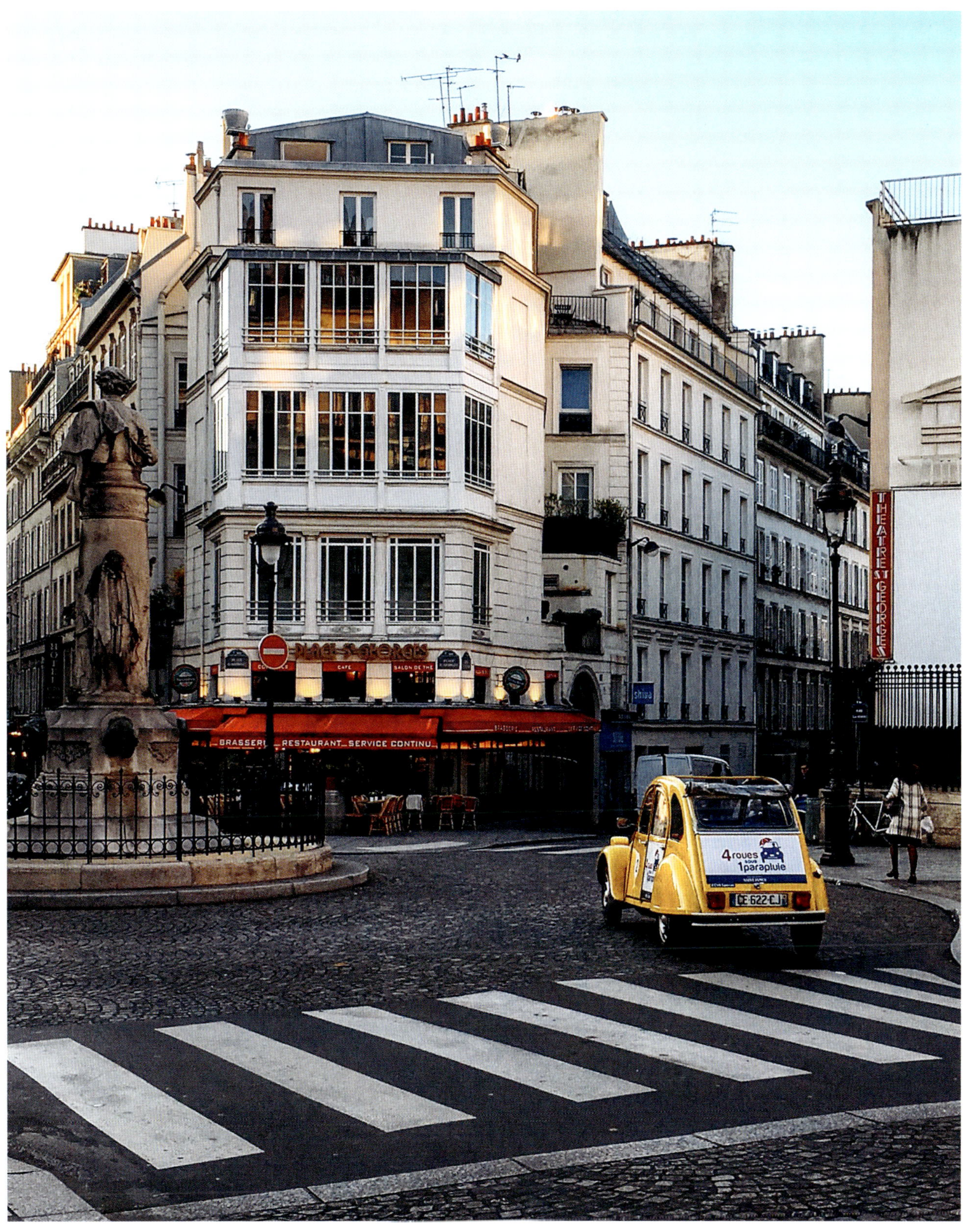

Place Saint-Georges
9e Arrondissement
Romain Figuiere

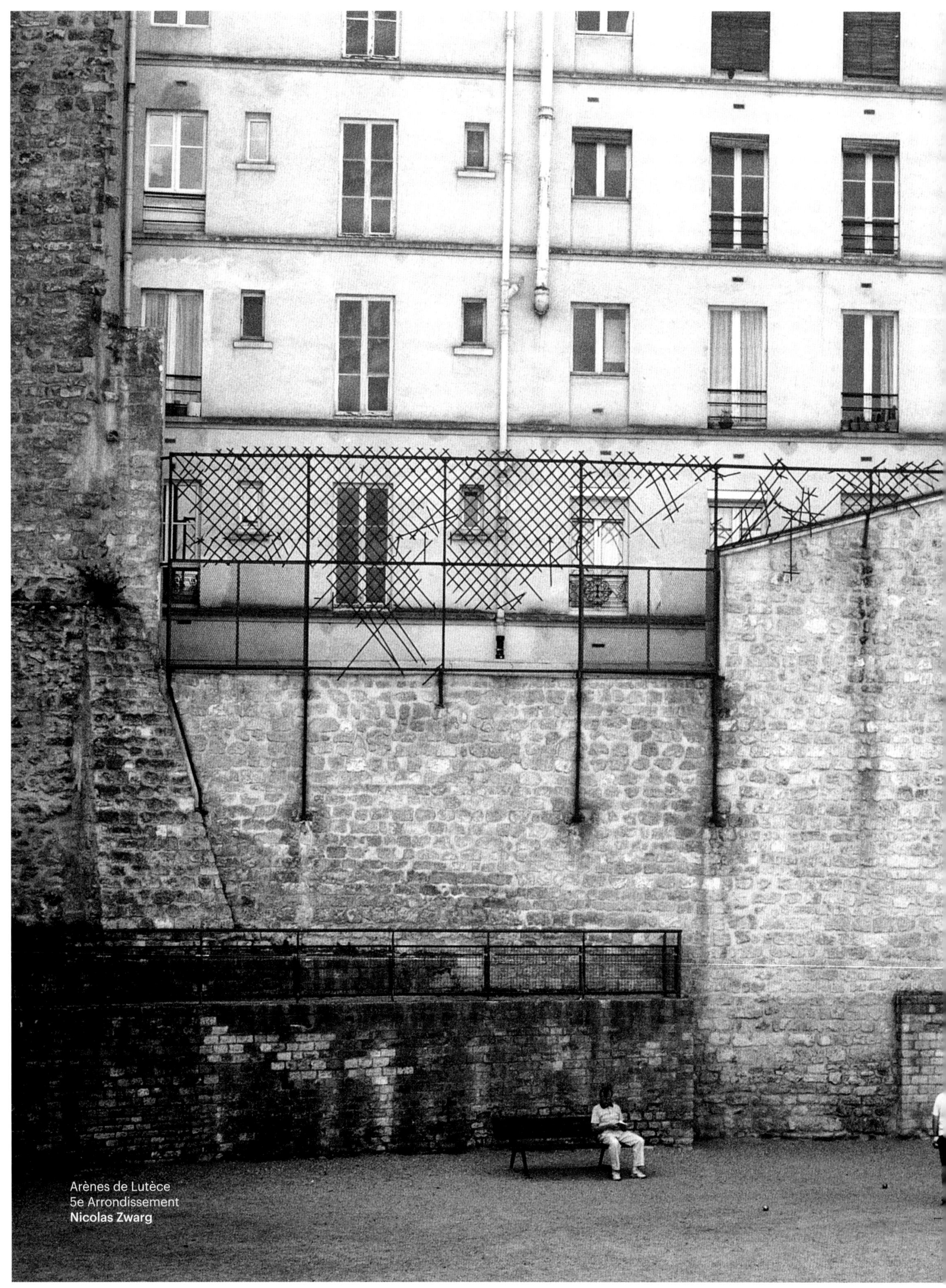

Arènes de Lutèce
5e Arrondissement
Nicolas Zwarg

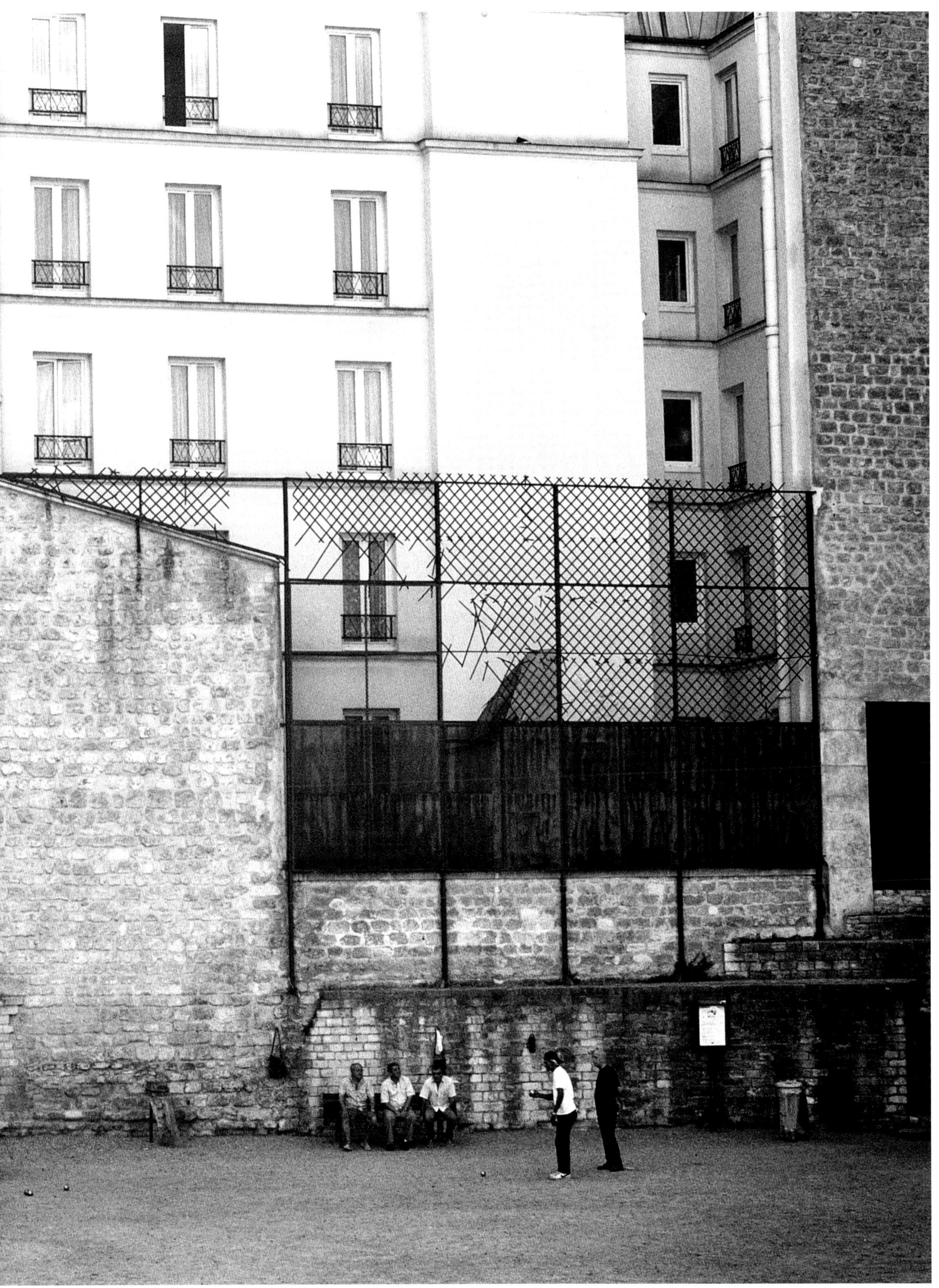

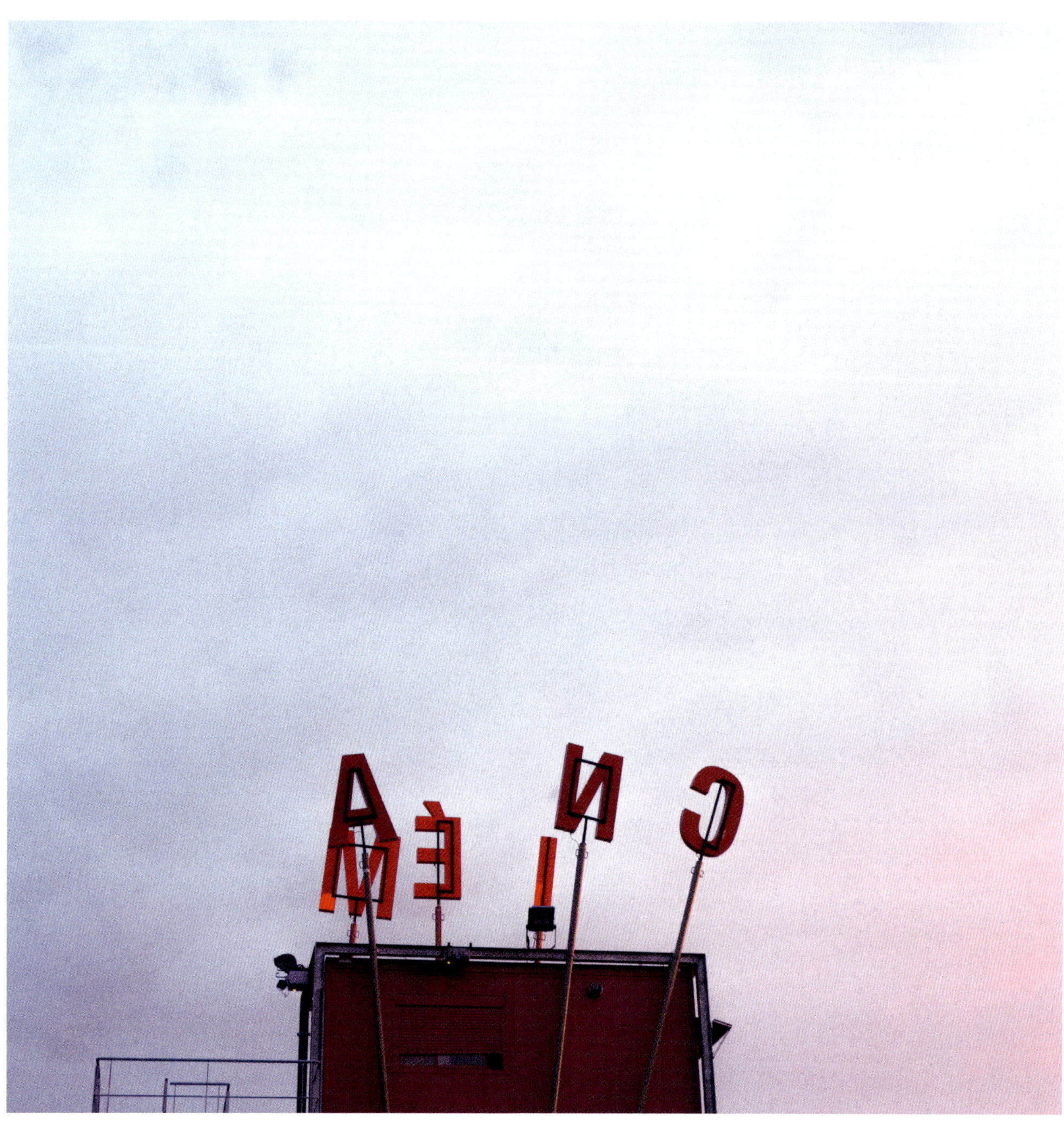

Cinéma en plein air
Parc la Villette
Hugo Katsumi

Grenelle Jasak
Dariusz Jasak —

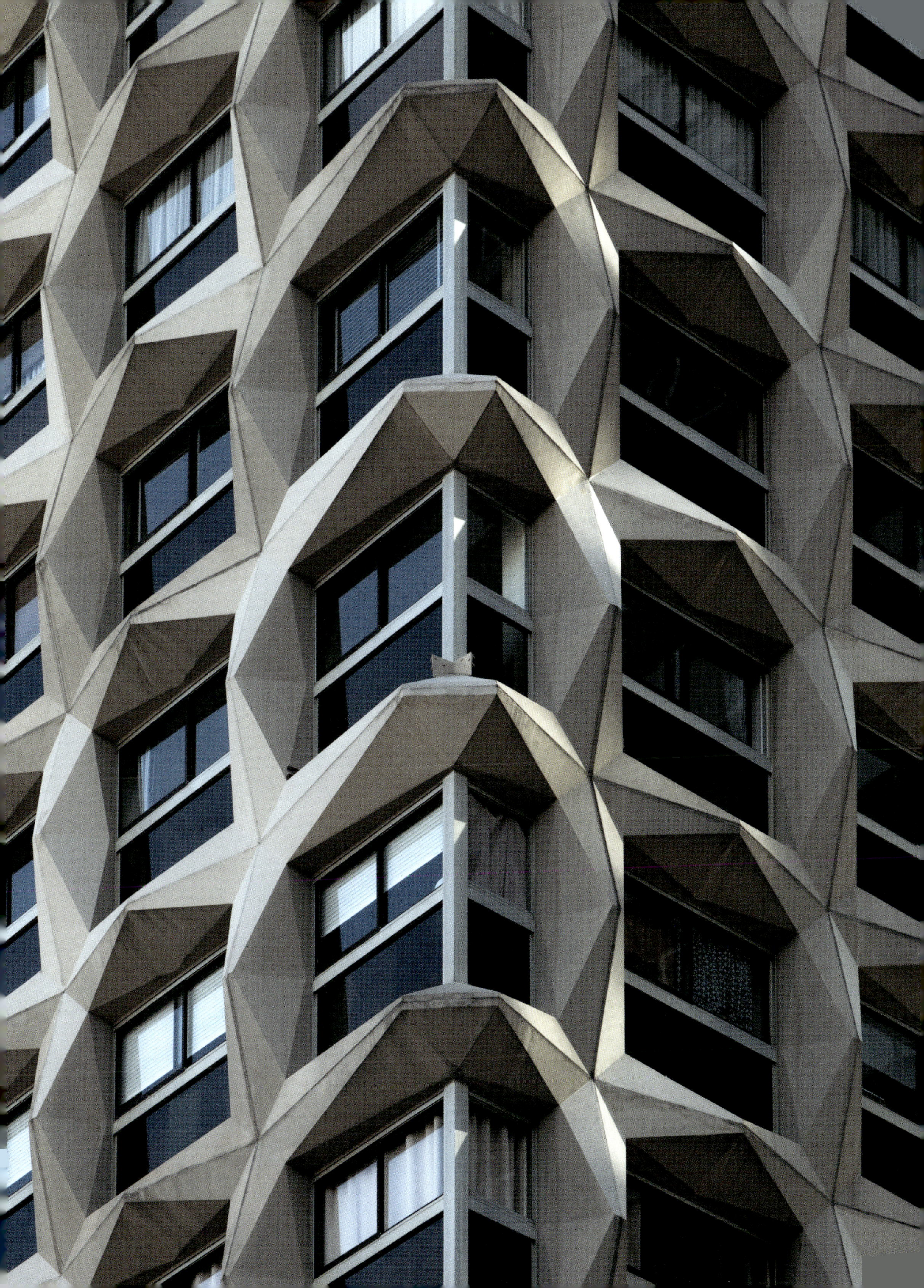

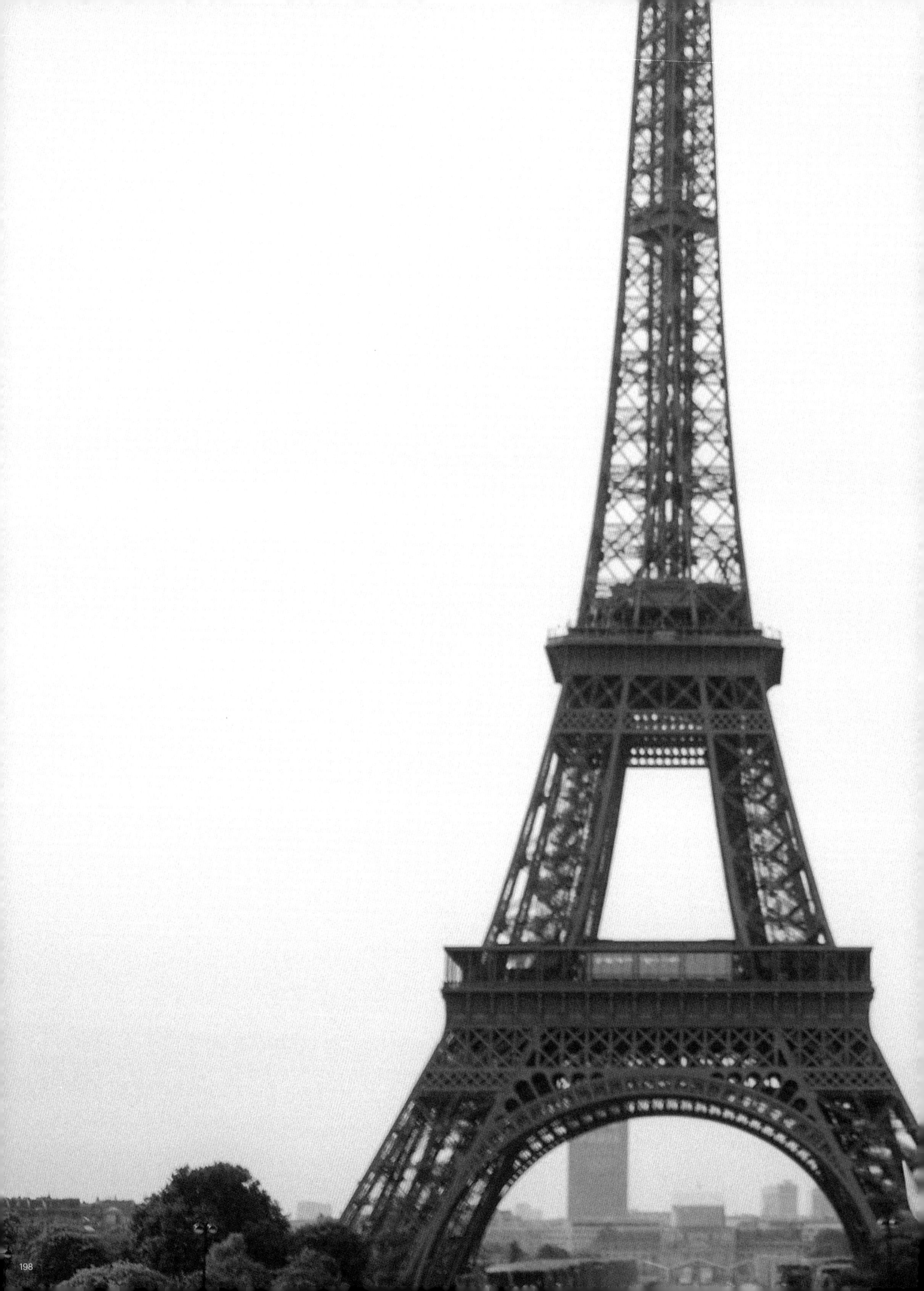

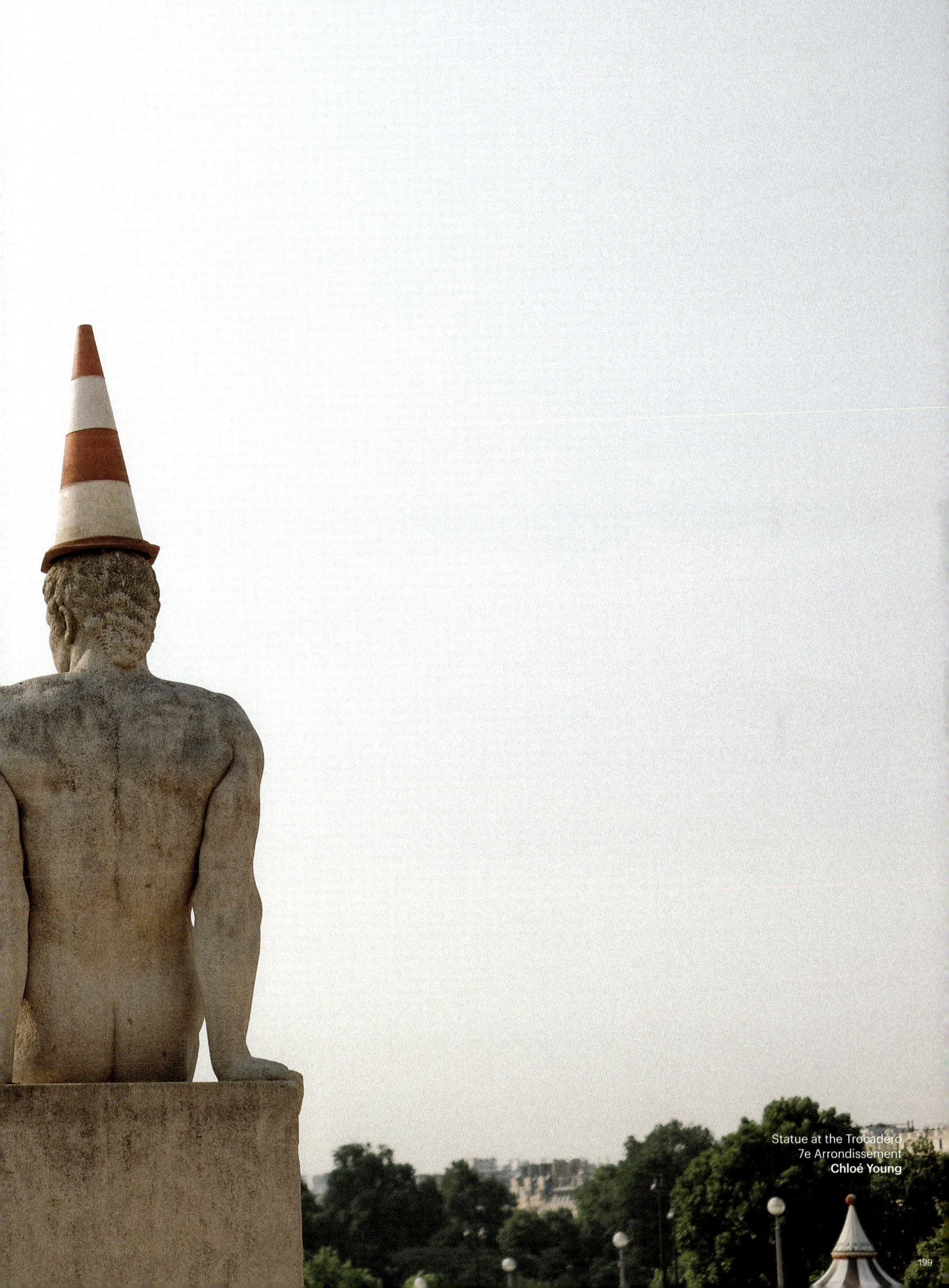

Statue at the Trocadéro
7e Arrondissement
Chloé Young

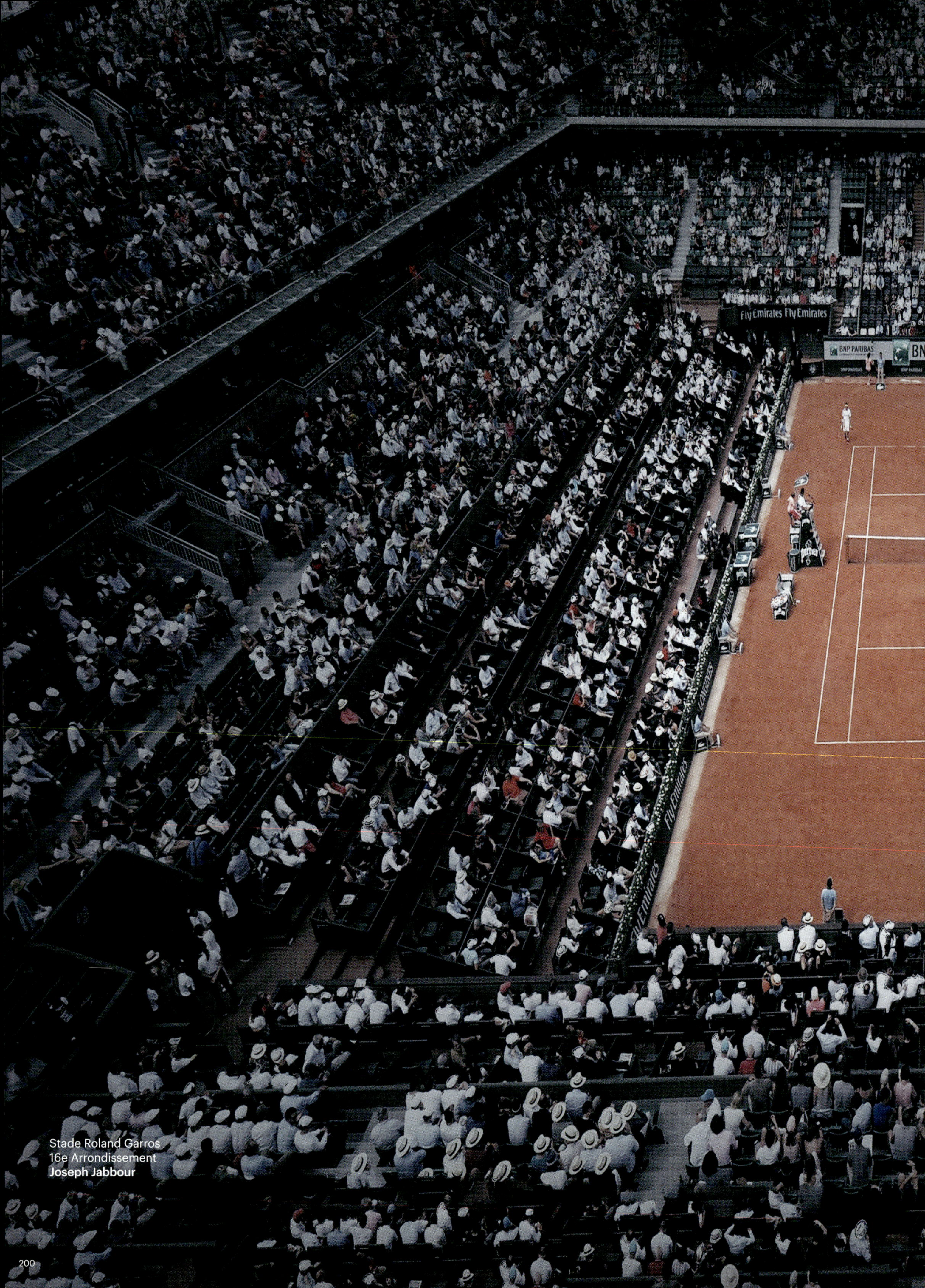

Stade Roland Garros
16e Arrondissement
Joseph Jabbour

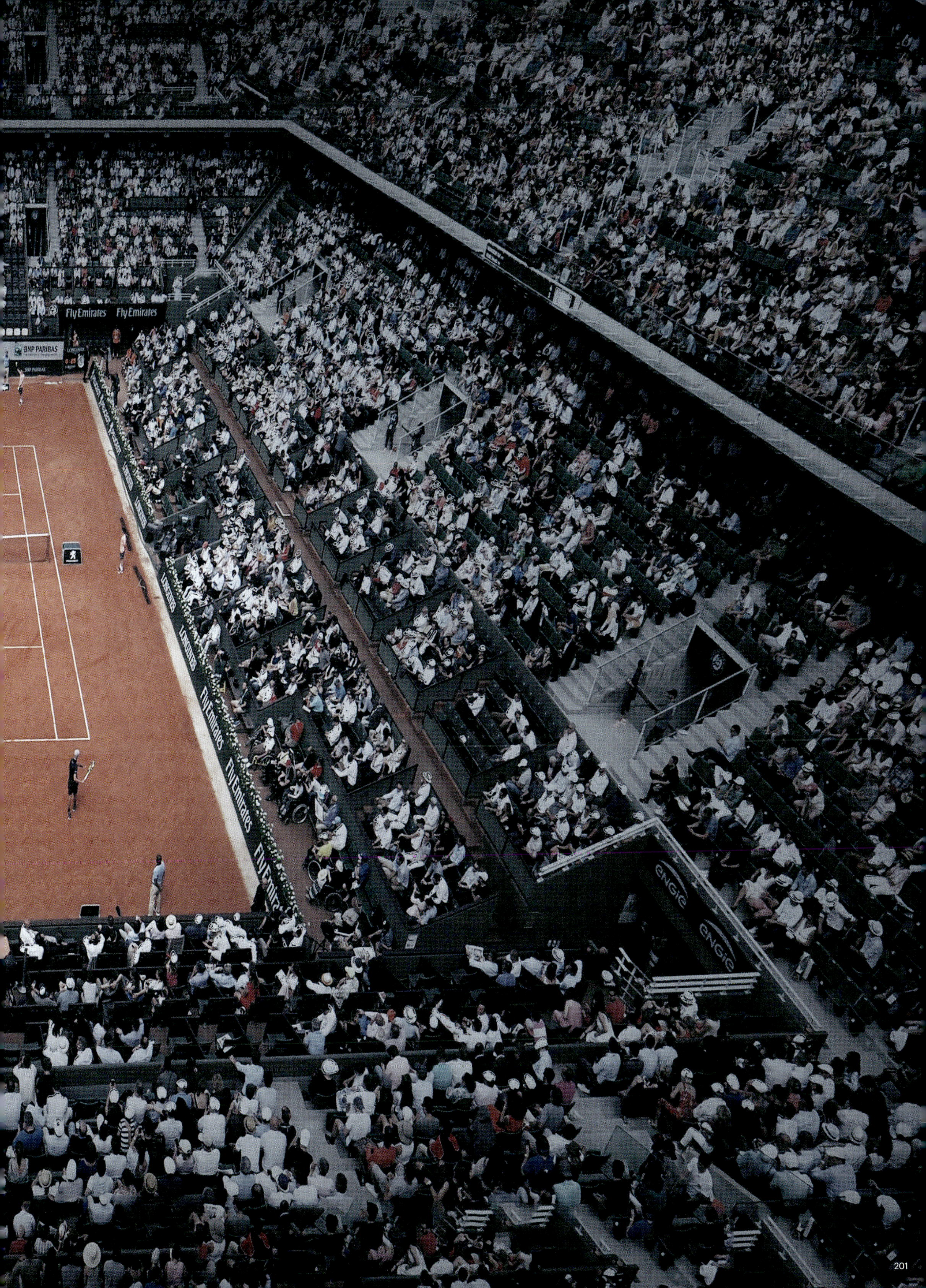
Fly Emirates
Fly Emirates
BNP PARIBAS
LONGINES
LONGINES
Fly Emirates
Fly Emirates
Fly Emirates
engie
engie

Boulevard Raspail
Today's Brew →

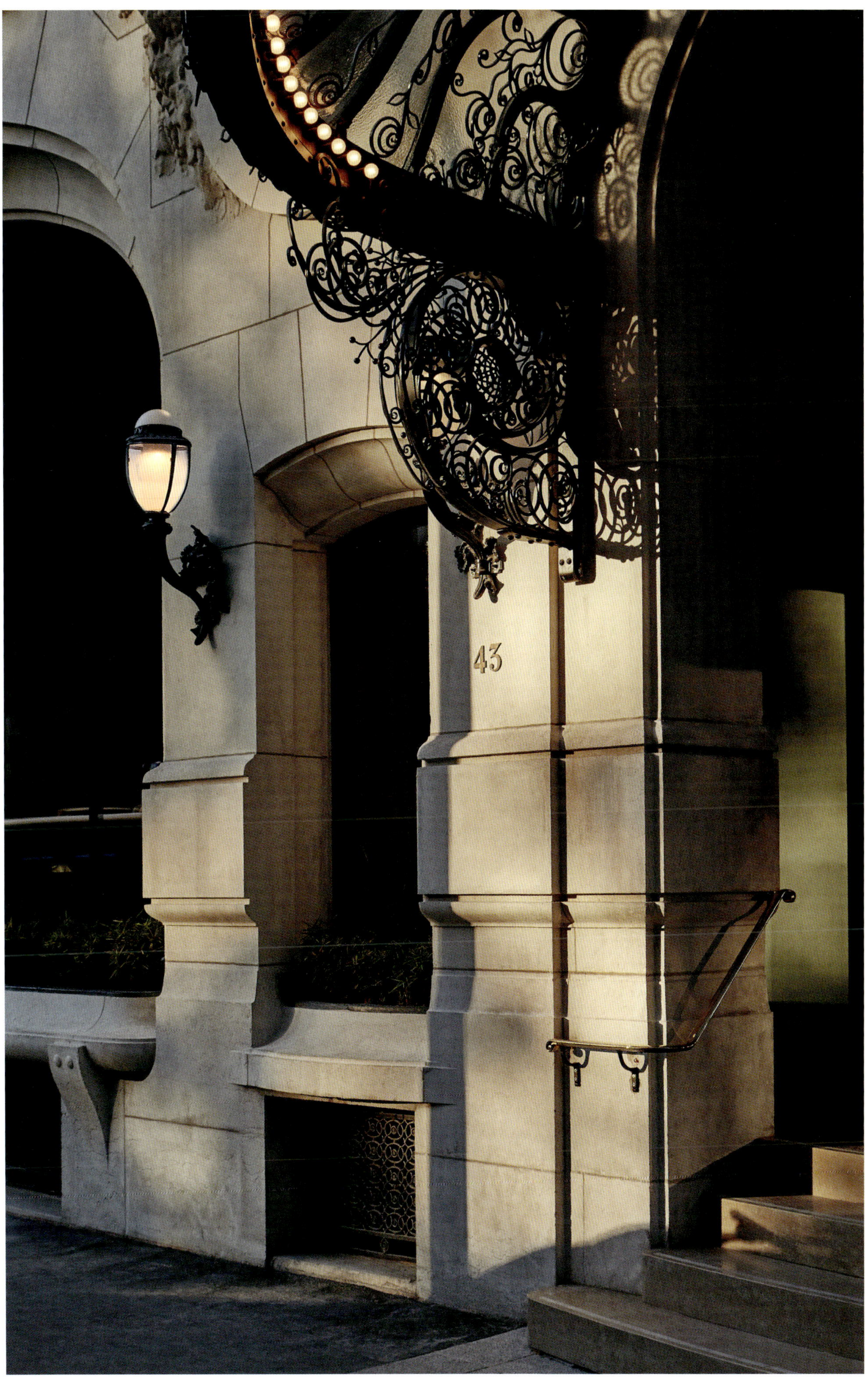
43

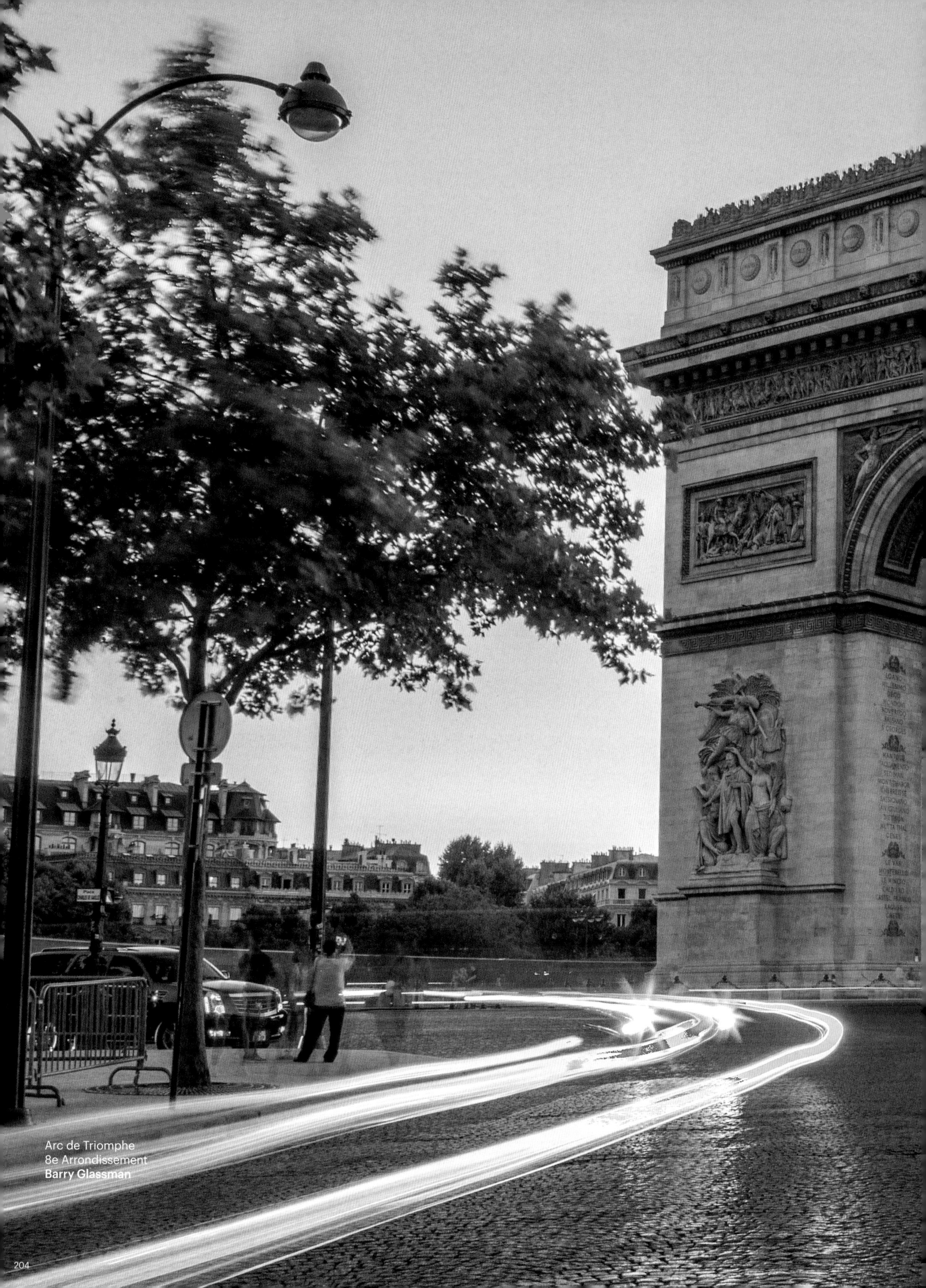

Arc de Triomphe
8e Arrondissement
Barry Glassman

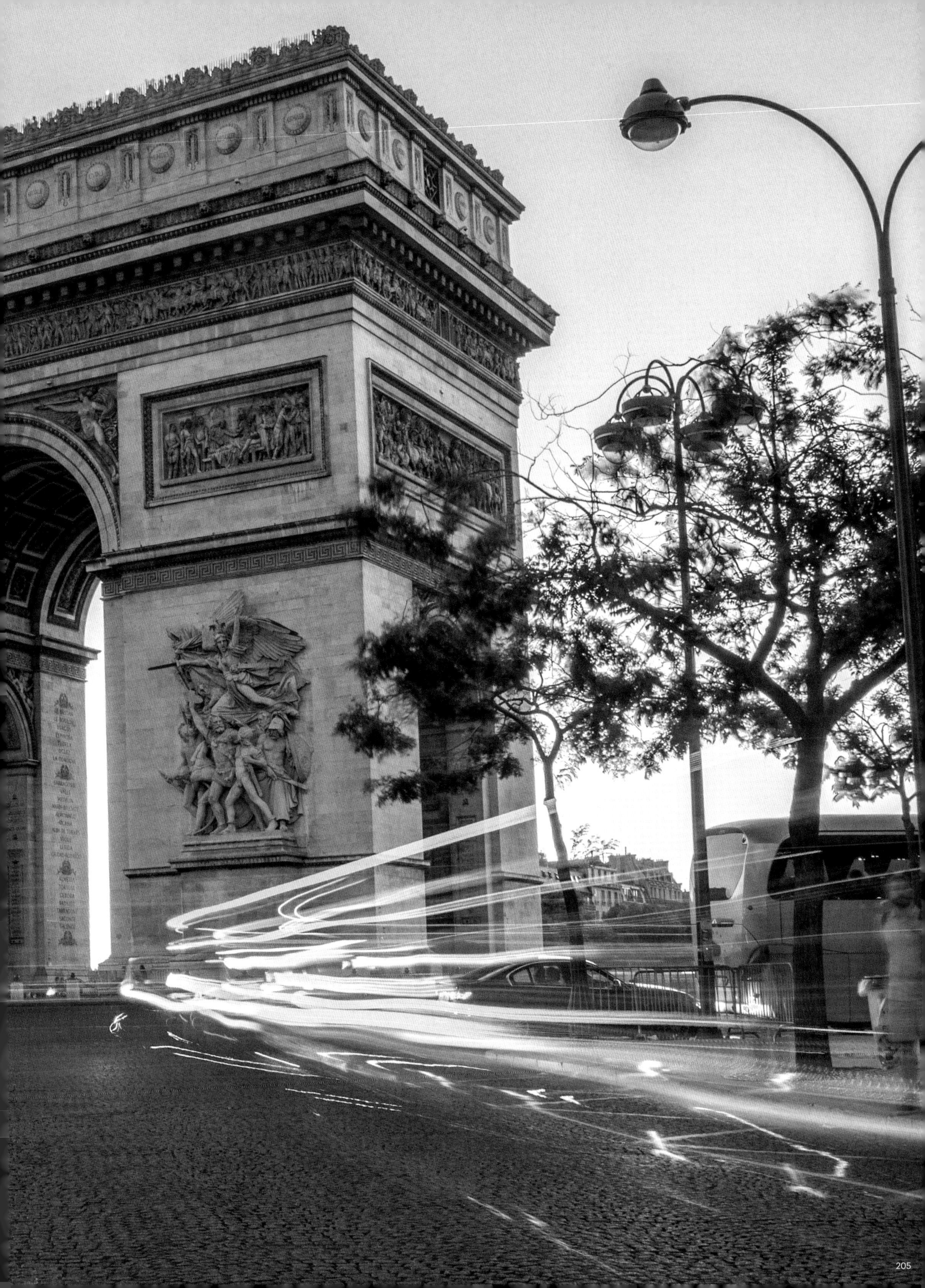

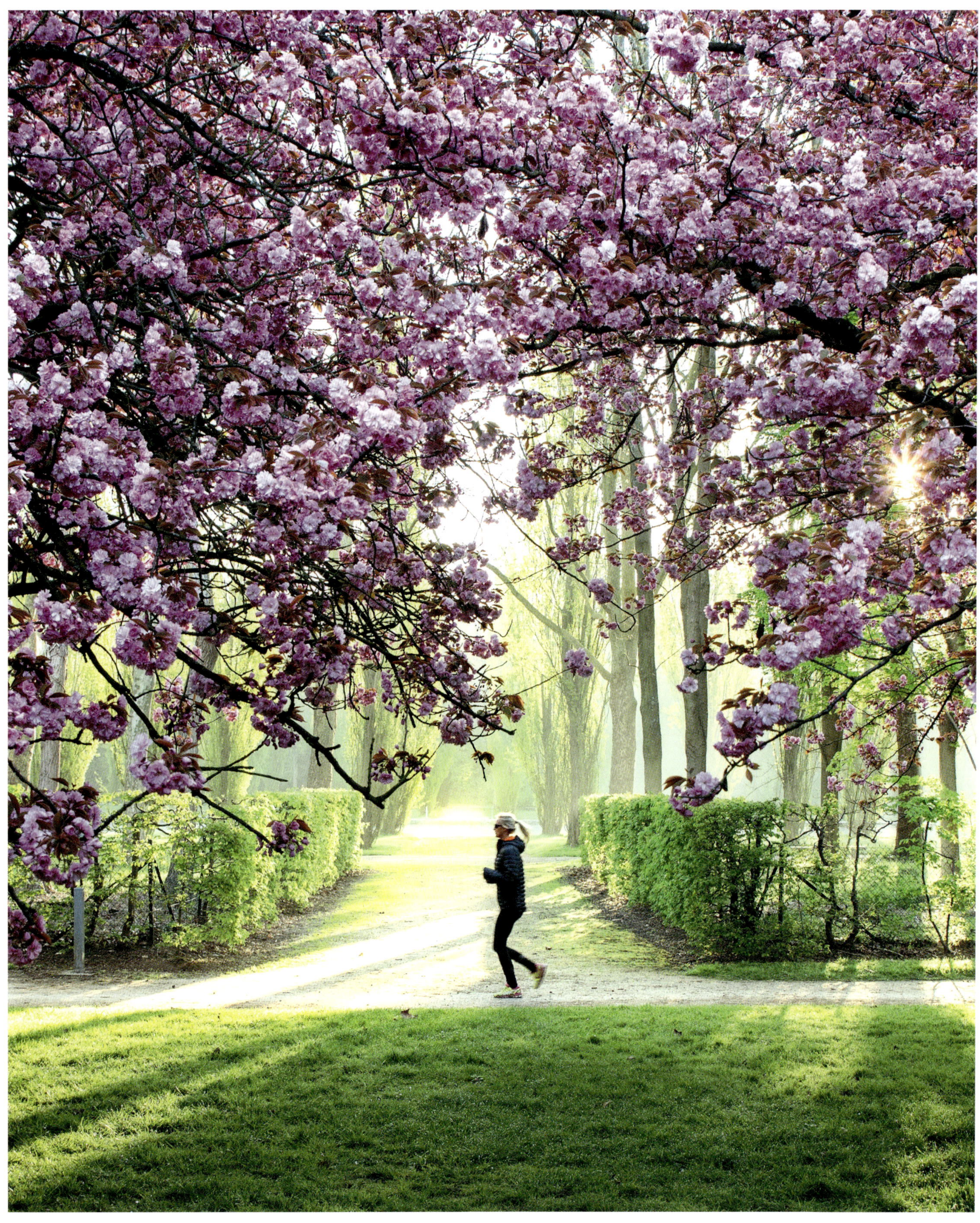

Parc de Sceaux
Romain Figuiere

All the different faces of this metropolis can be seen through the lenses of contemporary photographers.

—Joost Bastmeijer

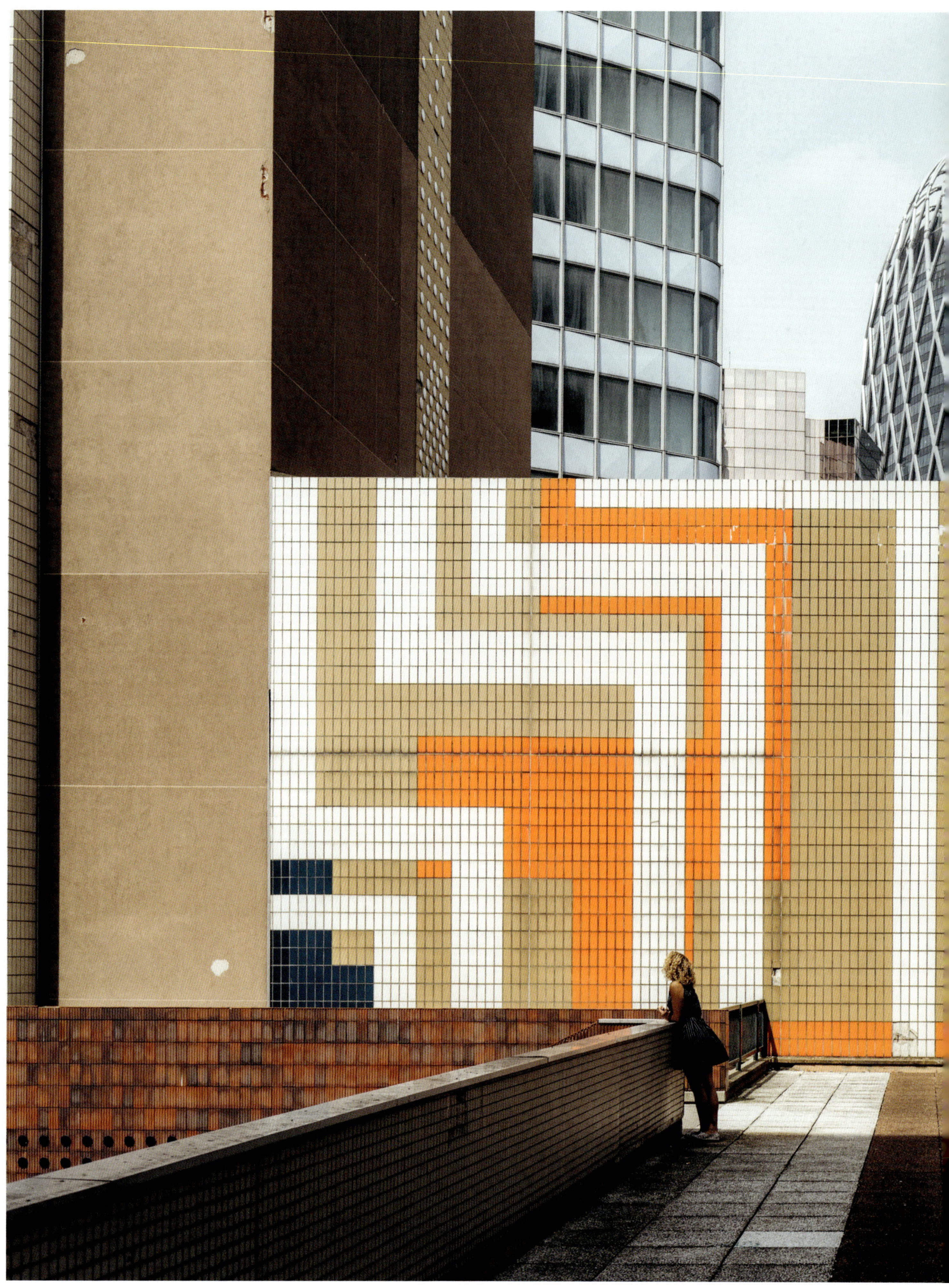

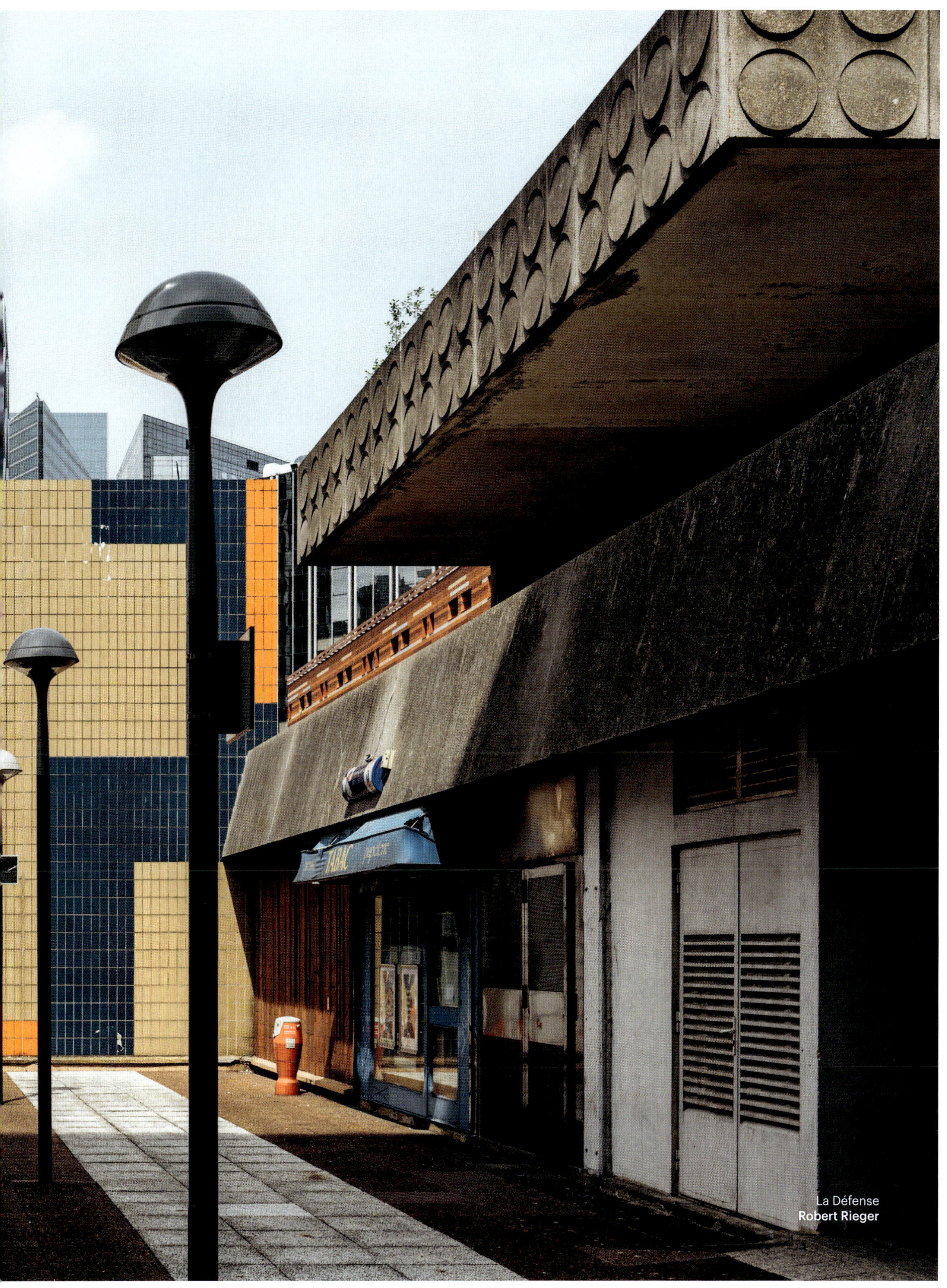

La Défense
Robert Rieger

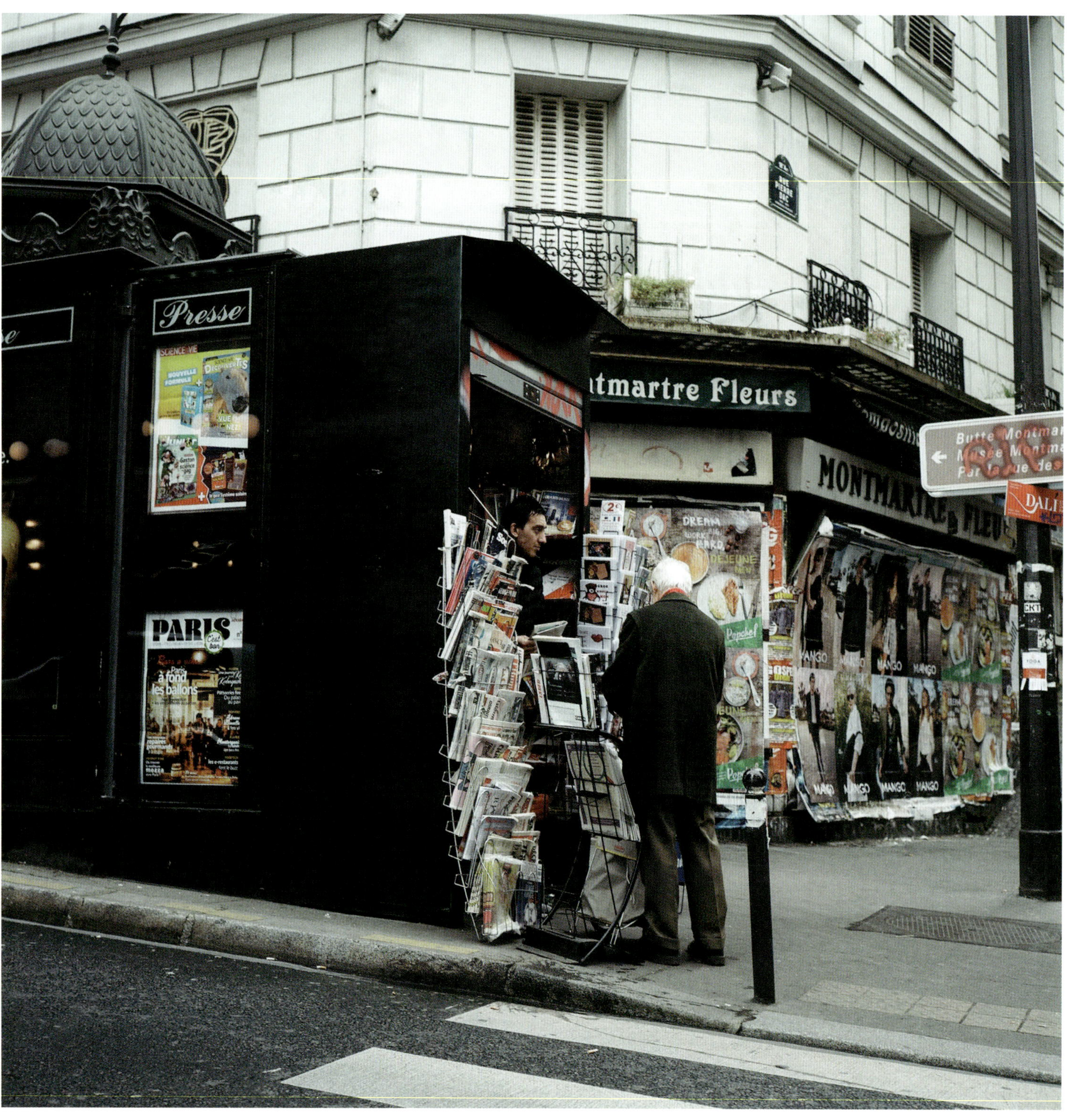

Rue Lamarck
Monmartre
Erica Gonzalez

Erica Gonzalez

hometown Seattle, USA
IG handle @filmandpixel

Erica Gonzalez is one of Paris' millions of visitors every year. Born in a Cuban family in Miami, she now resides in Seattle, USA and clearly remembers the first picture she took on French soil: "We were about to head into Paris via train. I took a photo of one of the platform officers. Just from what he was wearing alone, I knew I was going to have a field day in this beautiful place." Erica had always wanted to travel to Paris, because of her love for French cuisine, history, and fashion. "There is just a certain feel about Paris and France in general that screams love and romance," she says, "I wanted to feel that connection to emotion while experiencing the city." Moving through the capital, Erica focused on the people of Paris. "Like in any major city, everyone is stuck in their routine, moving at a fast pace, and they have no regard for you whatsoever." Still, she finds individuality and poetry amid the urban experience. "Every person is unique and that to me is something that no one can replicate. If you photograph someone right where they stand, at a specific time and in a specific place, you can just never replicate that photo again. It is all based on the chance or fate of that person being there, at that exact place and time. To me, there is nothing more exciting than capturing a photo of a person who has a unique look or happened to be placed in a striking composition. I just want to share the beauty that is sometimes found right there in the ordinary situation.

I want to show people that you don't have to have a beautiful person, incredible landscape with a sunset, or stunning architecture to take an interesting photo. I want people to know that they can photograph everyday things around them and bring something new or exciting to their work."

Erica Gonzalez gehört zu den Millionen Besuchern, die Paris jedes Jahr überschwemmen. Sie wurde als Kind einer kubanischen Familie in Miami geboren und lebt nun in Seattle, USA. Ganz deutlich erinnert sie sich an das erste Foto, das sie auf französischem Boden machte: „Wir fuhren mit dem Zug in Paris ein. Ich fotografierte einen der Beamten auf dem Bahnsteig. Allein schon von seiner Kleidung her wusste ich, dass in dieser wunderschönen Stadt ein weites Feld auf mich wartete." Erica wollte wegen ihrer Vorliebe für die französische Küche, Geschichte und Mode immer schon nach Paris reisen. „Paris und Frankreich haben einfach etwas an sich, das nach Liebe und Romantik schreit", sagt sie. „Ich wollte diese Verbindung zur Emotion bei meinen Entdeckungstouren in der Stadt erleben." Dabei richtete sie ihr Augenmerk auf die Menschen in Paris. „Wie in jeder Großstadt bewegen sie sich routinemäßig, hasten vorbei und niemand achtet auf dich." Doch mitten in dem städtischen Treiben findet sie viel Persönliches und Poetisches. „Jeder Mensch ist anders und für mich ist er damit unverwechselbar. Wenn du jemanden dort, wo er ist, zu einer bestimmten Zeit und an einem bestimmten Platz fotografierst, kannst du niemals das gleiche Foto noch mal machen. Alles beruht auf dem Zufall oder Schicksal, dass diese Person gerade dort ist, genau an diesem Ort und zu dieser Zeit. Für mich gibt es nichts Spannenderes, als ein Foto von einer Person zu machen, die einen ganz eigenen Blick hat oder in eine besondere Situation geraten ist. Ich möchte anderen einfach die Schönheit zeigen, die sich manchmal aus einer ganz normalen Situation ergibt, möchte den Menschen zeigen, dass man für interessante Bilder keine schönen Menschen braucht, keine außergewöhnliche Landschaft mit Sonnenuntergang oder keine besondere Architektur. Die Leute sollen einfach wissen, dass sie ganz alltägliche Dinge um sie herum fotografieren können und damit ihre Arbeit neu oder spannend machen können."

Erica Gonzalez fait partie des millions de visiteurs qui se rendent dans la capitale chaque année. Née dans une famille cubaine à Miami, elle vit actuellement à Seattle, aux Etats-Unis, et se souvient avec netteté de la première photographie prise sur le sol français : « Nous allions à Paris en train. J'ai photographié l'un des agents de la gare, et rien que d'après sa tenue, j'ai su que j'allais vivre un grand jour dans ce lieu magnifique ». Portée par son amour de la cuisine, de l'histoire et de la mode françaises, Erica voulait depuis toujours se rendre à Paris. « Il y a simplement cette sensation que Paris, et la France en général, exprime avec force l'amour et le romantisme, affirme-t-elle. J'avais envie d'éprouver ce rapport à l'émotion tout en faisant l'expérience de la ville ». Lorsqu'elle sillonne la capitale, Erica se concentre sur ses habitants. « Comme dans toute grande ville, chacun est pris par sa routine et se déplace rapidement, sans prêter aucune attention à autrui ». Dans cette expérience urbaine, pourtant, elle découvre individualité et poésie. « Chaque personne est unique, et c'est, à mes yeux, quelque chose que nul ne peut reproduire. Lorsque vous photographiez quelqu'un qui est simplement là où il est, à un moment et dans un lieu précis, jamais, vous ne pourrez reproduire cette image. Tout repose sur le hasard ou le destin qui veut que cette personne se soit trouvée là, en un lieu et un temps donné. Pour moi, il n'est rien de plus excitant que de capturer l'image d'une personne dont l'apparence est unique et qui se trouve être placée dans une composition étonnante. Je souhaite simplement partager la beauté qui peut émerger juste là, dans une situation ordinaire. Je veux montrer qu'il n'est pas besoin d'avoir un protagoniste séduisant, ni un paysage incroyable avec un coucher de soleil ou un édifice surprenant, pour obtenir une image intéressante. Je souhaite que chacun sache qu'il peut photographier le quotidien et en faire surgir quelque chose d'excitant ou de nouveau dans son travail ».

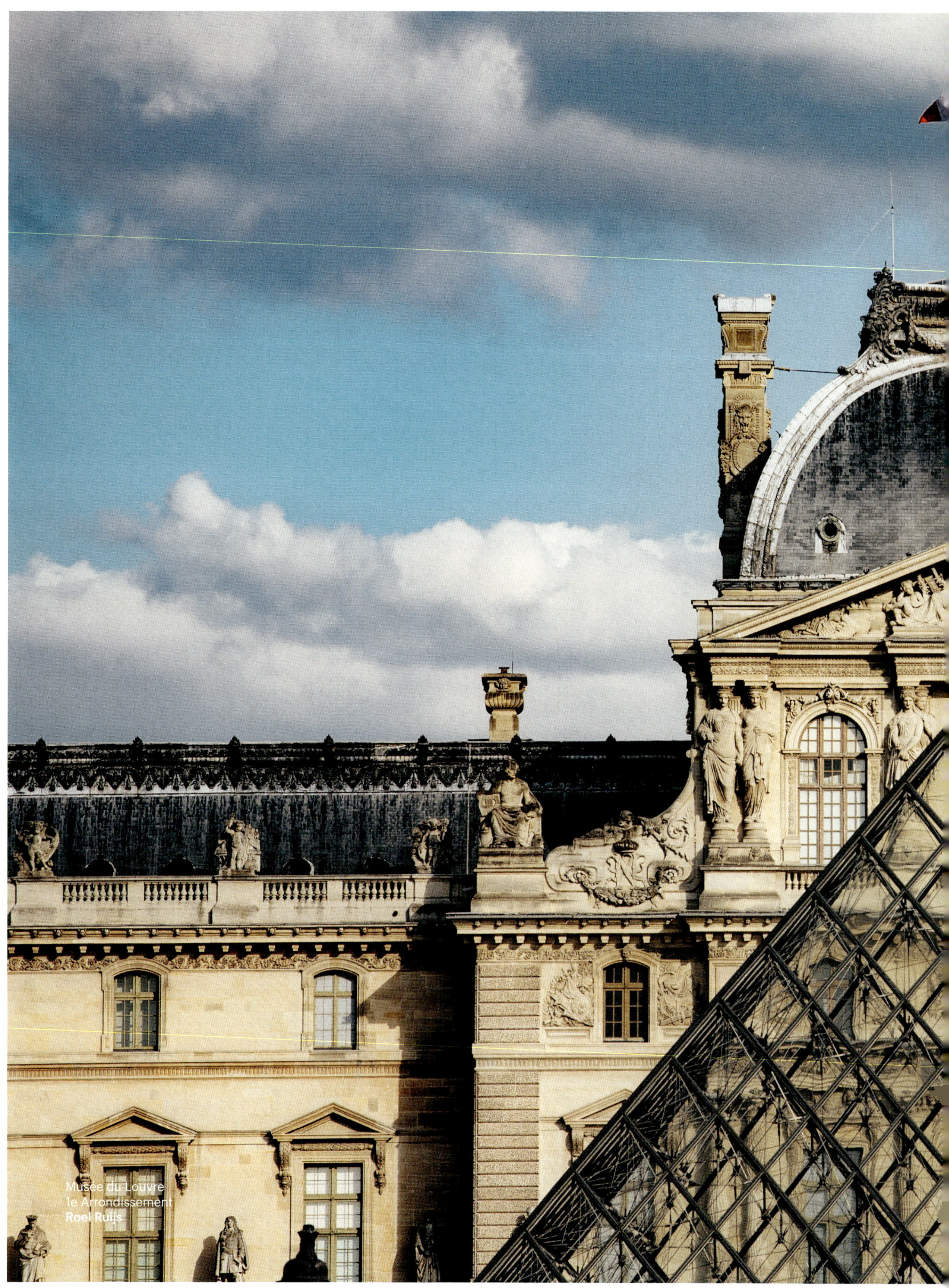

Musée du Louvre
1e Arrondissement
Roel Ruijs

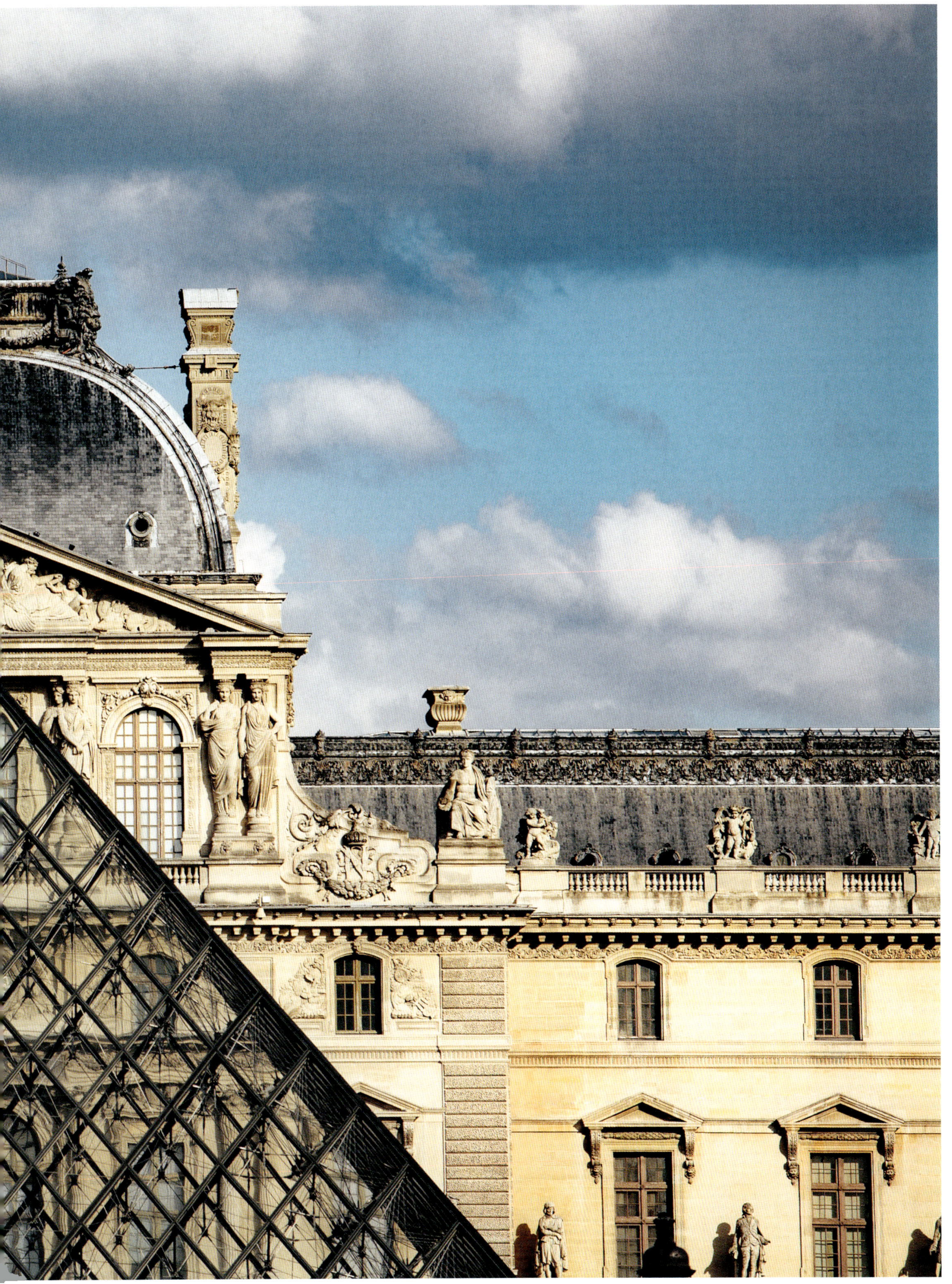

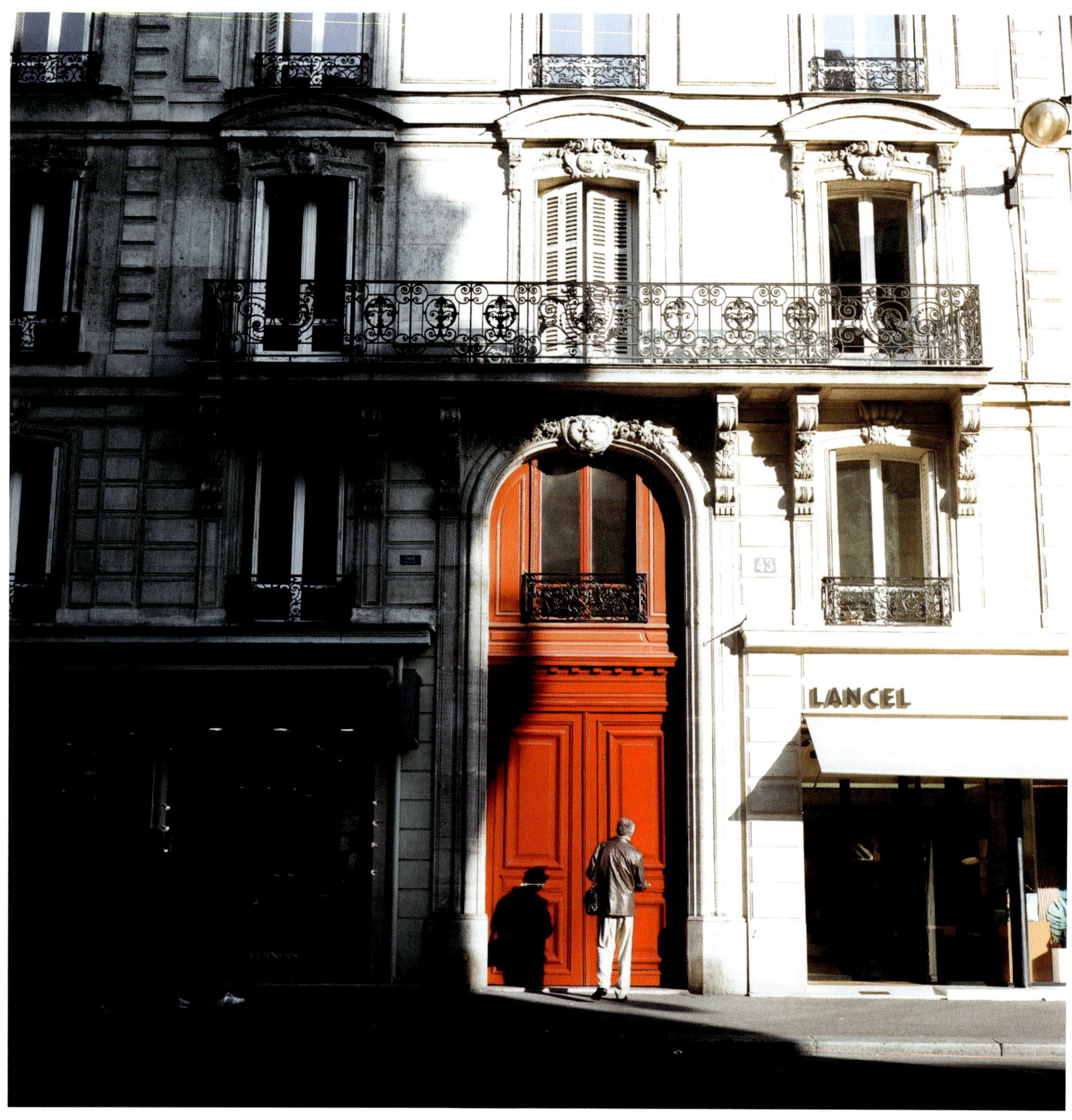

Rue de Rennes
6e Arrondissement
Erica Gonzalez

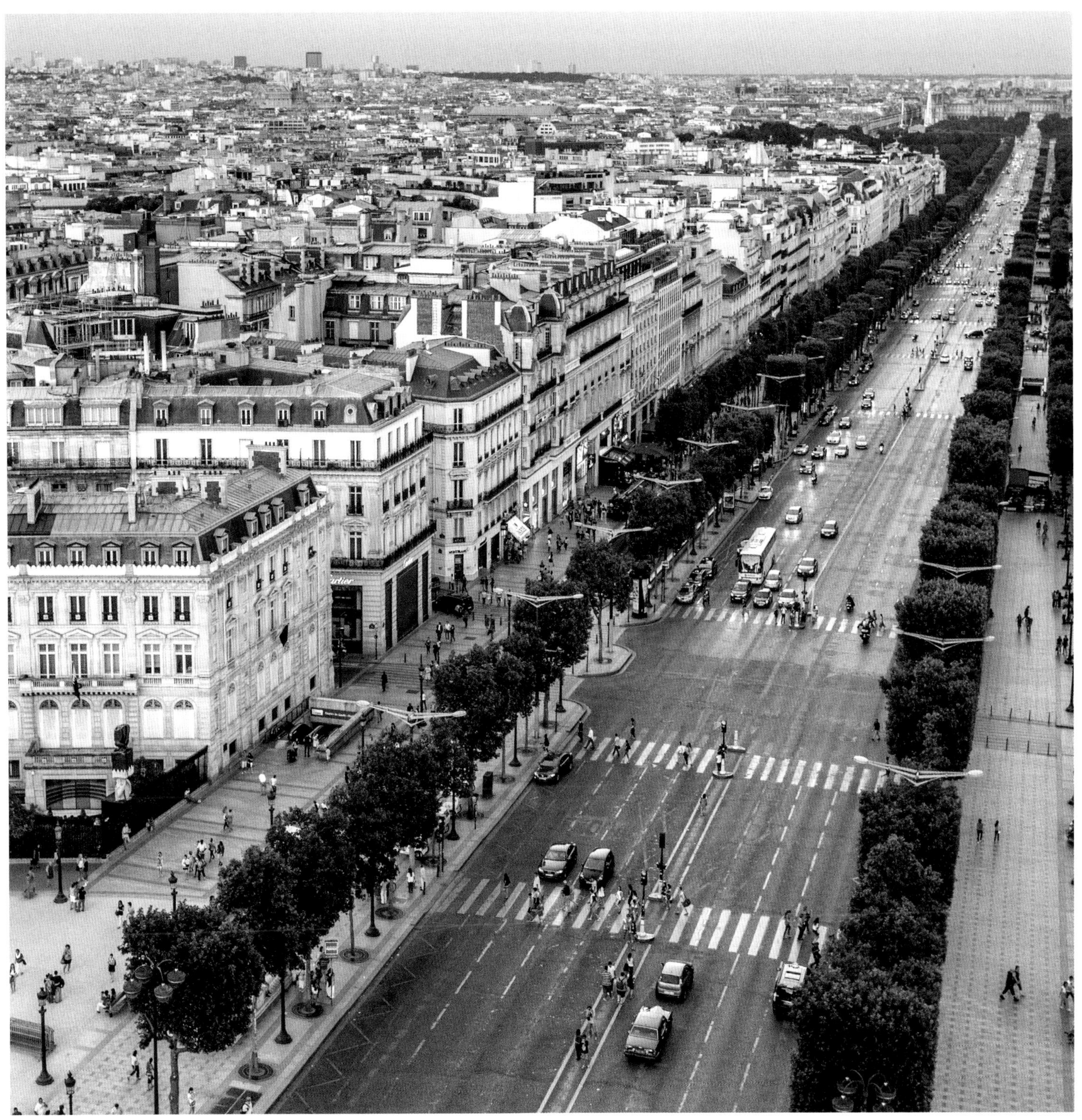

Avenue des Champs-Élysées
8e Arrondissement
Barry Glassman

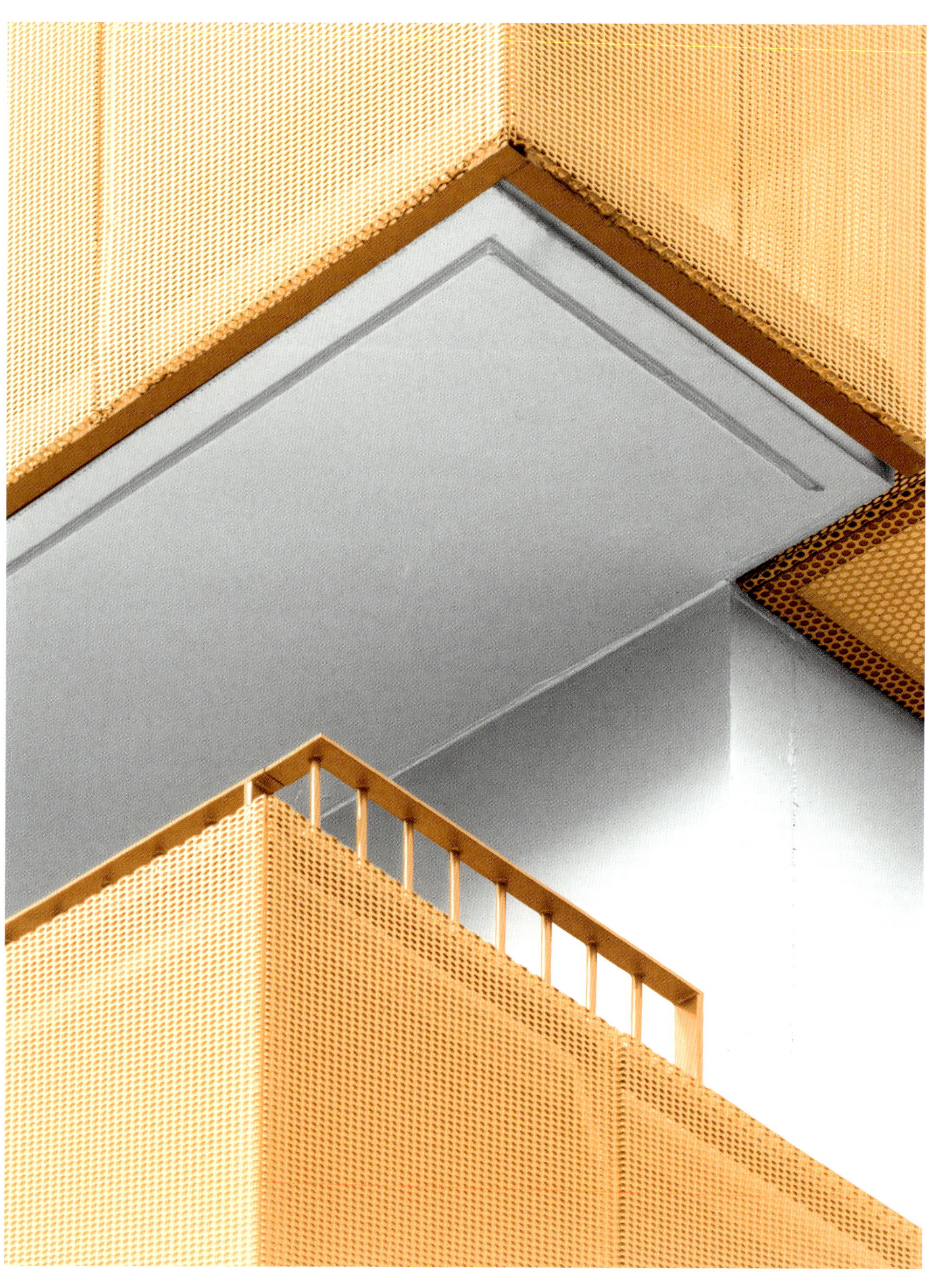

Student residence Boulogne Seguin
Billancourt–Rives de Seine
Olivier Morisse

Pont Alexandre III
Seine River
Baptiste Jayat →

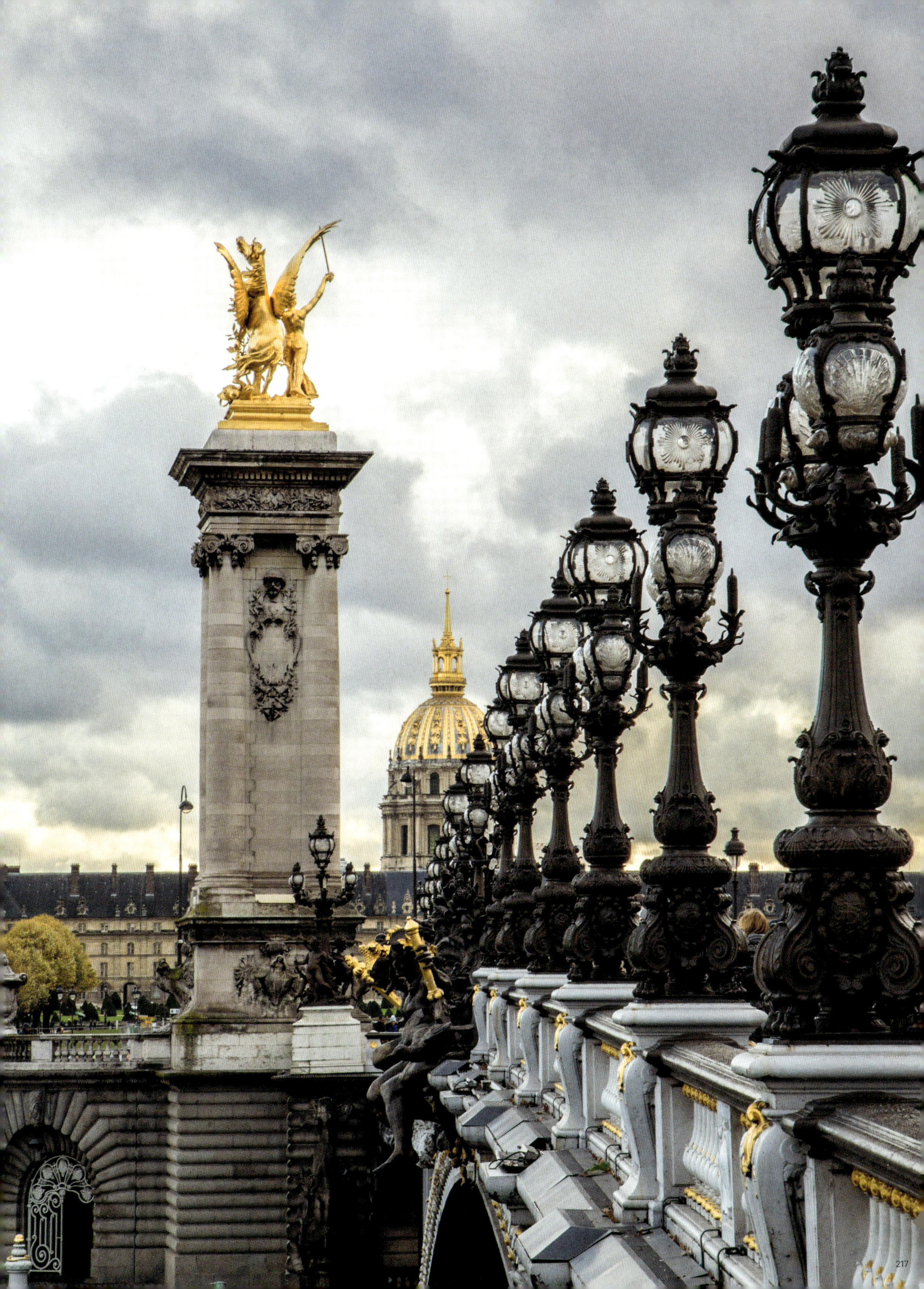

Seine River
Pie Aerts

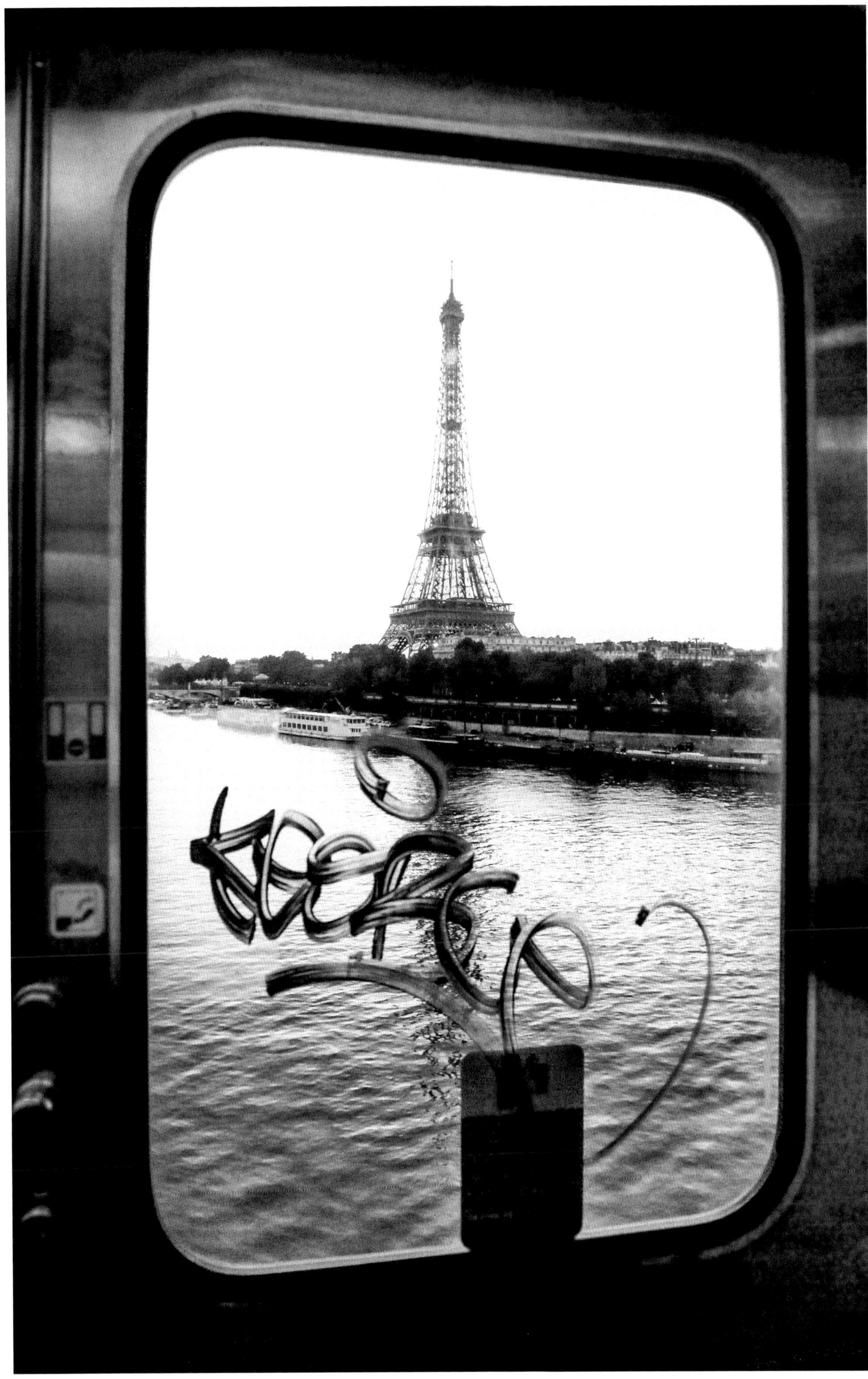

Photographers index a/z

Alena Cherepanova
@aliona_ch

Amedeo Abello
@amedeoabello

Baptiste Jayat
@dessinateurs

Barry Glassman
@barryglassman

Ben Cinetik
@bencinetik

Chloé Young
@almostharmless

Dariusz Jasak
@myfriendario

Denis Mamin
@by_qwerty

Erica Gonzalez
@filmandpixel

Gérard Trang
@superchinois801

Guillaume Dutreix
@guillaume_dx

Hugo Katsumi
@hugokatsumi

Hugo Michaudel
@limagigraphe

IZBERG
@izbergphotography

Jermain Cikic
@cikicjermain

Joann Pai
@sliceofpai

Joseph Jabbour
@jabbourjoseph

Juan Jerez del Valle
@juanjerez

Laetitia Modine
@laetitiamodine

Laurent Dassencourt
@loxilaux

Maxime Roig
@roigmax

Mikel van den Boogaard
@mikklz

Nicolas Zwarg
@nzphoto

Olivier Morisse
@oliviermorisse

Pie Aerts
@pie_aerts

Raul Cabrera
@raulcabrera

Robert Rieger
@robertrieger

Roel Ruijs
@roelservice

Romain Figuiere
@gl0be_trotter

Sarah van Rij
@sarahvanrij

Stéphanie Le Lay
@by.steph

Stijn Hoekstra
@stijnhoekstra

Sulay Kelly
@shoelayce

Today's Brew
@todaysbrew

Willem Evers
@freeaparis

Willem Sizoo
@willemsizoo

Yvan Des Costards
@canal_street55

Imprint

Streets of Paris – MENDO

First published in 2018 at
teNeues Media Verlag GmbH & Co. KG, Kempen

Edited and written by MENDO *mendo.nl*
Publisher: Gunifort Uwambaga, MENDO
Creative Director: Joeri Worm, MENDO
Editorial coordination: Joost Bastmeijer
and Roy Rietstap, MENDO
Copy: Joost Bastmeijer, MENDO

Published by gestalten, Berlin 2025

Editorial Management by Stephanie Rebel, gestalten
Production by Sandra Jansen-Dorn, gestalten
Color separation by Robert Kuhlendahl, gestalten
Copy editing & proofreading: Eliza Apperly, Cheryl Redmond
Translation: Alice Boucher (French);
Deman Übersetzungen/Anne Siebertz (German)

ISBN 978-3-96171-647-0

1st printing, 2025

Printed in the Czech Republic by PBtisk a.s.

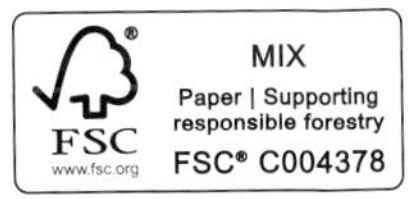

For more information and
to order books, please visit
www.teneues.com and www.gestalten.com

Die Gestalten Verlag GmbH & Co. KG
Mariannenstrasse 9–10
10999 Berlin, Germany
hello@gestalten.com

Düsseldorf Office
Waldenburger Straße 13
41564 Kaarst, Germany
verlag@teneues.com

teNeues Press Department
press@gestalten.com

Bibliographic information published by the Deutsche Nationalbibliothek. The Deutsche Nationalbibliothek lists this publication in the Deutsche Nationalbibliografie; detailed bibliographic data is available online at www.dnb.de

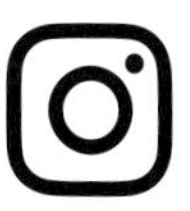

https://instagram.com/teneuespublishing

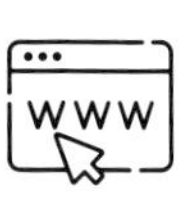

www.teneues.com

streets of paris

teNeues | MENDO